StormWatch
Post Human Division

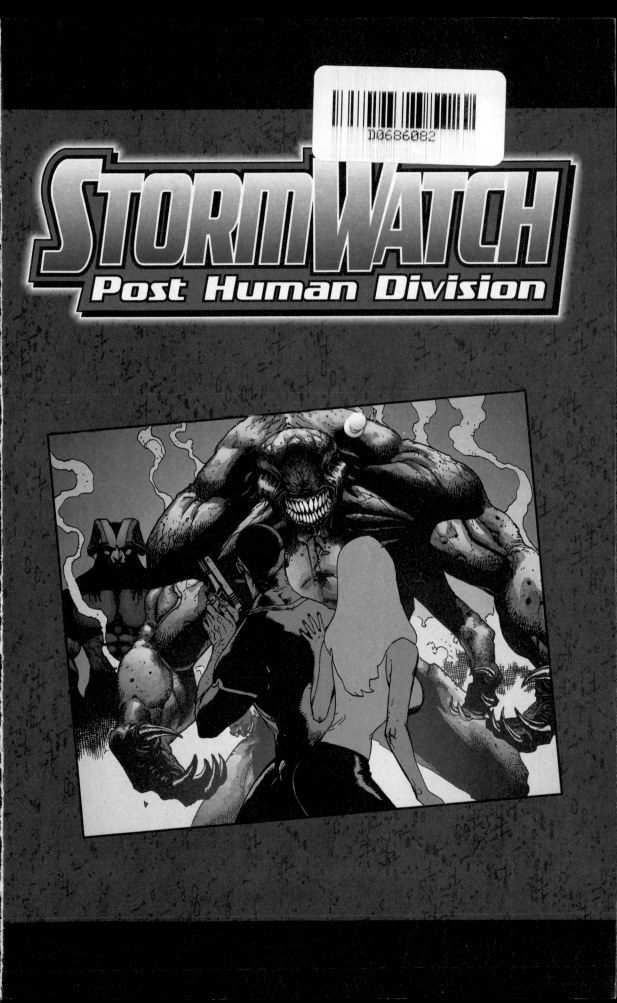

Writer: Christos Gage

Artist: Doug Mahnke

Colors: David Baron
Peter Pantazis (#4)

Letters: Jared K. Fletcher (#1-3)
Phil Balsman (#4)
Travis Lanham (#6-7)

STORMWATCH: P.H.D. published by WildStorm Productions. 888 Prospect St. #240, La Jolla, CA 92037. Compilation and sketchbook copyright © 2007 WildStorm Productions, an imprint of DC Comics. All Rights Reserved. WildStorm and logo, StormWatch, all characters, the distinctive likenesses thereof and all related elements are trademarks of DC Comics. Originally published in single magazine form as WORLDSTORM #1 © 2006 and STORMWATCH: PHD #1-4, 6-7 © 2006, 2007 WildStorm Productions, an imprint of DC Comics.

ISBN: 1-4012-1500-9
ISBN-13: 978-1-4012-1500-2

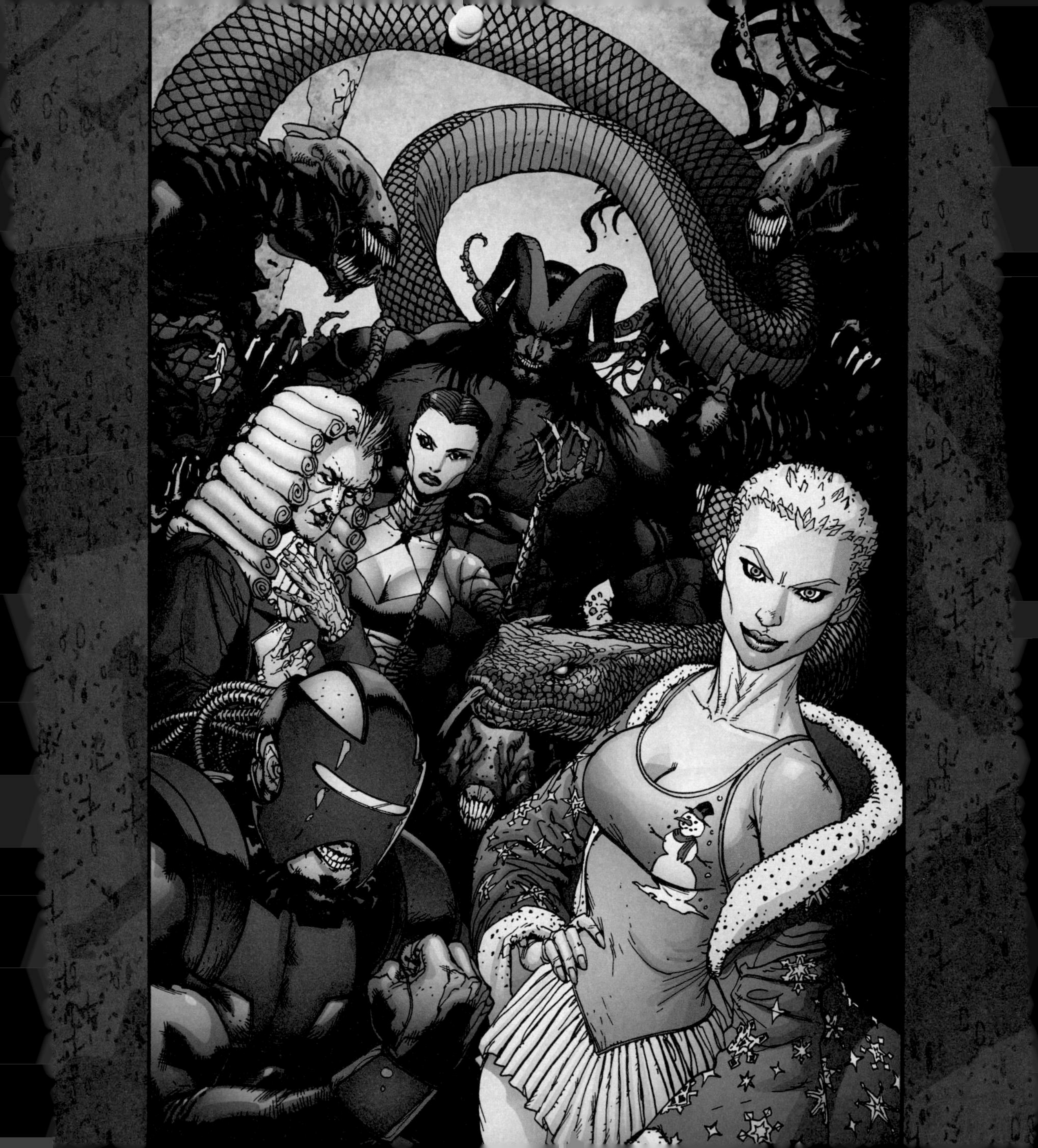

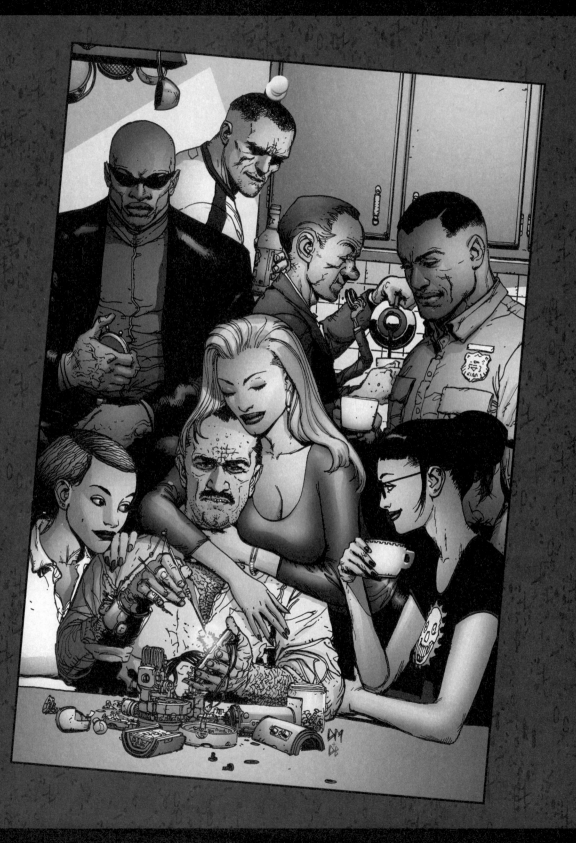

Doug Mahnke & David Baron

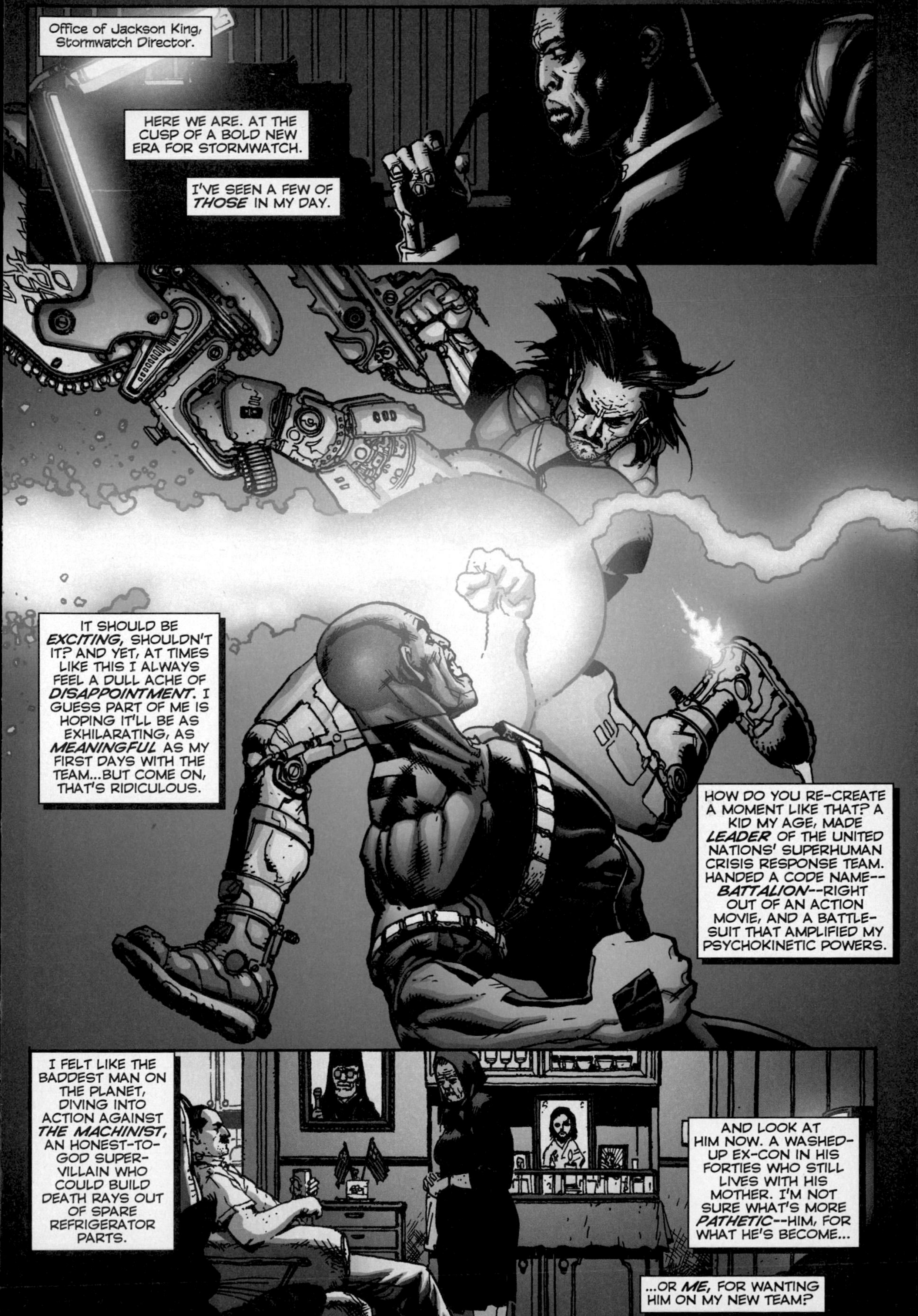
Office of Jackson King, Stormwatch Director.
HERE WE ARE. AT THE CUSP OF A BOLD NEW ERA FOR STORMWATCH.
I'VE SEEN A FEW OF *THOSE* IN MY DAY.
IT SHOULD BE *EXCITING,* SHOULDN'T IT? AND YET, AT TIMES LIKE THIS I ALWAYS FEEL A DULL ACHE OF *DISAPPOINTMENT.* I GUESS PART OF ME IS HOPING IT'LL BE AS EXHILARATING, AS *MEANINGFUL* AS MY FIRST DAYS WITH THE TEAM...BUT COME ON, THAT'S RIDICULOUS.
HOW DO YOU RE-CREATE A MOMENT LIKE THAT? A KID MY AGE, MADE *LEADER* OF THE UNITED NATIONS' SUPERHUMAN CRISIS RESPONSE TEAM. HANDED A CODE NAME--*BATTALION*--RIGHT OUT OF AN ACTION MOVIE, AND A BATTLE-SUIT THAT AMPLIFIED MY PSYCHOKINETIC POWERS.
I FELT LIKE THE BADDEST MAN ON THE PLANET, DIVING INTO ACTION AGAINST *THE MACHINIST,* AN HONEST-TO-GOD SUPER-VILLAIN WHO COULD BUILD DEATH RAYS OUT OF SPARE REFRIGERATOR PARTS.
AND LOOK AT HIM NOW. A WASHED-UP EX-CON IN HIS FORTIES WHO STILL LIVES WITH HIS MOTHER. I'M NOT SURE WHAT'S MORE *PATHETIC*--HIM, FOR WHAT HE'S BECOME...
...OR *ME,* FOR WANTING HIM ON MY NEW TEAM?

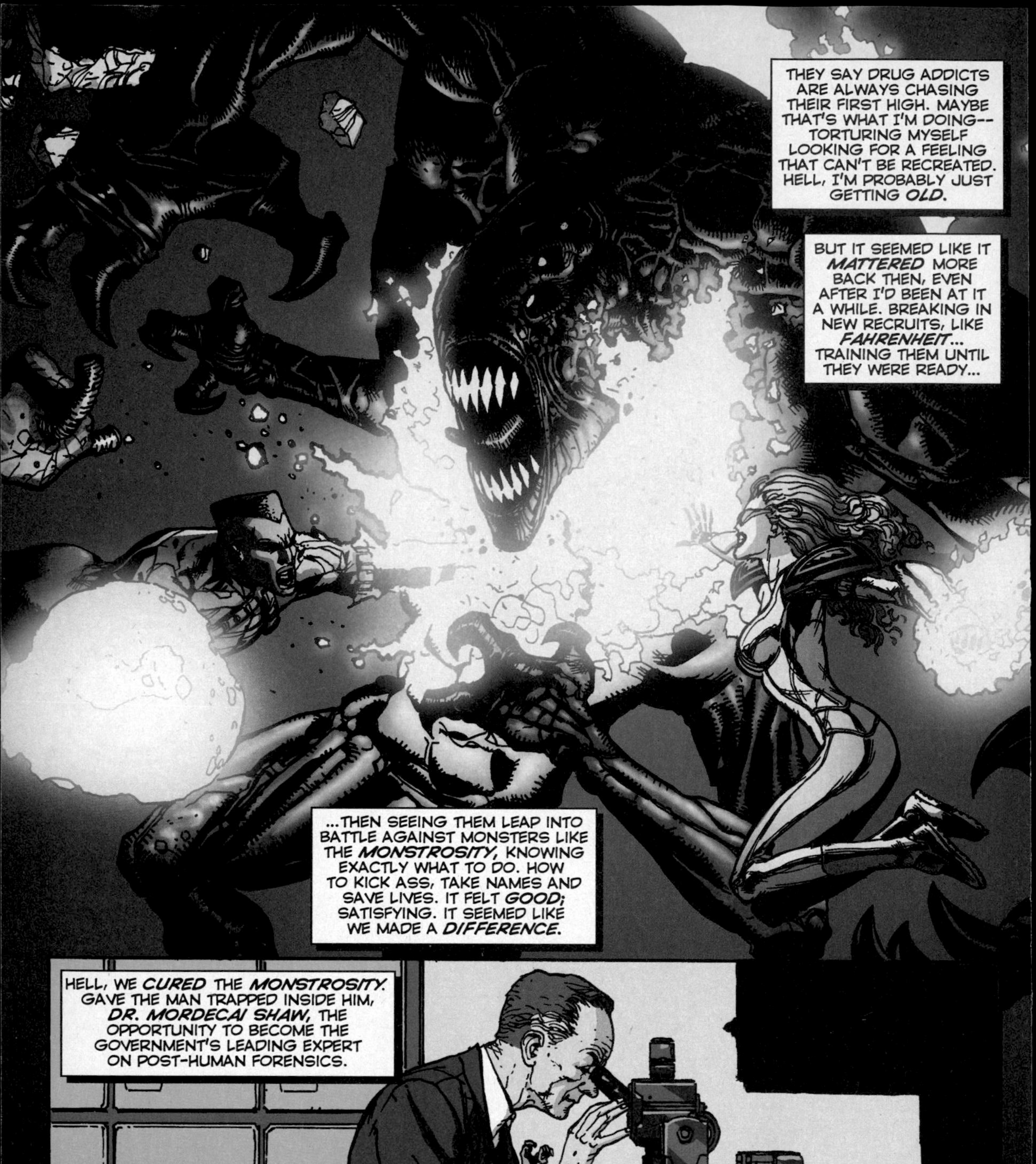
THEY SAY DRUG ADDICTS ARE ALWAYS CHASING THEIR FIRST HIGH. MAYBE THAT'S WHAT I'M DOING--TORTURING MYSELF LOOKING FOR A FEELING THAT CAN'T BE RECREATED. HELL, I'M PROBABLY JUST GETTING *OLD*.
BUT IT SEEMED LIKE IT *MATTERED* MORE BACK THEN, EVEN AFTER I'D BEEN AT IT A WHILE. BREAKING IN NEW RECRUITS, LIKE *FAHRENHEIT*... TRAINING THEM UNTIL THEY WERE READY...
...THEN SEEING THEM LEAP INTO BATTLE AGAINST MONSTERS LIKE THE *MONSTROSITY*, KNOWING EXACTLY WHAT TO DO. HOW TO KICK ASS, TAKE NAMES AND SAVE LIVES. IT FELT *GOOD*; SATISFYING. IT SEEMED LIKE WE MADE A *DIFFERENCE*.
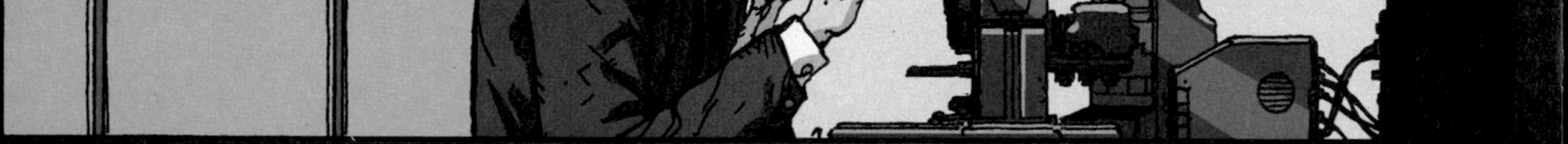
HELL, WE *CURED* THE *MONSTROSITY*. GAVE THE MAN TRAPPED INSIDE HIM, *DR. MORDECAI SHAW*, THE OPPORTUNITY TO BECOME THE GOVERNMENT'S LEADING EXPERT ON POST-HUMAN FORENSICS.
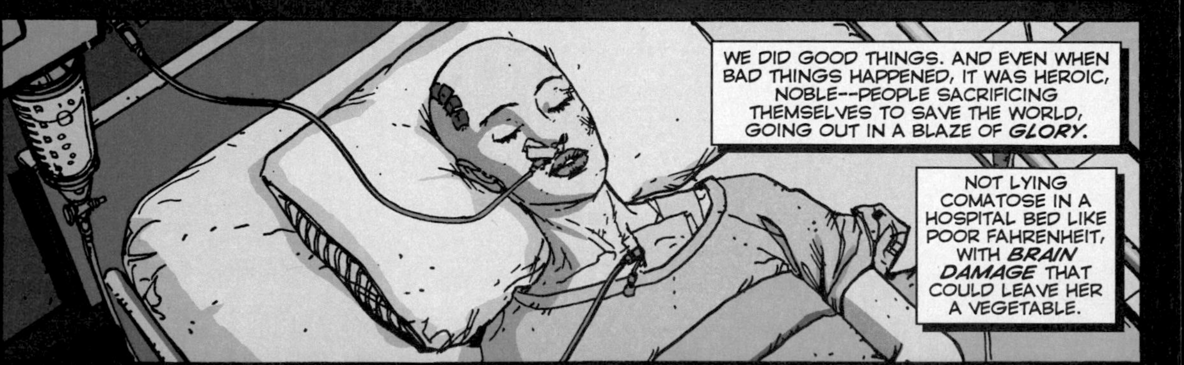
WE DID GOOD THINGS. AND EVEN WHEN BAD THINGS HAPPENED, IT WAS HEROIC, NOBLE--PEOPLE SACRIFICING THEMSELVES TO SAVE THE WORLD, GOING OUT IN A BLAZE OF *GLORY*.
NOT LYING COMATOSE IN A HOSPITAL BED LIKE POOR FAHRENHEIT, WITH *BRAIN DAMAGE* THAT COULD LEAVE HER A VEGETABLE.

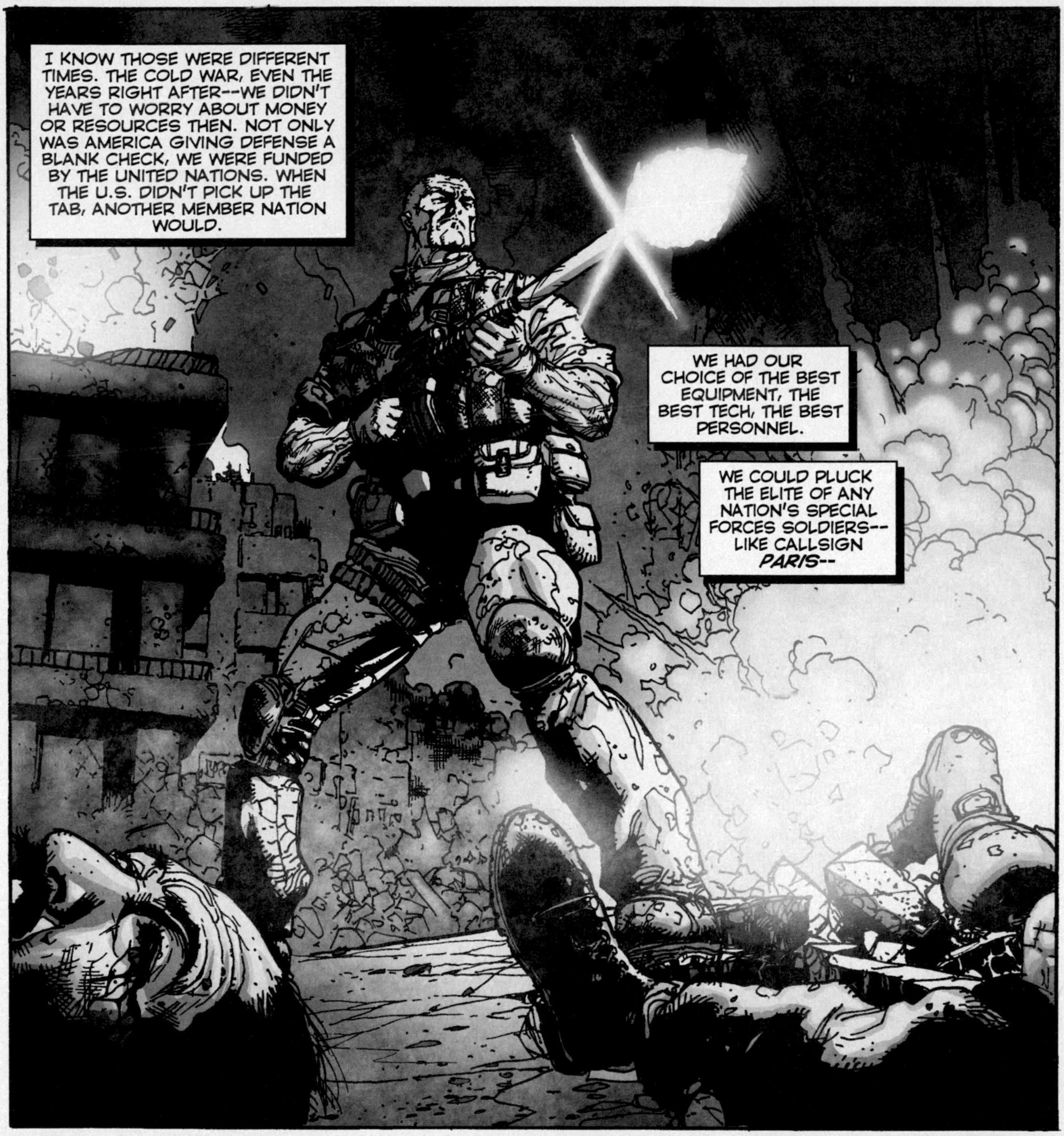
I KNOW THOSE WERE DIFFERENT TIMES. THE COLD WAR, EVEN THE YEARS RIGHT AFTER--WE DIDN'T HAVE TO WORRY ABOUT MONEY OR RESOURCES THEN. NOT ONLY WAS AMERICA GIVING DEFENSE A BLANK CHECK, WE WERE FUNDED BY THE UNITED NATIONS. WHEN THE U.S. DIDN'T PICK UP THE TAB, ANOTHER MEMBER NATION WOULD.
WE HAD OUR CHOICE OF THE BEST EQUIPMENT, THE BEST TECH, THE BEST PERSONNEL.
WE COULD PLUCK THE ELITE OF ANY NATION'S SPECIAL FORCES SOLDIERS--LIKE CALLSIGN *PARIS*--

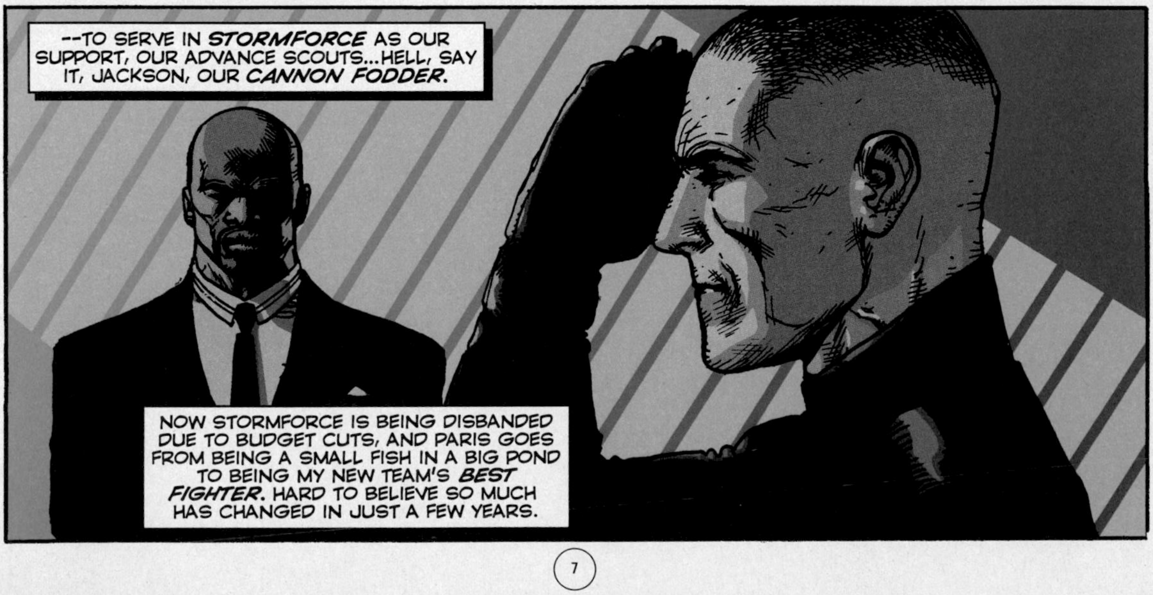
--TO SERVE IN *STORMFORCE* AS OUR SUPPORT, OUR ADVANCE SCOUTS...HELL, SAY IT, JACKSON, OUR *CANNON FODDER*.
NOW STORMFORCE IS BEING DISBANDED DUE TO BUDGET CUTS, AND PARIS GOES FROM BEING A SMALL FISH IN A BIG POND TO BEING MY NEW TEAM'S *BEST FIGHTER*. HARD TO BELIEVE SO MUCH HAS CHANGED IN JUST A FEW YEARS.

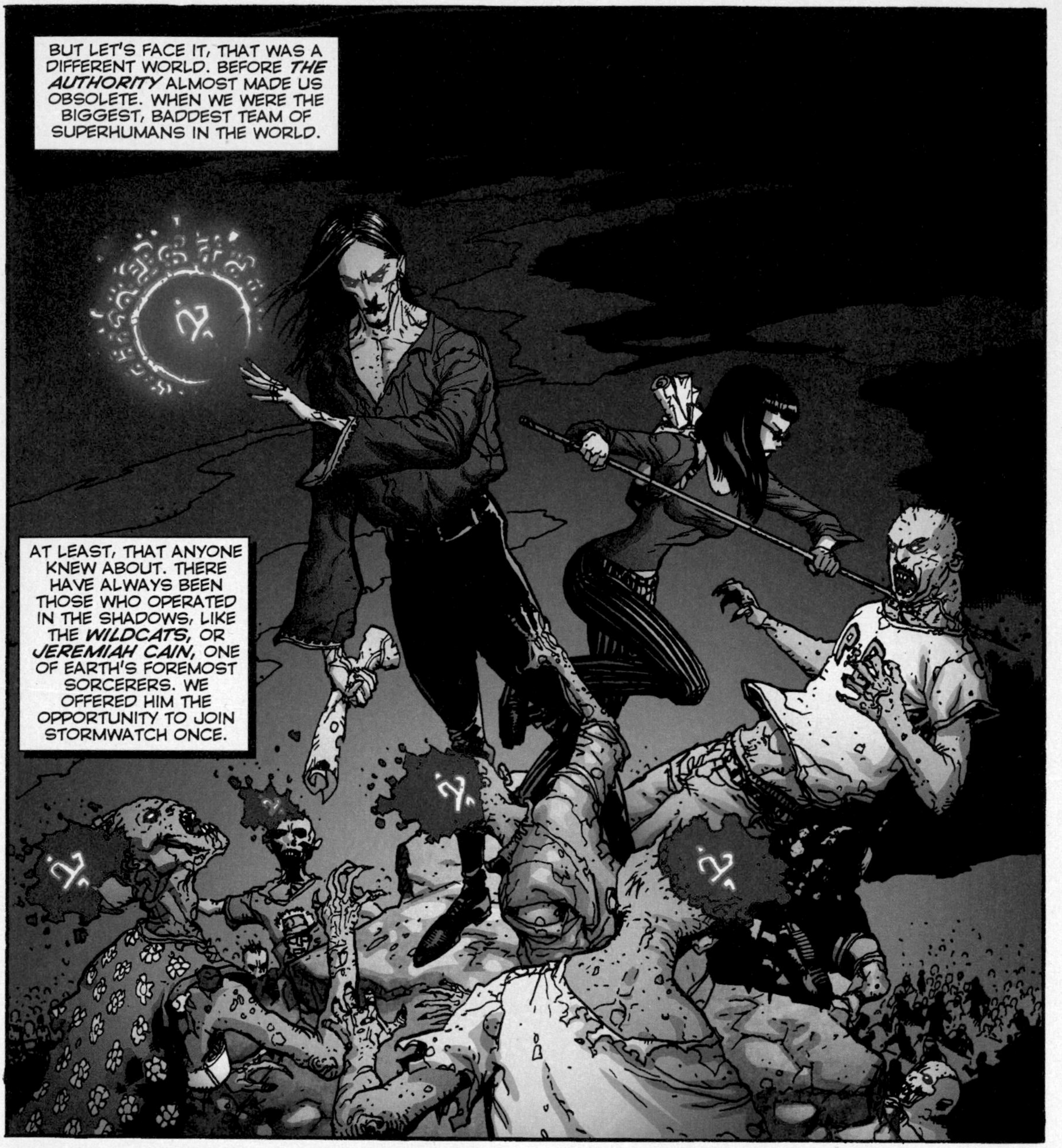
BUT LET'S FACE IT, THAT WAS A DIFFERENT WORLD. BEFORE *THE AUTHORITY* ALMOST MADE US OBSOLETE. WHEN WE WERE THE BIGGEST, BADDEST TEAM OF SUPERHUMANS IN THE WORLD.
AT LEAST, THAT ANYONE KNEW ABOUT. THERE HAVE ALWAYS BEEN THOSE WHO OPERATED IN THE SHADOWS, LIKE THE *WILDCATS,* OR *JEREMIAH CAIN,* ONE OF EARTH'S FOREMOST SORCERERS. WE OFFERED HIM THE OPPORTUNITY TO JOIN STORMWATCH ONCE.

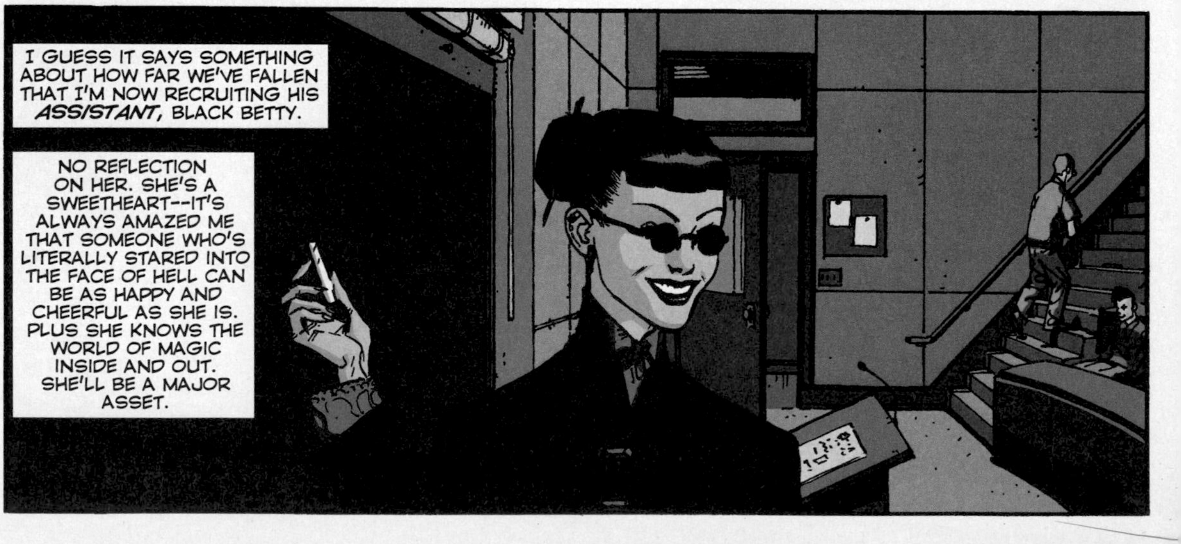
I GUESS IT SAYS SOMETHING ABOUT HOW FAR WE'VE FALLEN THAT I'M NOW RECRUITING HIS *ASSISTANT,* BLACK BETTY.
NO REFLECTION ON HER. SHE'S A SWEETHEART--IT'S ALWAYS AMAZED ME THAT SOMEONE WHO'S LITERALLY STARED INTO THE FACE OF HELL CAN BE AS HAPPY AND CHEERFUL AS SHE IS. PLUS SHE KNOWS THE WORLD OF MAGIC INSIDE AND OUT. SHE'LL BE A MAJOR ASSET.

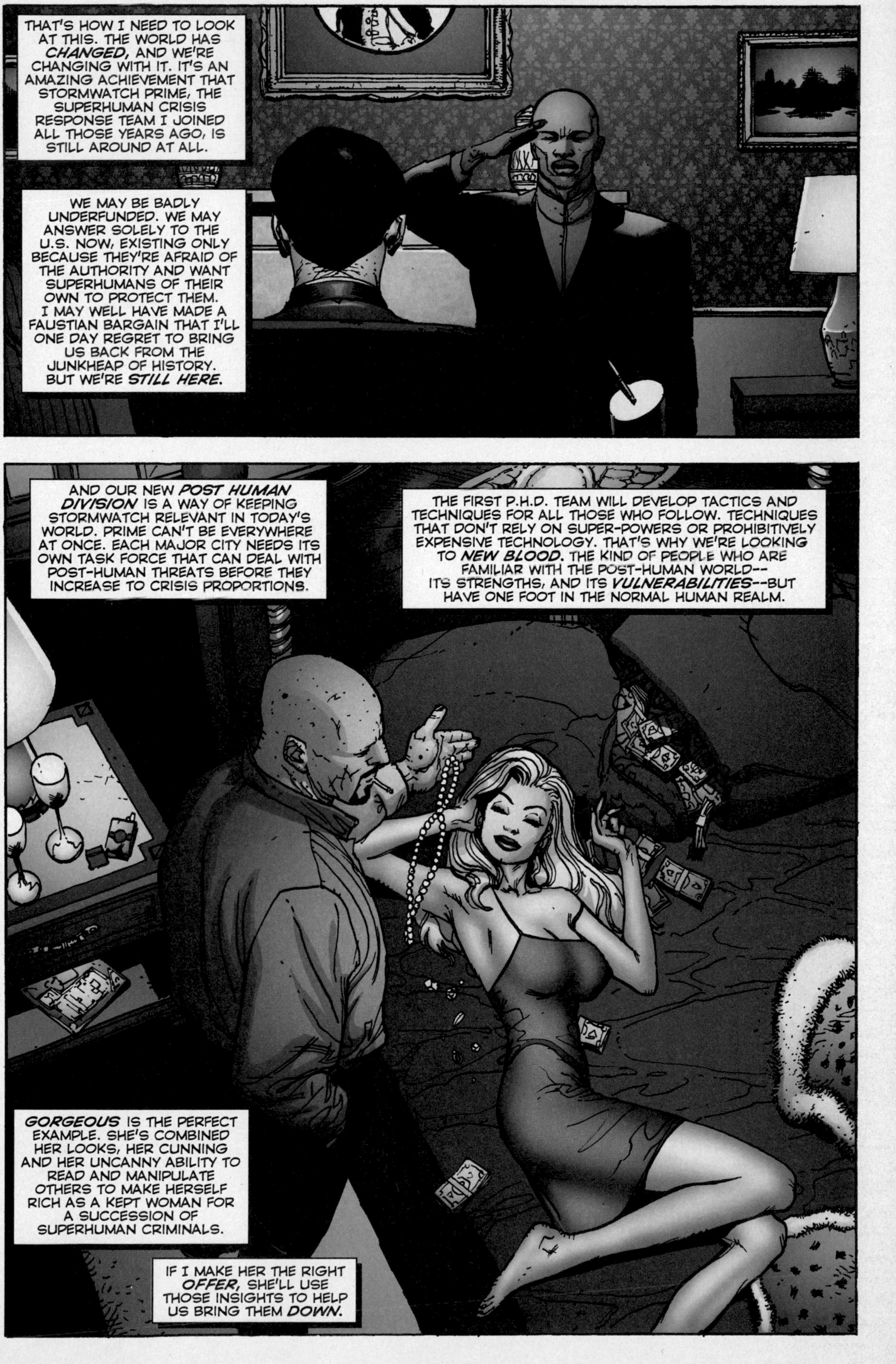
THAT'S HOW I NEED TO LOOK AT THIS. THE WORLD HAS CHANGED, AND WE'RE CHANGING WITH IT. IT'S AN AMAZING ACHIEVEMENT THAT STORMWATCH PRIME, THE SUPERHUMAN CRISIS RESPONSE TEAM I JOINED ALL THOSE YEARS AGO, IS STILL AROUND AT ALL.
WE MAY BE BADLY UNDERFUNDED. WE MAY ANSWER SOLELY TO THE U.S. NOW, EXISTING ONLY BECAUSE THEY'RE AFRAID OF THE AUTHORITY AND WANT SUPERHUMANS OF THEIR OWN TO PROTECT THEM. I MAY WELL HAVE MADE A FAUSTIAN BARGAIN THAT I'LL ONE DAY REGRET TO BRING US BACK FROM THE JUNKHEAP OF HISTORY. BUT WE'RE STILL HERE.
AND OUR NEW POST HUMAN DIVISION IS A WAY OF KEEPING STORMWATCH RELEVANT IN TODAY'S WORLD. PRIME CAN'T BE EVERYWHERE AT ONCE. EACH MAJOR CITY NEEDS ITS OWN TASK FORCE THAT CAN DEAL WITH POST-HUMAN THREATS BEFORE THEY INCREASE TO CRISIS PROPORTIONS.
THE FIRST P.H.D. TEAM WILL DEVELOP TACTICS AND TECHNIQUES FOR ALL THOSE WHO FOLLOW. TECHNIQUES THAT DON'T RELY ON SUPER-POWERS OR PROHIBITIVELY EXPENSIVE TECHNOLOGY. THAT'S WHY WE'RE LOOKING TO NEW BLOOD. THE KIND OF PEOPLE WHO ARE FAMILIAR WITH THE POST-HUMAN WORLD-- ITS STRENGTHS, AND ITS VULNERABILITIES--BUT HAVE ONE FOOT IN THE NORMAL HUMAN REALM.
GORGEOUS IS THE PERFECT EXAMPLE. SHE'S COMBINED HER LOOKS, HER CUNNING AND HER UNCANNY ABILITY TO READ AND MANIPULATE OTHERS TO MAKE HERSELF RICH AS A KEPT WOMAN FOR A SUCCESSION OF SUPERHUMAN CRIMINALS.
IF I MAKE HER THE RIGHT OFFER, SHE'LL USE THOSE INSIGHTS TO HELP US BRING THEM DOWN.

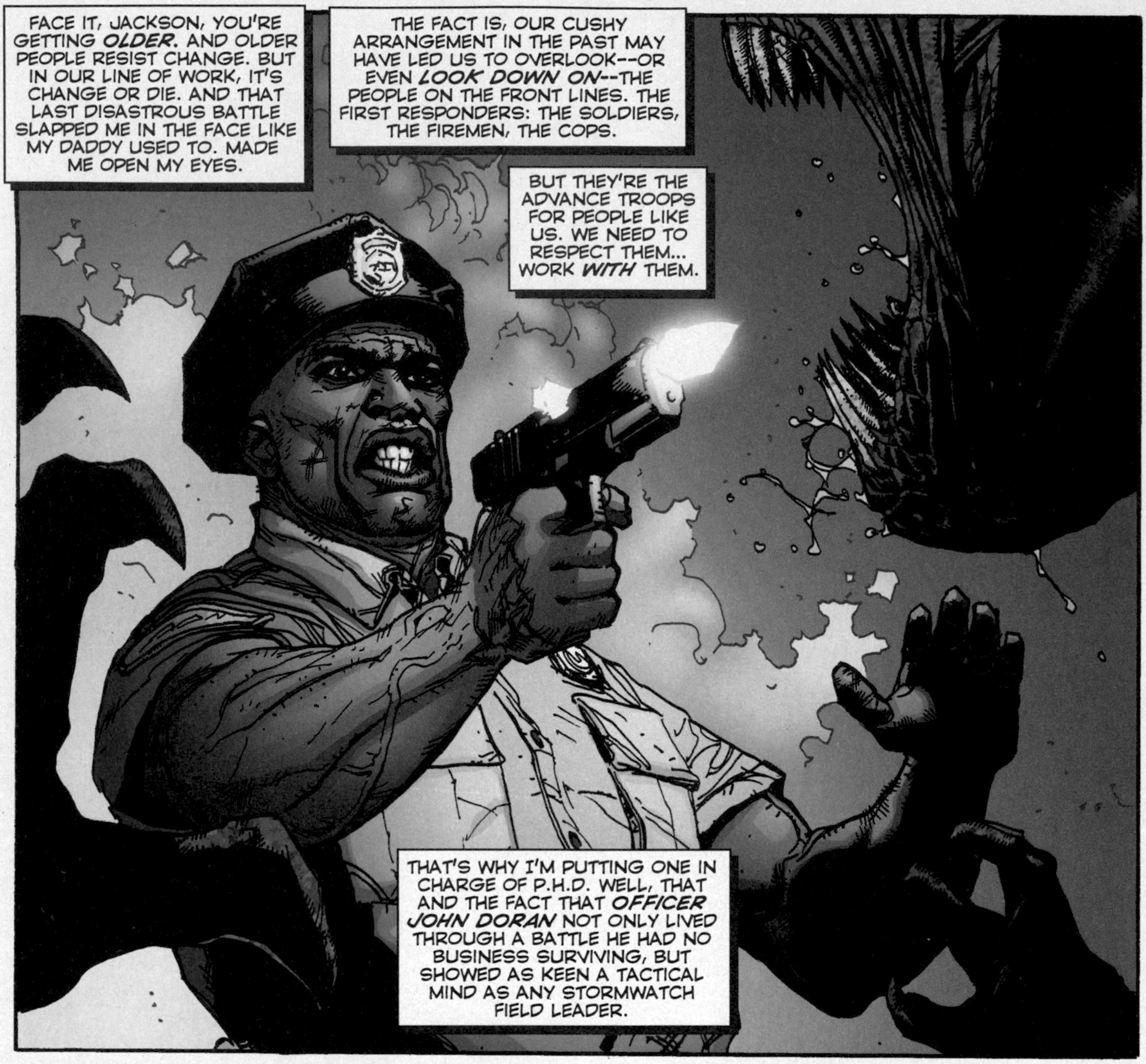
FACE IT, JACKSON, YOU'RE GETTING *OLDER*. AND OLDER PEOPLE RESIST CHANGE. BUT IN OUR LINE OF WORK, IT'S CHANGE OR DIE. AND THAT LAST DISASTROUS BATTLE SLAPPED ME IN THE FACE LIKE MY DADDY USED TO. MADE ME OPEN MY EYES.
THE FACT IS, OUR CUSHY ARRANGEMENT IN THE PAST MAY HAVE LED US TO OVERLOOK--OR EVEN *LOOK DOWN ON*--THE PEOPLE ON THE FRONT LINES. THE FIRST RESPONDERS: THE SOLDIERS, THE FIREMEN, THE COPS.
BUT THEY'RE THE ADVANCE TROOPS FOR PEOPLE LIKE US. WE NEED TO RESPECT THEM... WORK *WITH* THEM.
THAT'S WHY I'M PUTTING ONE IN CHARGE OF P.H.D. WELL, THAT AND THE FACT THAT *OFFICER JOHN DORAN* NOT ONLY LIVED THROUGH A BATTLE HE HAD NO BUSINESS SURVIVING, BUT SHOWED AS KEEN A TACTICAL MIND AS ANY STORMWATCH FIELD LEADER.

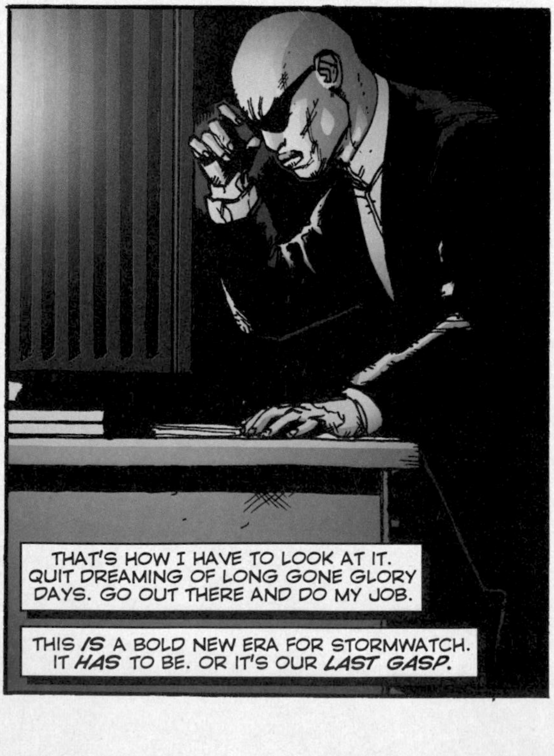
THAT'S HOW I HAVE TO LOOK AT IT. QUIT DREAMING OF LONG GONE GLORY DAYS. GO OUT THERE AND DO MY JOB.
THIS *IS* A BOLD NEW ERA FOR STORMWATCH. IT *HAS* TO BE. OR IT'S OUR *LAST GASP*.

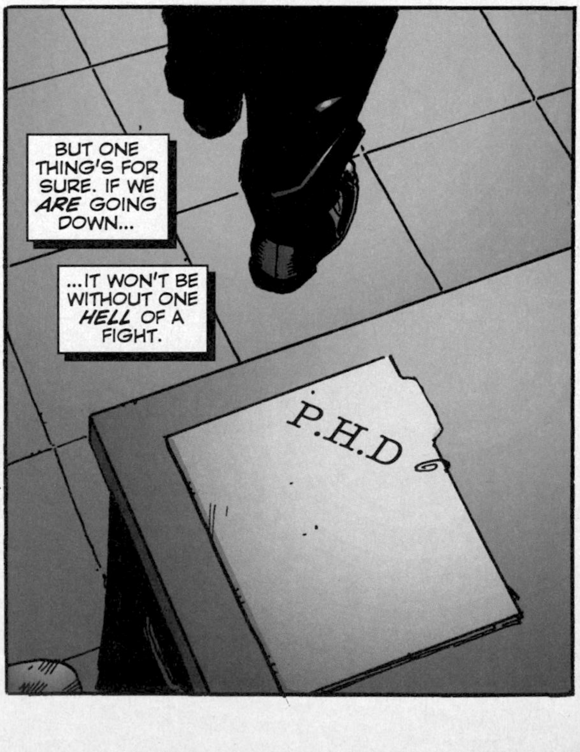
BUT ONE THING'S FOR SURE. IF WE *ARE* GOING DOWN...
...IT WON'T BE WITHOUT ONE *HELL* OF A FIGHT.
P.H.D

Chapter 1: In a New York Minute

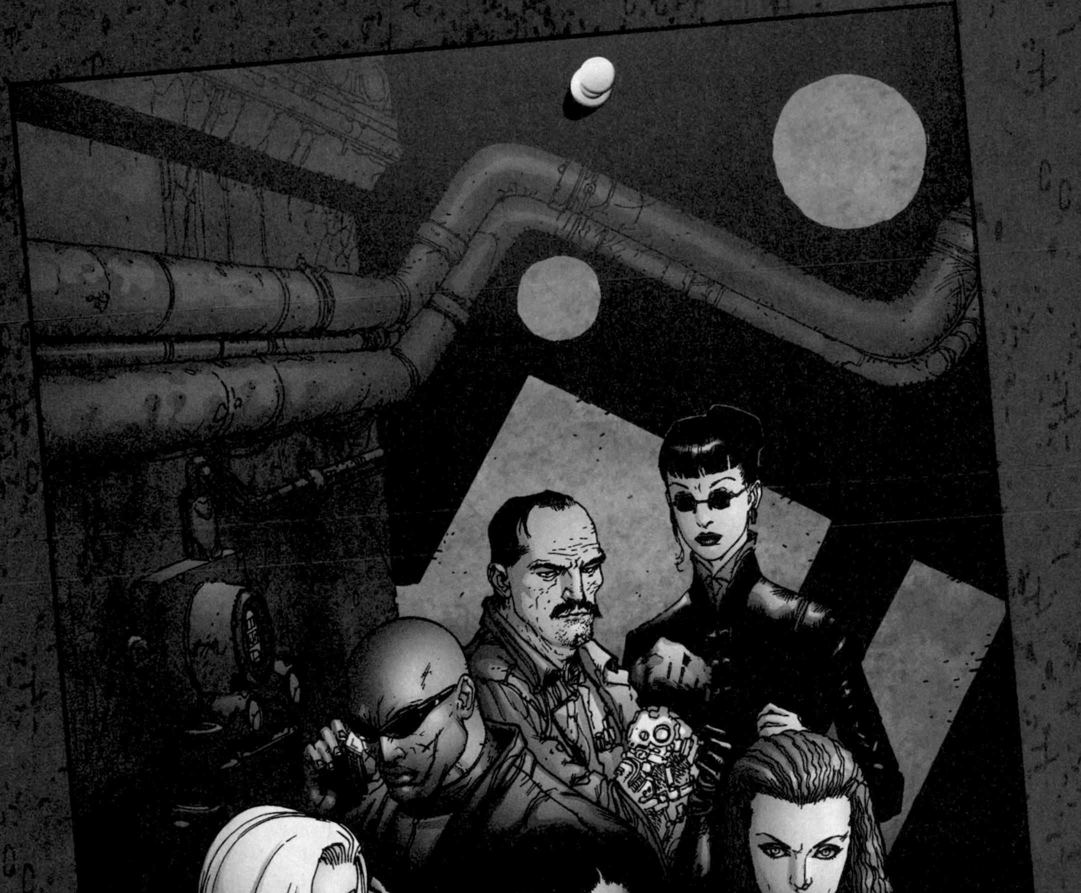

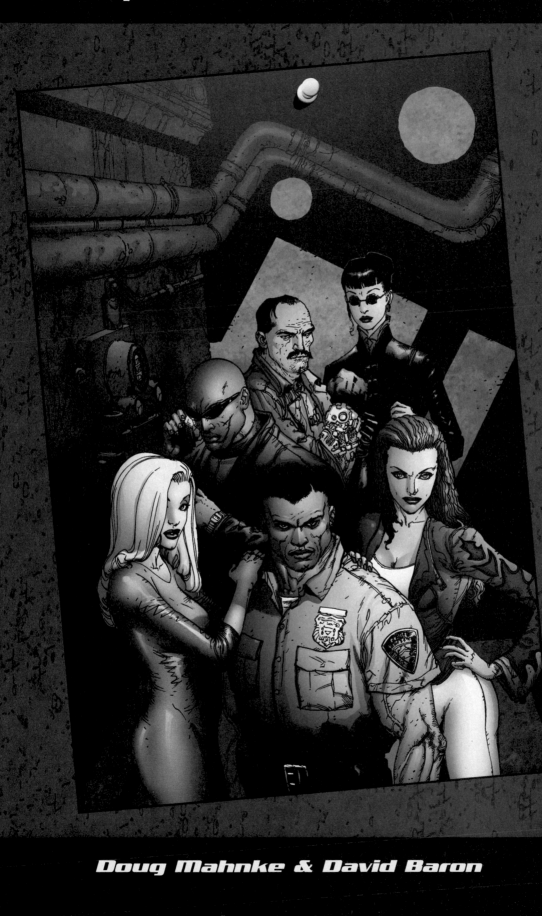

Doug Mahnke & David Baron

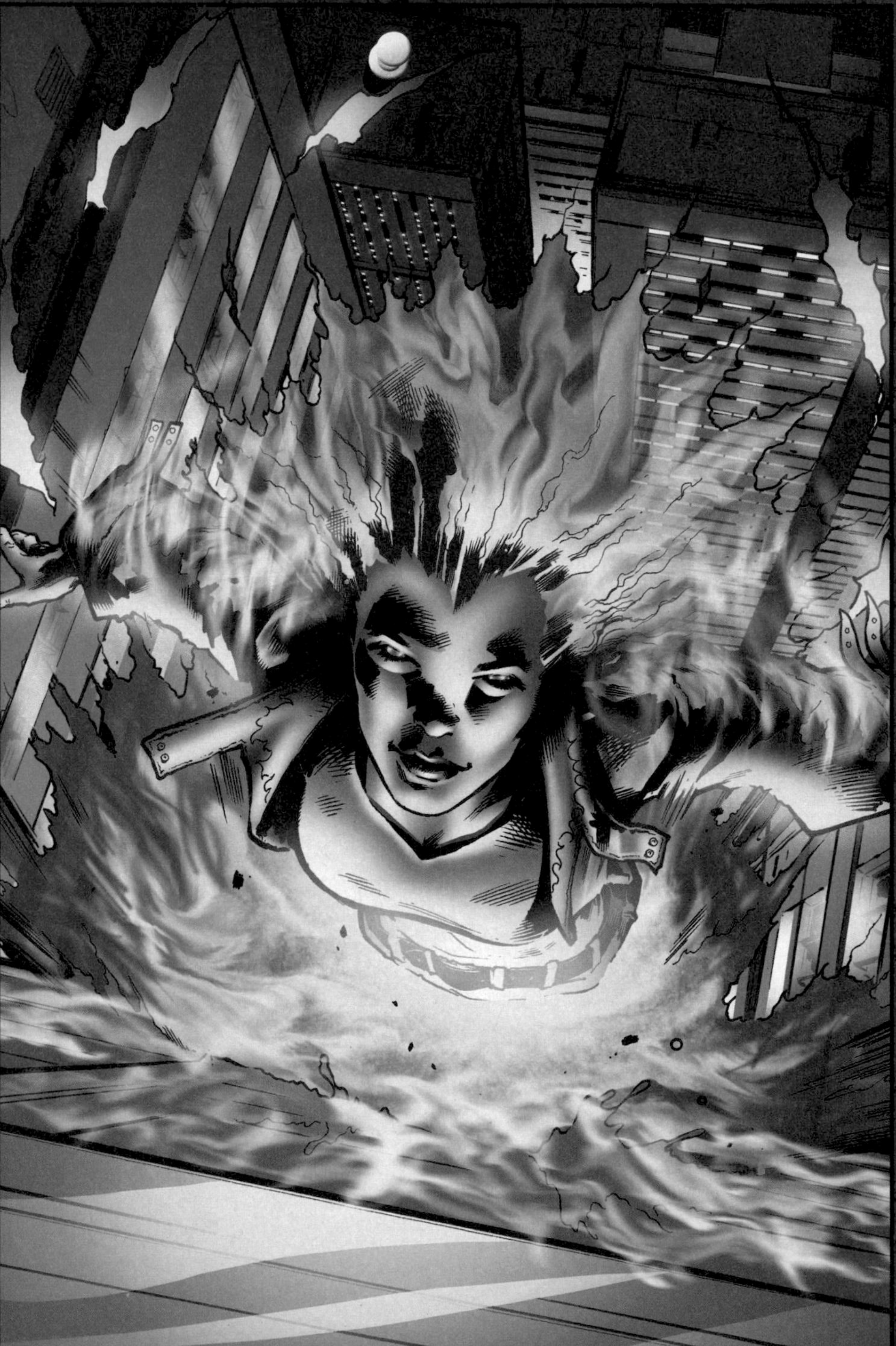

Trevor Hairsine & Randy Mayo

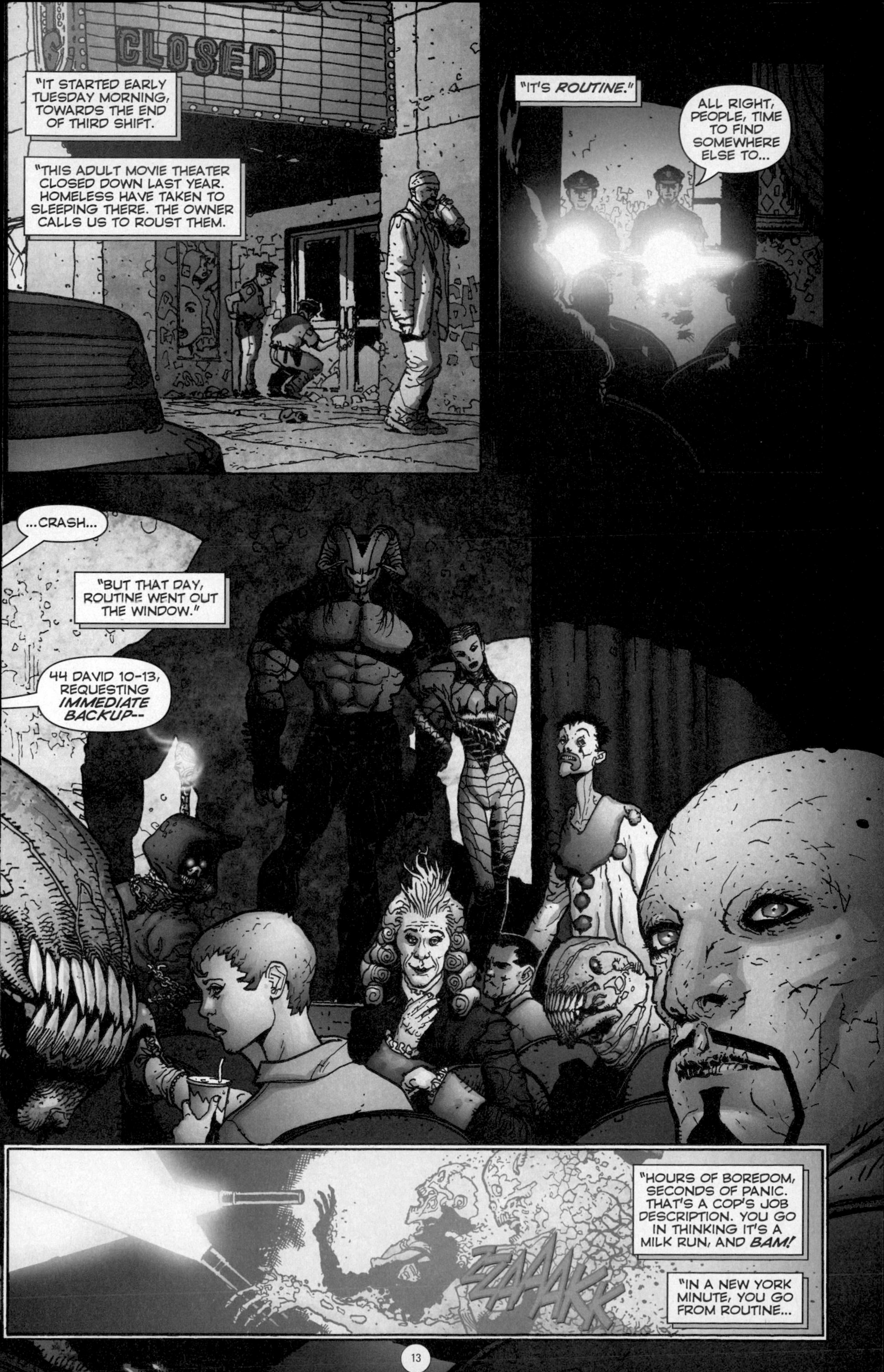
CLOSED
"IT STARTED EARLY TUESDAY MORNING, TOWARDS THE END OF THIRD SHIFT.
"THIS ADULT MOVIE THEATER CLOSED DOWN LAST YEAR. HOMELESS HAVE TAKEN TO SLEEPING THERE. THE OWNER CALLS US TO ROUST THEM.
"IT'S *ROUTINE.*"
ALL RIGHT, PEOPLE, TIME TO FIND SOMEWHERE ELSE TO...
...CRASH...
"BUT THAT DAY, ROUTINE WENT OUT THE WINDOW."
44 DAVID 10-13, REQUESTING *IMMEDIATE BACKUP*--
"HOURS OF BOREDOM, SECONDS OF PANIC. THAT'S A COP'S JOB DESCRIPTION. YOU GO IN THINKING IT'S A MILK RUN, AND *BAM!*
ZZAAAKK
"IN A NEW YORK MINUTE, YOU GO FROM ROUTINE...

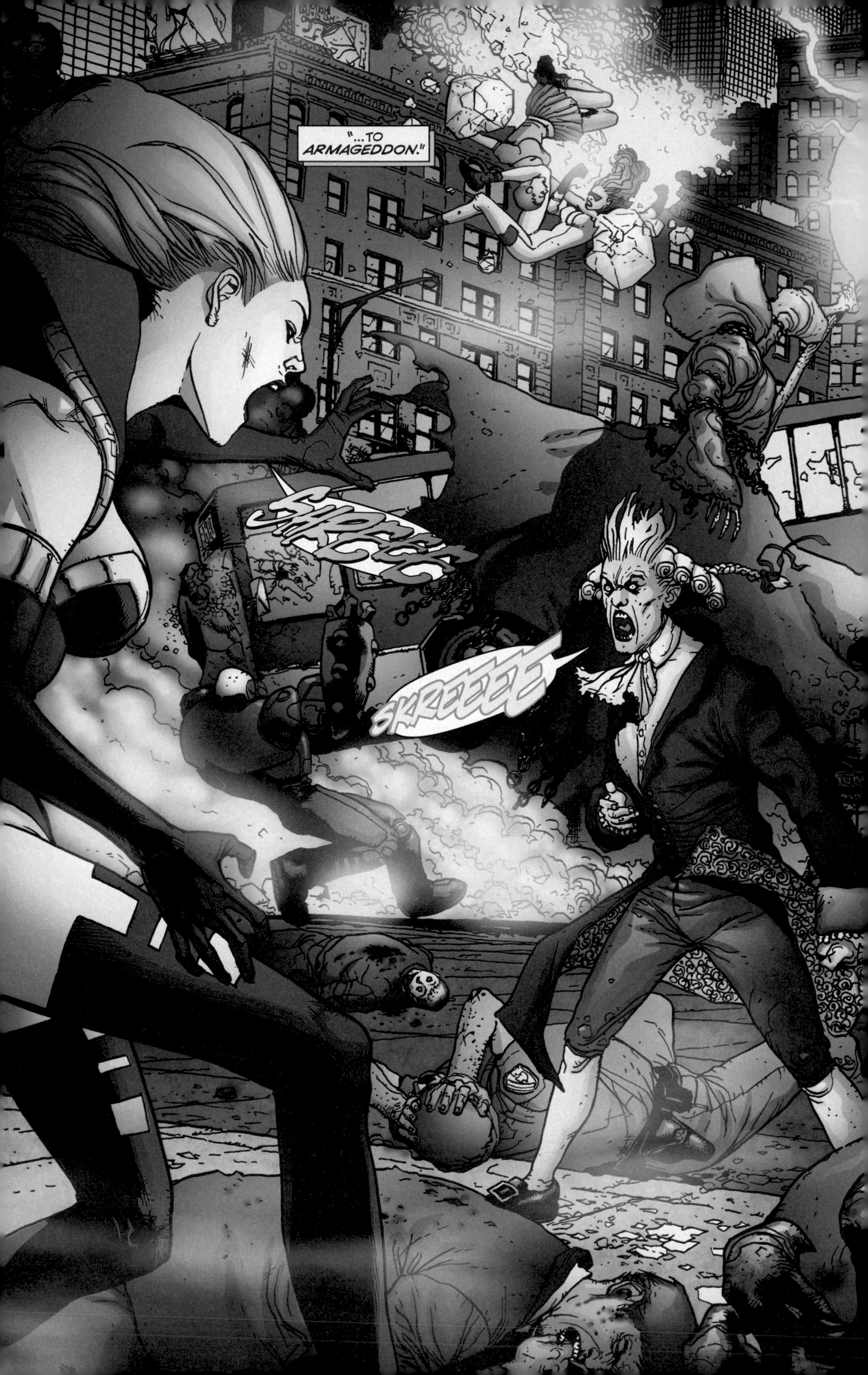
"...TO ARMAGEDDON."
SKREEEEE

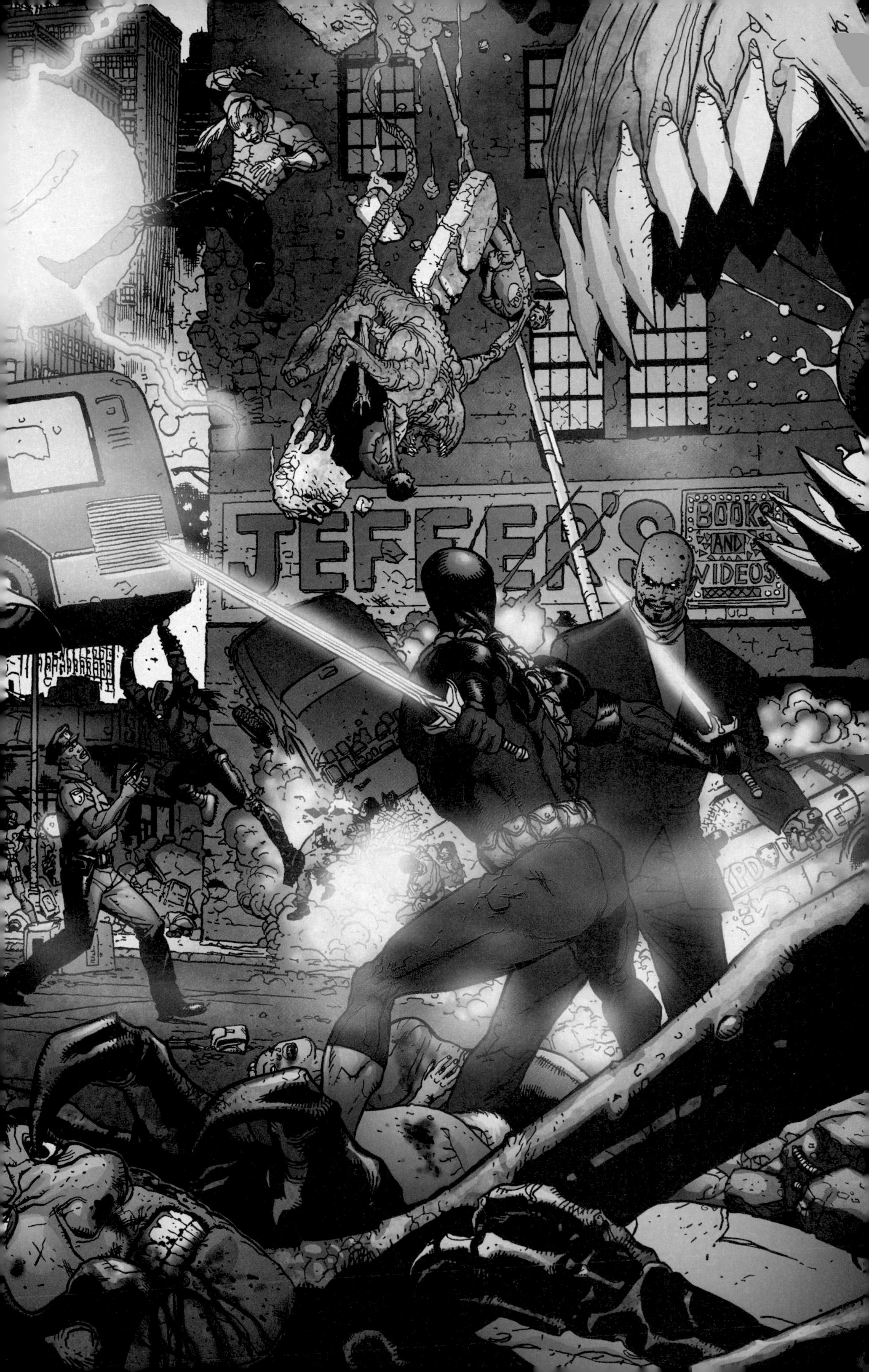
JEFFER'S
BOOK
AND
VIDEOS

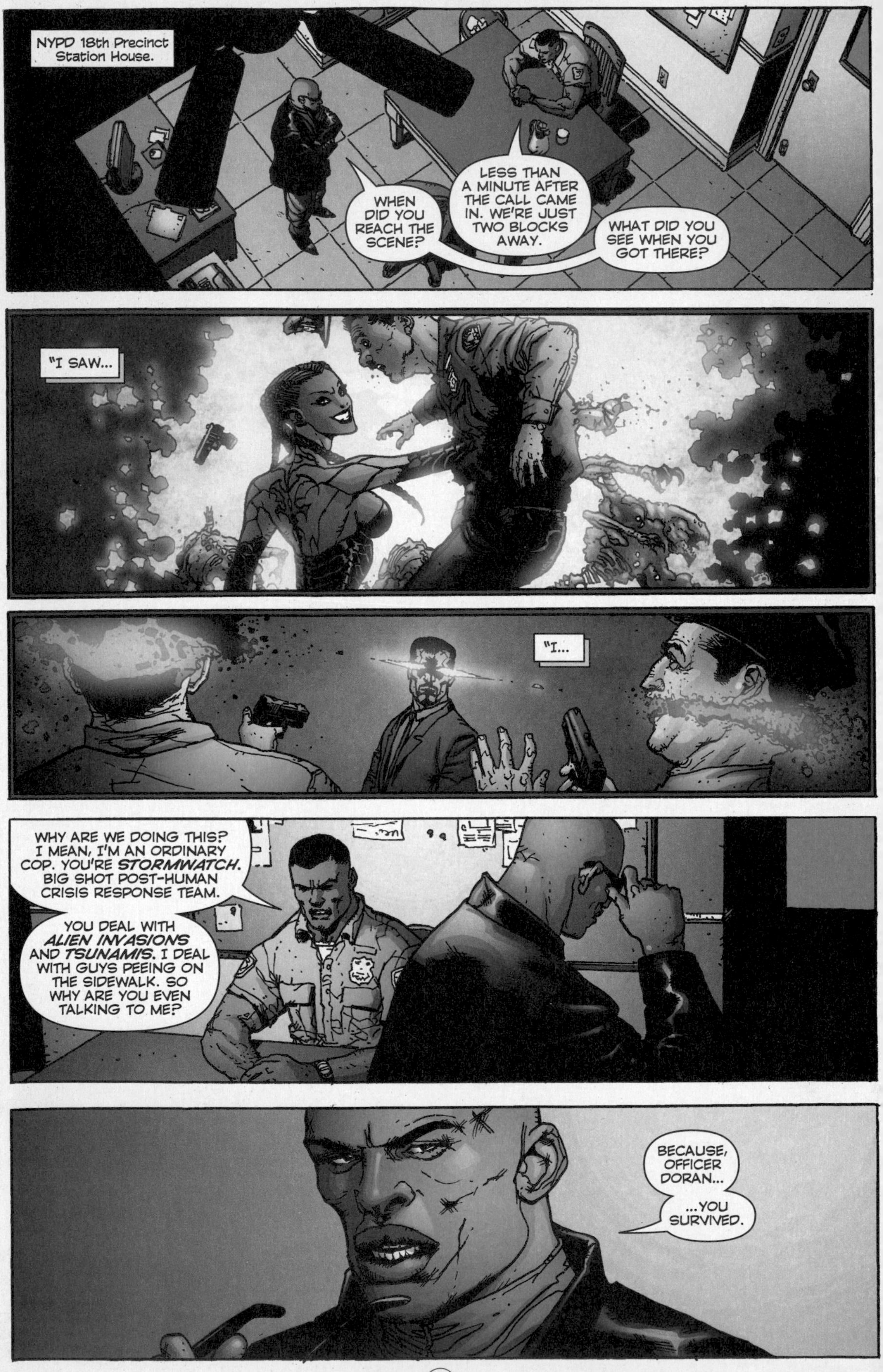
NYPD 18th Precinct Station House.
WHEN DID YOU REACH THE SCENE?
LESS THAN A MINUTE AFTER THE CALL CAME IN. WE'RE JUST TWO BLOCKS AWAY.
WHAT DID YOU SEE WHEN YOU GOT THERE?
"I SAW...
"I...
WHY ARE WE DOING THIS? I MEAN, I'M AN ORDINARY COP. YOU'RE STORMWATCH. BIG SHOT POST-HUMAN CRISIS RESPONSE TEAM.
YOU DEAL WITH ALIEN INVASIONS AND TSUNAMIS. I DEAL WITH GUYS PEEING ON THE SIDEWALK. SO WHY ARE YOU EVEN TALKING TO ME?
BECAUSE, OFFICER DORAN...
...YOU SURVIVED.

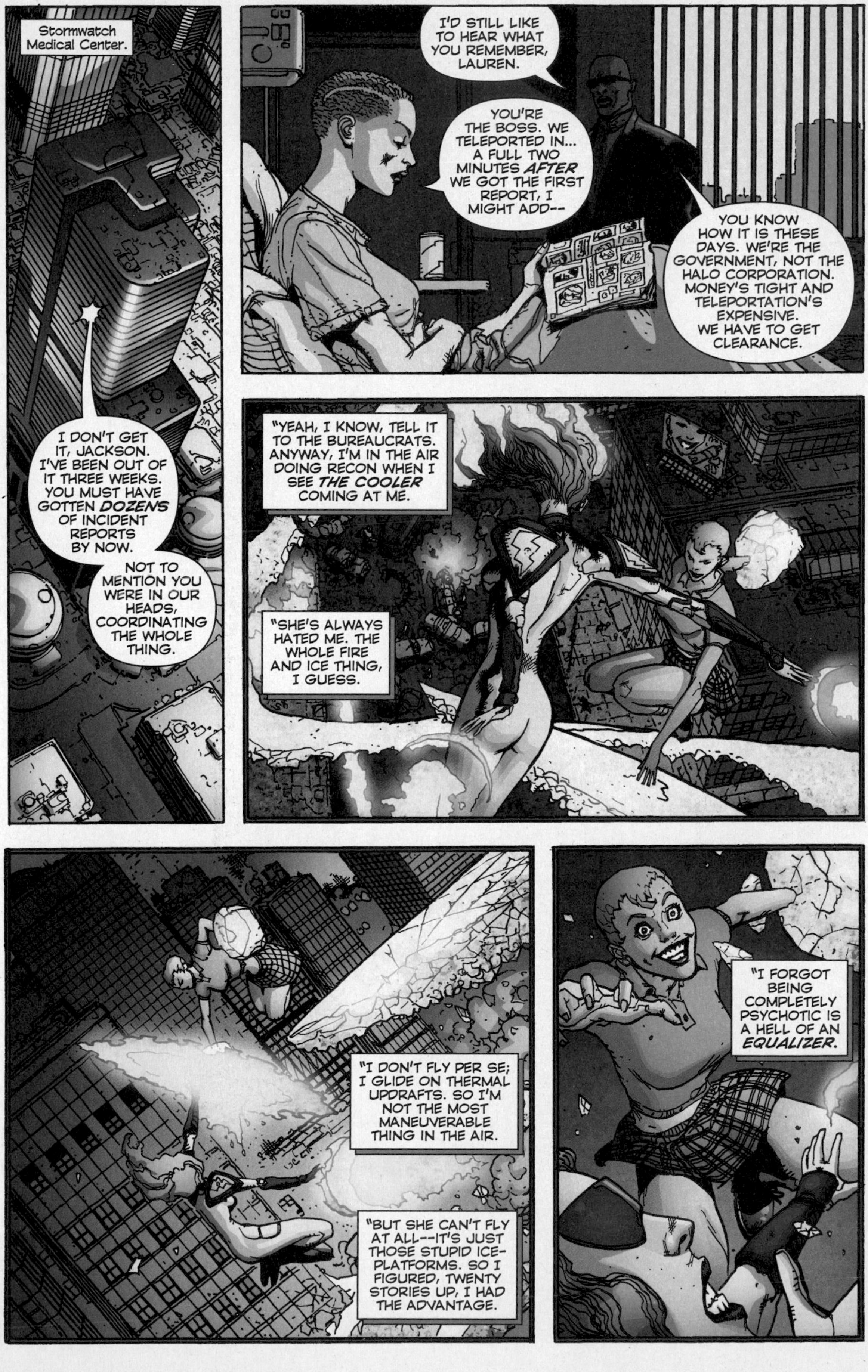
Stormwatch Medical Center.
I'D STILL LIKE TO HEAR WHAT YOU REMEMBER, LAUREN.
YOU'RE THE BOSS. WE TELEPORTED IN... A FULL TWO MINUTES AFTER WE GOT THE FIRST REPORT, I MIGHT ADD--
YOU KNOW HOW IT IS THESE DAYS. WE'RE THE GOVERNMENT, NOT THE HALO CORPORATION. MONEY'S TIGHT AND TELEPORTATION'S EXPENSIVE. WE HAVE TO GET CLEARANCE.
I DON'T GET IT, JACKSON. I'VE BEEN OUT OF IT THREE WEEKS. YOU MUST HAVE GOTTEN DOZENS OF INCIDENT REPORTS BY NOW.
NOT TO MENTION YOU WERE IN OUR HEADS, COORDINATING THE WHOLE THING.
"YEAH, I KNOW, TELL IT TO THE BUREAUCRATS. ANYWAY, I'M IN THE AIR DOING RECON WHEN I SEE THE COOLER COMING AT ME.
"SHE'S ALWAYS HATED ME. THE WHOLE FIRE AND ICE THING, I GUESS.
"I DON'T FLY PER SE; I GLIDE ON THERMAL UPDRAFTS. SO I'M NOT THE MOST MANEUVERABLE THING IN THE AIR.
"BUT SHE CAN'T FLY AT ALL--IT'S JUST THOSE STUPID ICE-PLATFORMS. SO I FIGURED, TWENTY STORIES UP, I HAD THE ADVANTAGE.
"I FORGOT BEING COMPLETELY PSYCHOTIC IS A HELL OF AN EQUALIZER.

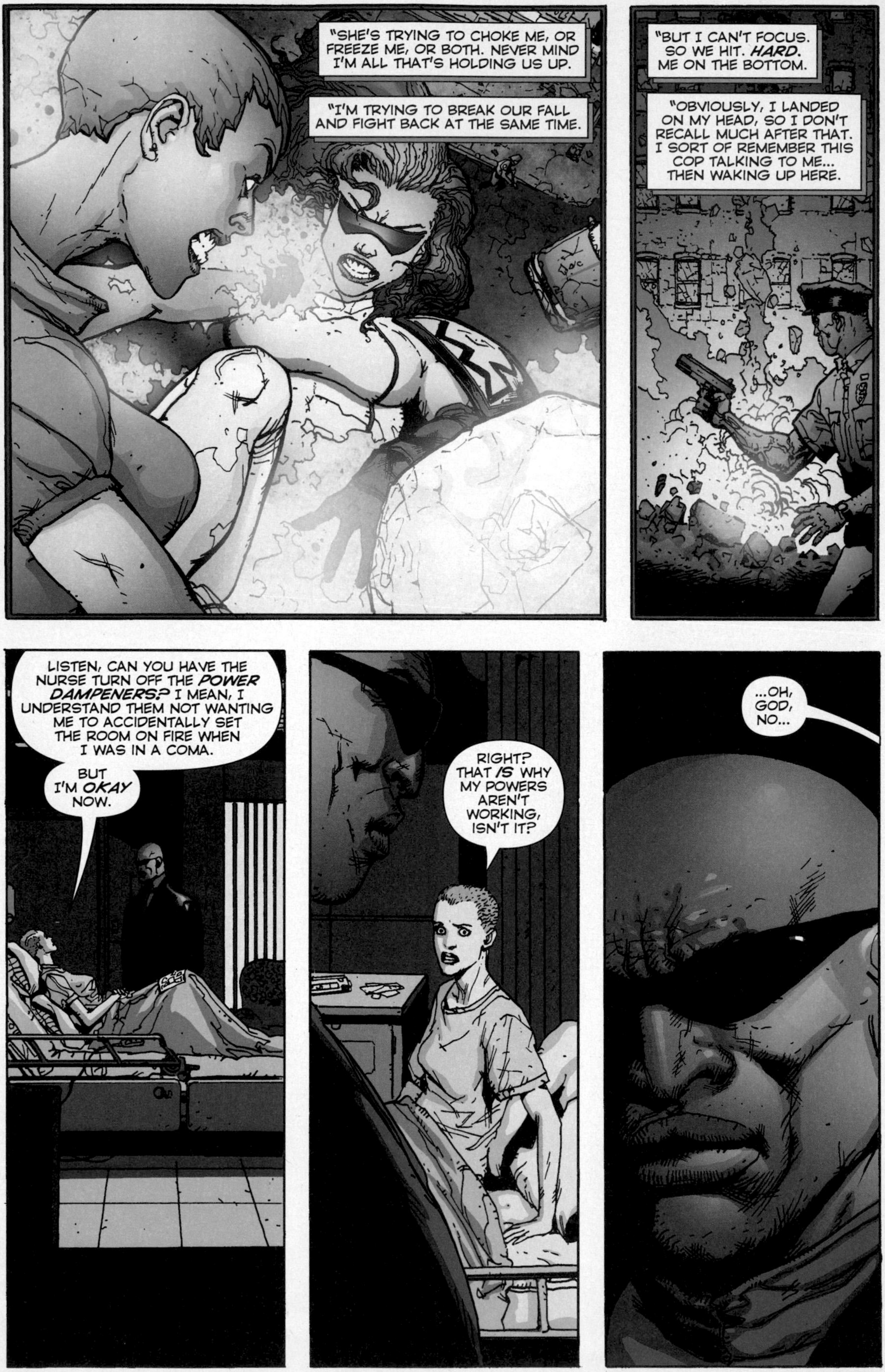
"SHE'S TRYING TO CHOKE ME, OR FREEZE ME, OR BOTH. NEVER MIND I'M ALL THAT'S HOLDING US UP.
"I'M TRYING TO BREAK OUR FALL AND FIGHT BACK AT THE SAME TIME.
"BUT I CAN'T FOCUS. SO WE HIT. HARD. ME ON THE BOTTOM.
"OBVIOUSLY, I LANDED ON MY HEAD, SO I DON'T RECALL MUCH AFTER THAT. I SORT OF REMEMBER THIS COP TALKING TO ME... THEN WAKING UP HERE.
LISTEN, CAN YOU HAVE THE NURSE TURN OFF THE POWER DAMPENERS? I MEAN, I UNDERSTAND THEM NOT WANTING ME TO ACCIDENTALLY SET THE ROOM ON FIRE WHEN I WAS IN A COMA.
BUT I'M OKAY NOW.
RIGHT? THAT IS WHY MY POWERS AREN'T WORKING, ISN'T IT?
...OH, GOD, NO...

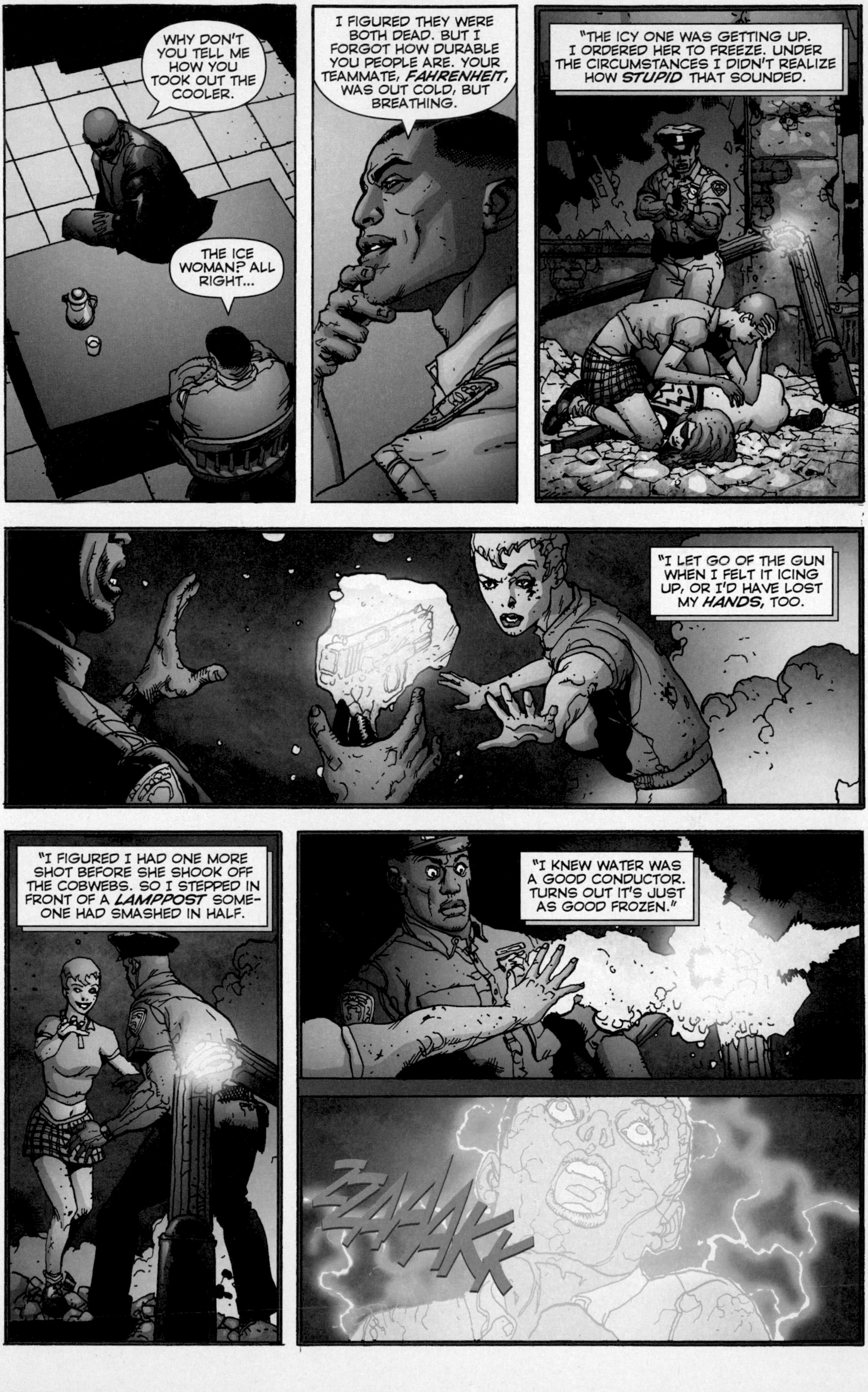

WHY DON'T YOU TELL ME HOW YOU TOOK OUT THE COOLER.
THE ICE WOMAN? ALL RIGHT...
I FIGURED THEY WERE BOTH DEAD. BUT I FORGOT HOW DURABLE YOU PEOPLE ARE. YOUR TEAMMATE, FAHRENHEIT, WAS OUT COLD, BUT BREATHING.
"THE ICY ONE WAS GETTING UP. I ORDERED HER TO FREEZE. UNDER THE CIRCUMSTANCES I DIDN'T REALIZE HOW STUPID THAT SOUNDED.
"I LET GO OF THE GUN WHEN I FELT IT ICING UP, OR I'D HAVE LOST MY HANDS, TOO.
"I FIGURED I HAD ONE MORE SHOT BEFORE SHE SHOOK OFF THE COBWEBS. SO I STEPPED IN FRONT OF A LAMPPOST SOME-ONE HAD SMASHED IN HALF.
"I KNEW WATER WAS A GOOD CONDUCTOR. TURNS OUT IT'S JUST AS GOOD FROZEN."
ZZAAAKK

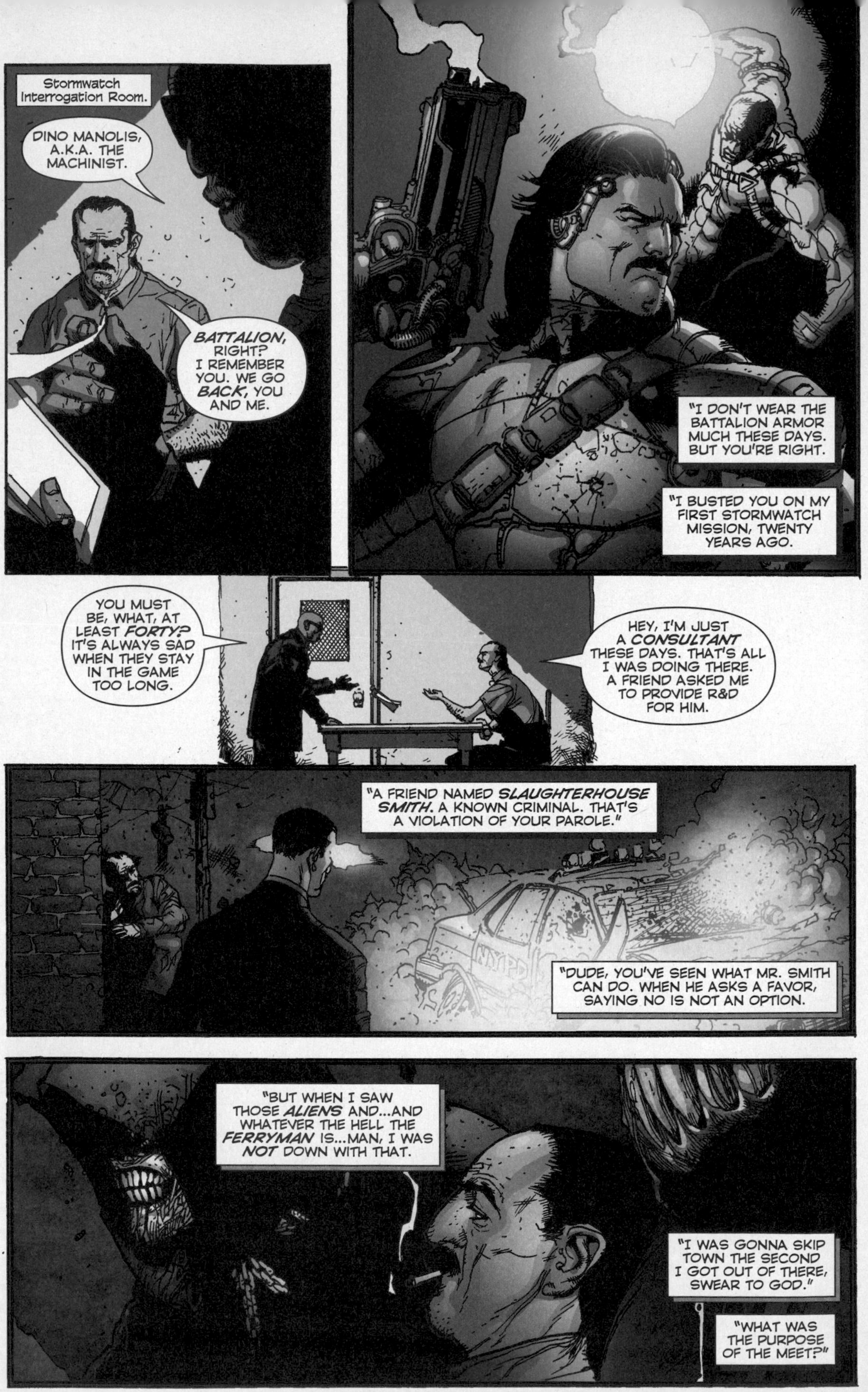
Stormwatch Interrogation Room.
DINO MANOLIS, A.K.A. THE MACHINIST.
BATTALION, RIGHT? I REMEMBER YOU. WE GO BACK, YOU AND ME.
"I DON'T WEAR THE BATTALION ARMOR MUCH THESE DAYS. BUT YOU'RE RIGHT.
"I BUSTED YOU ON MY FIRST STORMWATCH MISSION, TWENTY YEARS AGO.
YOU MUST BE, WHAT, AT LEAST FORTY? IT'S ALWAYS SAD WHEN THEY STAY IN THE GAME TOO LONG.
HEY, I'M JUST A CONSULTANT THESE DAYS. THAT'S ALL I WAS DOING THERE. A FRIEND ASKED ME TO PROVIDE R&D FOR HIM.
"A FRIEND NAMED SLAUGHTERHOUSE SMITH. A KNOWN CRIMINAL. THAT'S A VIOLATION OF YOUR PAROLE."
NYPD
"DUDE, YOU'VE SEEN WHAT MR. SMITH CAN DO. WHEN HE ASKS A FAVOR, SAYING NO IS NOT AN OPTION.
"BUT WHEN I SAW THOSE ALIENS AND...AND WHATEVER THE HELL THE FERRYMAN IS...MAN, I WAS NOT DOWN WITH THAT.
"I WAS GONNA SKIP TOWN THE SECOND I GOT OUT OF THERE, SWEAR TO GOD."
"WHAT WAS THE PURPOSE OF THE MEET?"

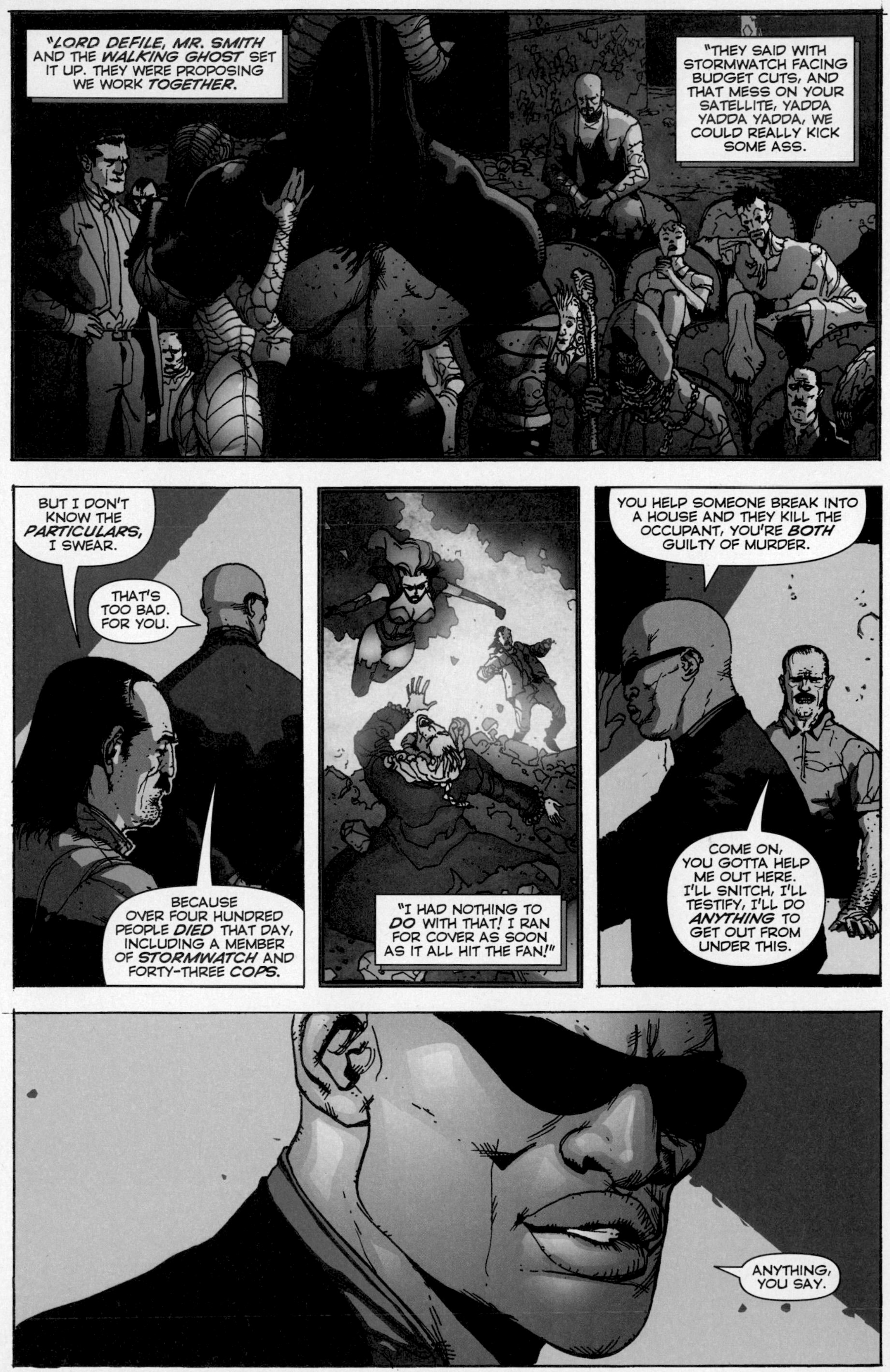
"LORD DEFILE, MR. SMITH AND THE WALKING GHOST SET IT UP. THEY WERE PROPOSING WE WORK TOGETHER.
"THEY SAID WITH STORMWATCH FACING BUDGET CUTS, AND THAT MESS ON YOUR SATELLITE, YADDA YADDA YADDA, WE COULD REALLY KICK SOME ASS.
BUT I DON'T KNOW THE PARTICULARS, I SWEAR.
THAT'S TOO BAD. FOR YOU.
BECAUSE OVER FOUR HUNDRED PEOPLE DIED THAT DAY, INCLUDING A MEMBER OF STORMWATCH AND FORTY-THREE COPS.
"I HAD NOTHING TO DO WITH THAT! I RAN FOR COVER AS SOON AS IT ALL HIT THE FAN!"
YOU HELP SOMEONE BREAK INTO A HOUSE AND THEY KILL THE OCCUPANT, YOU'RE BOTH GUILTY OF MURDER.
COME ON, YOU GOTTA HELP ME OUT HERE. I'LL SNITCH, I'LL TESTIFY, I'LL DO ANYTHING TO GET OUT FROM UNDER THIS.
ANYTHING, YOU SAY.

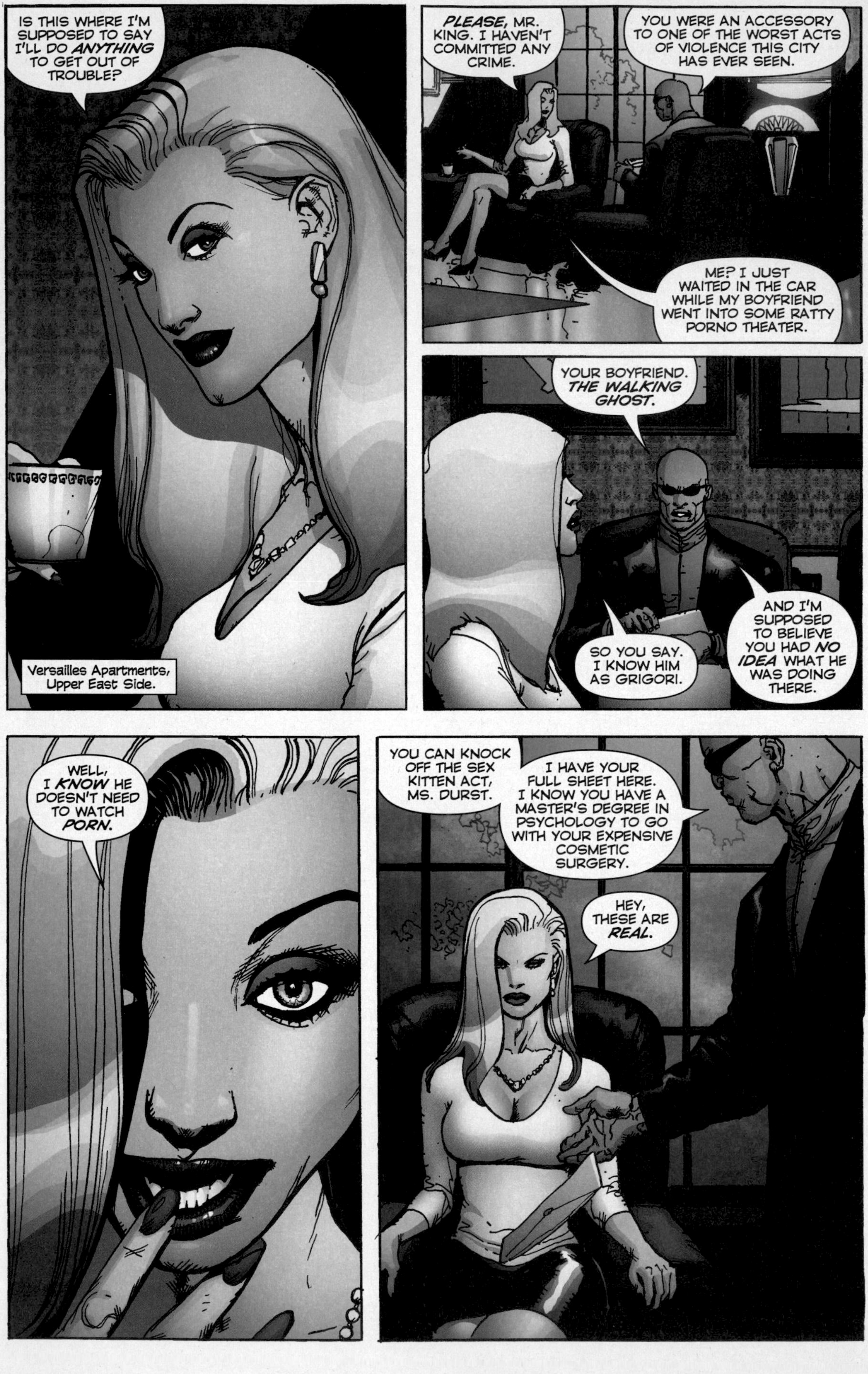
IS THIS WHERE I'M SUPPOSED TO SAY I'LL DO ANYTHING TO GET OUT OF TROUBLE?
Versailles Apartments, Upper East Side.
PLEASE, MR. KING. I HAVEN'T COMMITTED ANY CRIME.
YOU WERE AN ACCESSORY TO ONE OF THE WORST ACTS OF VIOLENCE THIS CITY HAS EVER SEEN.
ME? I JUST WAITED IN THE CAR WHILE MY BOYFRIEND WENT INTO SOME RATTY PORNO THEATER.
YOUR BOYFRIEND. THE WALKING GHOST.
SO YOU SAY. I KNOW HIM AS GRIGORI.
AND I'M SUPPOSED TO BELIEVE YOU HAD NO IDEA WHAT HE WAS DOING THERE.
WELL, I KNOW HE DOESN'T NEED TO WATCH PORN.
YOU CAN KNOCK OFF THE SEX KITTEN ACT, MS. DURST.
I HAVE YOUR FULL SHEET HERE. I KNOW YOU HAVE A MASTER'S DEGREE IN PSYCHOLOGY TO GO WITH YOUR EXPENSIVE COSMETIC SURGERY.
HEY, THESE ARE REAL.

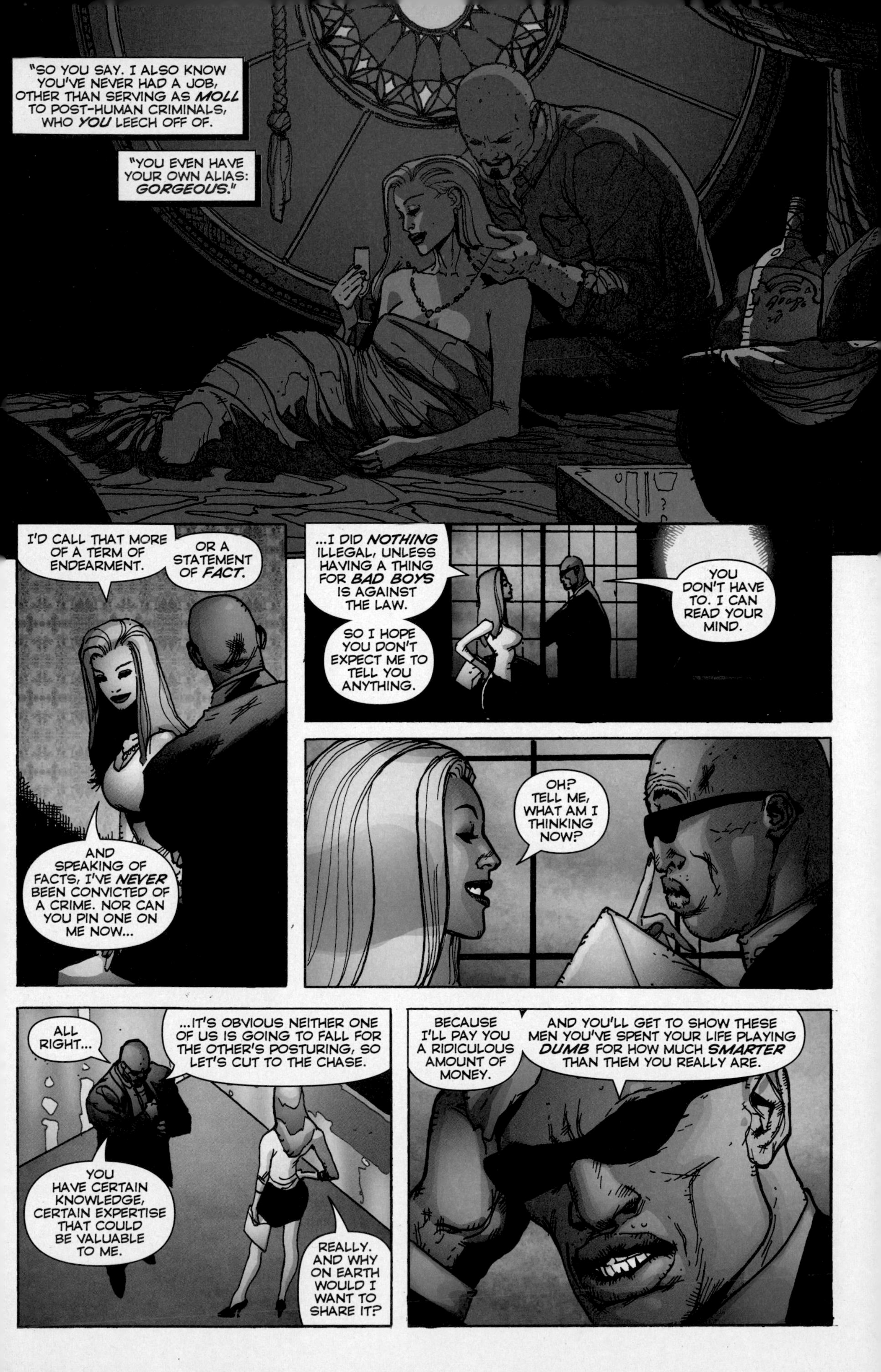
"SO YOU SAY. I ALSO KNOW YOU'VE NEVER HAD A JOB, OTHER THAN SERVING AS MOLL TO POST-HUMAN CRIMINALS, WHO YOU LEECH OFF OF.
"YOU EVEN HAVE YOUR OWN ALIAS: GORGEOUS."
I'D CALL THAT MORE OF A TERM OF ENDEARMENT.
OR A STATEMENT OF FACT.
AND SPEAKING OF FACTS, I'VE NEVER BEEN CONVICTED OF A CRIME. NOR CAN YOU PIN ONE ON ME NOW...
...I DID NOTHING ILLEGAL, UNLESS HAVING A THING FOR BAD BOYS IS AGAINST THE LAW.
SO I HOPE YOU DON'T EXPECT ME TO TELL YOU ANYTHING.
YOU DON'T HAVE TO. I CAN READ YOUR MIND.
OH? TELL ME, WHAT AM I THINKING NOW?
ALL RIGHT...
...IT'S OBVIOUS NEITHER ONE OF US IS GOING TO FALL FOR THE OTHER'S POSTURING, SO LET'S CUT TO THE CHASE.
YOU HAVE CERTAIN KNOWLEDGE, CERTAIN EXPERTISE THAT COULD BE VALUABLE TO ME.
REALLY. AND WHY ON EARTH WOULD I WANT TO SHARE IT?
BECAUSE I'LL PAY YOU A RIDICULOUS AMOUNT OF MONEY.
AND YOU'LL GET TO SHOW THESE MEN YOU'VE SPENT YOUR LIFE PLAYING DUMB FOR HOW MUCH SMARTER THAN THEM YOU REALLY ARE.

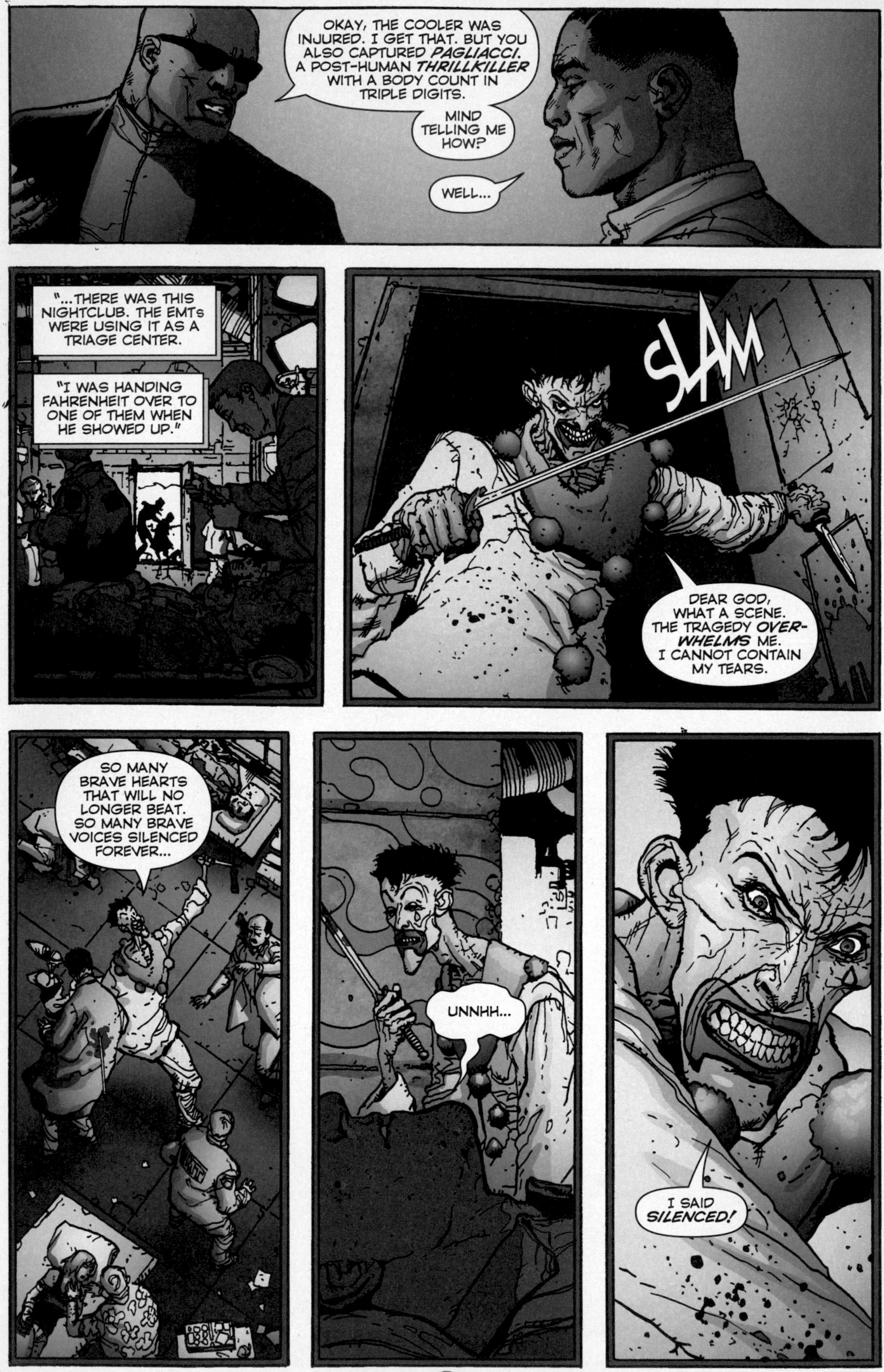
OKAY, THE COOLER WAS INJURED. I GET THAT. BUT YOU ALSO CAPTURED PAGLIACCI. A POST-HUMAN THRILLKILLER WITH A BODY COUNT IN TRIPLE DIGITS.
MIND TELLING ME HOW?
WELL...
"...THERE WAS THIS NIGHTCLUB. THE EMTs WERE USING IT AS A TRIAGE CENTER.
"I WAS HANDING FAHRENHEIT OVER TO ONE OF THEM WHEN HE SHOWED UP."
SLAM
DEAR GOD, WHAT A SCENE. THE TRAGEDY OVERWHELMS ME. I CANNOT CONTAIN MY TEARS.
SO MANY BRAVE HEARTS THAT WILL NO LONGER BEAT. SO MANY BRAVE VOICES SILENCED FOREVER...
UNNHH...
I SAID SILENCED!

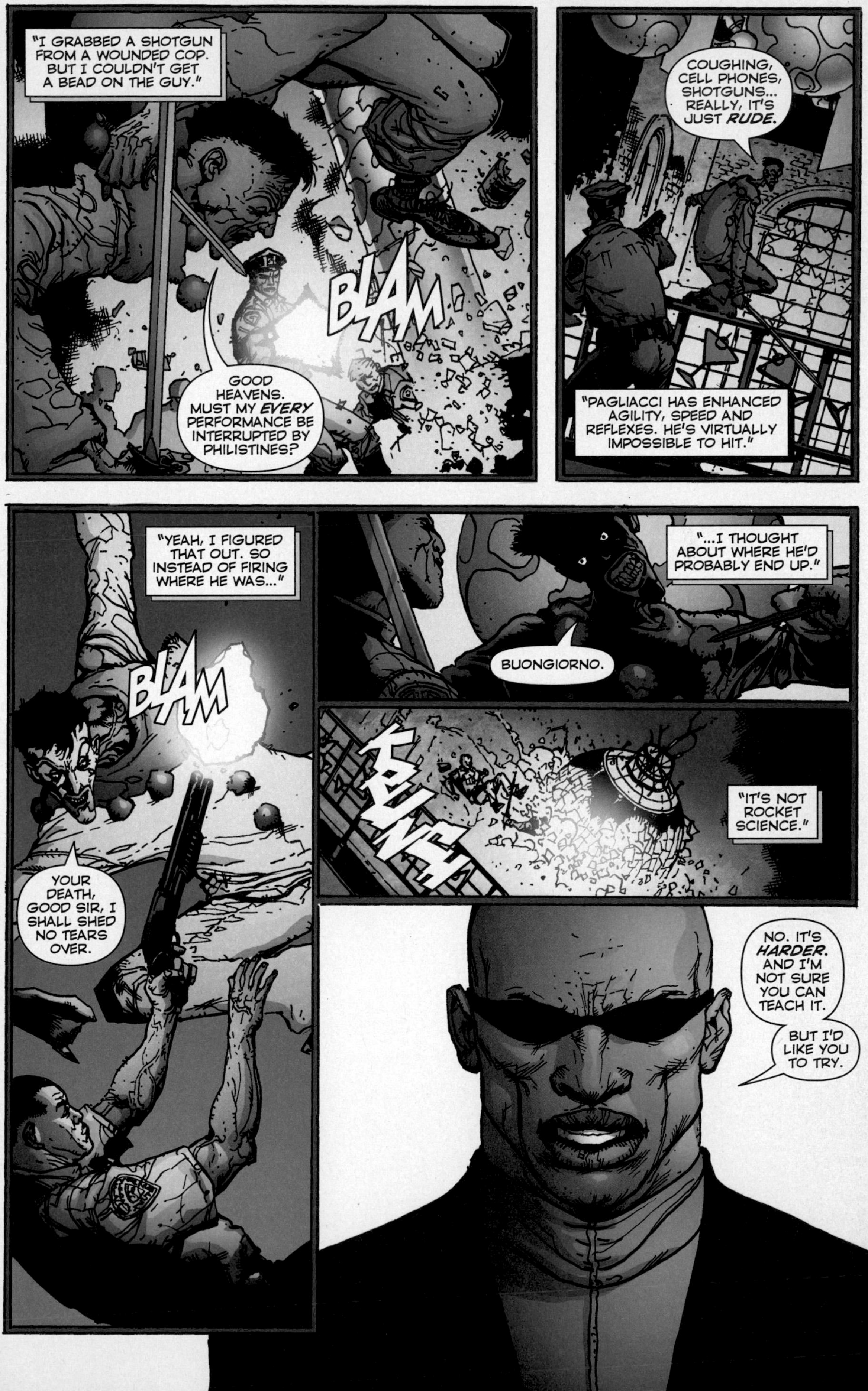
"I GRABBED A SHOTGUN FROM A WOUNDED COP. BUT I COULDN'T GET A BEAD ON THE GUY."
BLAM
GOOD HEAVENS. MUST MY *EVERY* PERFORMANCE BE INTERRUPTED BY PHILISTINES?
COUGHING, CELL PHONES, SHOTGUNS... REALLY, IT'S JUST *RUDE*.
"PAGLIACCI HAS ENHANCED AGILITY, SPEED AND REFLEXES. HE'S VIRTUALLY IMPOSSIBLE TO HIT."
"YEAH, I FIGURED THAT OUT. SO INSTEAD OF FIRING WHERE HE WAS..."
BLAM
YOUR DEATH, GOOD SIR, I SHALL SHED NO TEARS OVER.
"...I THOUGHT ABOUT WHERE HE'D PROBABLY END UP."
BUONGIORNO.
"IT'S NOT ROCKET SCIENCE."
NO. IT'S *HARDER*. AND I'M NOT SURE YOU CAN TEACH IT.
BUT I'D LIKE YOU TO TRY.

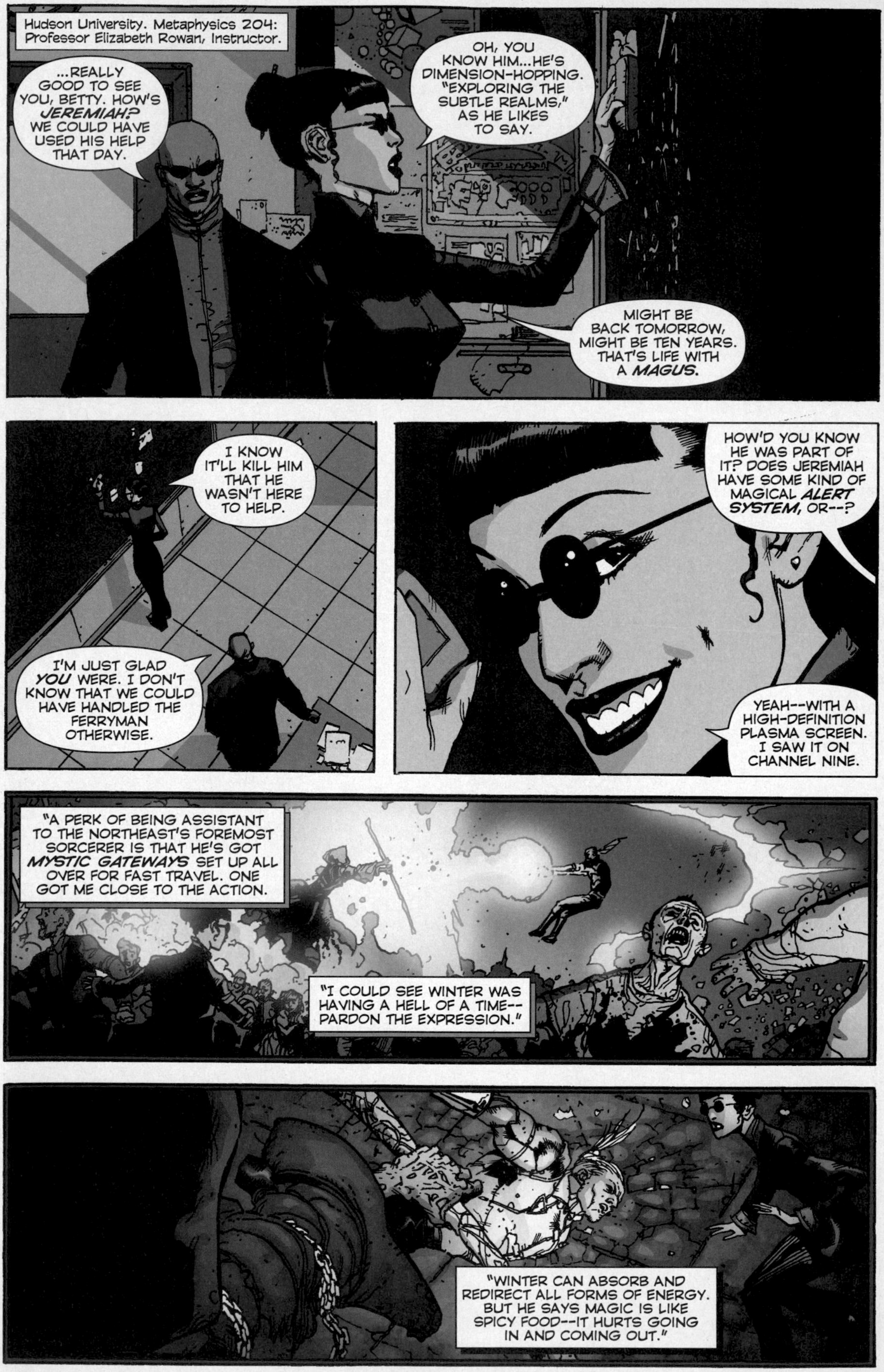
Hudson University. Metaphysics 204: Professor Elizabeth Rowan, Instructor.
...REALLY GOOD TO SEE YOU, BETTY. HOW'S JEREMIAH? WE COULD HAVE USED HIS HELP THAT DAY.
OH, YOU KNOW HIM...HE'S DIMENSION-HOPPING. "EXPLORING THE SUBTLE REALMS," AS HE LIKES TO SAY.
MIGHT BE BACK TOMORROW, MIGHT BE TEN YEARS. THAT'S LIFE WITH A MAGUS.
I KNOW IT'LL KILL HIM THAT HE WASN'T HERE TO HELP.
I'M JUST GLAD YOU WERE. I DON'T KNOW THAT WE COULD HAVE HANDLED THE FERRYMAN OTHERWISE.
HOW'D YOU KNOW HE WAS PART OF IT? DOES JEREMIAH HAVE SOME KIND OF MAGICAL ALERT SYSTEM, OR--?
YEAH--WITH A HIGH-DEFINITION PLASMA SCREEN. I SAW IT ON CHANNEL NINE.
"A PERK OF BEING ASSISTANT TO THE NORTHEAST'S FOREMOST SORCERER IS THAT HE'S GOT MYSTIC GATEWAYS SET UP ALL OVER FOR FAST TRAVEL. ONE GOT ME CLOSE TO THE ACTION.
"I COULD SEE WINTER WAS HAVING A HELL OF A TIME--PARDON THE EXPRESSION."
"WINTER CAN ABSORB AND REDIRECT ALL FORMS OF ENERGY. BUT HE SAYS MAGIC IS LIKE SPICY FOOD--IT HURTS GOING IN AND COMING OUT."

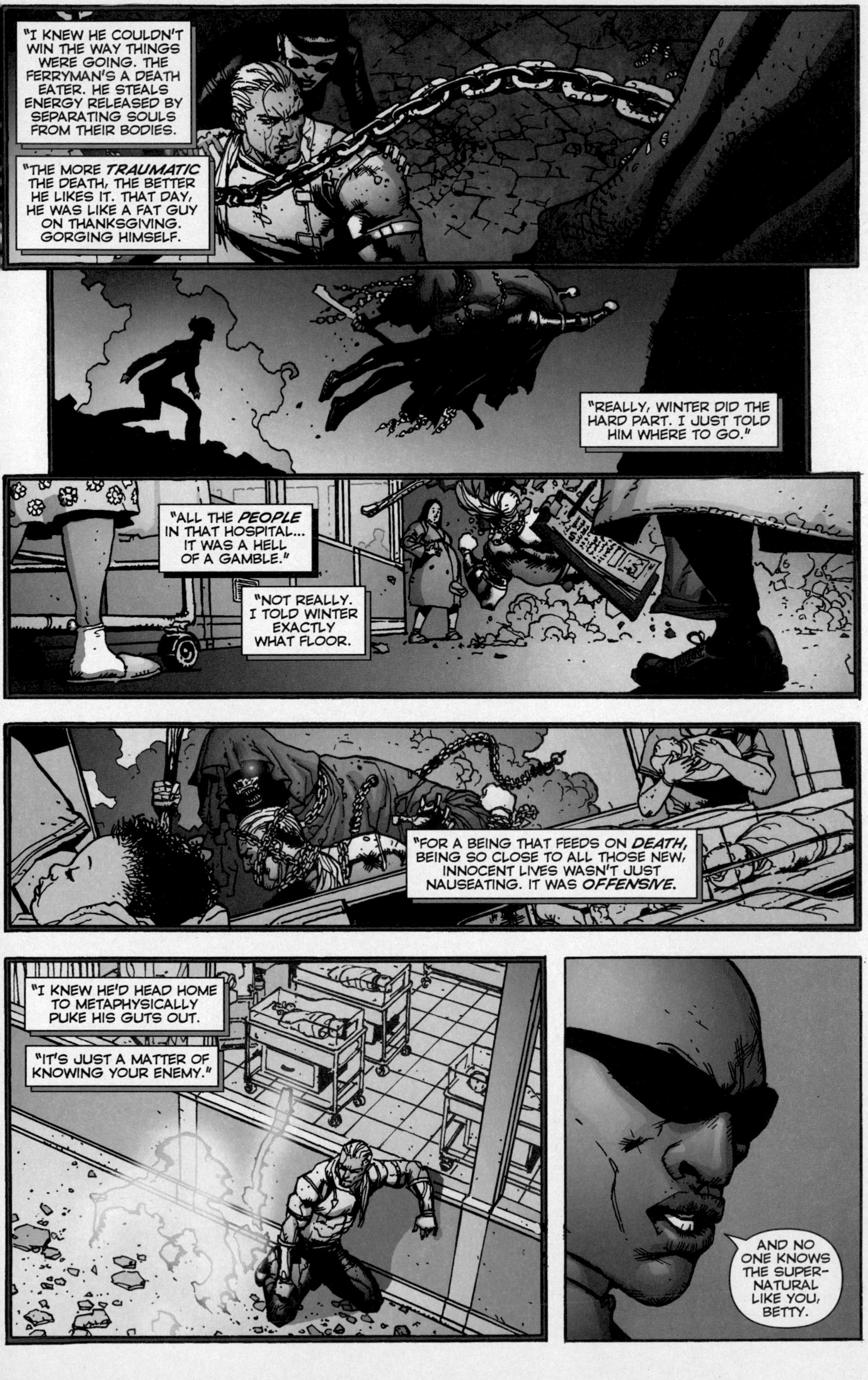
"I KNEW HE COULDN'T WIN THE WAY THINGS WERE GOING. THE FERRYMAN'S A DEATH EATER. HE STEALS ENERGY RELEASED BY SEPARATING SOULS FROM THEIR BODIES.
"THE MORE *TRAUMATIC* THE DEATH, THE BETTER HE LIKES IT. THAT DAY, HE WAS LIKE A FAT GUY ON THANKSGIVING. GORGING HIMSELF.
"REALLY, WINTER DID THE HARD PART. I JUST TOLD HIM WHERE TO GO."
"ALL THE *PEOPLE* IN THAT HOSPITAL... IT WAS A HELL OF A GAMBLE."
"NOT REALLY. I TOLD WINTER EXACTLY WHAT FLOOR.
"FOR A BEING THAT FEEDS ON *DEATH*, BEING SO CLOSE TO ALL THOSE NEW, INNOCENT LIVES WASN'T JUST NAUSEATING. IT WAS *OFFENSIVE*.
"I KNEW HE'D HEAD HOME TO METAPHYSICALLY PUKE HIS GUTS OUT.
"IT'S JUST A MATTER OF KNOWING YOUR ENEMY."
AND NO ONE KNOWS THE SUPER-NATURAL LIKE YOU, BETTY.

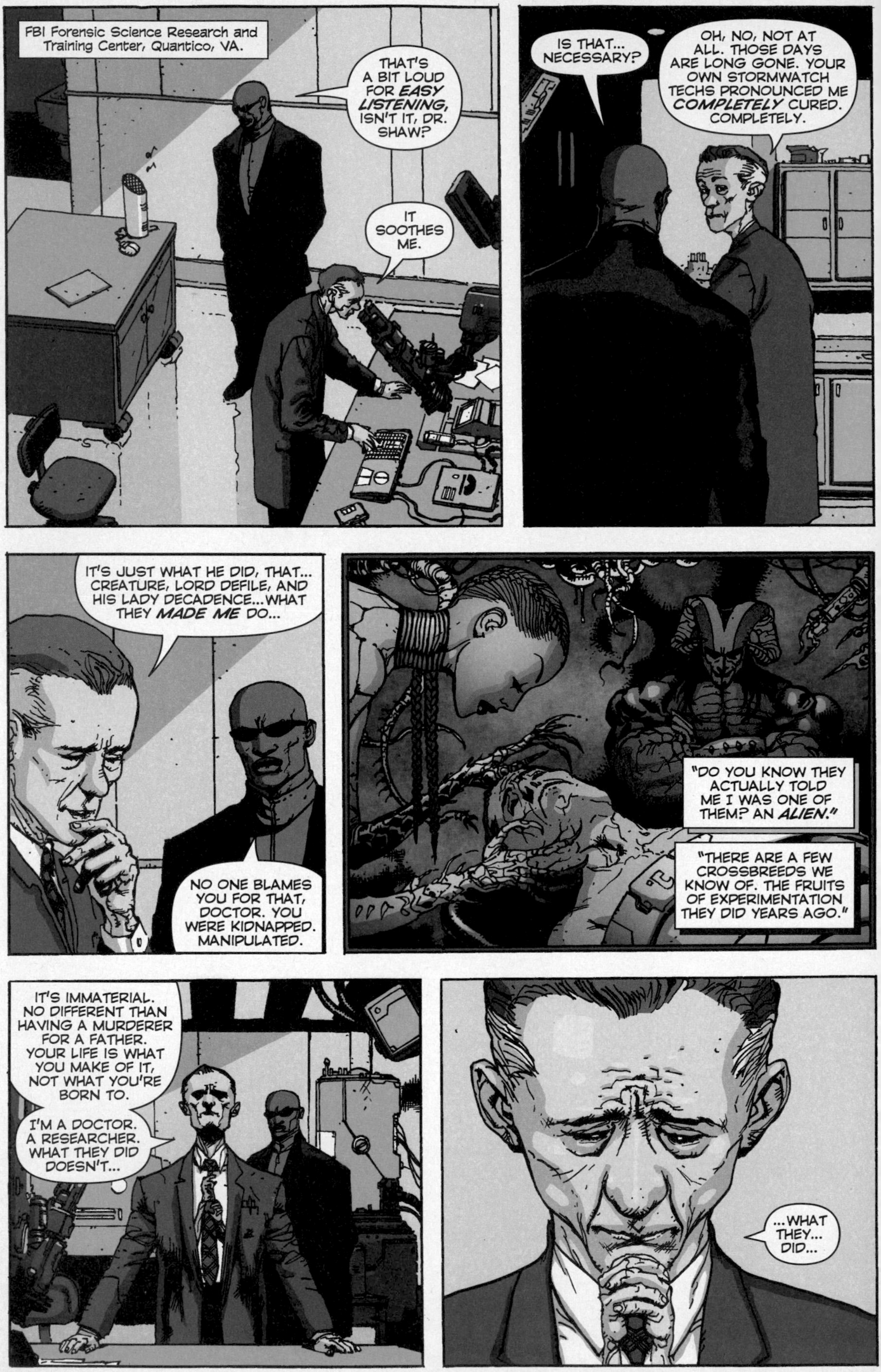
FBI Forensic Science Research and Training Center, Quantico, VA.
THAT'S A BIT LOUD FOR EASY LISTENING, ISN'T IT, DR. SHAW?
IT SOOTHES ME.
IS THAT... NECESSARY?
OH, NO, NOT AT ALL. THOSE DAYS ARE LONG GONE. YOUR OWN STORMWATCH TECHS PRONOUNCED ME COMPLETELY CURED. COMPLETELY.
IT'S JUST WHAT HE DID, THAT... CREATURE, LORD DEFILE, AND HIS LADY DECADENCE...WHAT THEY MADE ME DO...
NO ONE BLAMES YOU FOR THAT, DOCTOR. YOU WERE KIDNAPPED. MANIPULATED.
"DO YOU KNOW THEY ACTUALLY TOLD ME I WAS ONE OF THEM? AN ALIEN."
"THERE ARE A FEW CROSSBREEDS WE KNOW OF. THE FRUITS OF EXPERIMENTATION THEY DID YEARS AGO."
IT'S IMMATERIAL. NO DIFFERENT THAN HAVING A MURDERER FOR A FATHER. YOUR LIFE IS WHAT YOU MAKE OF IT, NOT WHAT YOU'RE BORN TO.
I'M A DOCTOR. A RESEARCHER. WHAT THEY DID DOESN'T...
...WHAT THEY... DID...

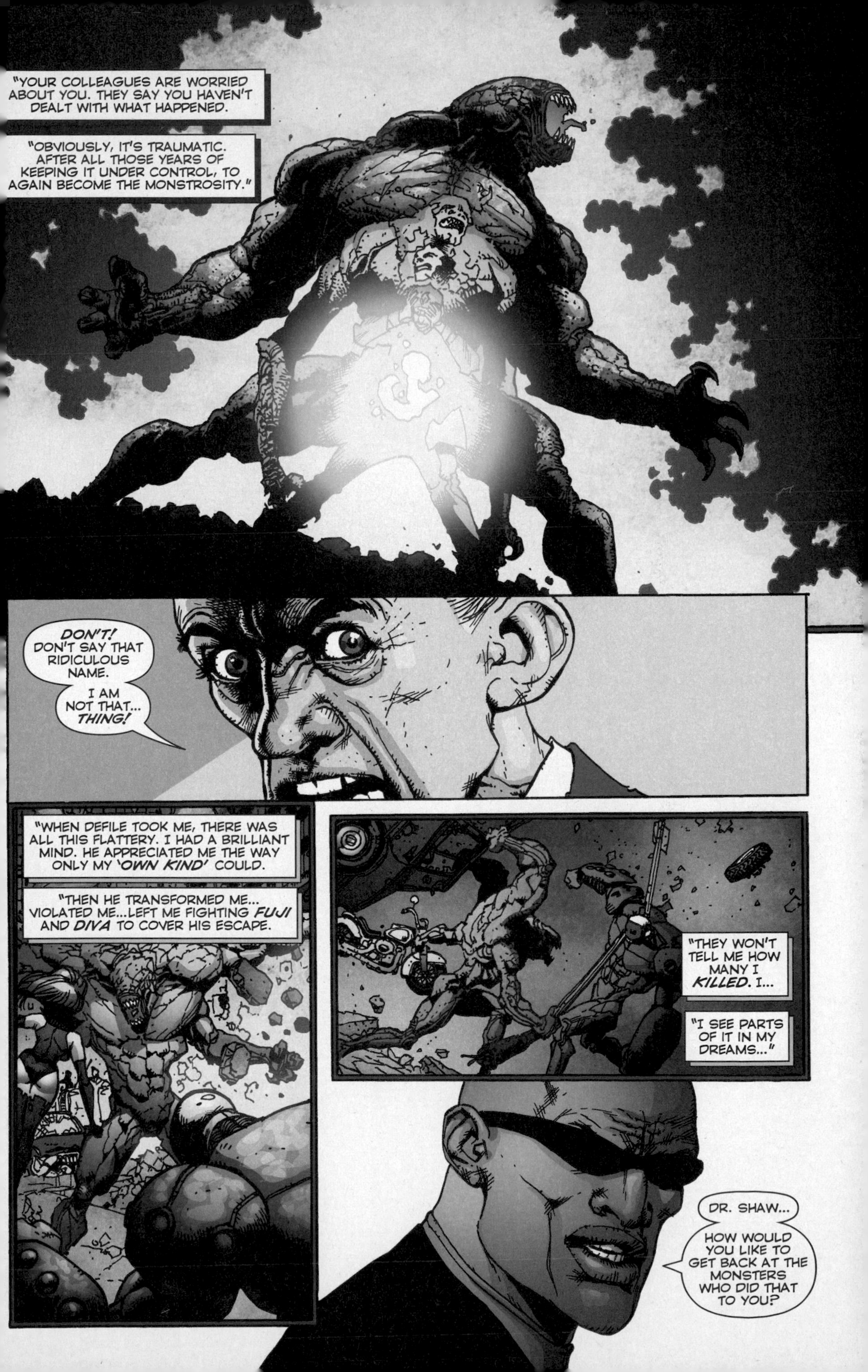
"YOUR COLLEAGUES ARE WORRIED ABOUT YOU. THEY SAY YOU HAVEN'T DEALT WITH WHAT HAPPENED.
"OBVIOUSLY, IT'S TRAUMATIC. AFTER ALL THOSE YEARS OF KEEPING IT UNDER CONTROL, TO AGAIN BECOME THE MONSTROSITY."
DON'T! DON'T SAY THAT RIDICULOUS NAME.
I AM NOT THAT... *THING!*
"WHEN DEFILE TOOK ME, THERE WAS ALL THIS FLATTERY. I HAD A BRILLIANT MIND. HE APPRECIATED ME THE WAY ONLY MY *'OWN KIND'* COULD.
"THEN HE TRANSFORMED ME... VIOLATED ME...LEFT ME FIGHTING *FUJI* AND *DIVA* TO COVER HIS ESCAPE.
"THEY WON'T TELL ME HOW MANY I *KILLED*. I...
"I SEE PARTS OF IT IN MY DREAMS..."
DR. SHAW...
HOW WOULD YOU LIKE TO GET BACK AT THE MONSTERS WHO DID THAT TO YOU?

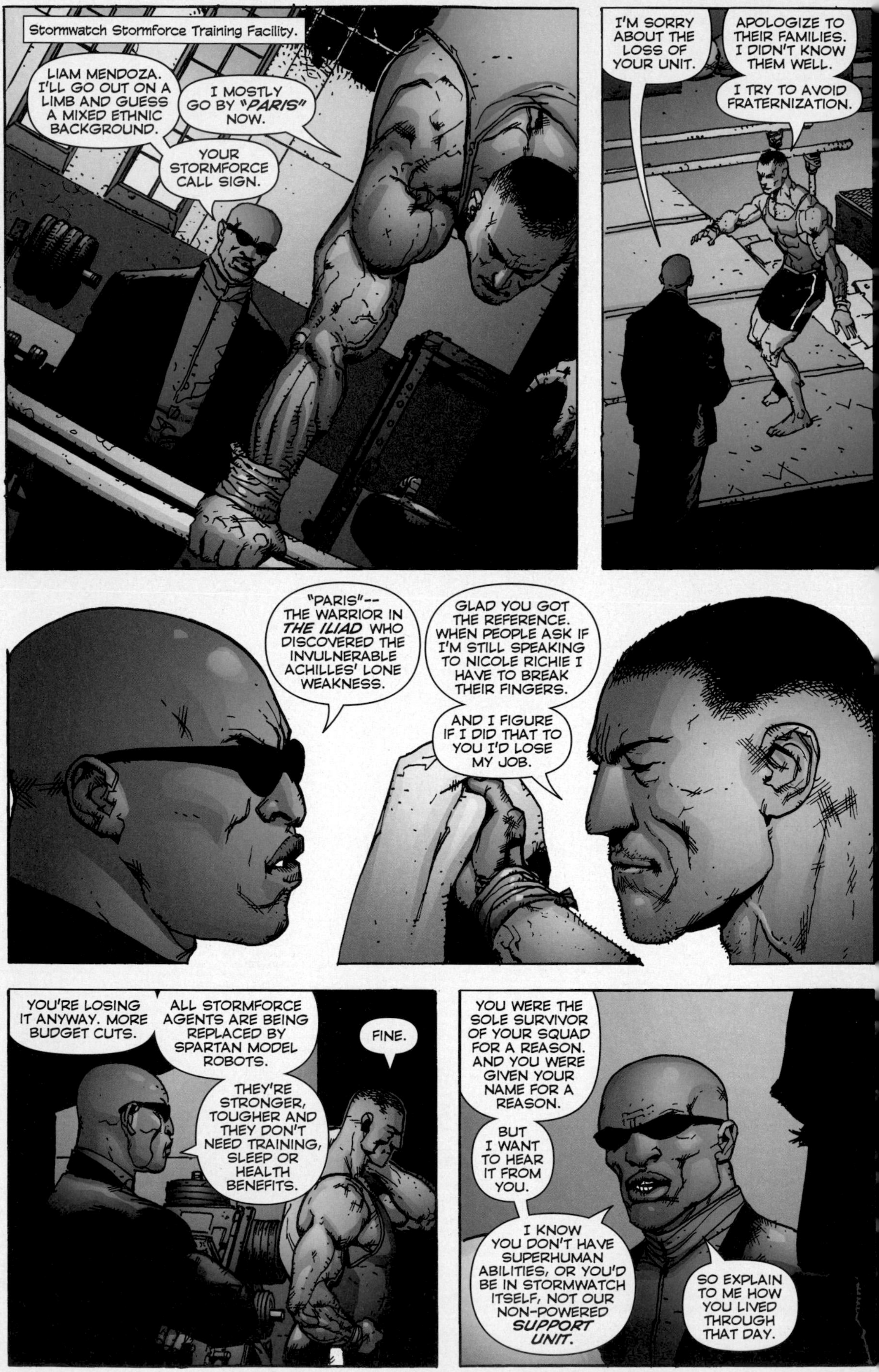
Stormwatch Stormforce Training Facility.
LIAM MENDOZA. I'LL GO OUT ON A LIMB AND GUESS A MIXED ETHNIC BACKGROUND.
I MOSTLY GO BY "PARIS" NOW.
YOUR STORMFORCE CALL SIGN.
I'M SORRY ABOUT THE LOSS OF YOUR UNIT.
APOLOGIZE TO THEIR FAMILIES. I DIDN'T KNOW THEM WELL.
I TRY TO AVOID FRATERNIZATION.
"PARIS"-- THE WARRIOR IN THE ILIAD WHO DISCOVERED THE INVULNERABLE ACHILLES' LONE WEAKNESS.
GLAD YOU GOT THE REFERENCE. WHEN PEOPLE ASK IF I'M STILL SPEAKING TO NICOLE RICHIE I HAVE TO BREAK THEIR FINGERS.
AND I FIGURE IF I DID THAT TO YOU I'D LOSE MY JOB.
YOU'RE LOSING IT ANYWAY. MORE BUDGET CUTS.
ALL STORMFORCE AGENTS ARE BEING REPLACED BY SPARTAN MODEL ROBOTS.
THEY'RE STRONGER, TOUGHER AND THEY DON'T NEED TRAINING, SLEEP OR HEALTH BENEFITS.
FINE.
YOU WERE THE SOLE SURVIVOR OF YOUR SQUAD FOR A REASON. AND YOU WERE GIVEN YOUR NAME FOR A REASON.
BUT I WANT TO HEAR IT FROM YOU.
I KNOW YOU DON'T HAVE SUPERHUMAN ABILITIES, OR YOU'D BE IN STORMWATCH ITSELF, NOT OUR NON-POWERED SUPPORT UNIT.
SO EXPLAIN TO ME HOW YOU LIVED THROUGH THAT DAY.

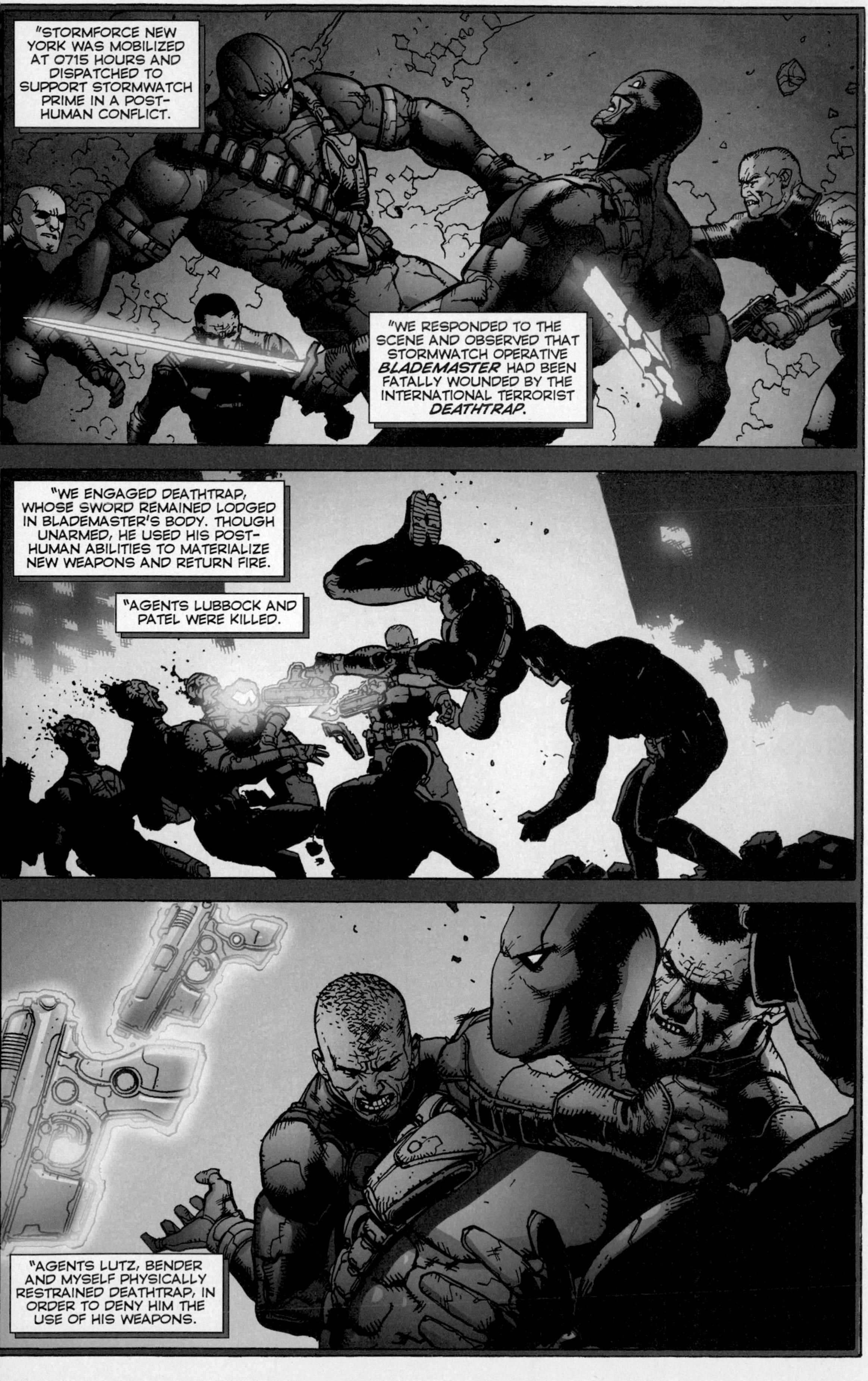
"STORMFORCE NEW YORK WAS MOBILIZED AT 0715 HOURS AND DISPATCHED TO SUPPORT STORMWATCH PRIME IN A POST-HUMAN CONFLICT.
"WE RESPONDED TO THE SCENE AND OBSERVED THAT STORMWATCH OPERATIVE BLADEMASTER HAD BEEN FATALLY WOUNDED BY THE INTERNATIONAL TERRORIST DEATHTRAP.
"WE ENGAGED DEATHTRAP, WHOSE SWORD REMAINED LODGED IN BLADEMASTER'S BODY. THOUGH UNARMED, HE USED HIS POST-HUMAN ABILITIES TO MATERIALIZE NEW WEAPONS AND RETURN FIRE.
"AGENTS LUBBOCK AND PATEL WERE KILLED.
"AGENTS LUTZ, BENDER AND MYSELF PHYSICALLY RESTRAINED DEATHTRAP, IN ORDER TO DENY HIM THE USE OF HIS WEAPONS.

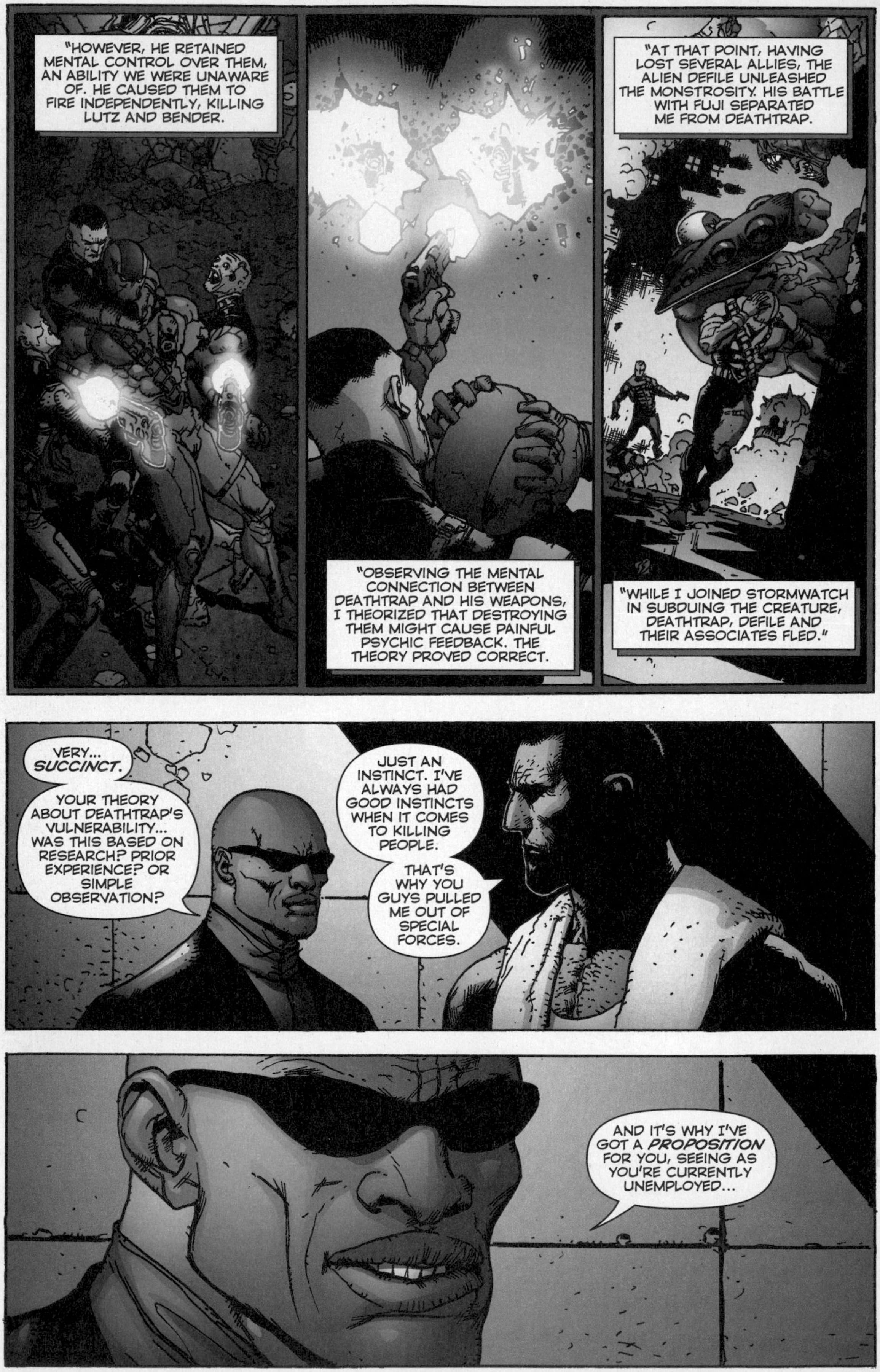
"HOWEVER, HE RETAINED MENTAL CONTROL OVER THEM, AN ABILITY WE WERE UNAWARE OF. HE CAUSED THEM TO FIRE INDEPENDENTLY, KILLING LUTZ AND BENDER.
"OBSERVING THE MENTAL CONNECTION BETWEEN DEATHTRAP AND HIS WEAPONS, I THEORIZED THAT DESTROYING THEM MIGHT CAUSE PAINFUL PSYCHIC FEEDBACK. THE THEORY PROVED CORRECT.
"AT THAT POINT, HAVING LOST SEVERAL ALLIES, THE ALIEN DEFILE UNLEASHED THE MONSTROSITY. HIS BATTLE WITH FUJI SEPARATED ME FROM DEATHTRAP.
"WHILE I JOINED STORMWATCH IN SUBDUING THE CREATURE, DEATHTRAP, DEFILE AND THEIR ASSOCIATES FLED."
VERY... *SUCCINCT.*
YOUR THEORY ABOUT DEATHTRAP'S VULNERABILITY... WAS THIS BASED ON RESEARCH? PRIOR EXPERIENCE? OR SIMPLE OBSERVATION?
JUST AN INSTINCT. I'VE ALWAYS HAD GOOD INSTINCTS WHEN IT COMES TO KILLING PEOPLE.
THAT'S WHY YOU GUYS PULLED ME OUT OF SPECIAL FORCES.
AND IT'S WHY I'VE GOT A *PROPOSITION* FOR YOU, SEEING AS YOU'RE CURRENTLY UNEMPLOYED...

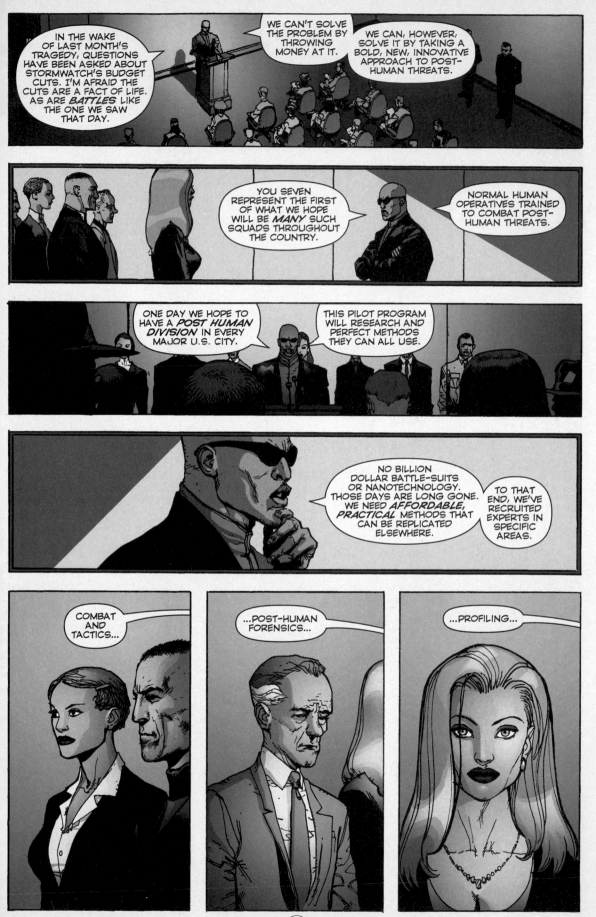

IN THE WAKE OF LAST MONTH'S TRAGEDY, QUESTIONS HAVE BEEN ASKED ABOUT STORMWATCH'S BUDGET CUTS. I'M AFRAID THE CUTS ARE A FACT OF LIFE. AS ARE *BATTLES* LIKE THE ONE WE SAW THAT DAY.

WE CAN'T SOLVE THE PROBLEM BY THROWING MONEY AT IT.

WE CAN, HOWEVER, SOLVE IT BY TAKING A BOLD, NEW, INNOVATIVE APPROACH TO POST-HUMAN THREATS.

YOU SEVEN REPRESENT THE FIRST OF WHAT WE HOPE WILL BE *MANY* SUCH SQUADS THROUGHOUT THE COUNTRY.

NORMAL HUMAN OPERATIVES TRAINED TO COMBAT POST-HUMAN THREATS.

ONE DAY WE HOPE TO HAVE A *POST HUMAN DIVISION* IN EVERY MAJOR U.S. CITY.

THIS PILOT PROGRAM WILL RESEARCH AND PERFECT METHODS THEY CAN ALL USE.

NO BILLION DOLLAR BATTLE-SUITS OR NANOTECHNOLOGY. THOSE DAYS ARE LONG GONE. WE NEED *AFFORDABLE, PRACTICAL* METHODS THAT CAN BE REPLICATED ELSEWHERE.

TO THAT END, WE'VE RECRUITED EXPERTS IN SPECIFIC AREAS.

COMBAT AND TACTICS...

...POST-HUMAN FORENSICS...

...PROFILING...

33

...THE SUPERNATURAL...

...AND TECHNOLOGY.

WHILE RECEIVING SUPPORT AND COOPERATION FROM STORMWATCH, PHD IS A COMPLETELY *AUTONOMOUS* BRANCH OF LOCAL LAW ENFORCEMENT.

IT WILL BE HOUSED IN THE 18TH PRECINCT, LED BY ONE OF ITS *OWN* WHO DISPLAYED UNCOMMON *HEROISM* ON THAT TERRIBLE DAY. OFFICER *JOHN DORAN.*

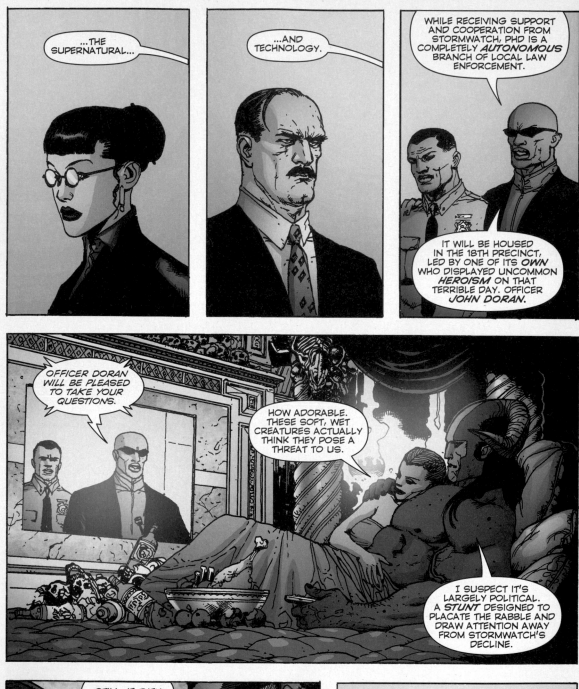

OFFICER DORAN WILL BE PLEASED TO *TAKE YOUR QUESTIONS.*

HOW ADORABLE. THESE SOFT, WET CREATURES ACTUALLY THINK THEY POSE A THREAT TO US.

I SUSPECT IT'S LARGELY POLITICAL. A *STUNT* DESIGNED TO PLACATE THE RABBLE AND DRAW ATTENTION AWAY FROM STORMWATCH'S DECLINE.

STILL, IF THEY PROVE TO BE AN ANNOYANCE...

...THE MOLE I'VE PLANTED AMONG THEM WILL MAKE THEM EASY ENOUGH TO CRUSH.

OFFICER DORAN, WHAT CAN YOU DO THAT SPARTAN ROBOTS CAN'T?

GUYS, GUYS. I'M KIND OF NEW AT THIS.

SO GO *EASY* ON ME, ALL RIGHT?

OFFICER DORAN, DO YOU THINK *RACE* WAS A FACTOR IN YOUR HIRING?

Chapter 2: Ghosts

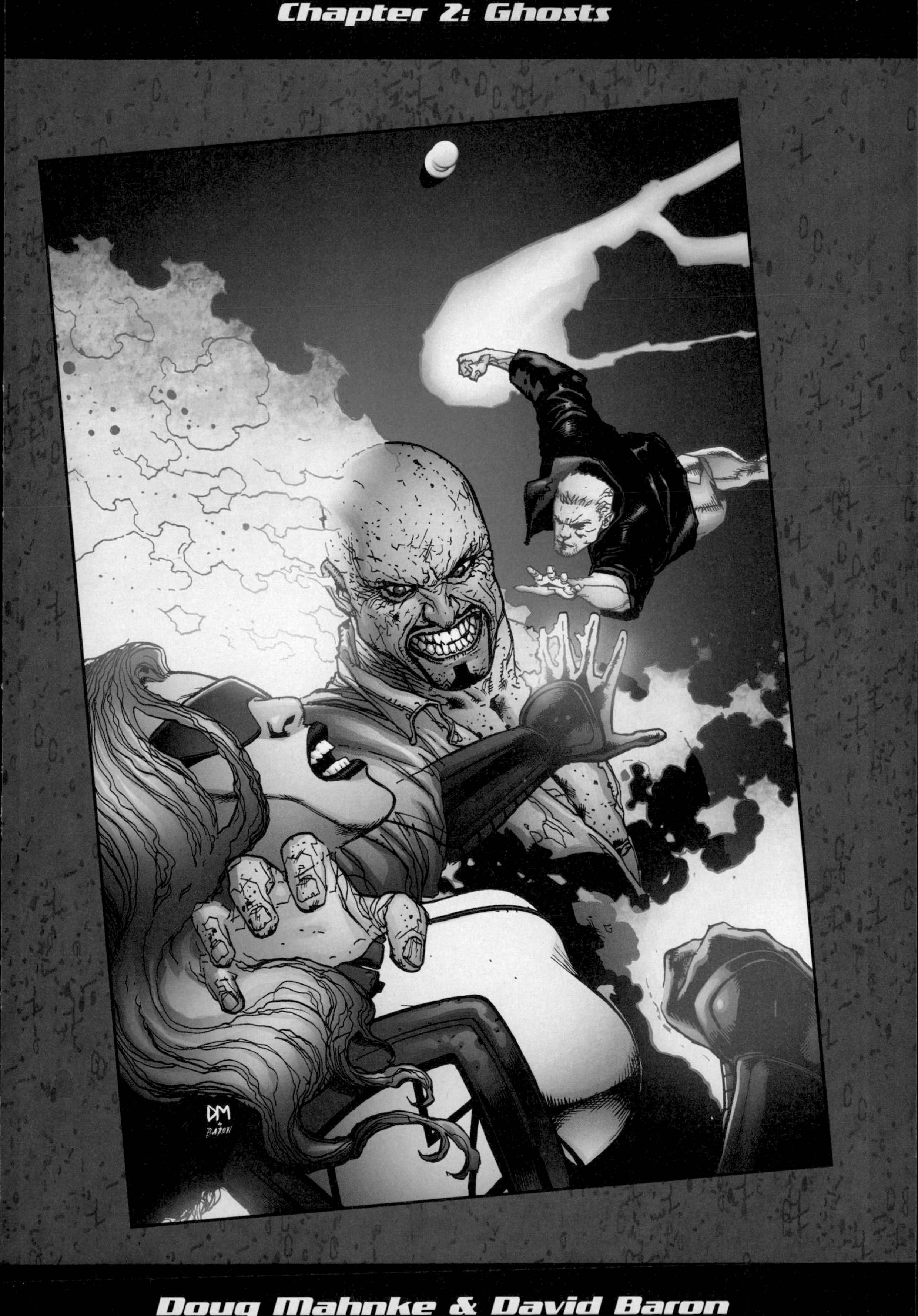

DM
BARON

Doug Mahnke & David Baron

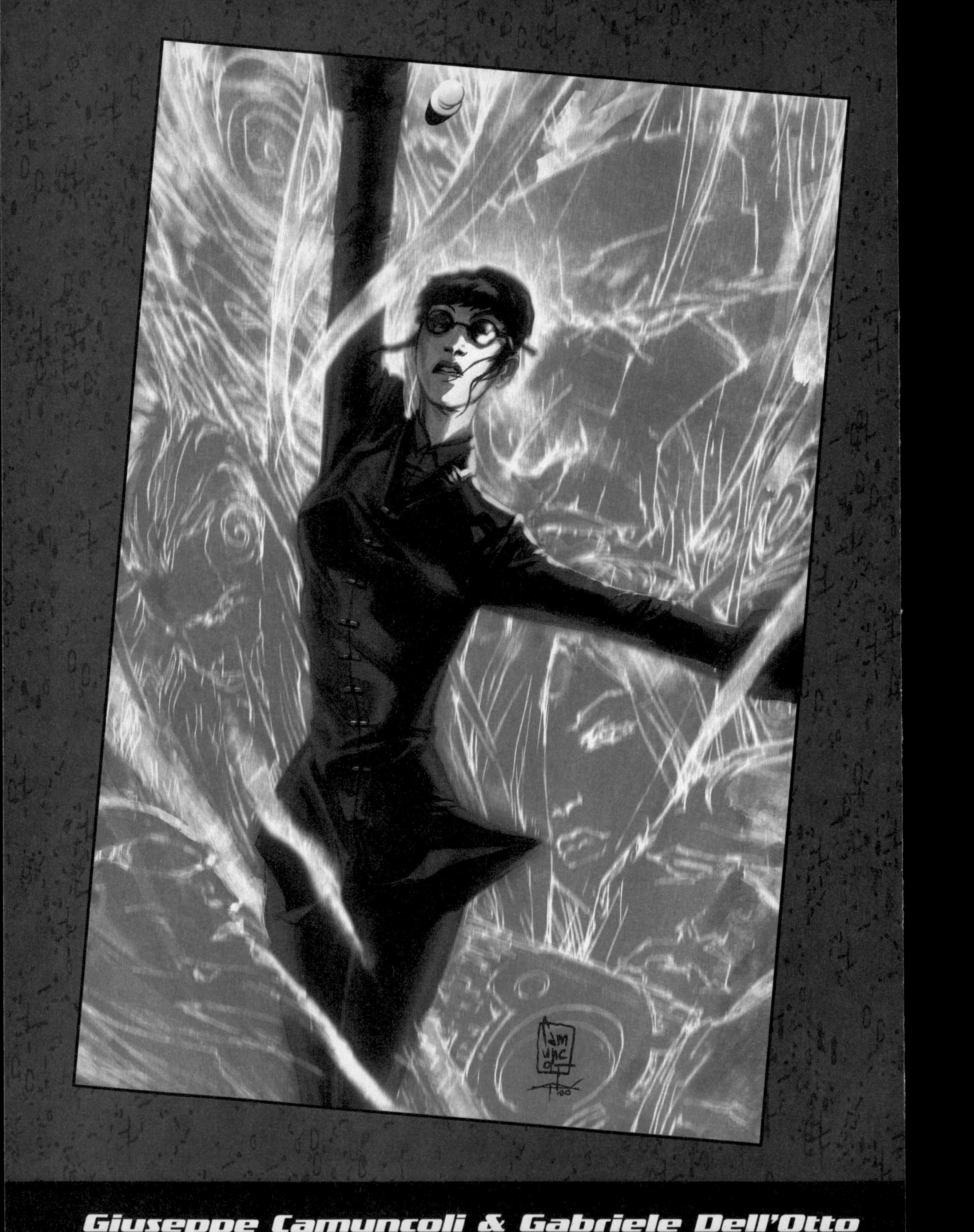

Giuseppe Camuncoli & Gabriele Dell'Otto

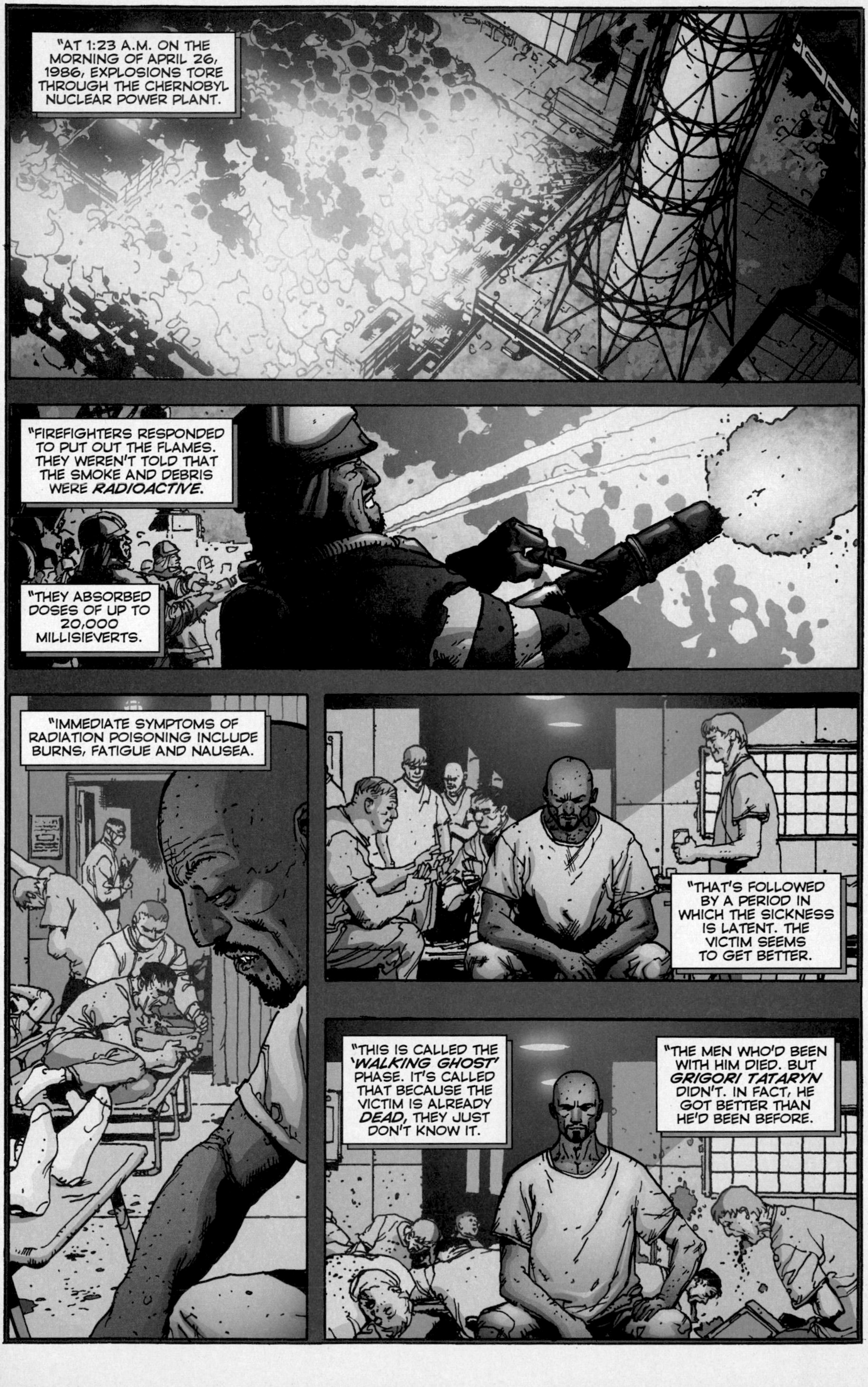
"AT 1:23 A.M. ON THE MORNING OF APRIL 26, 1986, EXPLOSIONS TORE THROUGH THE CHERNOBYL NUCLEAR POWER PLANT.
"FIREFIGHTERS RESPONDED TO PUT OUT THE FLAMES. THEY WEREN'T TOLD THAT THE SMOKE AND DEBRIS WERE *RADIOACTIVE*.
"THEY ABSORBED DOSES OF UP TO 20,000 MILLISIEVERTS.
"IMMEDIATE SYMPTOMS OF RADIATION POISONING INCLUDE BURNS, FATIGUE AND NAUSEA.
"THAT'S FOLLOWED BY A PERIOD IN WHICH THE SICKNESS IS LATENT. THE VICTIM SEEMS TO GET BETTER.
"THIS IS CALLED THE '*WALKING GHOST*' PHASE. IT'S CALLED THAT BECAUSE THE VICTIM IS ALREADY *DEAD*, THEY JUST DON'T KNOW IT.
"THE MEN WHO'D BEEN WITH HIM DIED. BUT *GRIGORI TATARYN* DIDN'T. IN FACT, HE GOT BETTER THAN HE'D BEEN BEFORE.

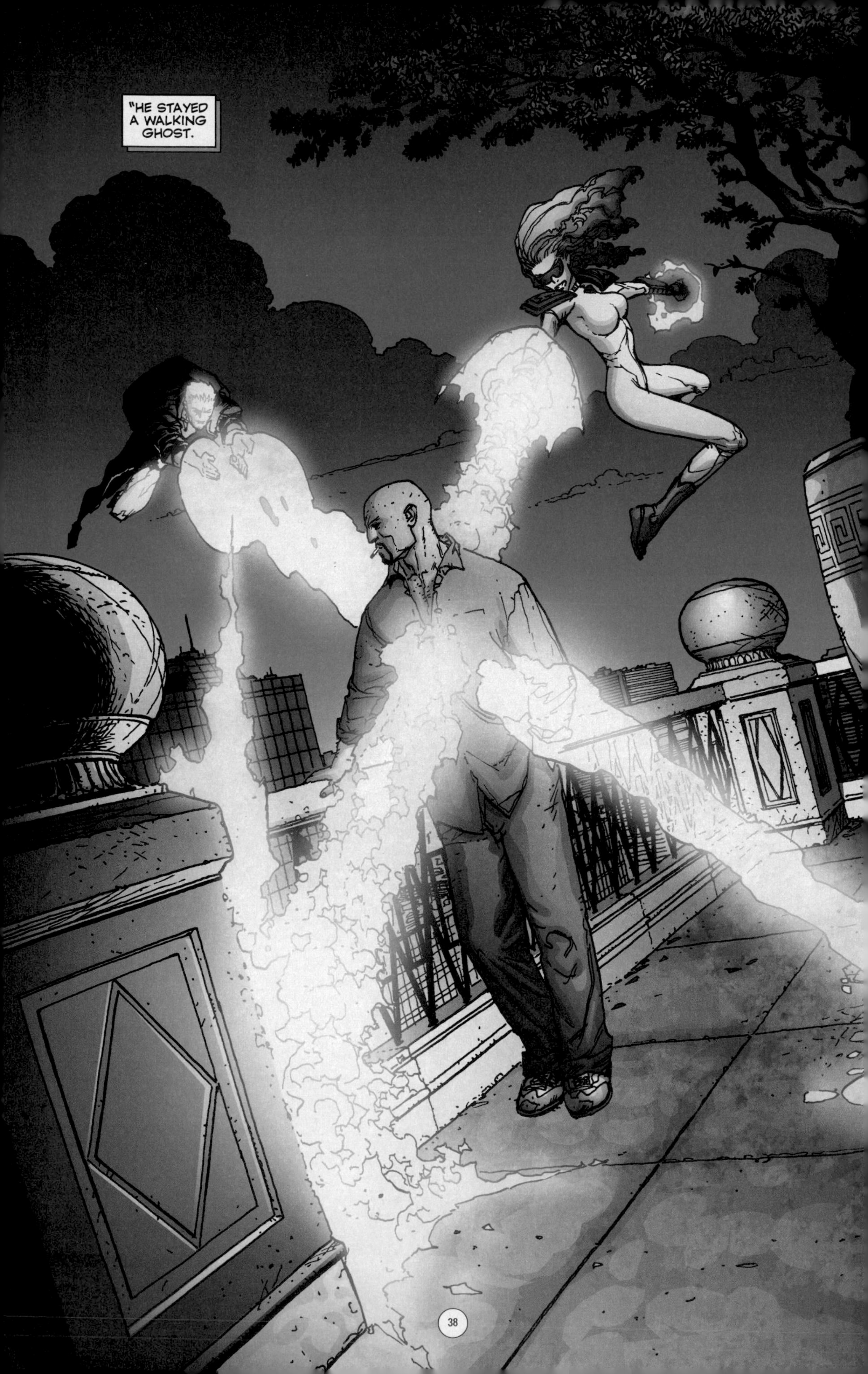
"HE STAYED A WALKING GHOST.

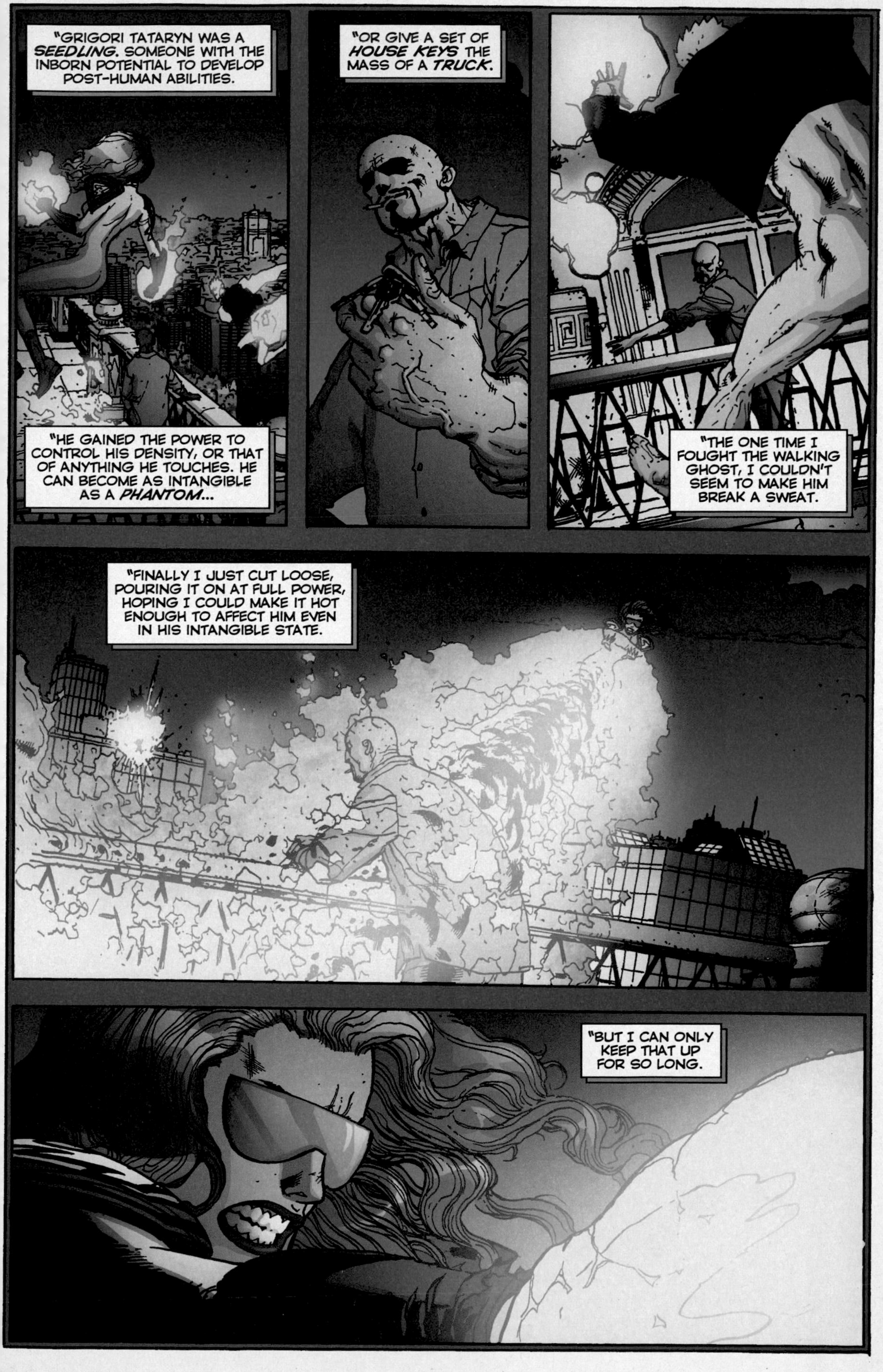
"GRIGORI TATARYN WAS A SEEDLING. SOMEONE WITH THE INBORN POTENTIAL TO DEVELOP POST-HUMAN ABILITIES.
"HE GAINED THE POWER TO CONTROL HIS DENSITY, OR THAT OF ANYTHING HE TOUCHES. HE CAN BECOME AS INTANGIBLE AS A PHANTOM...
"OR GIVE A SET OF HOUSE KEYS THE MASS OF A TRUCK.
"THE ONE TIME I FOUGHT THE WALKING GHOST, I COULDN'T SEEM TO MAKE HIM BREAK A SWEAT.
"FINALLY I JUST CUT LOOSE, POURING IT ON AT FULL POWER, HOPING I COULD MAKE IT HOT ENOUGH TO AFFECT HIM EVEN IN HIS INTANGIBLE STATE.
"BUT I CAN ONLY KEEP THAT UP FOR SO LONG.

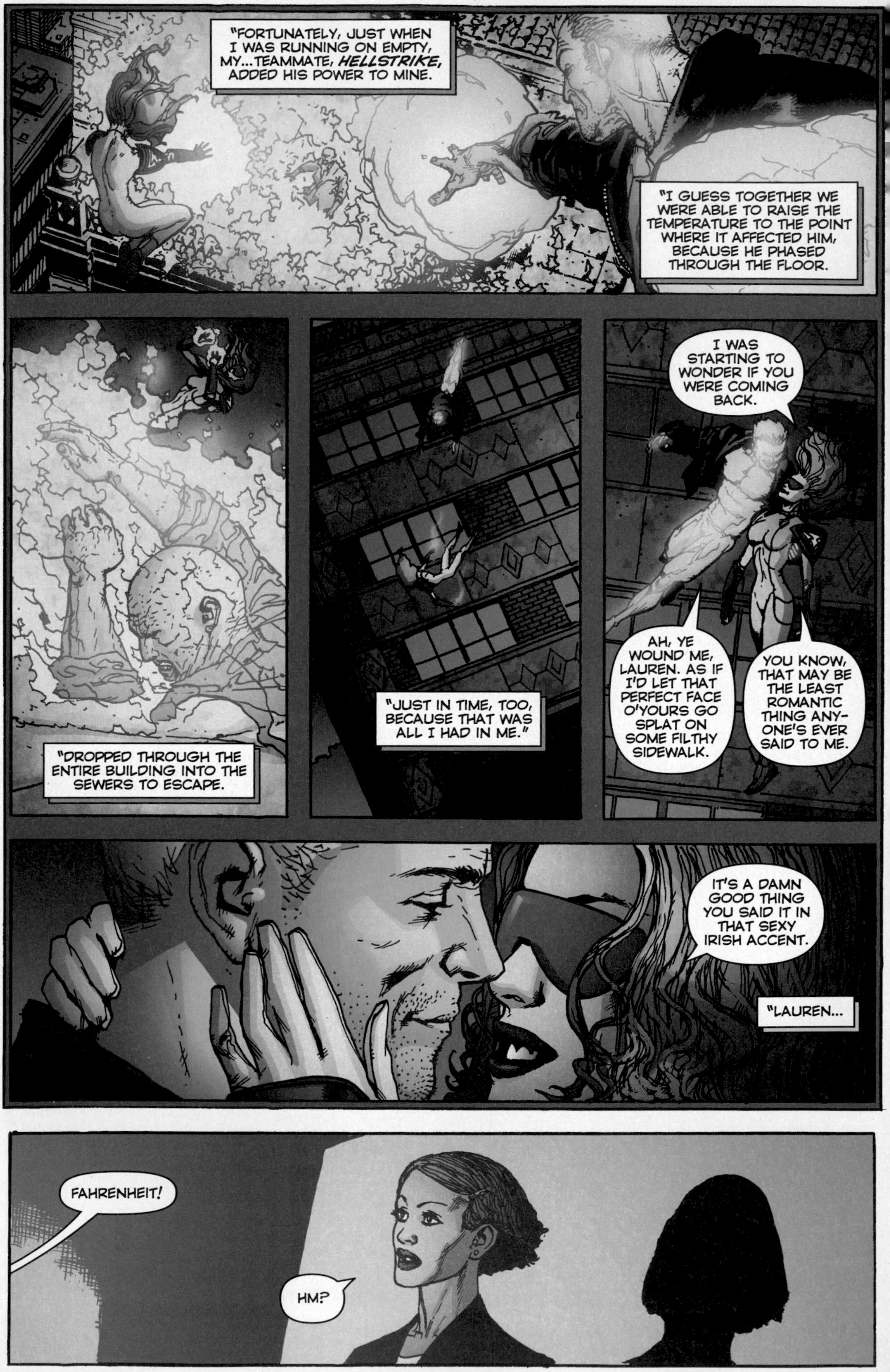
"FORTUNATELY, JUST WHEN I WAS RUNNING ON EMPTY, MY...TEAMMATE, ***HELLSTRIKE,*** ADDED HIS POWER TO MINE.
"I GUESS TOGETHER WE WERE ABLE TO RAISE THE TEMPERATURE TO THE POINT WHERE IT AFFECTED HIM, BECAUSE HE PHASED THROUGH THE FLOOR.
"DROPPED THROUGH THE ENTIRE BUILDING INTO THE SEWERS TO ESCAPE.
"JUST IN TIME, TOO, BECAUSE THAT WAS ALL I HAD IN ME."
I WAS STARTING TO WONDER IF YOU WERE COMING BACK.
AH, YE WOUND ME, LAUREN. AS IF I'D LET THAT PERFECT FACE O'YOURS GO SPLAT ON SOME FILTHY SIDEWALK.
YOU KNOW, THAT MAY BE THE LEAST ROMANTIC THING ANYONE'S EVER SAID TO ME.
IT'S A DAMN GOOD THING YOU SAID IT IN THAT SEXY IRISH ACCENT.
"LAUREN...
FAHRENHEIT!
HM?

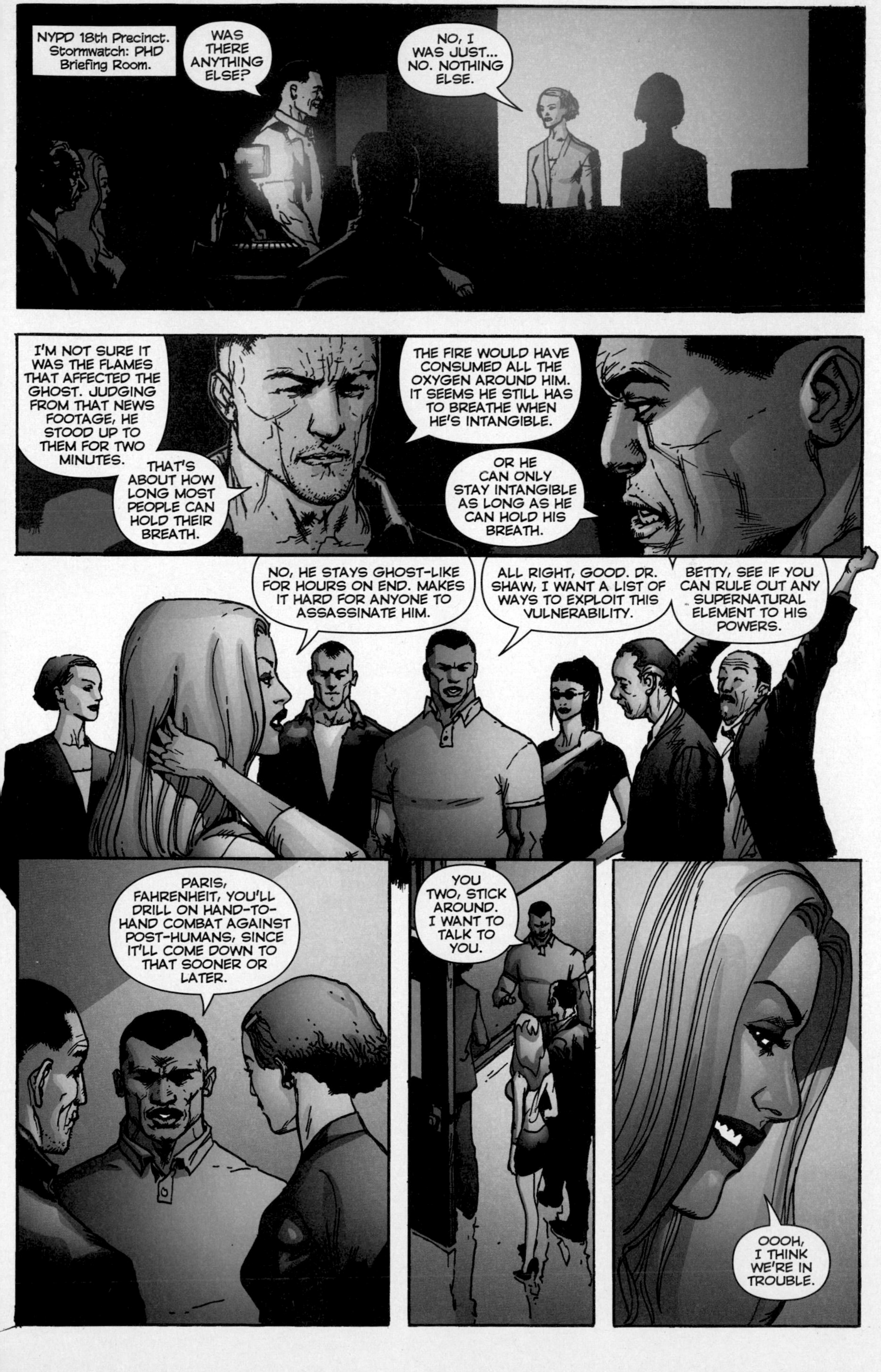
NYPD 18th Precinct. Stormwatch: PHD Briefing Room.
WAS THERE ANYTHING ELSE?
NO, I WAS JUST... NO. NOTHING ELSE.
I'M NOT SURE IT WAS THE FLAMES THAT AFFECTED THE GHOST. JUDGING FROM THAT NEWS FOOTAGE, HE STOOD UP TO THEM FOR TWO MINUTES.
THAT'S ABOUT HOW LONG MOST PEOPLE CAN HOLD THEIR BREATH.
THE FIRE WOULD HAVE CONSUMED ALL THE OXYGEN AROUND HIM. IT SEEMS HE STILL HAS TO BREATHE WHEN HE'S INTANGIBLE.
OR HE CAN ONLY STAY INTANGIBLE AS LONG AS HE CAN HOLD HIS BREATH.
NO, HE STAYS GHOST-LIKE FOR HOURS ON END. MAKES IT HARD FOR ANYONE TO ASSASSINATE HIM.
ALL RIGHT, GOOD. DR. SHAW, I WANT A LIST OF WAYS TO EXPLOIT THIS VULNERABILITY.
BETTY, SEE IF YOU CAN RULE OUT ANY SUPERNATURAL ELEMENT TO HIS POWERS.
PARIS, FAHRENHEIT, YOU'LL DRILL ON HAND-TO-HAND COMBAT AGAINST POST-HUMANS, SINCE IT'LL COME DOWN TO THAT SOONER OR LATER.
YOU TWO, STICK AROUND. I WANT TO TALK TO YOU.
OOOH, I THINK WE'RE IN TROUBLE.

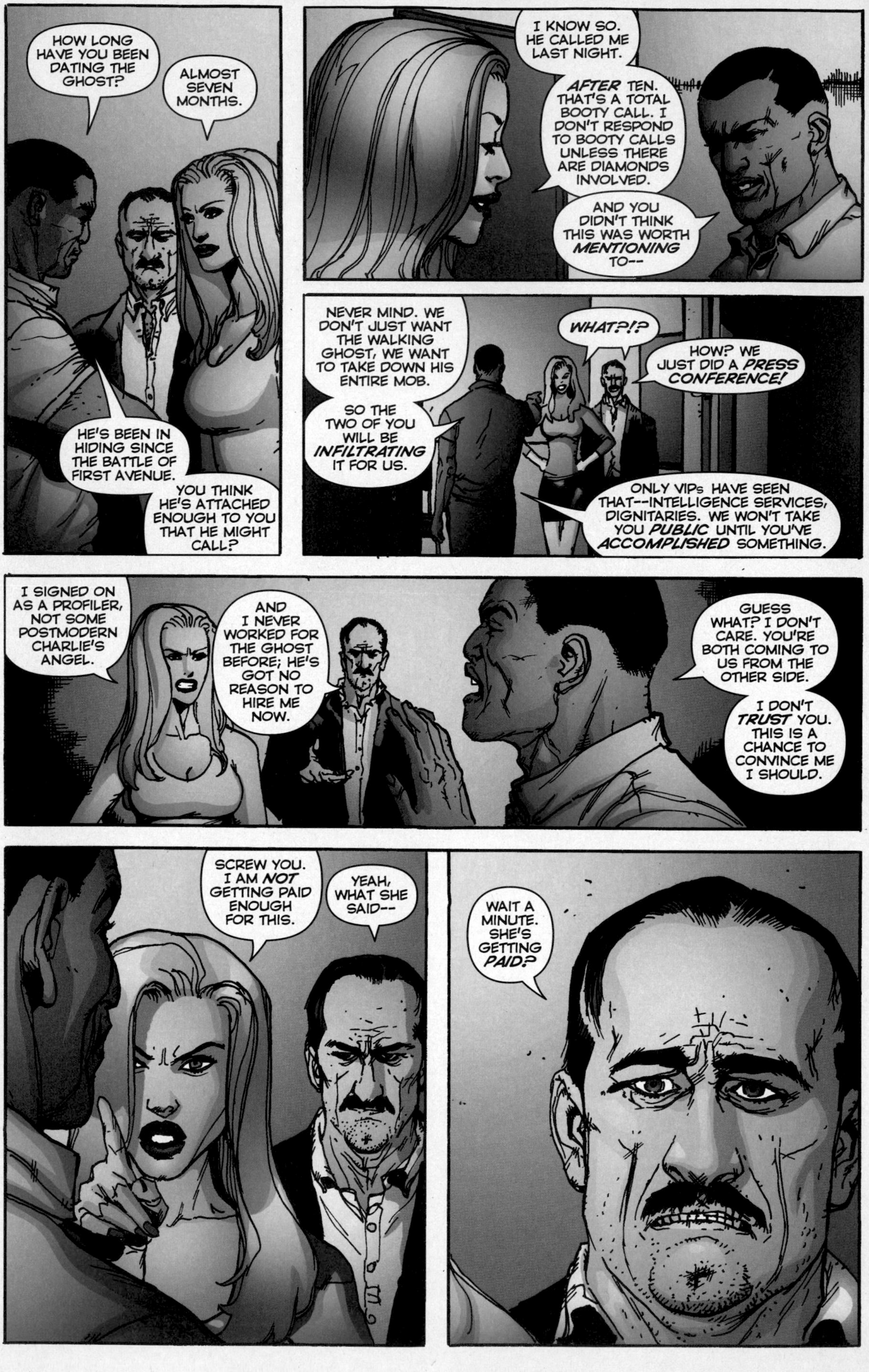
HOW LONG HAVE YOU BEEN DATING THE GHOST?
ALMOST SEVEN MONTHS.
HE'S BEEN IN HIDING SINCE THE BATTLE OF FIRST AVENUE.
YOU THINK HE'S ATTACHED ENOUGH TO YOU THAT HE MIGHT CALL?
I KNOW SO. HE CALLED ME LAST NIGHT.
AFTER TEN. THAT'S A TOTAL BOOTY CALL. I DON'T RESPOND TO BOOTY CALLS UNLESS THERE ARE DIAMONDS INVOLVED.
AND YOU DIDN'T THINK THIS WAS WORTH MENTIONING TO--
NEVER MIND. WE DON'T JUST WANT THE WALKING GHOST, WE WANT TO TAKE DOWN HIS ENTIRE MOB.
SO THE TWO OF YOU WILL BE INFILTRATING IT FOR US.
WHAT?!?
HOW? WE JUST DID A PRESS CONFERENCE!
ONLY VIPs HAVE SEEN THAT--INTELLIGENCE SERVICES, DIGNITARIES. WE WON'T TAKE YOU PUBLIC UNTIL YOU'VE ACCOMPLISHED SOMETHING.
I SIGNED ON AS A PROFILER, NOT SOME POSTMODERN CHARLIE'S ANGEL.
AND I NEVER WORKED FOR THE GHOST BEFORE; HE'S GOT NO REASON TO HIRE ME NOW.
GUESS WHAT? I DON'T CARE. YOU'RE BOTH COMING TO US FROM THE OTHER SIDE.
I DON'T TRUST YOU. THIS IS A CHANCE TO CONVINCE ME I SHOULD.
SCREW YOU. I AM NOT GETTING PAID ENOUGH FOR THIS.
YEAH, WHAT SHE SAID--
WAIT A MINUTE. SHE'S GETTING PAID?

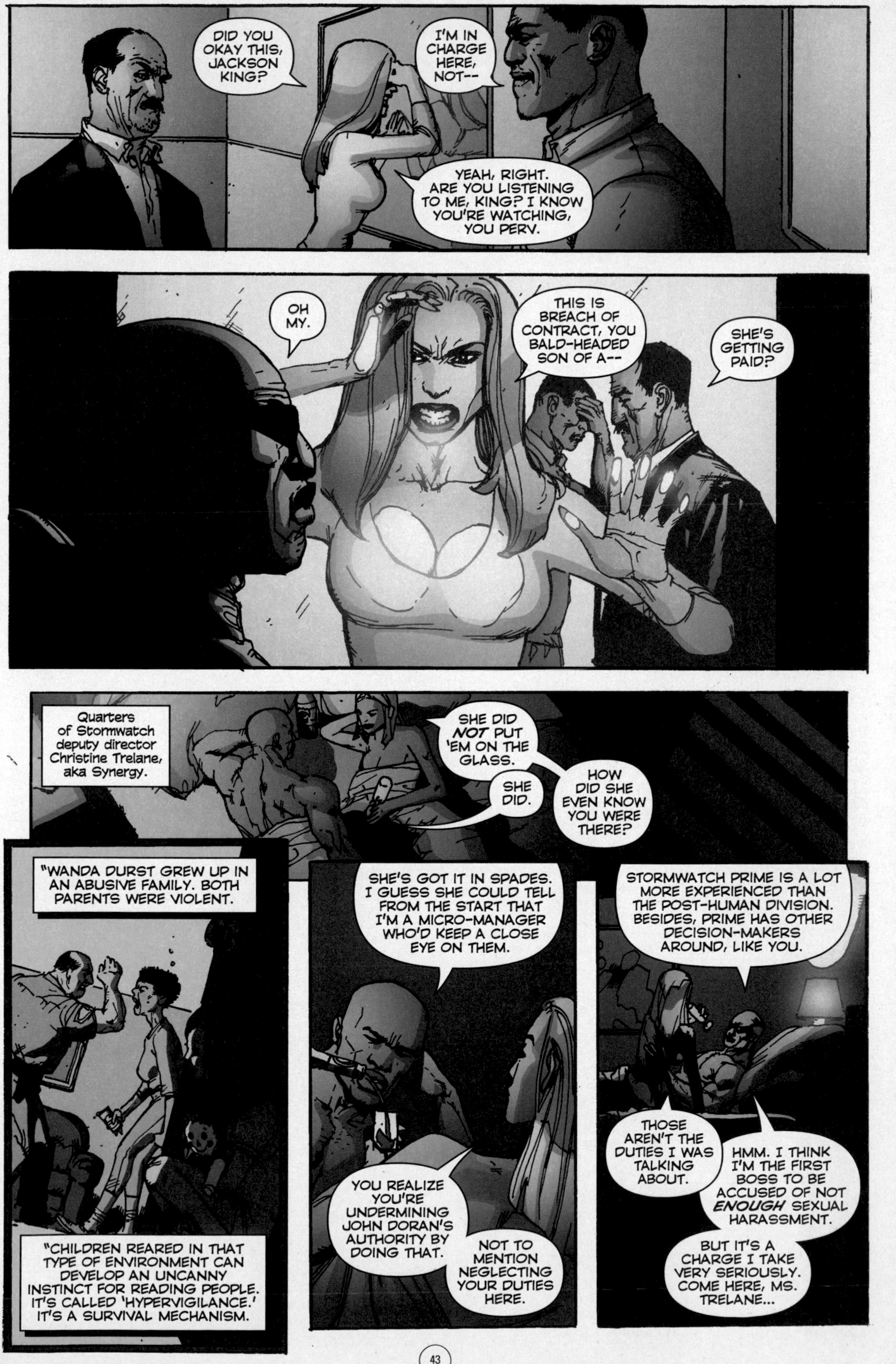
DID YOU OKAY THIS, JACKSON KING?
I'M IN CHARGE HERE, NOT--
YEAH, RIGHT. ARE YOU LISTENING TO ME, KING? I KNOW YOU'RE WATCHING, YOU PERV.
OH MY.
THIS IS BREACH OF CONTRACT, YOU BALD-HEADED SON OF A--
SHE'S GETTING PAID?
Quarters of Stormwatch deputy director Christine Trelane, aka Synergy.
SHE DID *NOT* PUT 'EM ON THE GLASS.
SHE DID.
HOW DID SHE EVEN KNOW YOU WERE THERE?
"WANDA DURST GREW UP IN AN ABUSIVE FAMILY. BOTH PARENTS WERE VIOLENT.
"CHILDREN REARED IN THAT TYPE OF ENVIRONMENT CAN DEVELOP AN UNCANNY INSTINCT FOR READING PEOPLE. IT'S CALLED 'HYPERVIGILANCE.' IT'S A SURVIVAL MECHANISM.
SHE'S GOT IT IN SPADES. I GUESS SHE COULD TELL FROM THE START THAT I'M A MICRO-MANAGER WHO'D KEEP A CLOSE EYE ON THEM.
YOU REALIZE YOU'RE UNDERMINING JOHN DORAN'S AUTHORITY BY DOING THAT.
NOT TO MENTION NEGLECTING YOUR DUTIES HERE.
STORMWATCH PRIME IS A LOT MORE EXPERIENCED THAN THE POST-HUMAN DIVISION. BESIDES, PRIME HAS OTHER DECISION-MAKERS AROUND, LIKE YOU.
THOSE AREN'T THE DUTIES I WAS TALKING ABOUT.
HMM. I THINK I'M THE FIRST BOSS TO BE ACCUSED OF NOT *ENOUGH* SEXUAL HARASSMENT.
BUT IT'S A CHARGE I TAKE VERY SERIOUSLY. COME HERE, MS. TRELANE...

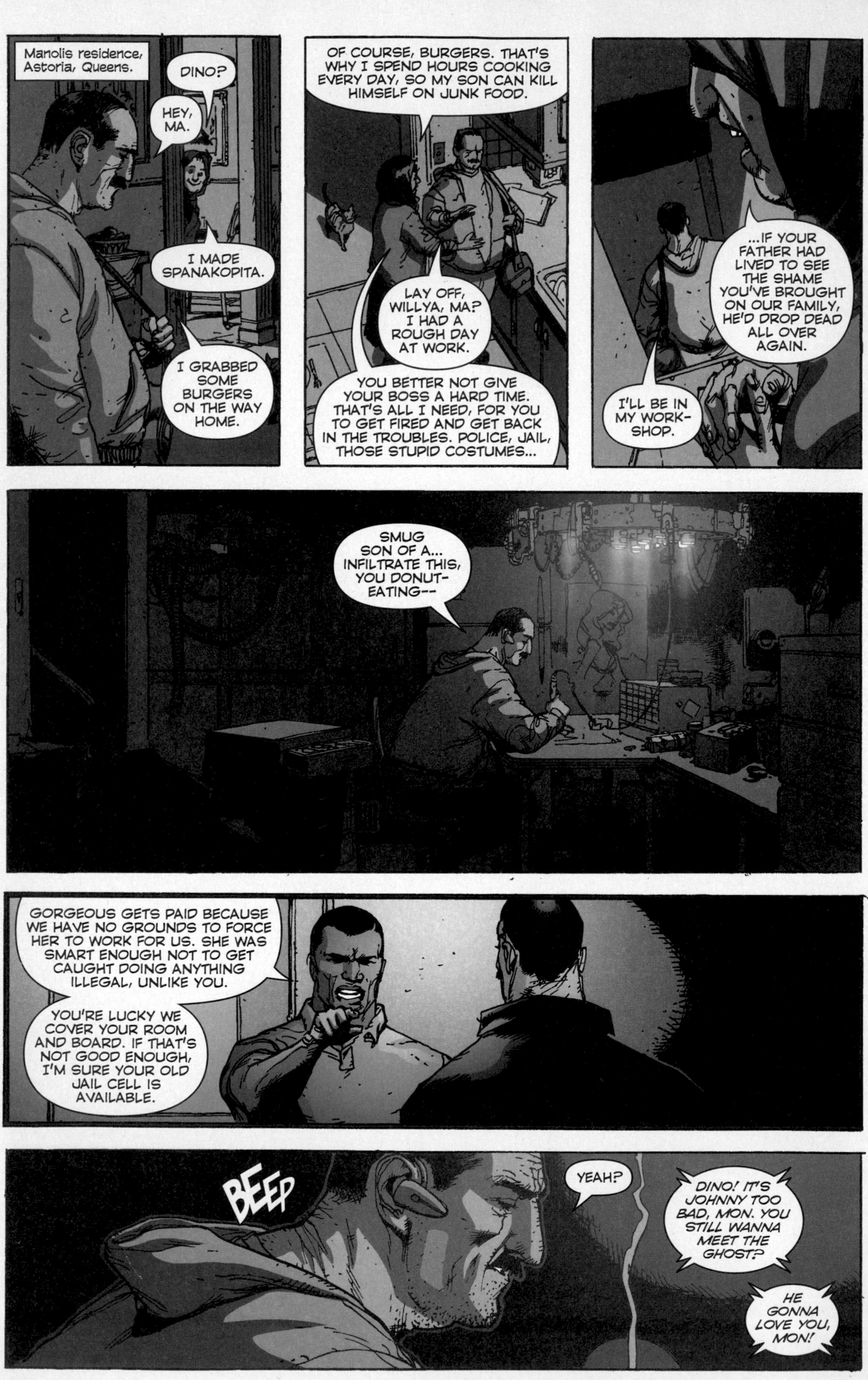
Manolis residence, Astoria, Queens.
DINO?
HEY, MA.
I MADE SPANAKOPITA.
I GRABBED SOME BURGERS ON THE WAY HOME.
OF COURSE, BURGERS. THAT'S WHY I SPEND HOURS COOKING EVERY DAY, SO MY SON CAN KILL HIMSELF ON JUNK FOOD.
LAY OFF, WILLYA, MA? I HAD A ROUGH DAY AT WORK.
YOU BETTER NOT GIVE YOUR BOSS A HARD TIME. THAT'S ALL I NEED, FOR YOU TO GET FIRED AND GET BACK IN THE TROUBLES. POLICE, JAIL, THOSE STUPID COSTUMES...
...IF YOUR FATHER HAD LIVED TO SEE THE SHAME YOU'VE BROUGHT ON OUR FAMILY, HE'D DROP DEAD ALL OVER AGAIN.
I'LL BE IN MY WORK-SHOP.
SMUG SON OF A... INFILTRATE THIS, YOU DONUT-EATING--
GORGEOUS GETS PAID BECAUSE WE HAVE NO GROUNDS TO FORCE HER TO WORK FOR US. SHE WAS SMART ENOUGH NOT TO GET CAUGHT DOING ANYTHING ILLEGAL, UNLIKE YOU.
YOU'RE LUCKY WE COVER YOUR ROOM AND BOARD. IF THAT'S NOT GOOD ENOUGH, I'M SURE YOUR OLD JAIL CELL IS AVAILABLE.
BEEP
YEAH?
DINO! IT'S JOHNNY TOO BAD, MON. YOU STILL WANNA MEET THE GHOST?
HE GONNA LOVE YOU, MON!

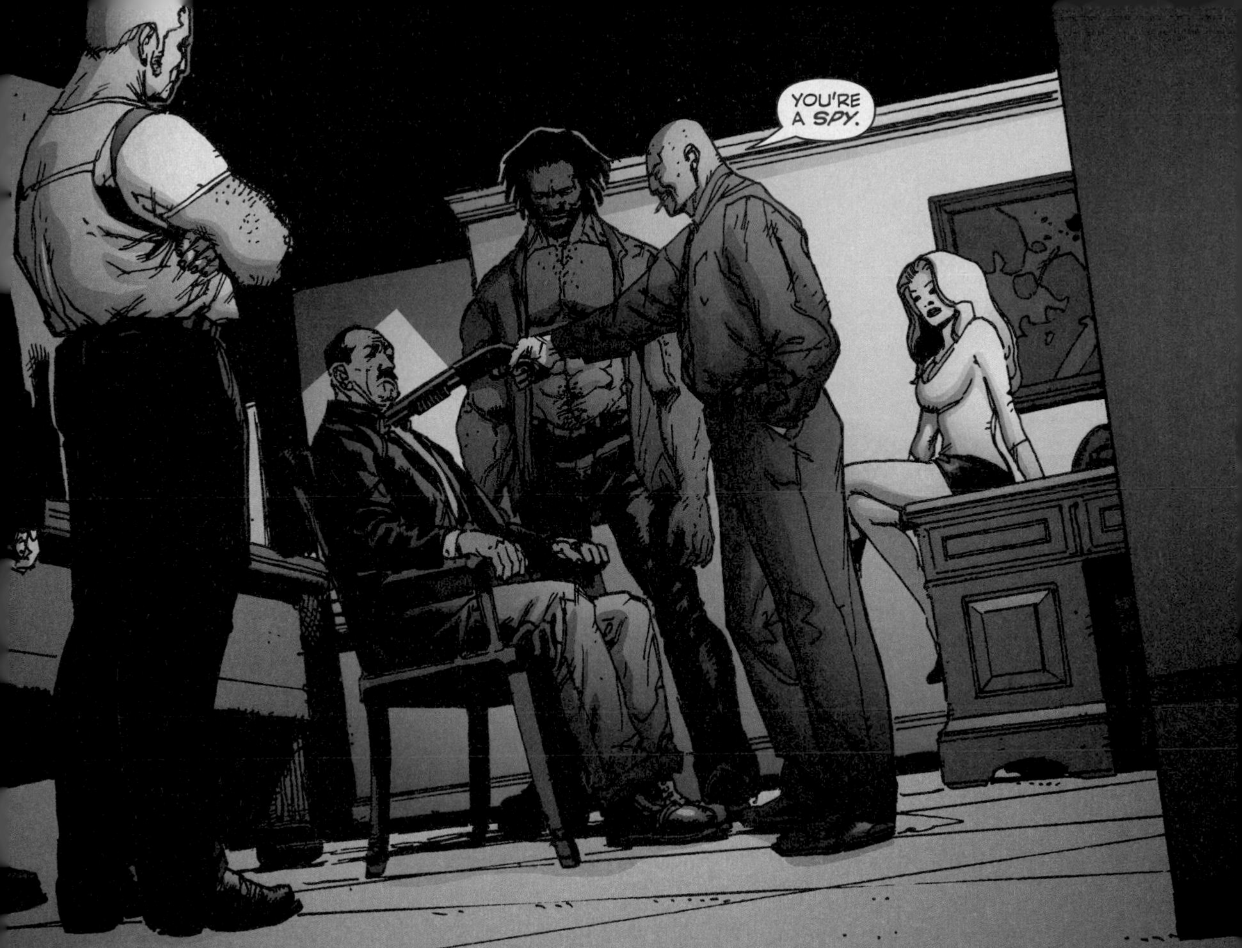
YOU'RE A SPY.
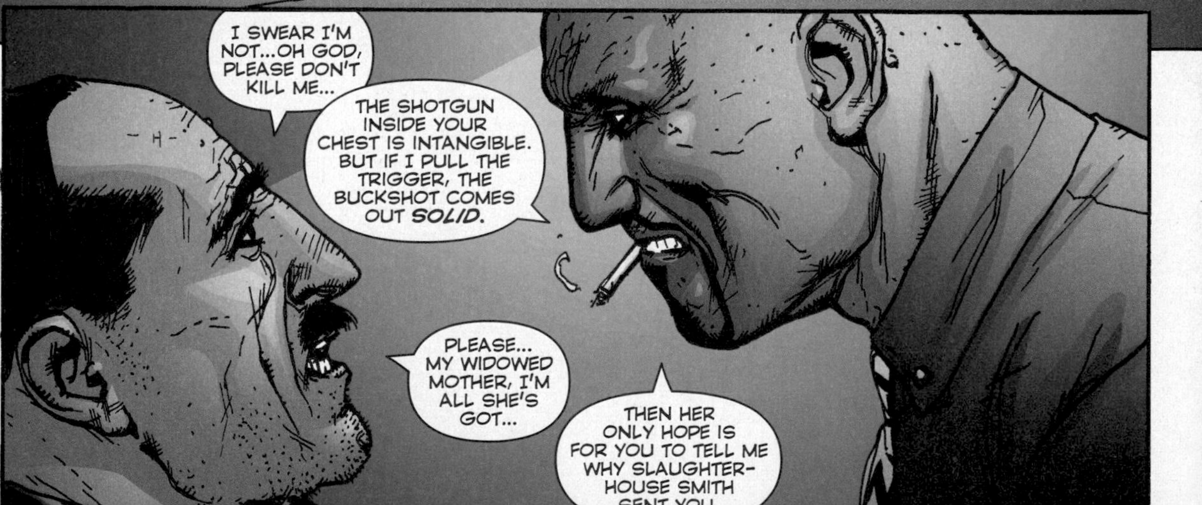
I SWEAR I'M NOT...OH GOD, PLEASE DON'T KILL ME...
THE SHOTGUN INSIDE YOUR CHEST IS INTANGIBLE. BUT IF I PULL THE TRIGGER, THE BUCKSHOT COMES OUT SOLID.
PLEASE... MY WIDOWED MOTHER, I'M ALL SHE'S GOT...
THEN HER ONLY HOPE IS FOR YOU TO TELL ME WHY SLAUGHTER-HOUSE SMITH SENT YOU.
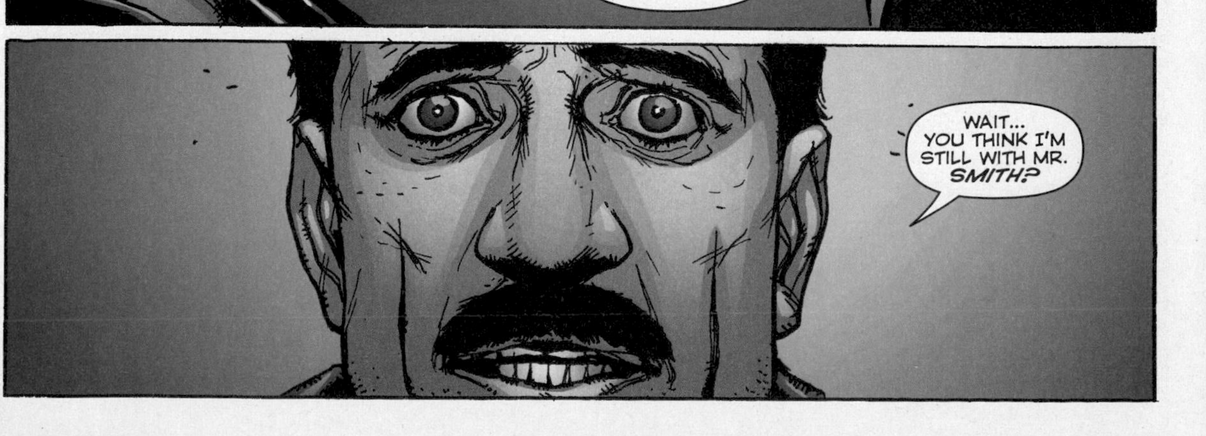
WAIT... YOU THINK I'M STILL WITH MR. SMITH?

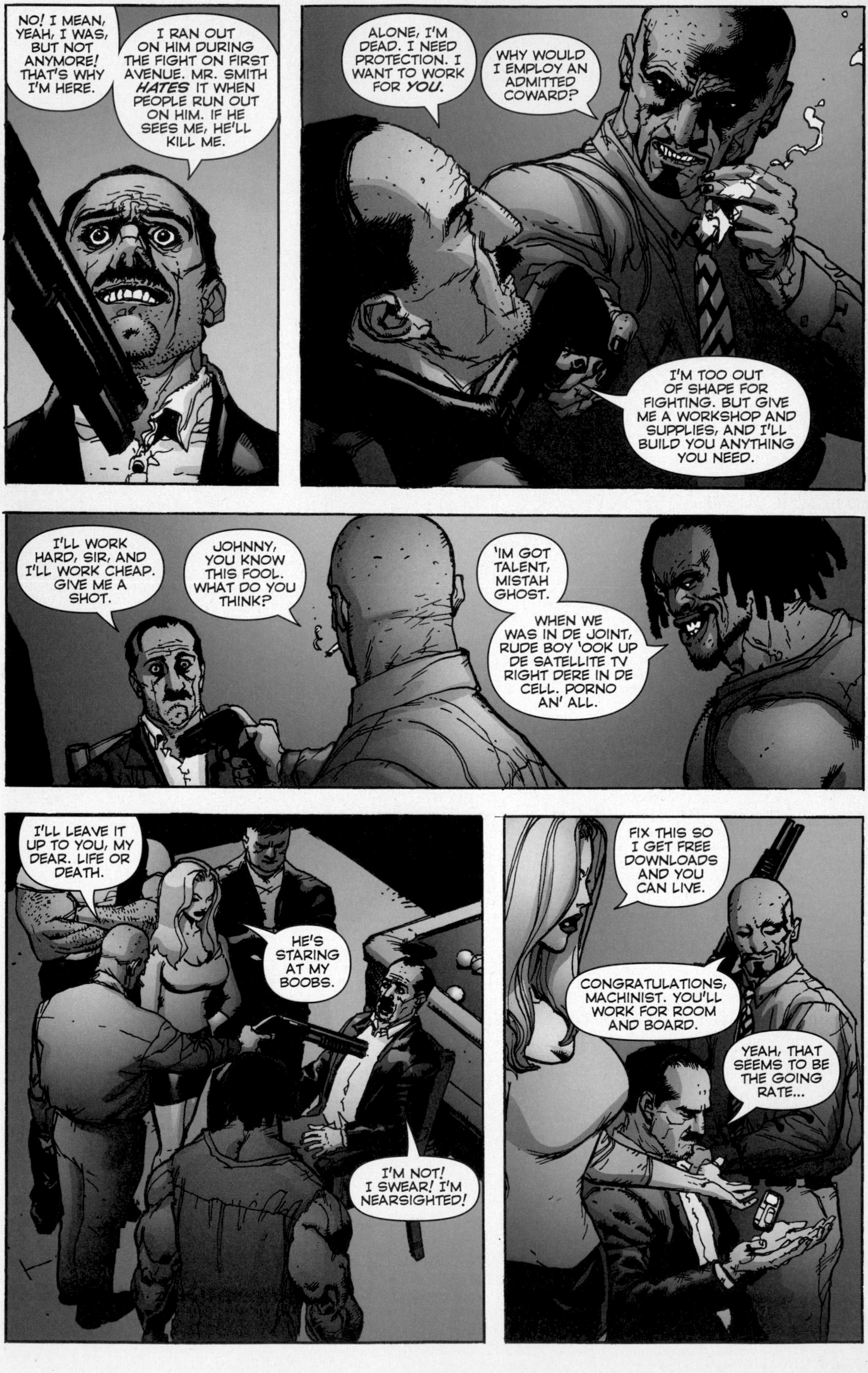
NO! I MEAN, YEAH, I WAS, BUT NOT ANYMORE! THAT'S WHY I'M HERE.
I RAN OUT ON HIM DURING THE FIGHT ON FIRST AVENUE. MR. SMITH *HATES* IT WHEN PEOPLE RUN OUT ON HIM. IF HE SEES ME, HE'LL KILL ME.
ALONE, I'M DEAD. I NEED PROTECTION. I WANT TO WORK FOR *YOU*.
WHY WOULD I EMPLOY AN ADMITTED COWARD?
I'M TOO OUT OF SHAPE FOR FIGHTING. BUT GIVE ME A WORKSHOP AND SUPPLIES, AND I'LL BUILD YOU ANYTHING YOU NEED.
I'LL WORK HARD, SIR, AND I'LL WORK CHEAP. GIVE ME A SHOT.
JOHNNY, YOU KNOW THIS FOOL. WHAT DO YOU THINK?
'IM GOT TALENT, MISTAH GHOST.
WHEN WE WAS IN DE JOINT, RUDE BOY 'OOK UP DE SATELLITE TV RIGHT DERE IN DE CELL. PORNO AN' ALL.
I'LL LEAVE IT UP TO YOU, MY DEAR. LIFE OR DEATH.
HE'S STARING AT MY BOOBS.
I'M NOT! I SWEAR! I'M NEARSIGHTED!
FIX THIS SO I GET FREE DOWNLOADS AND YOU CAN LIVE.
CONGRATULATIONS, MACHINIST. YOU'LL WORK FOR ROOM AND BOARD.
YEAH, THAT SEEMS TO BE THE GOING RATE...

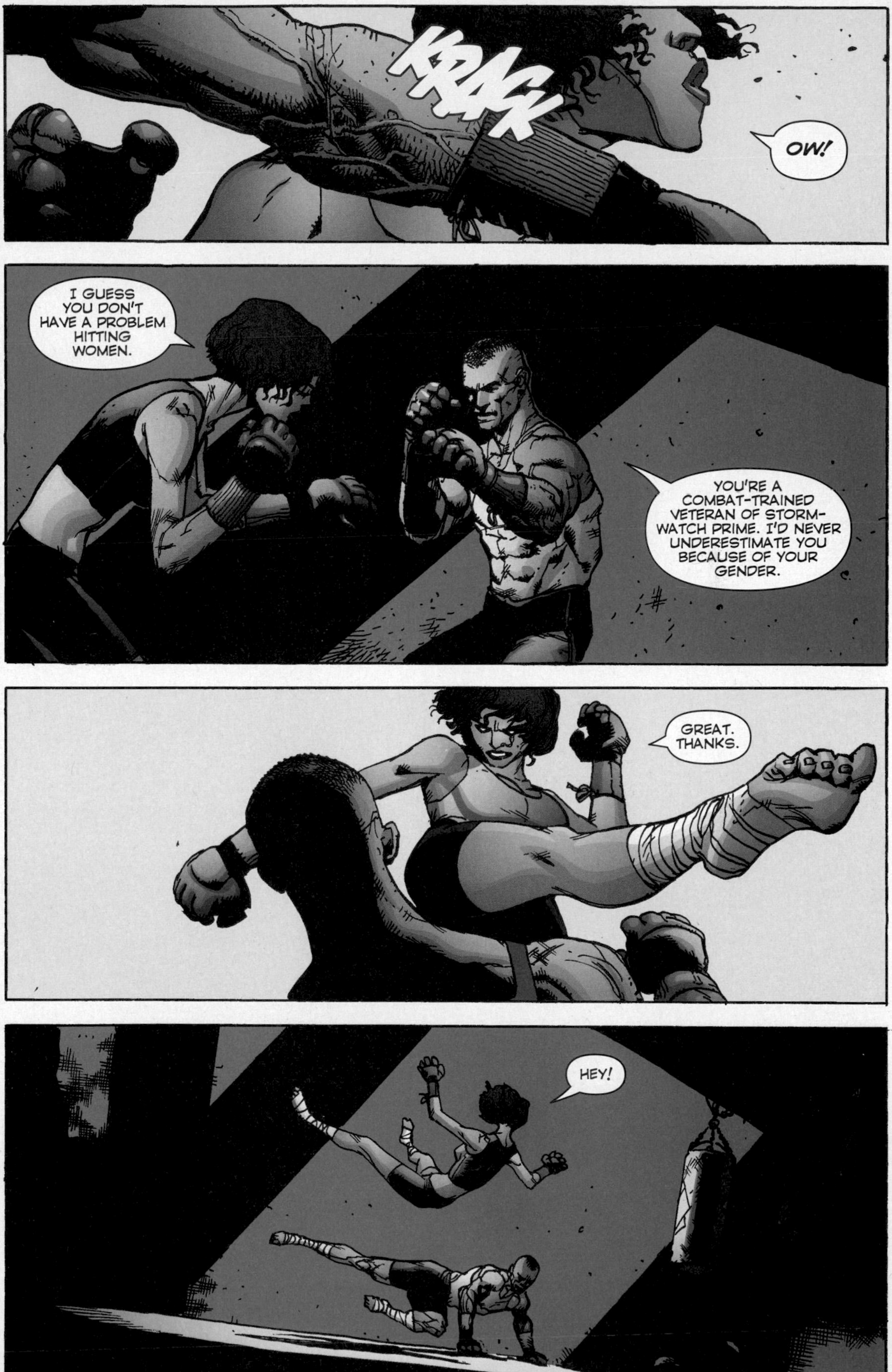
KRACK
OW!
I GUESS YOU DON'T HAVE A PROBLEM HITTING WOMEN.
YOU'RE A COMBAT-TRAINED VETERAN OF STORM-WATCH PRIME. I'D NEVER UNDERESTIMATE YOU BECAUSE OF YOUR GENDER.
GREAT. THANKS.
HEY!

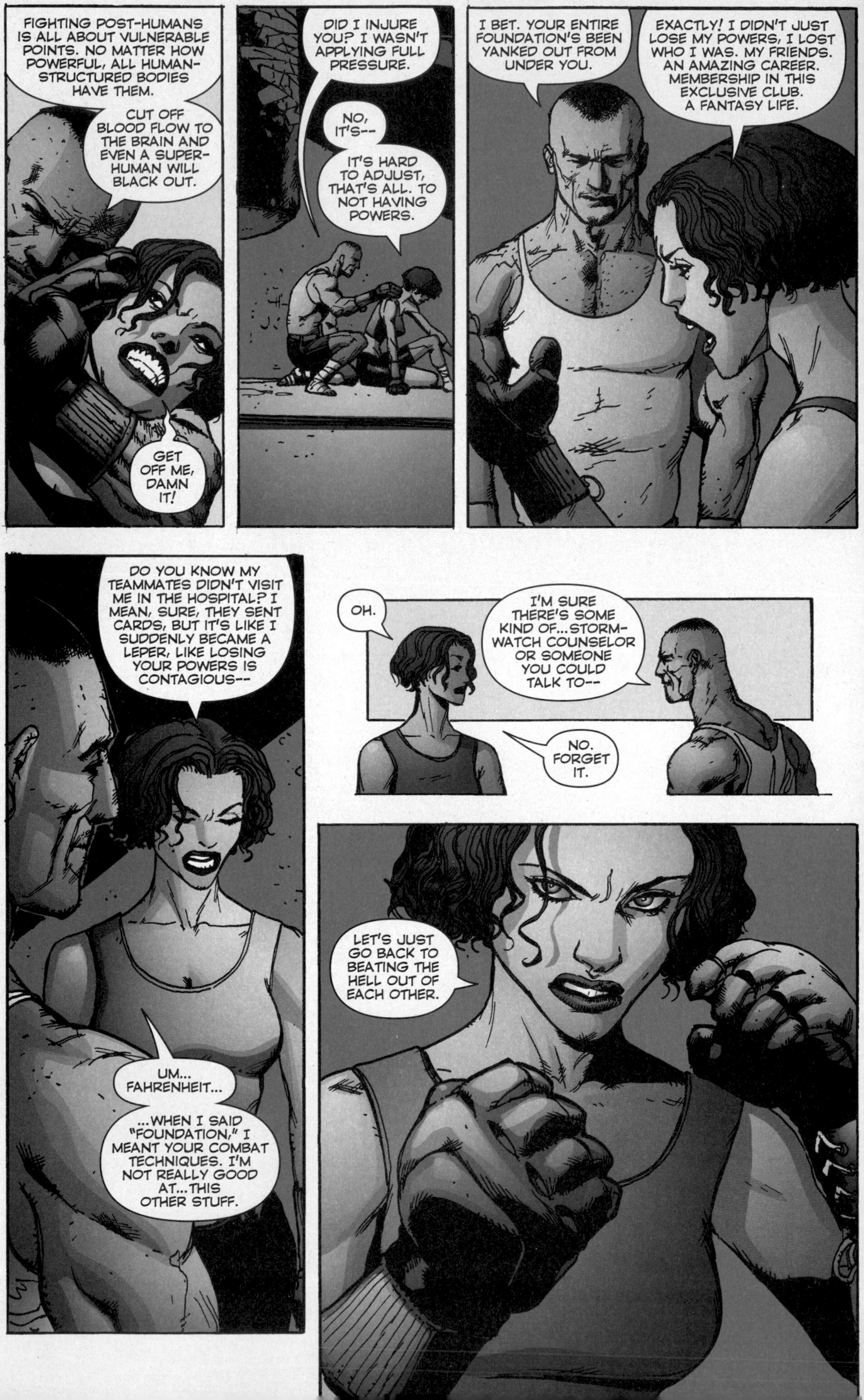

FIGHTING POST-HUMANS IS ALL ABOUT VULNERABLE POINTS. NO MATTER HOW POWERFUL, ALL HUMAN-STRUCTURED BODIES HAVE THEM.
CUT OFF BLOOD FLOW TO THE BRAIN AND EVEN A SUPER-HUMAN WILL BLACK OUT.
GET OFF ME, DAMN IT!
DID I INJURE YOU? I WASN'T APPLYING FULL PRESSURE.
NO, IT'S--
IT'S HARD TO ADJUST, THAT'S ALL. TO NOT HAVING POWERS.
I BET. YOUR ENTIRE FOUNDATION'S BEEN YANKED OUT FROM UNDER YOU.
EXACTLY! I DIDN'T JUST LOSE MY POWERS, I LOST WHO I WAS. MY FRIENDS. AN AMAZING CAREER. MEMBERSHIP IN THIS EXCLUSIVE CLUB. A FANTASY LIFE.
DO YOU KNOW MY TEAMMATES DIDN'T VISIT ME IN THE HOSPITAL? I MEAN, SURE, THEY SENT CARDS, BUT IT'S LIKE I SUDDENLY BECAME A LEPER, LIKE LOSING YOUR POWERS IS CONTAGIOUS--
UM... FAHRENHEIT...
...WHEN I SAID "FOUNDATION," I MEANT YOUR COMBAT TECHNIQUES. I'M NOT REALLY GOOD AT...THIS OTHER STUFF.
OH.
I'M SURE THERE'S SOME KIND OF...STORM-WATCH COUNSELOR OR SOMEONE YOU COULD TALK TO--
NO. FORGET IT.
LET'S JUST GO BACK TO BEATING THE HELL OUT OF EACH OTHER.

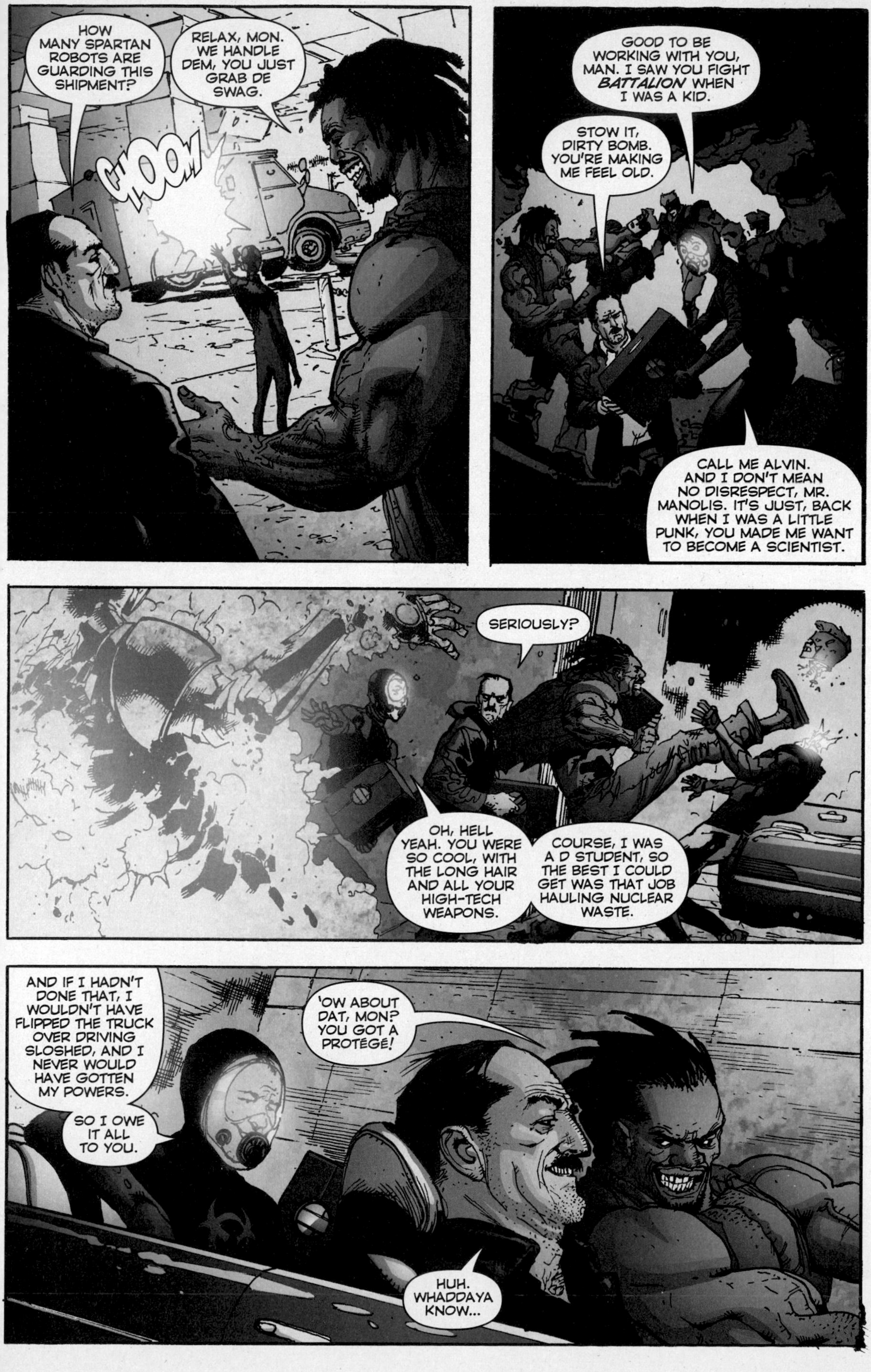

HOW MANY SPARTAN ROBOTS ARE GUARDING THIS SHIPMENT?
RELAX, MON. WE HANDLE DEM, YOU JUST GRAB DE SWAG.
CHOOM
GOOD TO BE WORKING WITH YOU, MAN. I SAW YOU FIGHT BATTALION WHEN I WAS A KID.
STOW IT, DIRTY BOMB. YOU'RE MAKING ME FEEL OLD.
CALL ME ALVIN. AND I DON'T MEAN NO DISRESPECT, MR. MANOLIS. IT'S JUST, BACK WHEN I WAS A LITTLE PUNK, YOU MADE ME WANT TO BECOME A SCIENTIST.
SERIOUSLY?
OH, HELL YEAH. YOU WERE SO COOL, WITH THE LONG HAIR AND ALL YOUR HIGH-TECH WEAPONS.
COURSE, I WAS A D STUDENT, SO THE BEST I COULD GET WAS THAT JOB HAULING NUCLEAR WASTE.
AND IF I HADN'T DONE THAT, I WOULDN'T HAVE FLIPPED THE TRUCK OVER DRIVING SLOSHED, AND I NEVER WOULD HAVE GOTTEN MY POWERS.
SO I OWE IT ALL TO YOU.
'OW ABOUT DAT, MON? YOU GOT A PROTÉGÉ!
HUH. WHADDAYA KNOW...

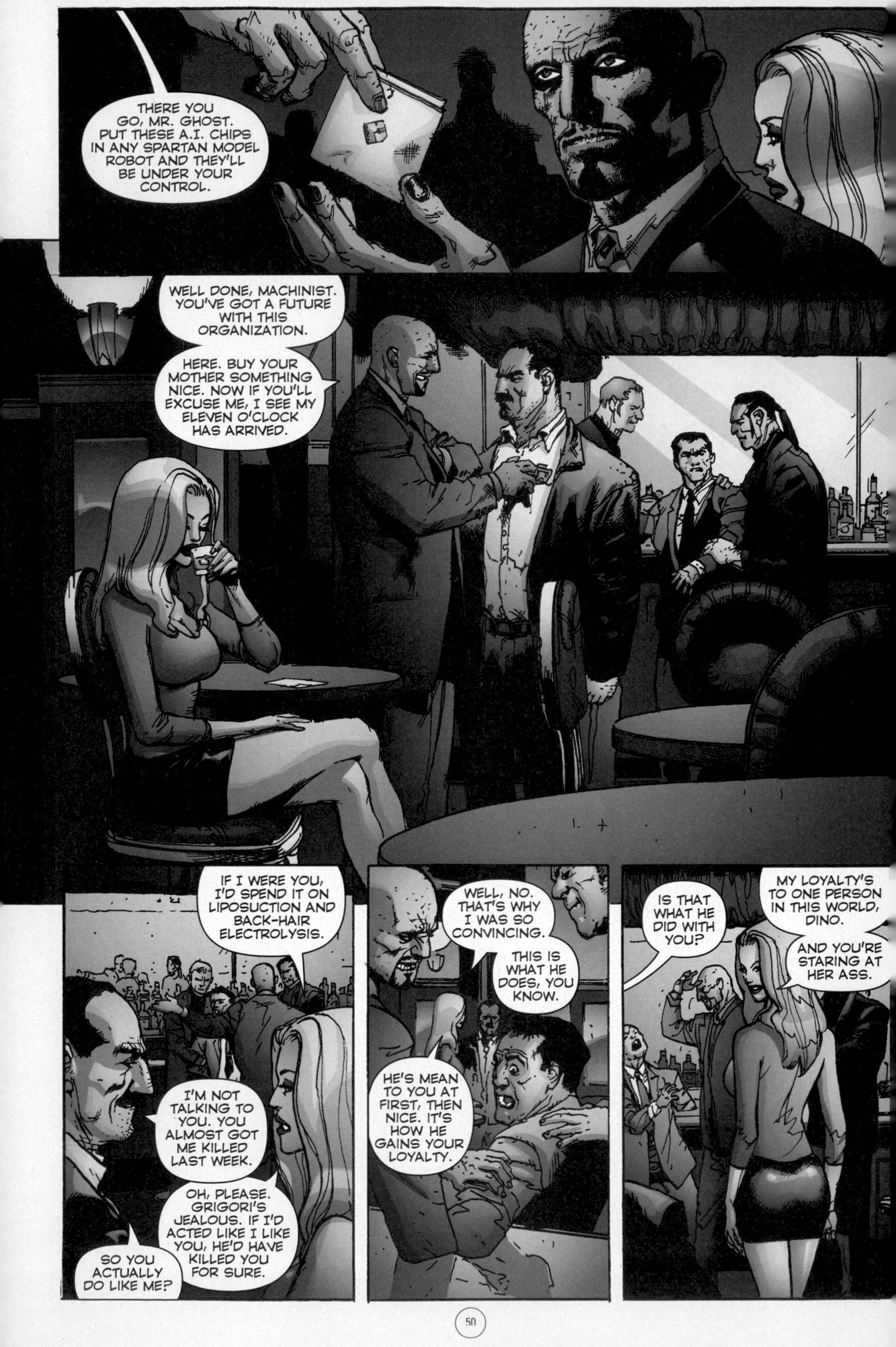
THERE YOU GO, MR. GHOST. PUT THESE A.I. CHIPS IN ANY SPARTAN MODEL ROBOT AND THEY'LL BE UNDER YOUR CONTROL.
WELL DONE, MACHINIST. YOU'VE GOT A FUTURE WITH THIS ORGANIZATION.
HERE. BUY YOUR MOTHER SOMETHING NICE. NOW IF YOU'LL EXCUSE ME, I SEE MY ELEVEN O'CLOCK HAS ARRIVED.
IF I WERE YOU, I'D SPEND IT ON LIPOSUCTION AND BACK-HAIR ELECTROLYSIS.
I'M NOT TALKING TO YOU. YOU ALMOST GOT ME KILLED LAST WEEK.
OH, PLEASE. GRIGORI'S JEALOUS. IF I'D ACTED LIKE I LIKE YOU, HE'D HAVE KILLED YOU FOR SURE.
SO YOU ACTUALLY DO LIKE ME?
WELL, NO. THAT'S WHY I WAS SO CONVINCING.
THIS IS WHAT HE DOES, YOU KNOW.
HE'S MEAN TO YOU AT FIRST, THEN NICE. IT'S HOW HE GAINS YOUR LOYALTY.
IS THAT WHAT HE DID WITH YOU?
MY LOYALTY'S TO ONE PERSON IN THIS WORLD, DINO.
AND YOU'RE STARING AT HER ASS.

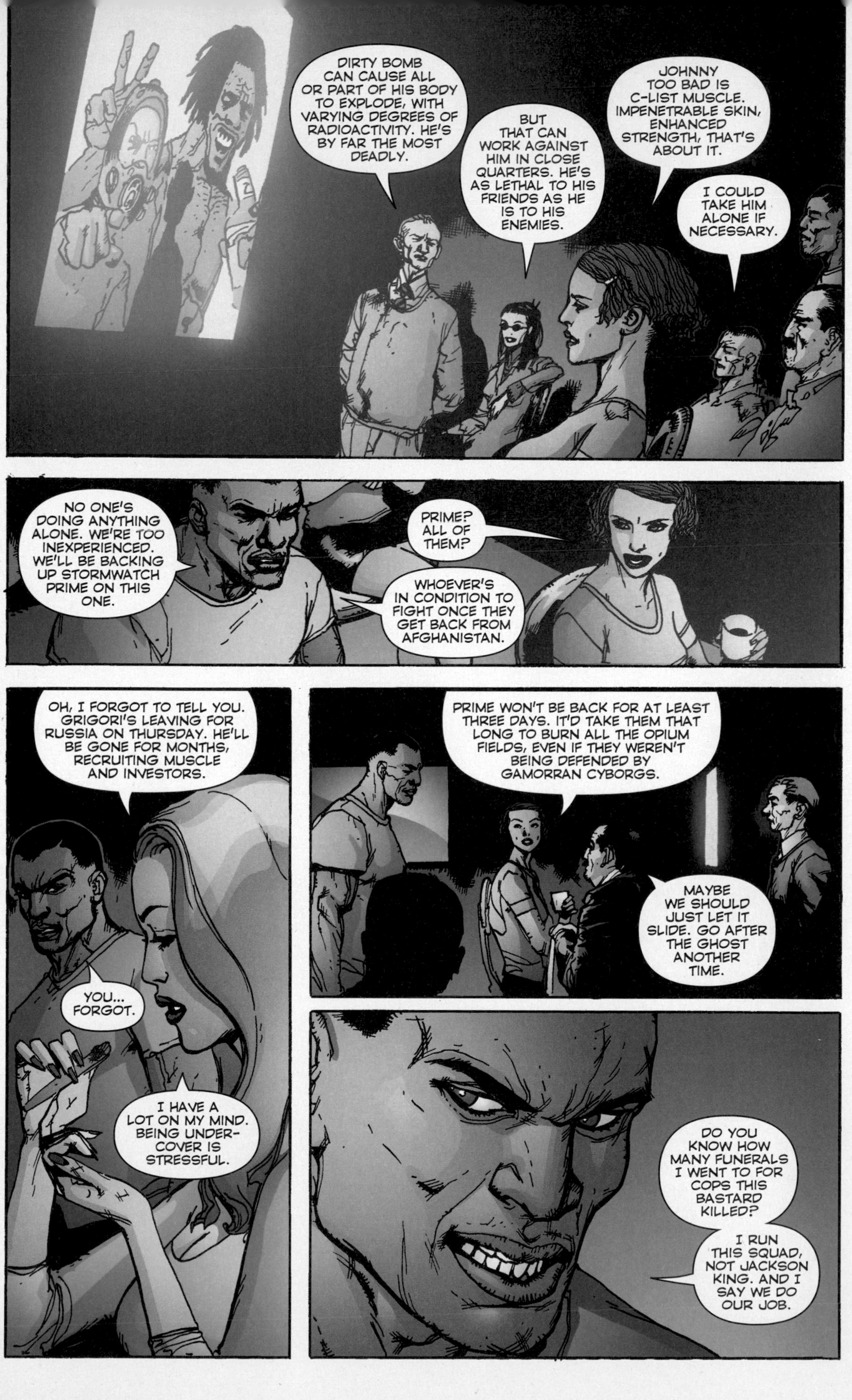
DIRTY BOMB CAN CAUSE ALL OR PART OF HIS BODY TO EXPLODE, WITH VARYING DEGREES OF RADIOACTIVITY. HE'S BY FAR THE MOST DEADLY.
BUT THAT CAN WORK AGAINST HIM IN CLOSE QUARTERS. HE'S AS LETHAL TO HIS FRIENDS AS HE IS TO HIS ENEMIES.
JOHNNY TOO BAD IS C-LIST MUSCLE. IMPENETRABLE SKIN, ENHANCED STRENGTH, THAT'S ABOUT IT.
I COULD TAKE HIM ALONE IF NECESSARY.
NO ONE'S DOING ANYTHING ALONE. WE'RE TOO INEXPERIENCED. WE'LL BE BACKING UP STORMWATCH PRIME ON THIS ONE.
PRIME? ALL OF THEM?
WHOEVER'S IN CONDITION TO FIGHT ONCE THEY GET BACK FROM AFGHANISTAN.
OH, I FORGOT TO TELL YOU. GRIGORI'S LEAVING FOR RUSSIA ON THURSDAY. HE'LL BE GONE FOR MONTHS, RECRUITING MUSCLE AND INVESTORS.
YOU... FORGOT.
I HAVE A LOT ON MY MIND. BEING UNDER-COVER IS STRESSFUL.
PRIME WON'T BE BACK FOR AT LEAST THREE DAYS. IT'D TAKE THEM THAT LONG TO BURN ALL THE OPIUM FIELDS, EVEN IF THEY WEREN'T BEING DEFENDED BY GAMORRAN CYBORGS.
MAYBE WE SHOULD JUST LET IT SLIDE. GO AFTER THE GHOST ANOTHER TIME.
DO YOU KNOW HOW MANY FUNERALS I WENT TO FOR COPS THIS BASTARD KILLED?
I RUN THIS SQUAD, NOT JACKSON KING. AND I SAY WE DO OUR JOB.

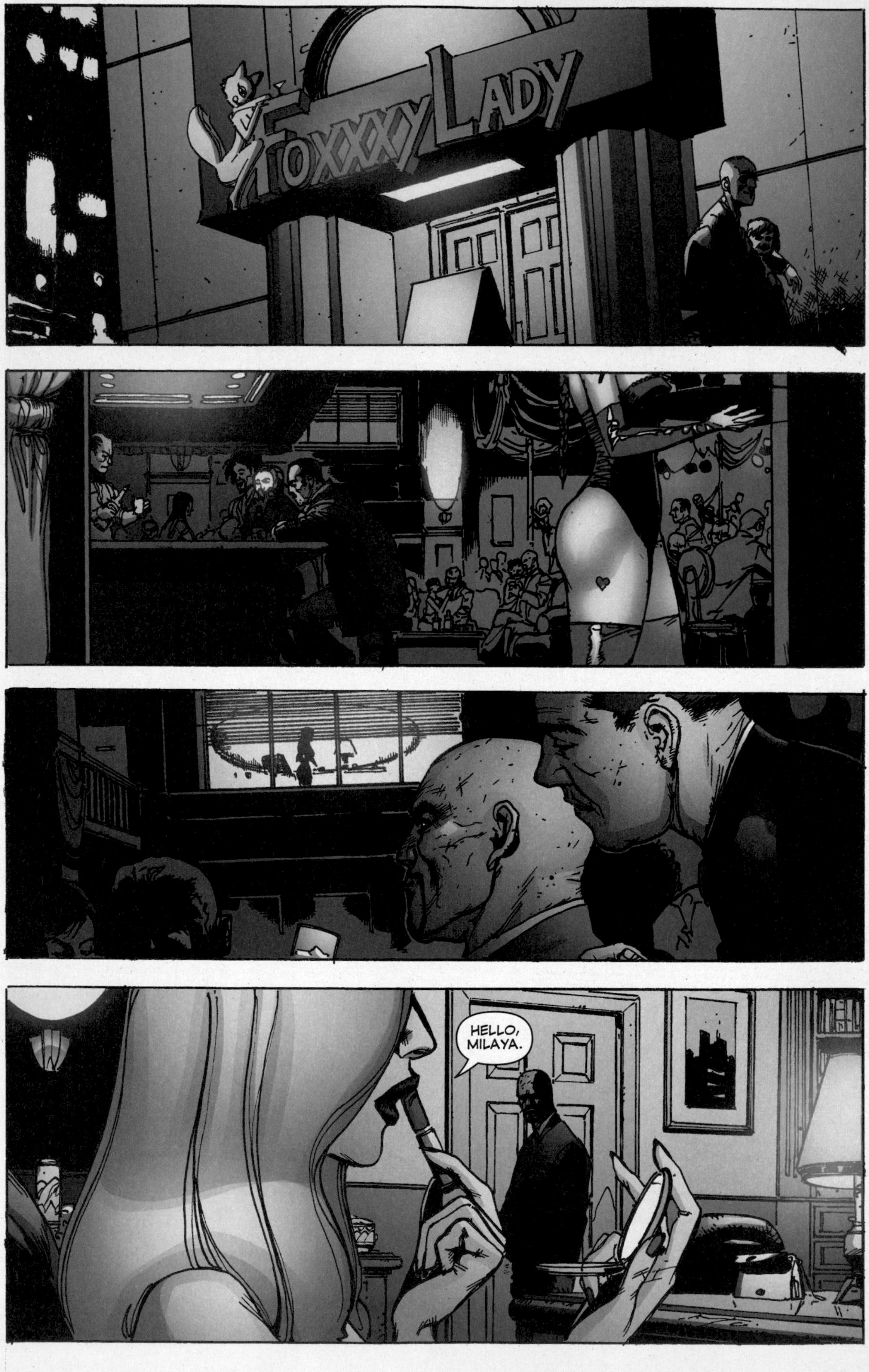
FOXXXY LADY
HELLO, MILAYA.

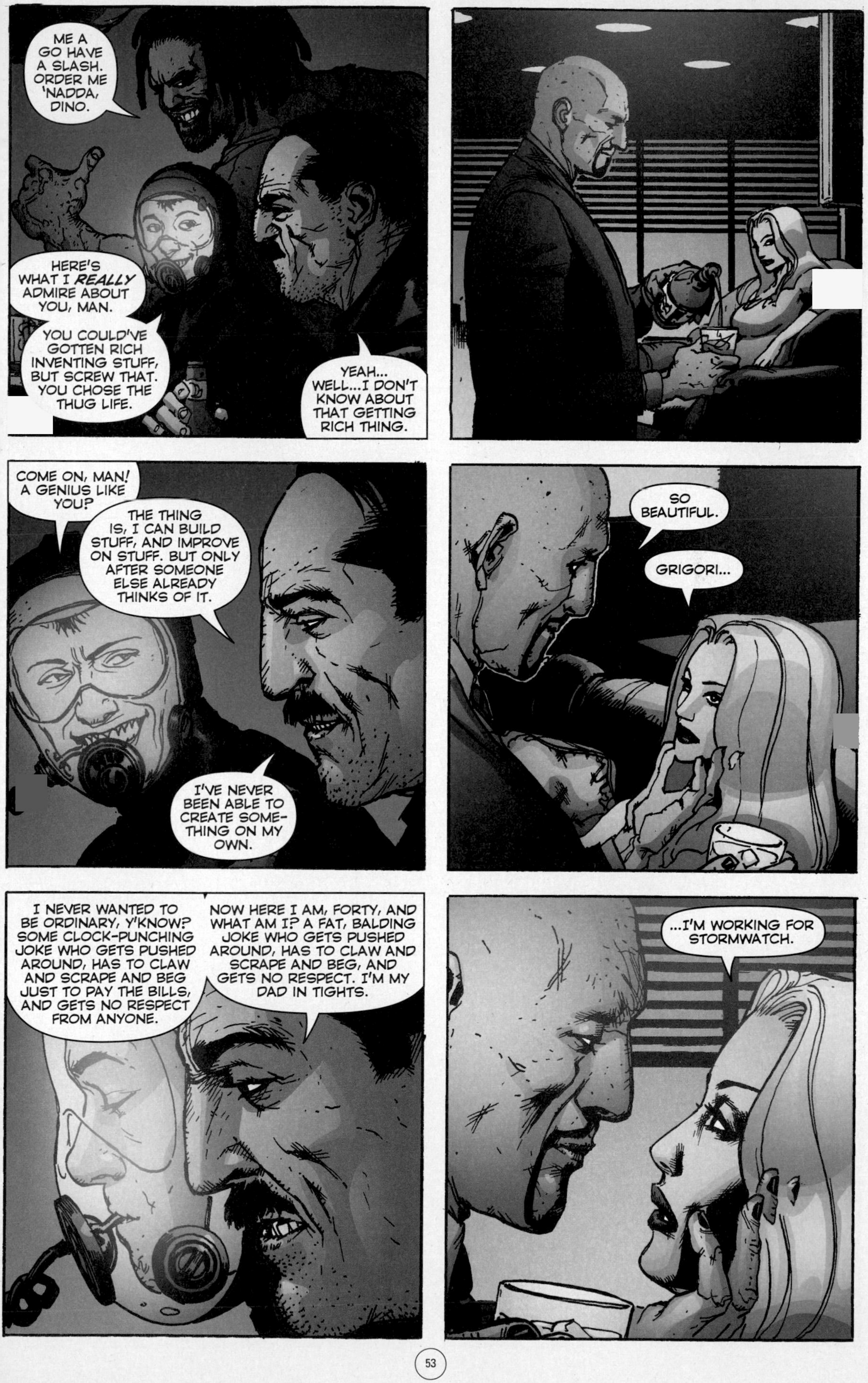

ME A GO HAVE A SLASH. ORDER ME 'NADDA, DINO.
HERE'S WHAT I REALLY ADMIRE ABOUT YOU, MAN.
YOU COULD'VE GOTTEN RICH INVENTING STUFF, BUT SCREW THAT. YOU CHOSE THE THUG LIFE.
YEAH... WELL...I DON'T KNOW ABOUT THAT GETTING RICH THING.
COME ON, MAN! A GENIUS LIKE YOU?
THE THING IS, I CAN BUILD STUFF, AND IMPROVE ON STUFF. BUT ONLY AFTER SOMEONE ELSE ALREADY THINKS OF IT.
I'VE NEVER BEEN ABLE TO CREATE SOME-THING ON MY OWN.
SO BEAUTIFUL.
GRIGORI...
I NEVER WANTED TO BE ORDINARY, Y'KNOW? SOME CLOCK-PUNCHING JOKE WHO GETS PUSHED AROUND, HAS TO CLAW AND SCRAPE AND BEG JUST TO PAY THE BILLS, AND GETS NO RESPECT FROM ANYONE.
NOW HERE I AM, FORTY, AND WHAT AM I? A FAT, BALDING JOKE WHO GETS PUSHED AROUND, HAS TO CLAW AND SCRAPE AND BEG, AND GETS NO RESPECT. I'M MY DAD IN TIGHTS.
...I'M WORKING FOR STORMWATCH.

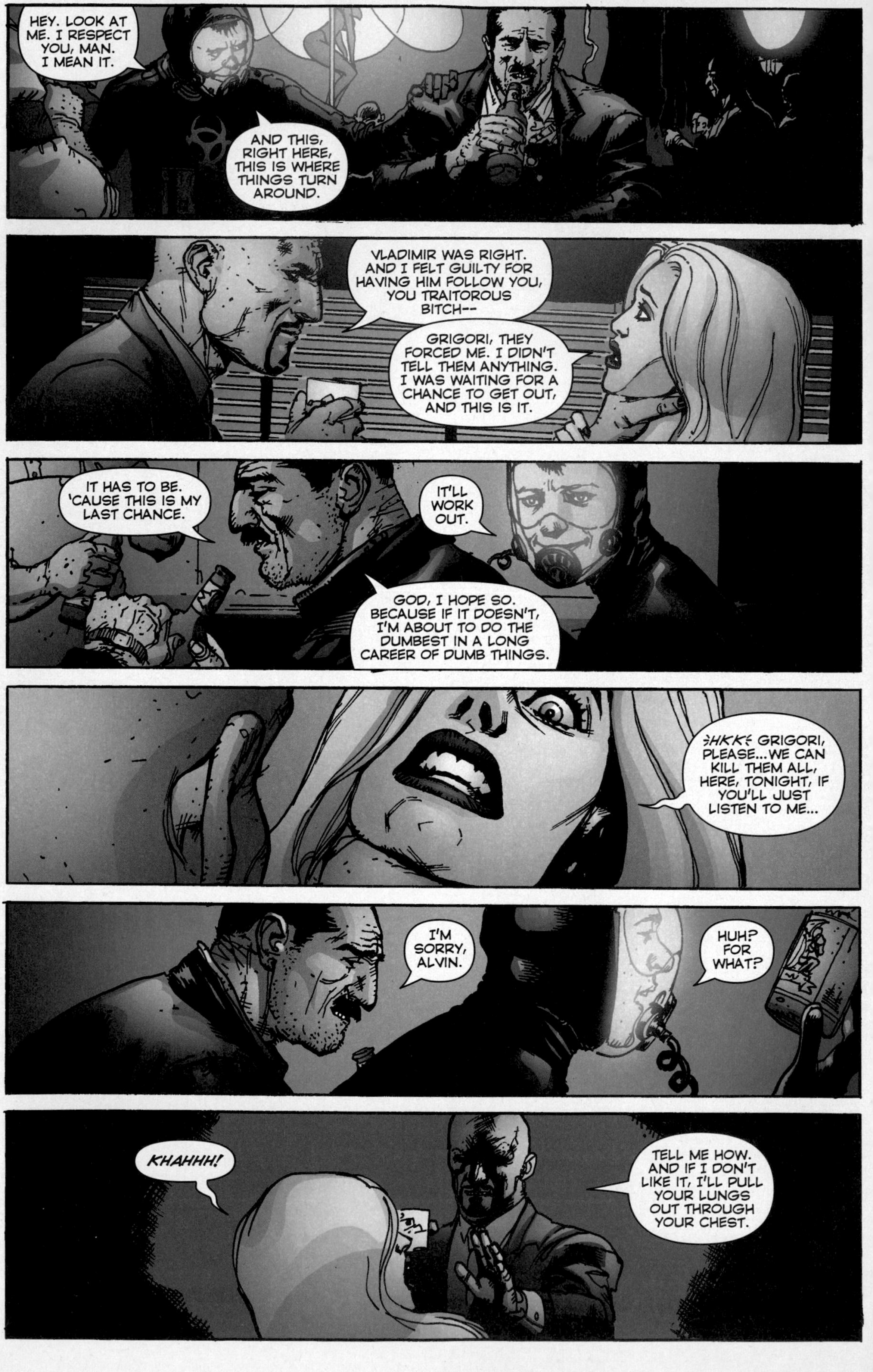
HEY. LOOK AT ME. I RESPECT YOU, MAN. I MEAN IT.
AND THIS, RIGHT HERE, THIS IS WHERE THINGS TURN AROUND.
VLADIMIR WAS RIGHT. AND I FELT GUILTY FOR HAVING HIM FOLLOW YOU, YOU TRAITOROUS BITCH--
GRIGORI, THEY FORCED ME. I DIDN'T TELL THEM ANYTHING. I WAS WAITING FOR A CHANCE TO GET OUT, AND THIS IS IT.
IT HAS TO BE. 'CAUSE THIS IS MY LAST CHANCE.
IT'LL WORK OUT.
GOD, I HOPE SO. BECAUSE IF IT DOESN'T, I'M ABOUT TO DO THE DUMBEST IN A LONG CAREER OF DUMB THINGS.
ƷHKKƸ GRIGORI, PLEASE...WE CAN KILL THEM ALL, HERE, TONIGHT, IF YOU'LL JUST LISTEN TO ME...
I'M SORRY, ALVIN.
HUH? FOR WHAT?
KHAHHH!
TELL ME HOW. AND IF I DON'T LIKE IT, I'LL PULL YOUR LUNGS OUT THROUGH YOUR CHEST.

I REALLY AM SORRY.
TSSSSSS
WHAT THE HELL--?
NNH... WHAT--?
ABOUT TIME. HOW MUCH OF THAT STUFF CAN ONE GUY INHALE?
EVEN WITH THE OXYGEN FILTERS IN MY NOSTRILS, I'M ABOUT TO KEEL OVER.
COMBINATION OF FIRE RETARDANT FOAM AND THE ARGONNE LABORATORY'S RADIATION-ABSORBING SUPERGEL.
YOU WON'T BE ABLE TO BUILD ENOUGH OF A CHARGE TO EXPLODE.
I CAN'T BELIEVE IT! YOU BACKSTABBING SONOFA--
CARBON MONOXIDE. UNLIKE THE GAS COMPANY, WE DIDN'T ADD ANY ODOR TO IT. YOU'VE BEEN BREATHING IT SINCE YOU WALKED IN.
YOUR POKER FACE NEEDS WORK. I COULD TELL RIGHT AWAY YOU WERE ON TO ME. BUT YOU FOUND OUT A LITTLE TOO LATE.
WHO'S THE BITCH NOW, SWEETIE?
OH, BODDERATION.

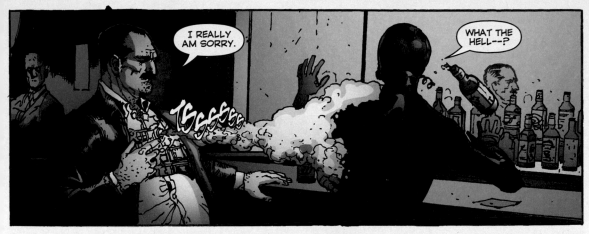

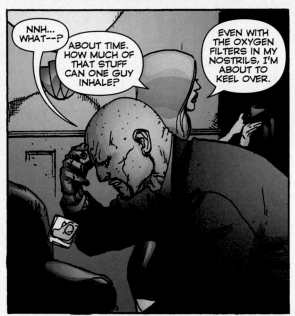

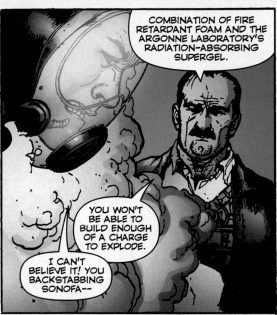

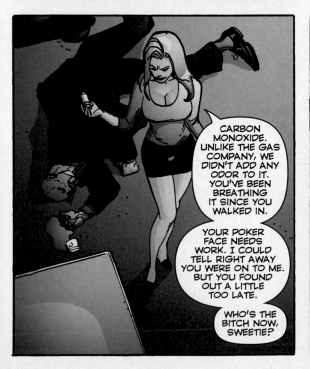

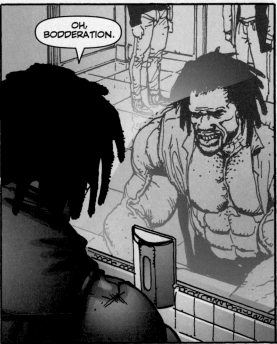

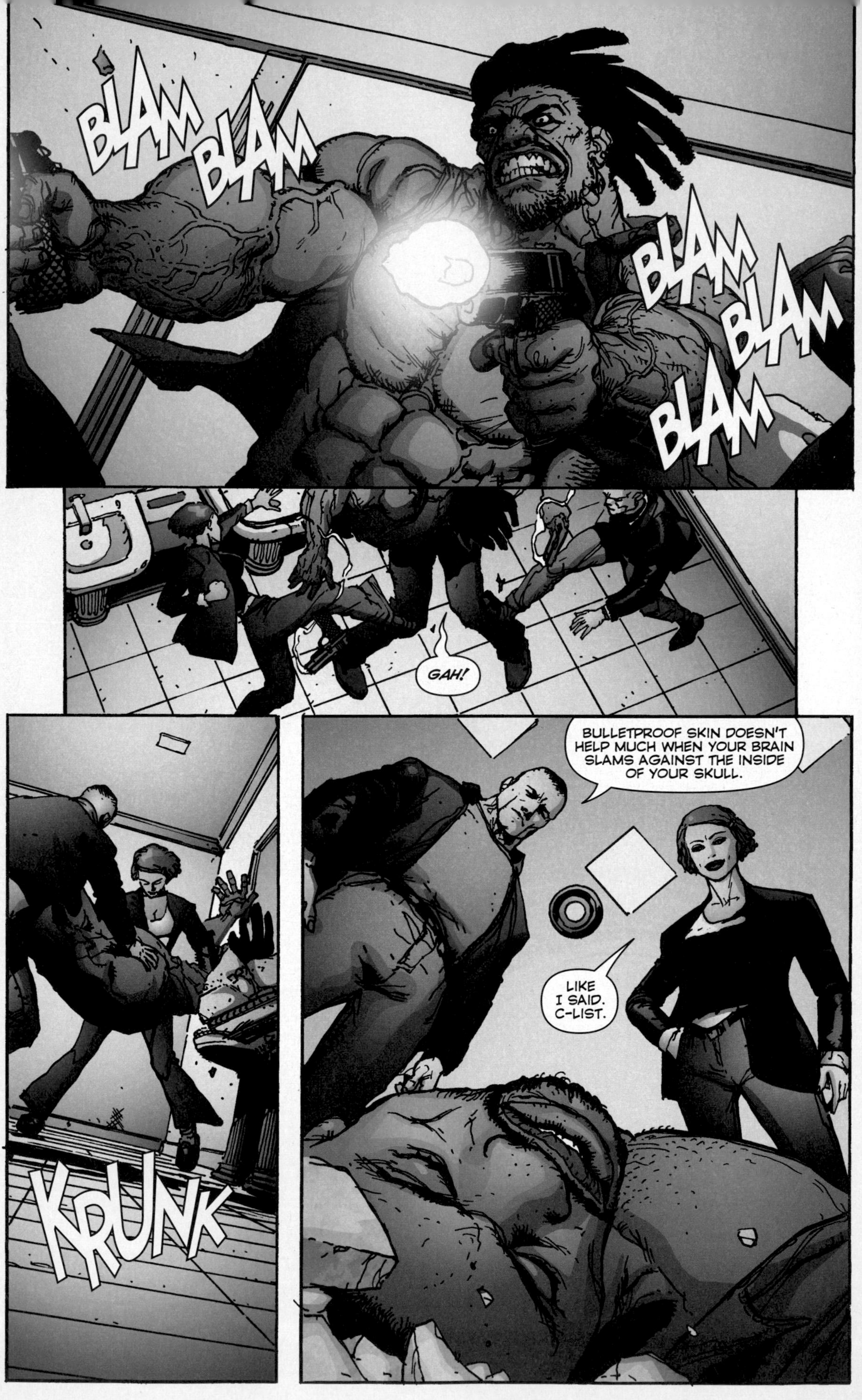
BLAM BLAM
BLAM BLAM BLAM
GAH!
KRUNK
BULLETPROOF SKIN DOESN'T HELP MUCH WHEN YOUR BRAIN SLAMS AGAINST THE INSIDE OF YOUR SKULL.
LIKE I SAID. C-LIST.

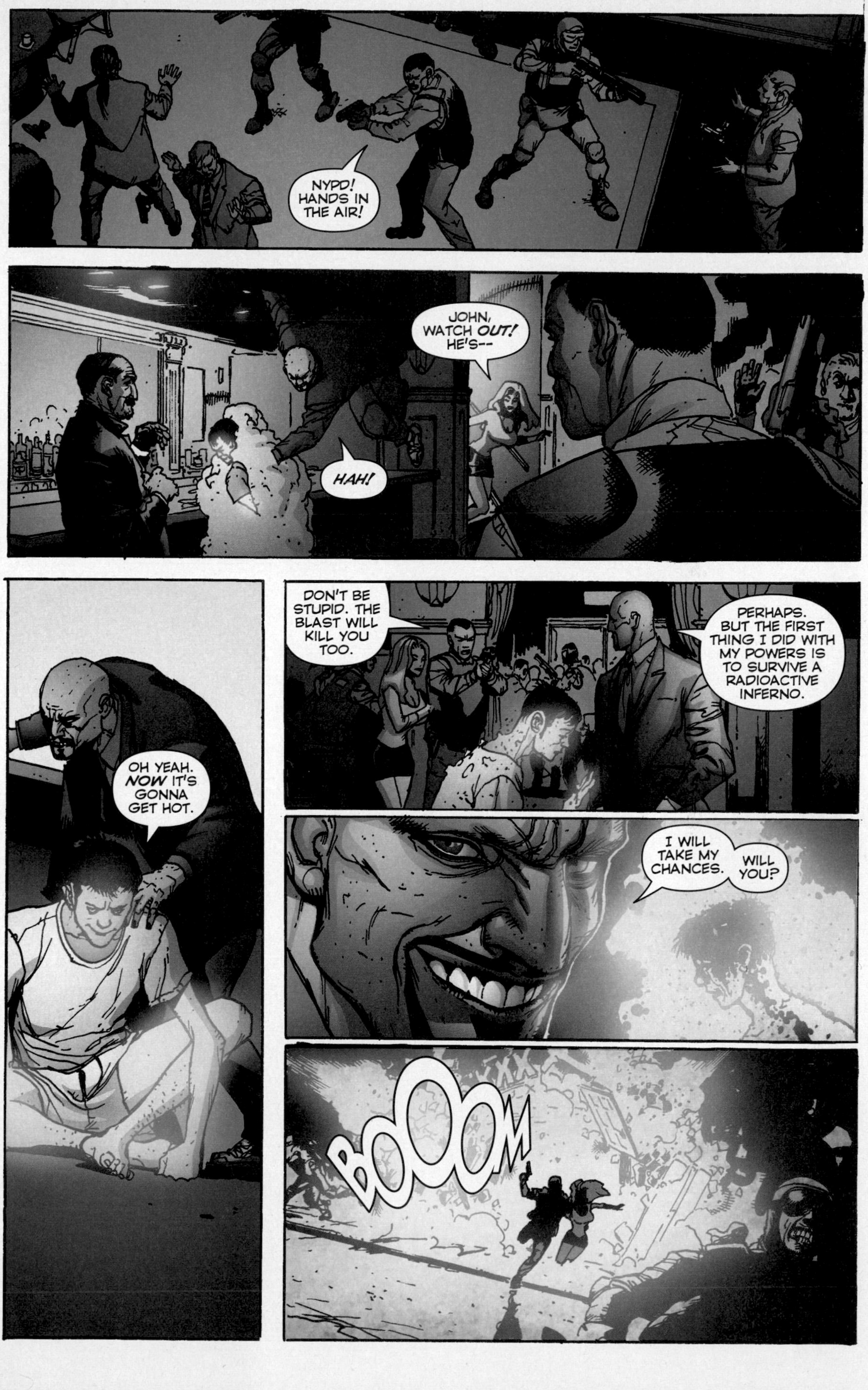
NYPD! HANDS IN THE AIR!
JOHN, WATCH OUT! HE'S--
HAH!
OH YEAH. NOW IT'S GONNA GET HOT.
DON'T BE STUPID. THE BLAST WILL KILL YOU TOO.
PERHAPS. BUT THE FIRST THING I DID WITH MY POWERS IS TO SURVIVE A RADIOACTIVE INFERNO.
I WILL TAKE MY CHANCES.
WILL YOU?
BOOOOM

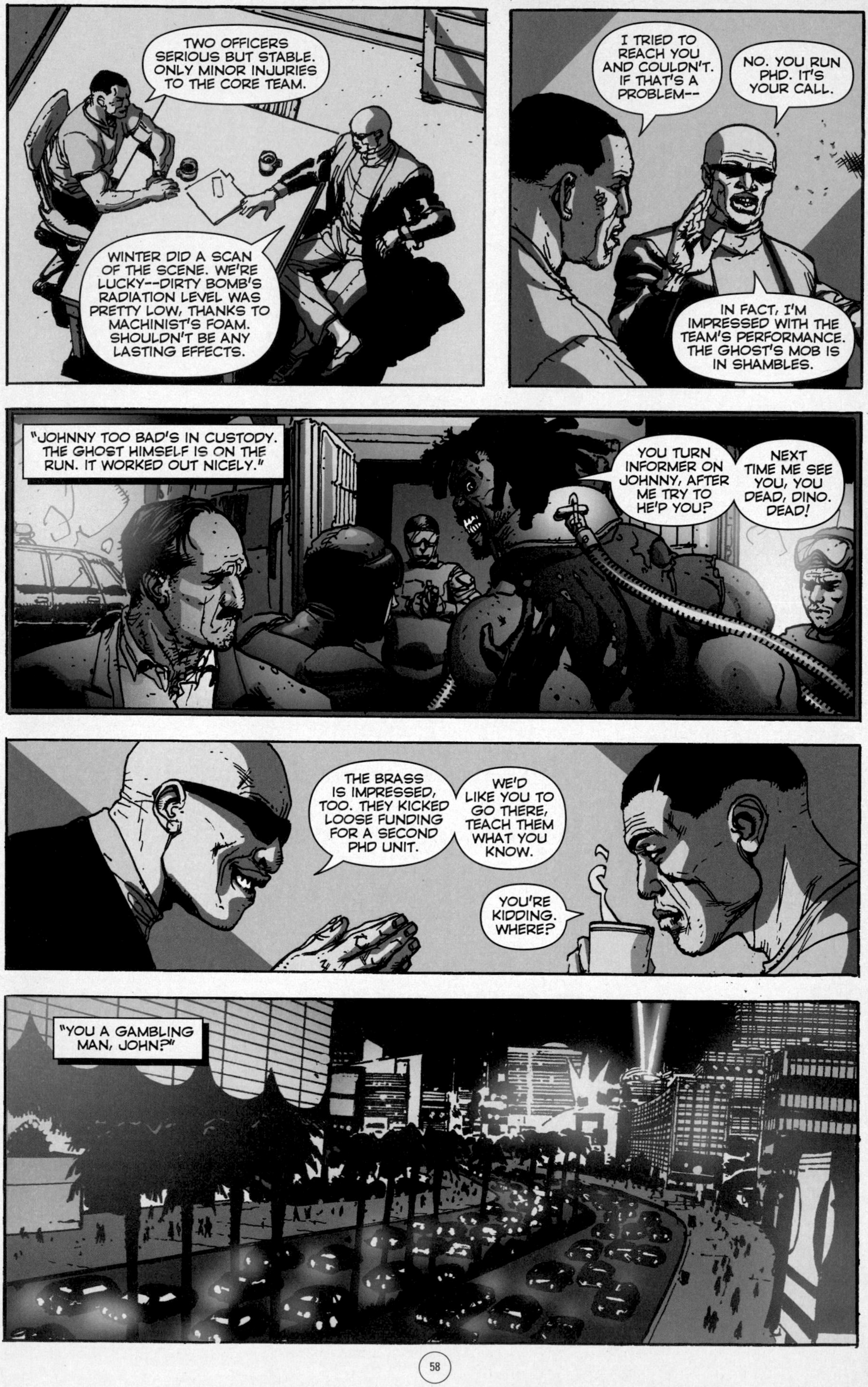
TWO OFFICERS SERIOUS BUT STABLE. ONLY MINOR INJURIES TO THE CORE TEAM.
WINTER DID A SCAN OF THE SCENE. WE'RE LUCKY--DIRTY BOMB'S RADIATION LEVEL WAS PRETTY LOW, THANKS TO MACHINIST'S FOAM. SHOULDN'T BE ANY LASTING EFFECTS.
I TRIED TO REACH YOU AND COULDN'T. IF THAT'S A PROBLEM--
NO. YOU RUN PHD. IT'S YOUR CALL.
IN FACT, I'M IMPRESSED WITH THE TEAM'S PERFORMANCE. THE GHOST'S MOB IS IN SHAMBLES.
"JOHNNY TOO BAD'S IN CUSTODY. THE GHOST HIMSELF IS ON THE RUN. IT WORKED OUT NICELY."
YOU TURN INFORMER ON JOHNNY, AFTER ME TRY TO HE'P YOU?
NEXT TIME ME SEE YOU, YOU DEAD, DINO. DEAD!
THE BRASS IS IMPRESSED, TOO. THEY KICKED LOOSE FUNDING FOR A SECOND PHD UNIT.
WE'D LIKE YOU TO GO THERE, TEACH THEM WHAT YOU KNOW.
YOU'RE KIDDING. WHERE?
"YOU A GAMBLING MAN, JOHN?"

chapter 3: what happens in vegas

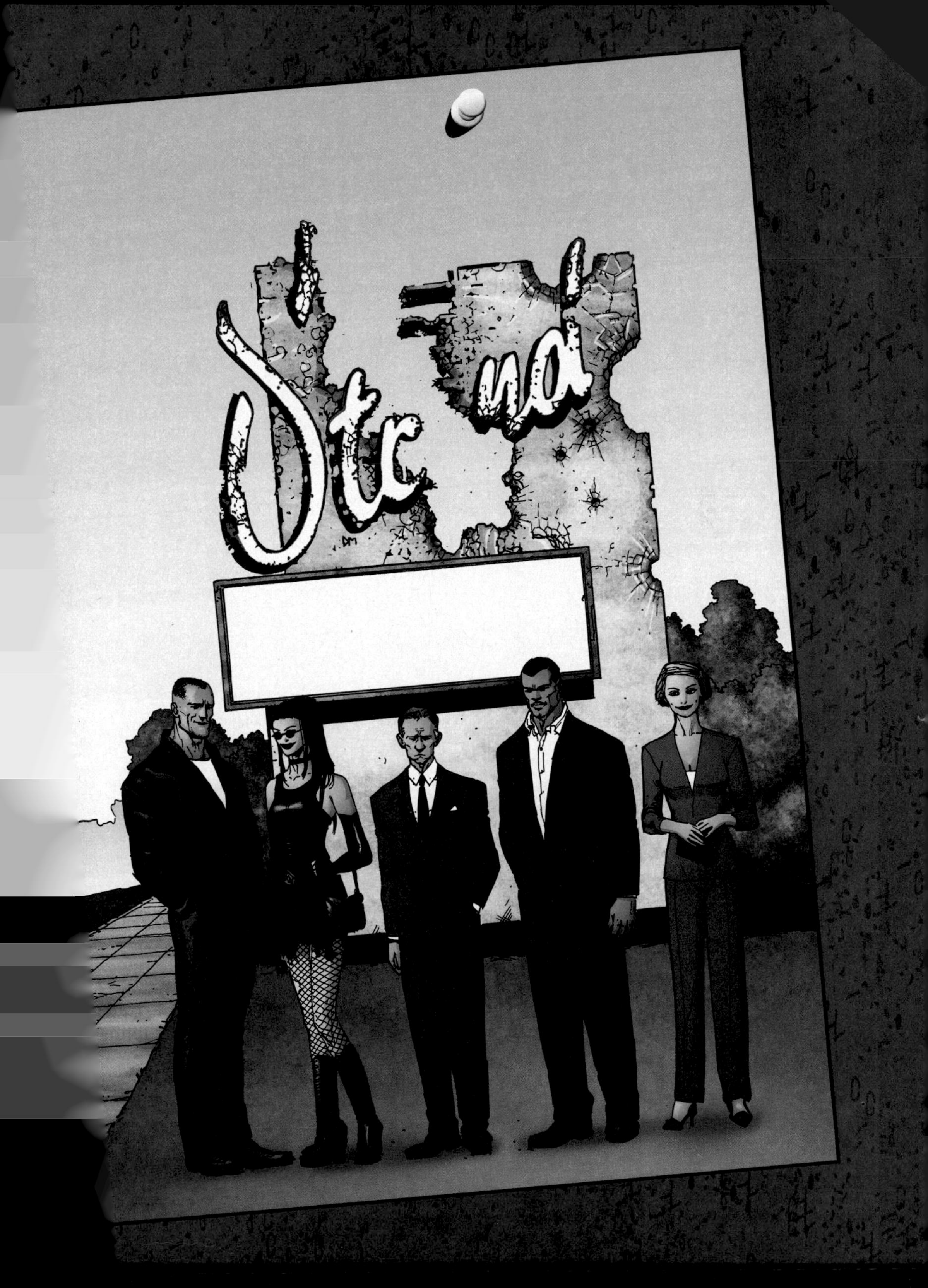

Doug Mahnke & David Baron

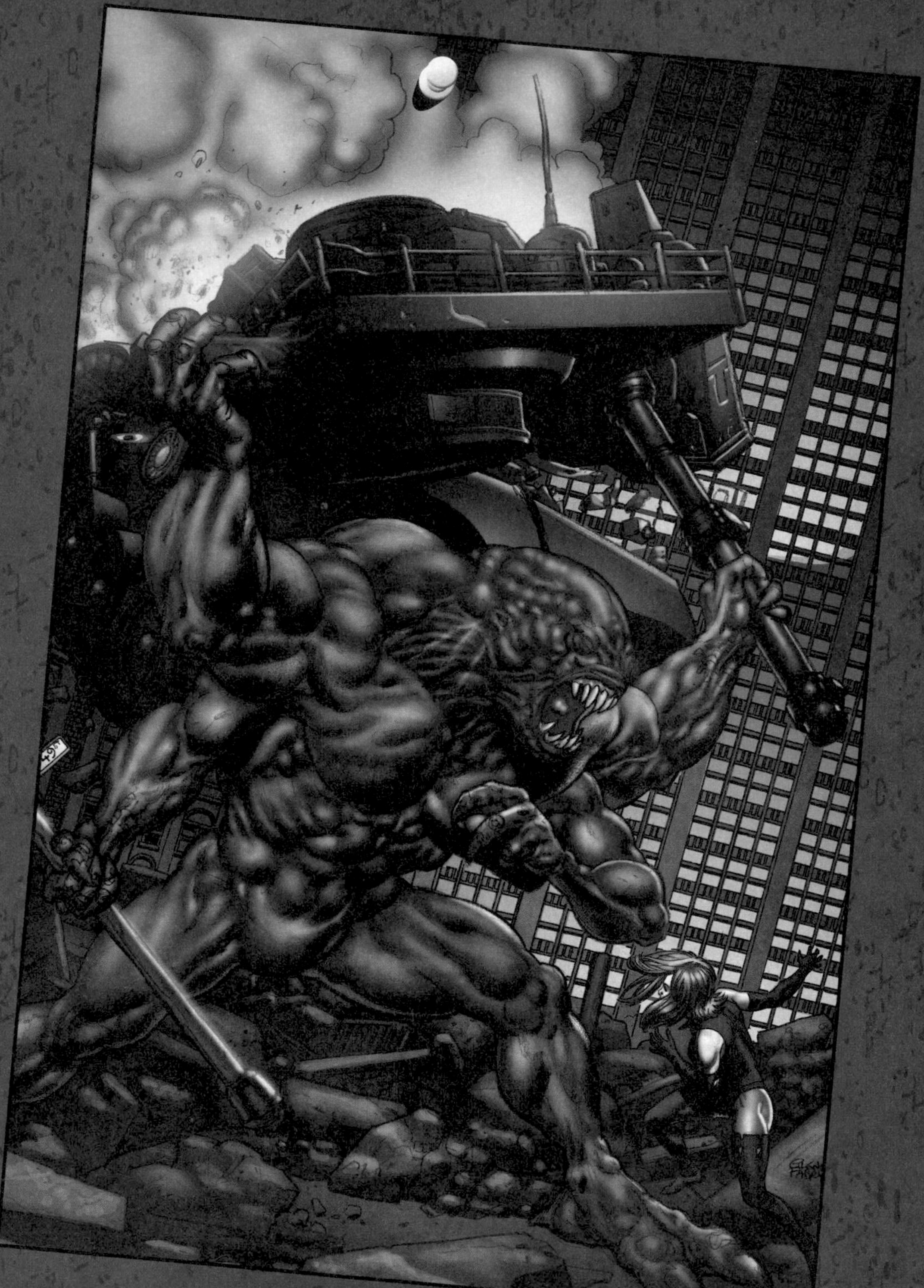

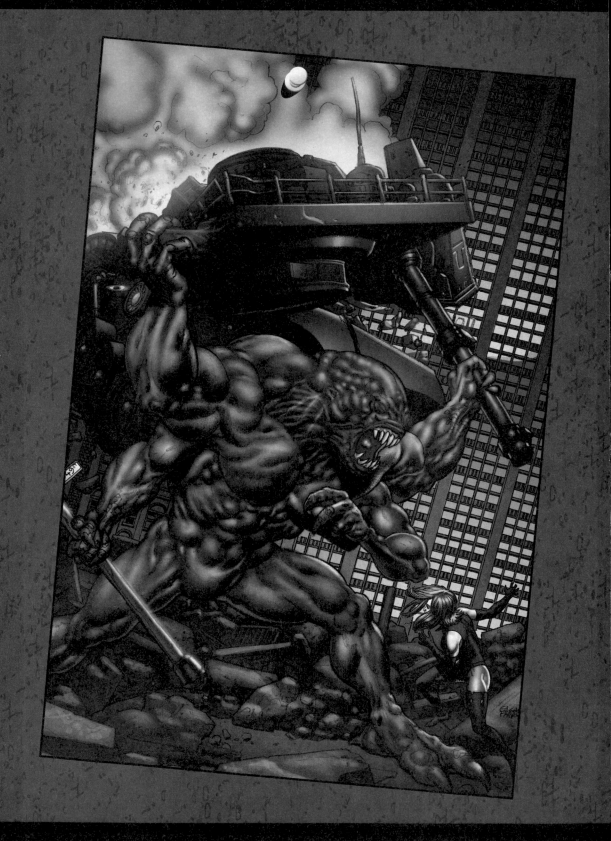

Glenn Fabry & David Baron

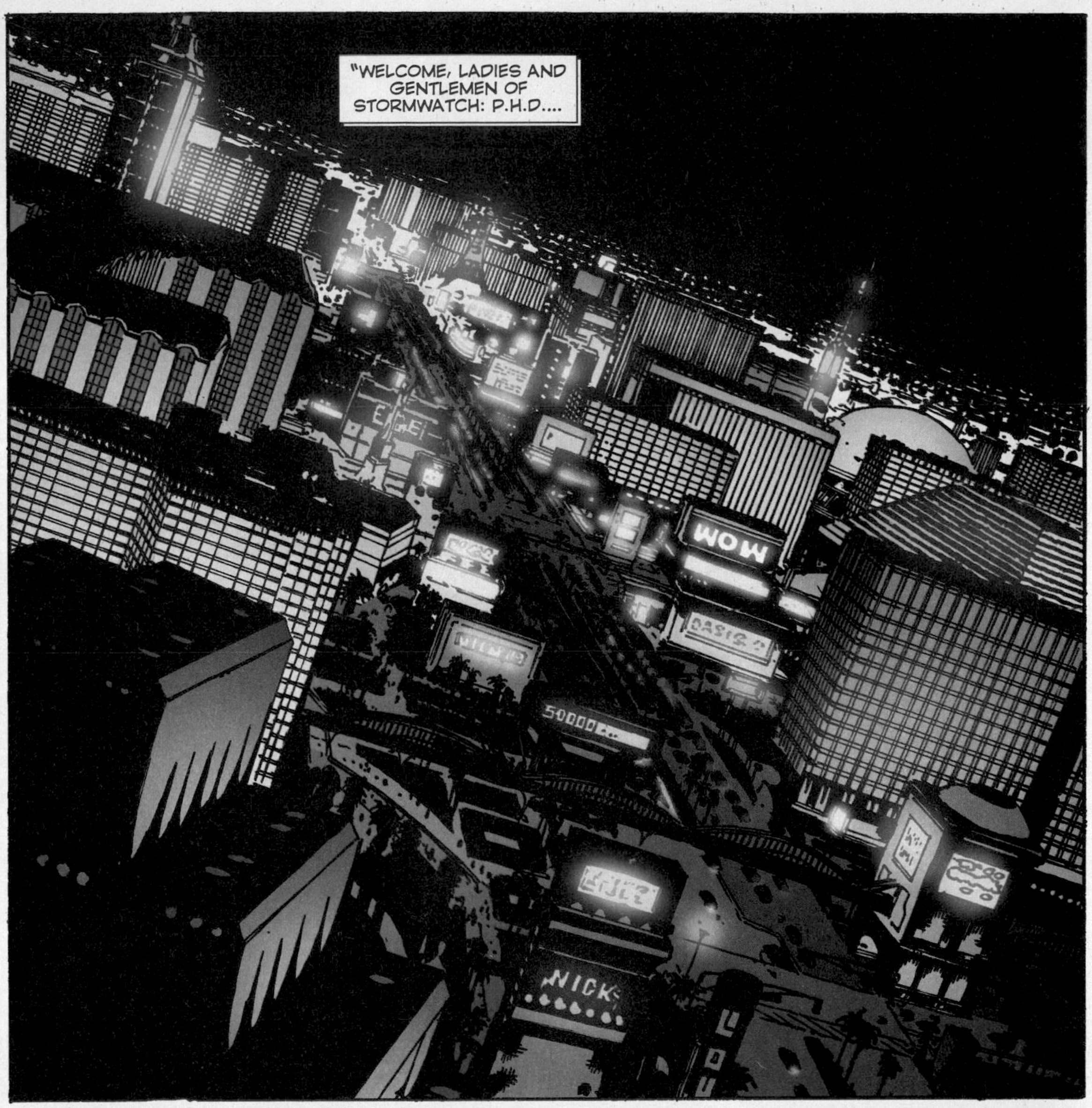
"WELCOME, LADIES AND GENTLEMEN OF STORMWATCH: P.H.D....
WOW
NICK

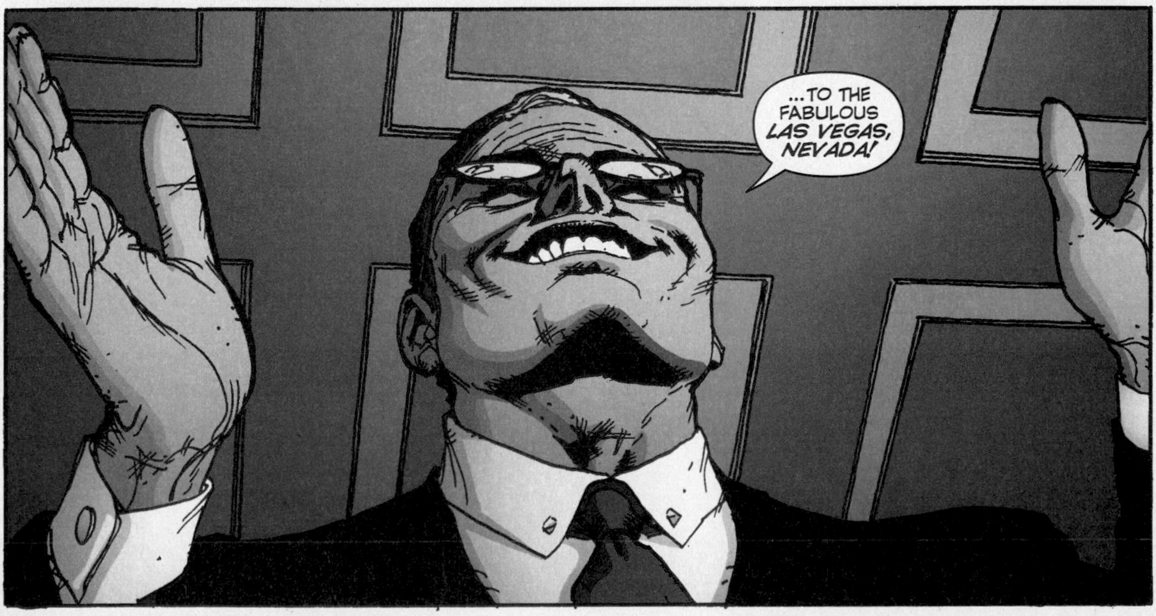
...TO THE FABULOUS *LAS VEGAS, NEVADA!*

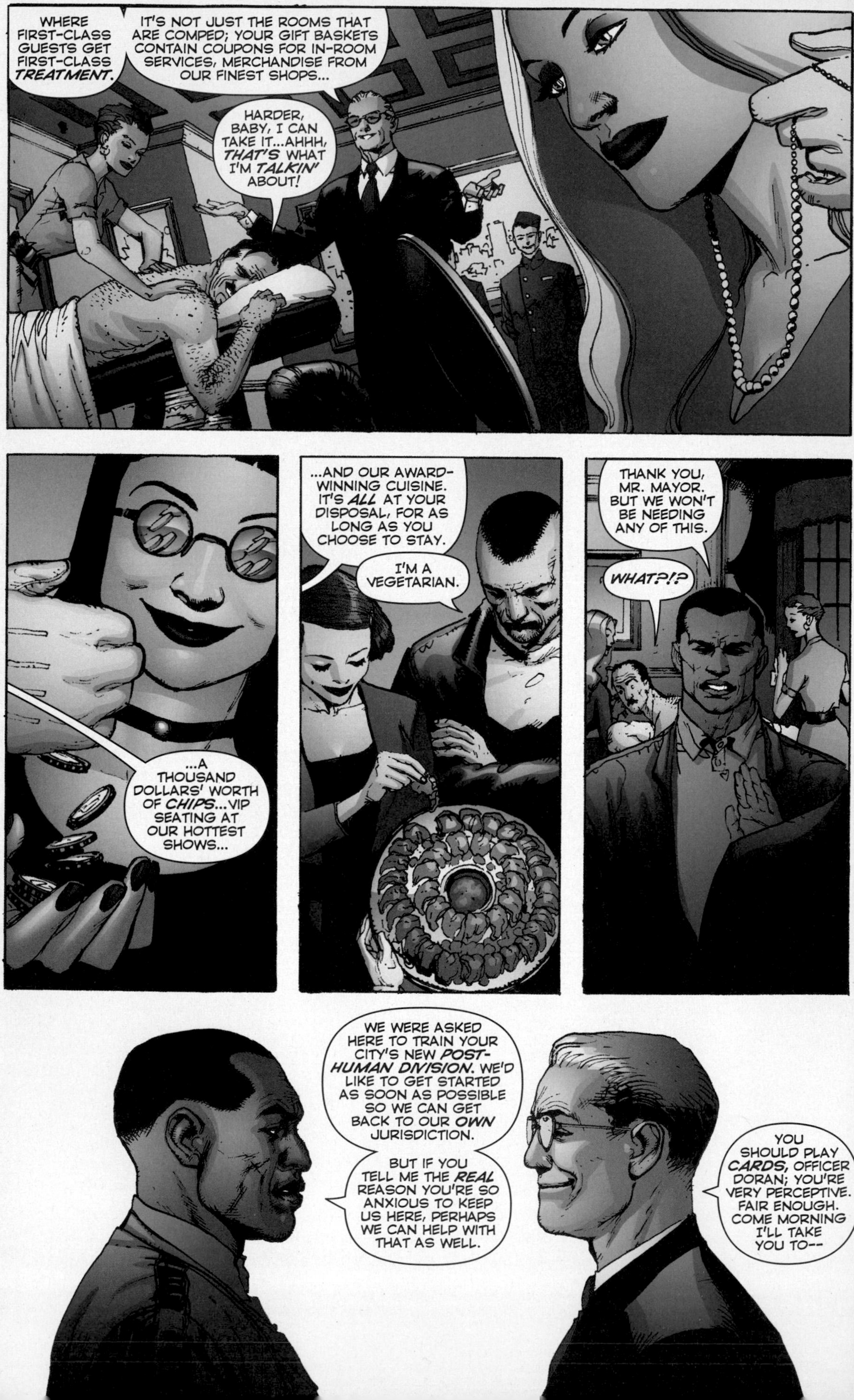
WHERE FIRST-CLASS GUESTS GET FIRST-CLASS *TREATMENT*.
IT'S NOT JUST THE ROOMS THAT ARE COMPED; YOUR GIFT BASKETS CONTAIN COUPONS FOR IN-ROOM SERVICES, MERCHANDISE FROM OUR FINEST SHOPS...
HARDER, BABY, I CAN TAKE IT...AHHH, *THAT'S* WHAT I'M *TALKIN'* ABOUT!
...A THOUSAND DOLLARS' WORTH OF *CHIPS*...VIP SEATING AT OUR HOTTEST SHOWS...
...AND OUR AWARD-WINNING CUISINE. IT'S *ALL* AT YOUR DISPOSAL, FOR AS LONG AS YOU CHOOSE TO STAY.
I'M A VEGETARIAN.
THANK YOU, MR. MAYOR. BUT WE WON'T BE NEEDING ANY OF THIS.
WHAT?!?
WE WERE ASKED HERE TO TRAIN YOUR CITY'S NEW *POST-HUMAN DIVISION*. WE'D LIKE TO GET STARTED AS SOON AS POSSIBLE SO WE CAN GET BACK TO OUR *OWN* JURISDICTION.
BUT IF YOU TELL ME THE *REAL* REASON YOU'RE SO ANXIOUS TO KEEP US HERE, PERHAPS WE CAN HELP WITH THAT AS WELL.
YOU SHOULD PLAY *CARDS*, OFFICER DORAN; YOU'RE VERY PERCEPTIVE. FAIR ENOUGH. COME MORNING I'LL TAKE YOU TO--

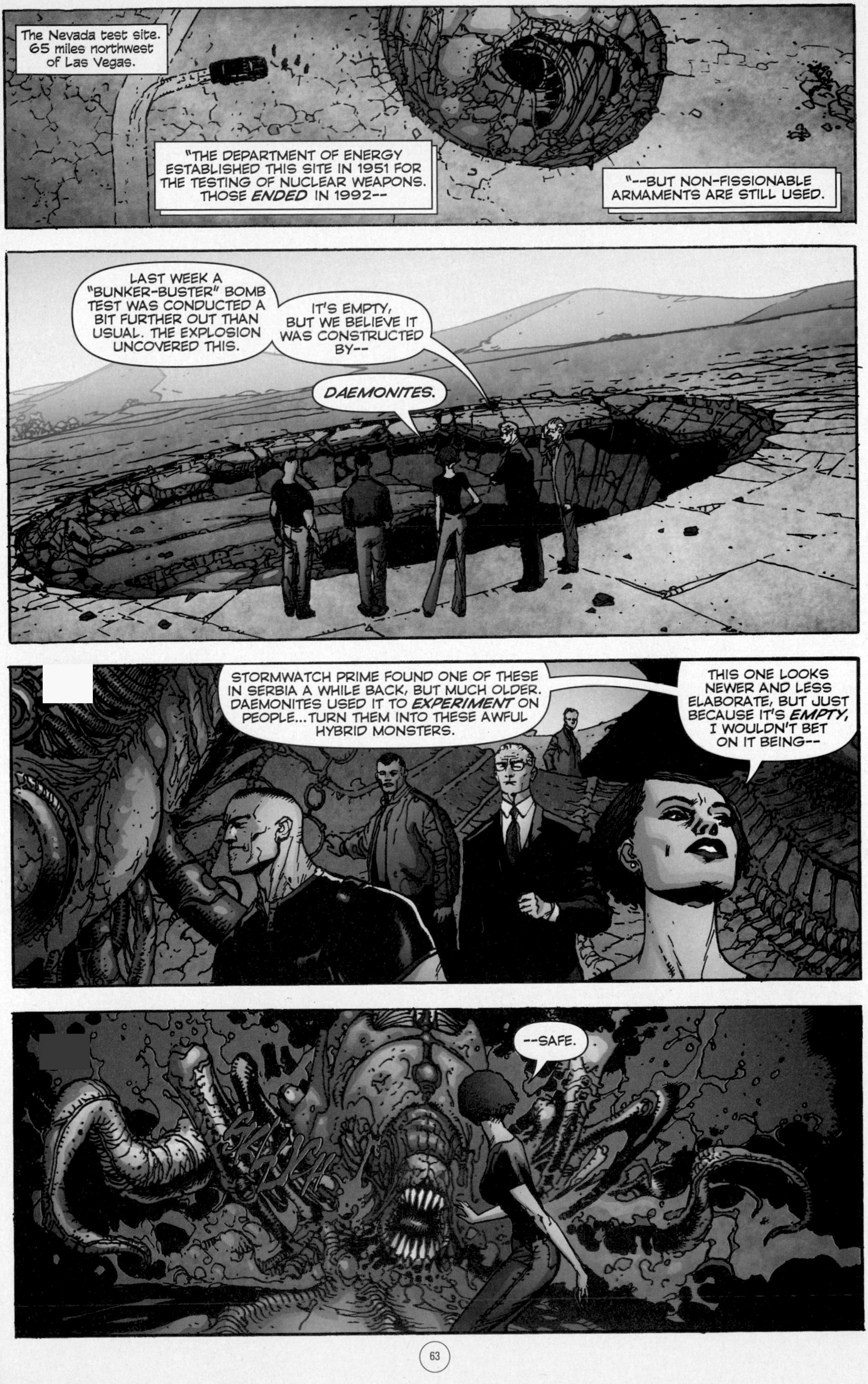
The Nevada test site. 65 miles northwest of Las Vegas.
"THE DEPARTMENT OF ENERGY ESTABLISHED THIS SITE IN 1951 FOR THE TESTING OF NUCLEAR WEAPONS. THOSE *ENDED* IN 1992--
"--BUT NON-FISSIONABLE ARMAMENTS ARE STILL USED.
LAST WEEK A "BUNKER-BUSTER" BOMB TEST WAS CONDUCTED A BIT FURTHER OUT THAN USUAL. THE EXPLOSION UNCOVERED THIS.
IT'S EMPTY, BUT WE BELIEVE IT WAS CONSTRUCTED BY--
DAEMONITES.
STORMWATCH PRIME FOUND ONE OF THESE IN SERBIA A WHILE BACK, BUT MUCH OLDER. DAEMONITES USED IT TO *EXPERIMENT* ON PEOPLE...TURN THEM INTO THESE AWFUL HYBRID MONSTERS.
THIS ONE LOOKS NEWER AND LESS ELABORATE, BUT JUST BECAUSE IT'S *EMPTY,* I WOULDN'T BET ON IT BEING--
--SAFE.

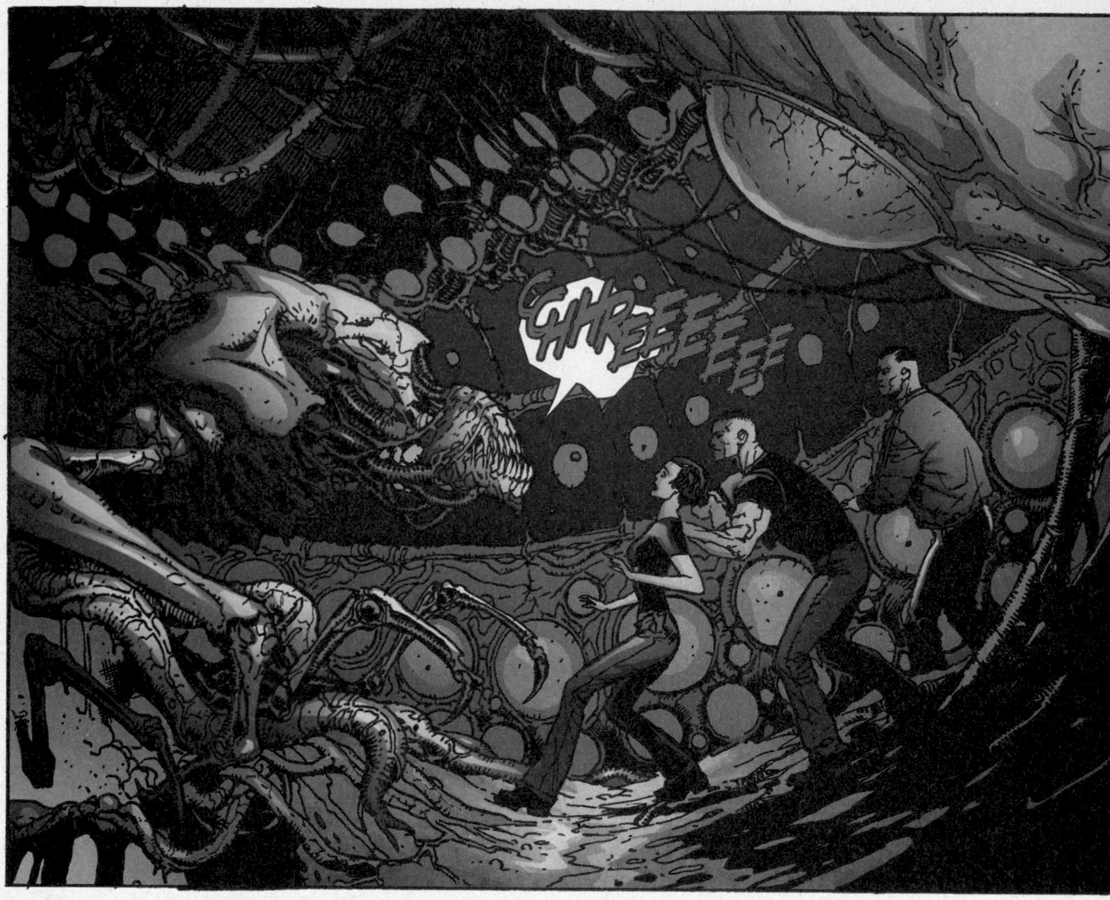
CHREEEEEEEE

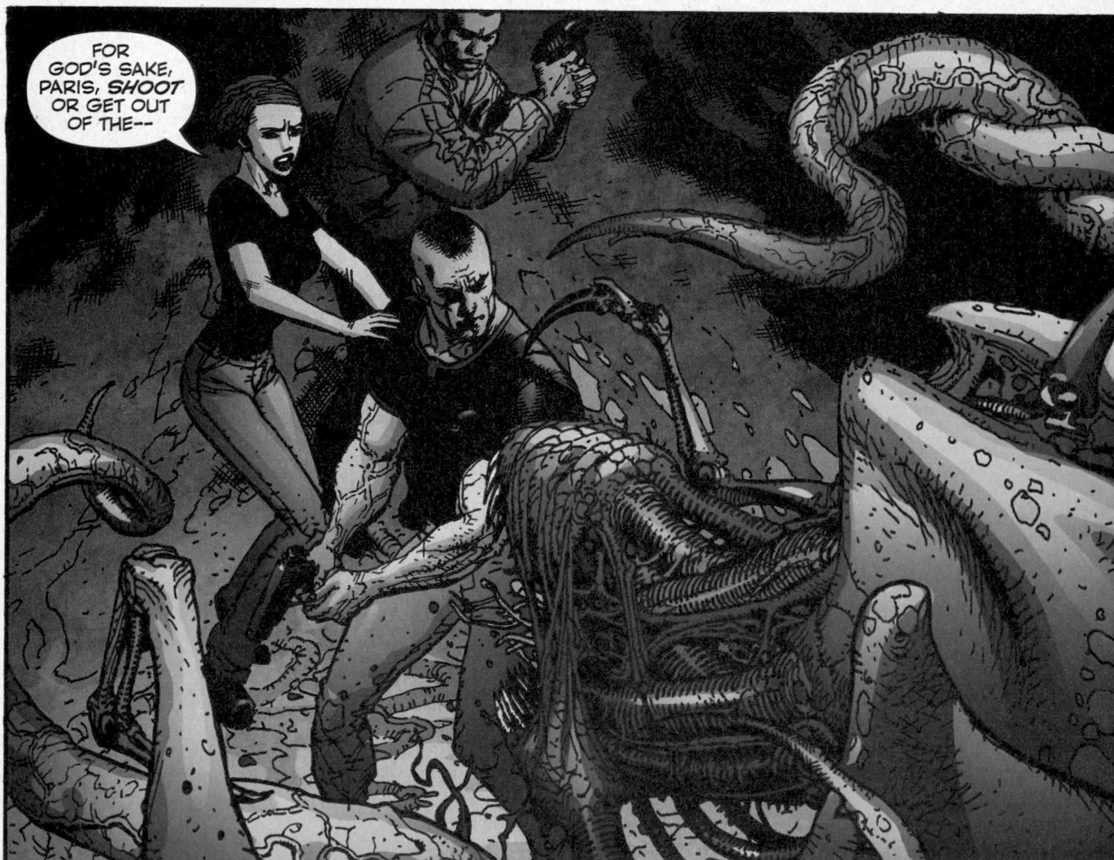
FOR GOD'S SAKE, PARIS, *SHOOT* OR GET OUT OF THE--

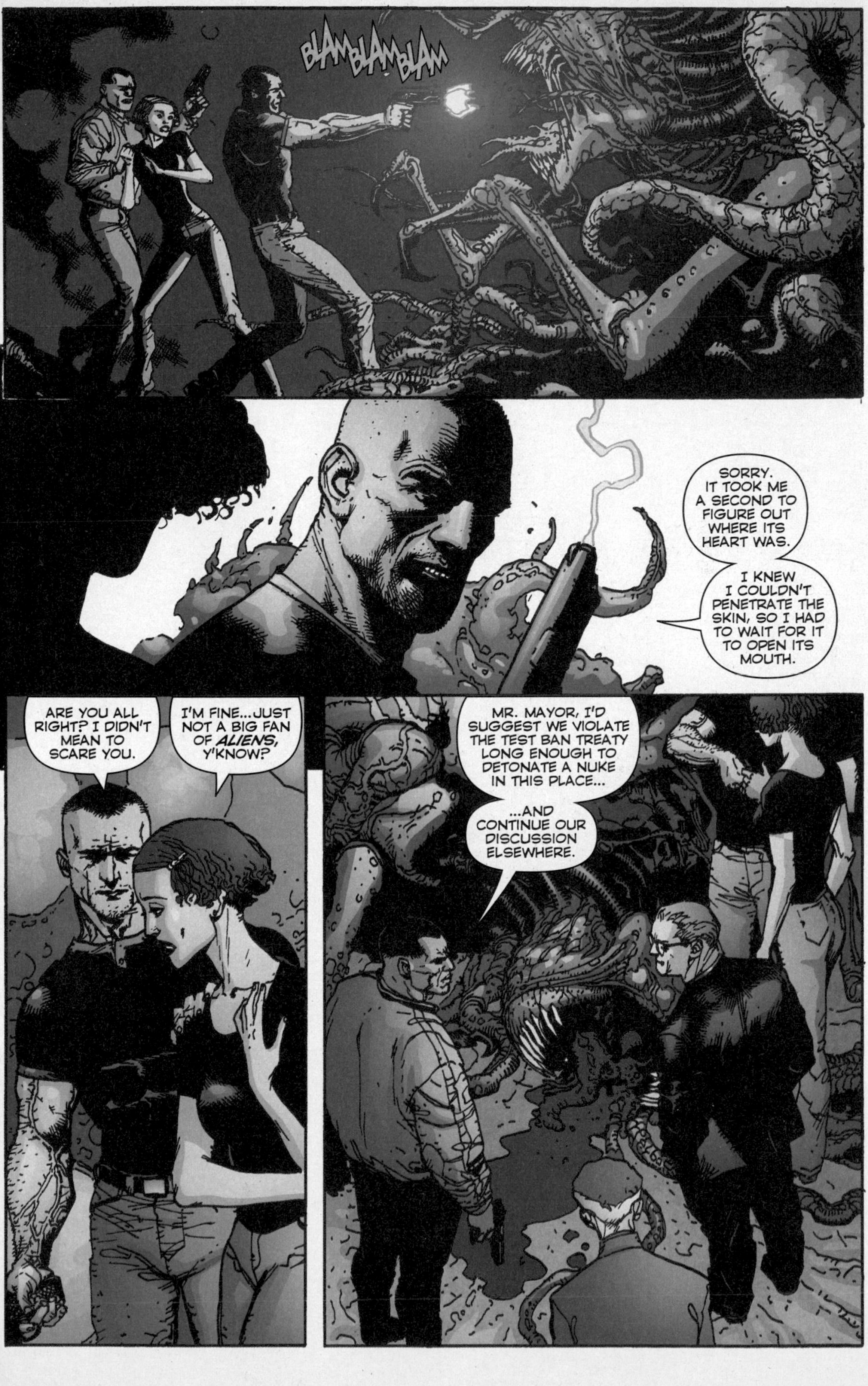
BLAMBLAMBLAM
SORRY. IT TOOK ME A SECOND TO FIGURE OUT WHERE ITS HEART WAS.
I KNEW I COULDN'T PENETRATE THE SKIN, SO I HAD TO WAIT FOR IT TO OPEN ITS MOUTH.
ARE YOU ALL RIGHT? I DIDN'T MEAN TO SCARE YOU.
I'M FINE...JUST NOT A BIG FAN OF *ALIENS,* Y'KNOW?
MR. MAYOR, I'D SUGGEST WE VIOLATE THE TEST BAN TREATY LONG ENOUGH TO DETONATE A NUKE IN THIS PLACE...
...AND CONTINUE OUR DISCUSSION ELSEWHERE.

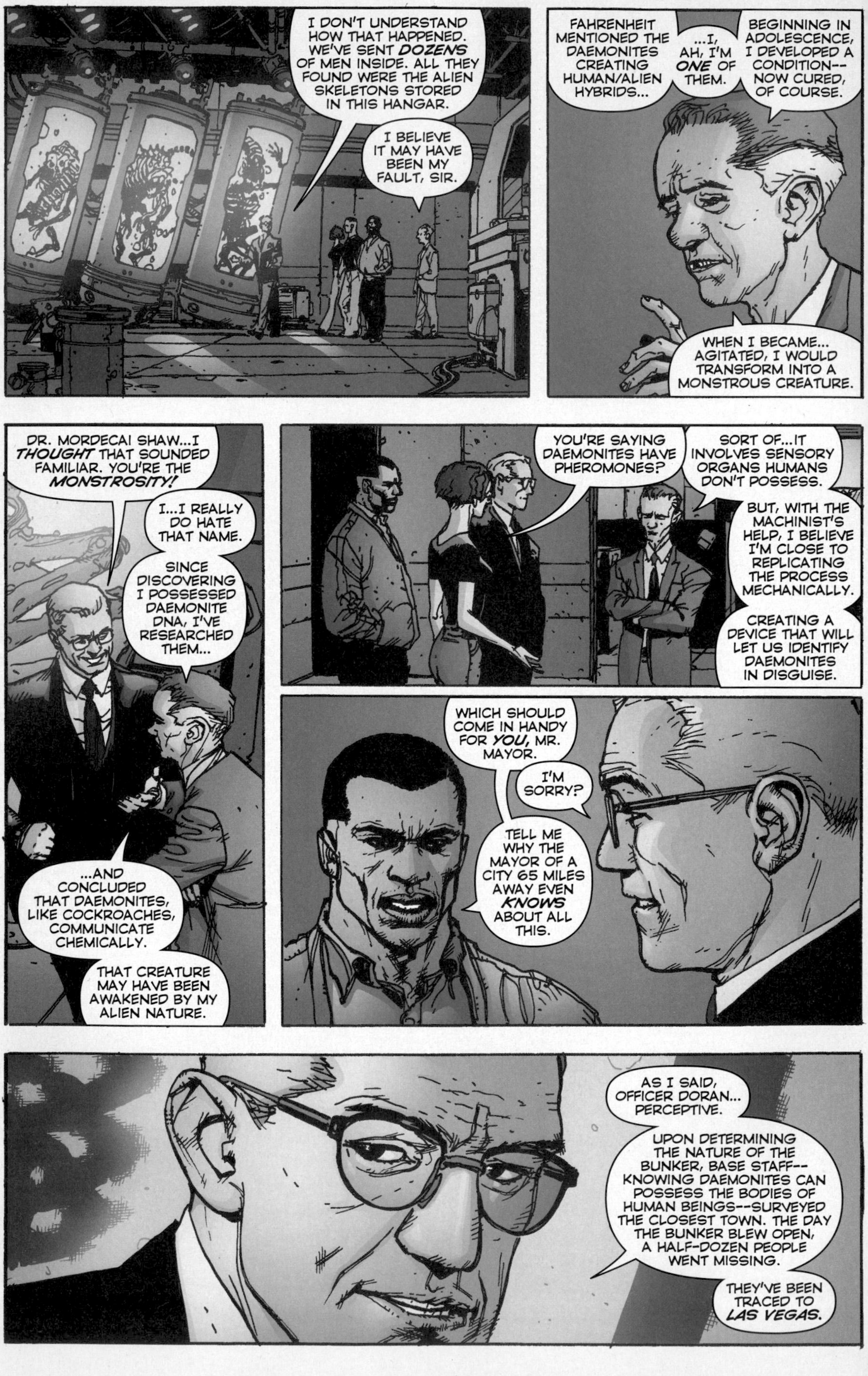
I DON'T UNDERSTAND HOW THAT HAPPENED. WE'VE SENT DOZENS OF MEN INSIDE. ALL THEY FOUND WERE THE ALIEN SKELETONS STORED IN THIS HANGAR.
I BELIEVE IT MAY HAVE BEEN MY FAULT, SIR.
FAHRENHEIT MENTIONED THE DAEMONITES CREATING HUMAN/ALIEN HYBRIDS...
...I, AH, I'M ONE OF THEM.
BEGINNING IN ADOLESCENCE, I DEVELOPED A CONDITION-- NOW CURED, OF COURSE.
WHEN I BECAME... AGITATED, I WOULD TRANSFORM INTO A MONSTROUS CREATURE.
DR. MORDECAI SHAW...I THOUGHT THAT SOUNDED FAMILIAR. YOU'RE THE MONSTROSITY!
I...I REALLY DO HATE THAT NAME.
SINCE DISCOVERING I POSSESSED DAEMONITE DNA, I'VE RESEARCHED THEM...
...AND CONCLUDED THAT DAEMONITES, LIKE COCKROACHES, COMMUNICATE CHEMICALLY.
THAT CREATURE MAY HAVE BEEN AWAKENED BY MY ALIEN NATURE.
YOU'RE SAYING DAEMONITES HAVE PHEROMONES?
SORT OF...IT INVOLVES SENSORY ORGANS HUMANS DON'T POSSESS.
BUT, WITH THE MACHINIST'S HELP, I BELIEVE I'M CLOSE TO REPLICATING THE PROCESS MECHANICALLY.
CREATING A DEVICE THAT WILL LET US IDENTIFY DAEMONITES IN DISGUISE.
WHICH SHOULD COME IN HANDY FOR YOU, MR. MAYOR.
I'M SORRY?
TELL ME WHY THE MAYOR OF A CITY 65 MILES AWAY EVEN KNOWS ABOUT ALL THIS.
AS I SAID, OFFICER DORAN... PERCEPTIVE.
UPON DETERMINING THE NATURE OF THE BUNKER, BASE STAFF-- KNOWING DAEMONITES CAN POSSESS THE BODIES OF HUMAN BEINGS--SURVEYED THE CLOSEST TOWN. THE DAY THE BUNKER BLEW OPEN, A HALF-DOZEN PEOPLE WENT MISSING.
THEY'VE BEEN TRACED TO LAS VEGAS.

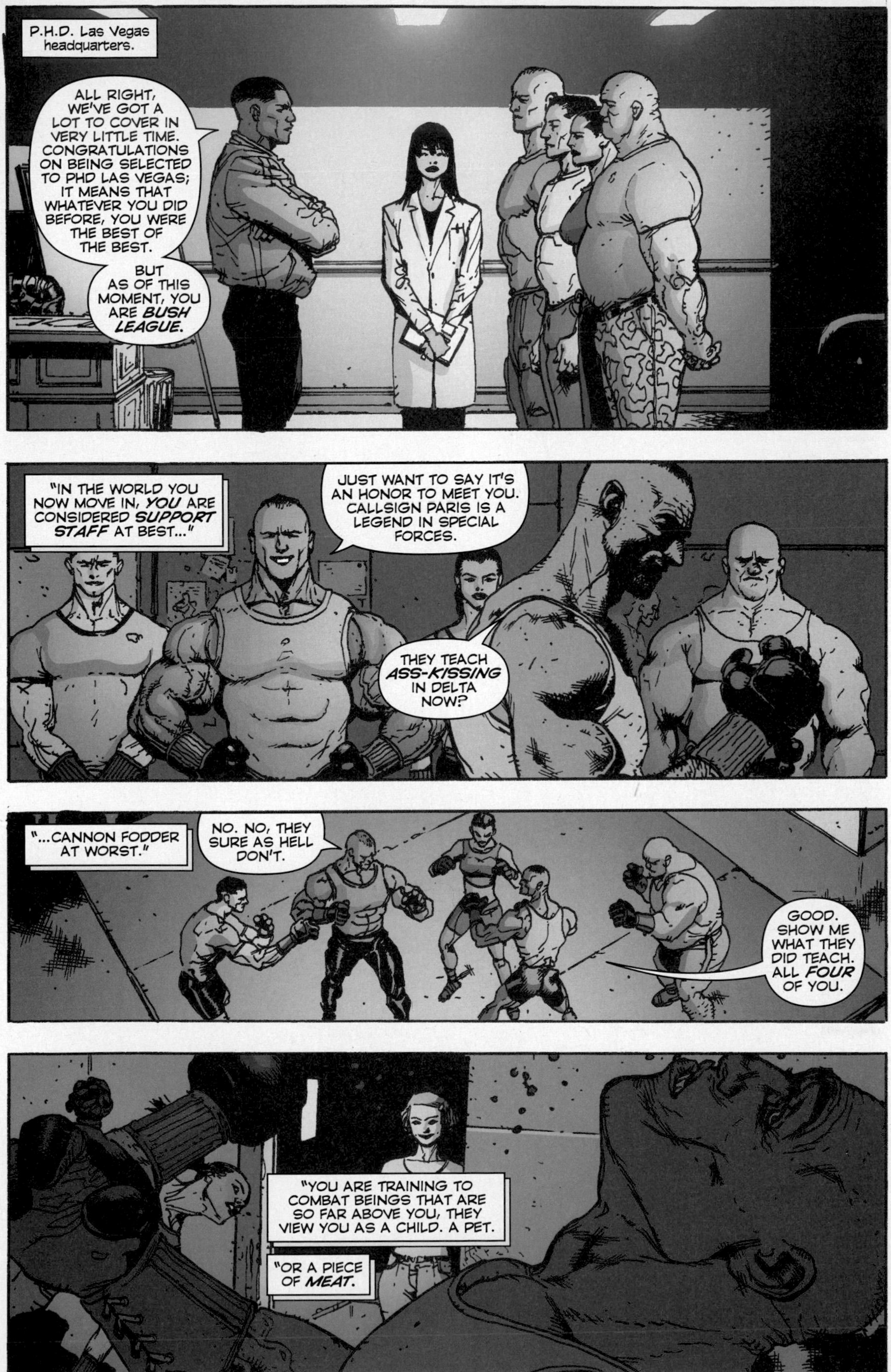
P.H.D. Las Vegas headquarters.
ALL RIGHT, WE'VE GOT A LOT TO COVER IN VERY LITTLE TIME. CONGRATULATIONS ON BEING SELECTED TO PHD LAS VEGAS; IT MEANS THAT WHATEVER YOU DID BEFORE, YOU WERE THE BEST OF THE BEST.
BUT AS OF THIS MOMENT, YOU ARE *BUSH LEAGUE*.
"IN THE WORLD YOU NOW MOVE IN, *YOU* ARE CONSIDERED *SUPPORT STAFF* AT BEST..."
JUST WANT TO SAY IT'S AN HONOR TO MEET YOU. CALLSIGN PARIS IS A LEGEND IN SPECIAL FORCES.
THEY TEACH *ASS-KISSING* IN DELTA NOW?
"...CANNON FODDER AT WORST."
NO. NO, THEY SURE AS HELL DON'T.
GOOD. SHOW ME WHAT THEY DID TEACH. ALL *FOUR* OF YOU.
"YOU ARE TRAINING TO COMBAT BEINGS THAT ARE SO FAR ABOVE YOU, THEY VIEW YOU AS A CHILD. A PET.
"OR A PIECE OF *MEAT*.

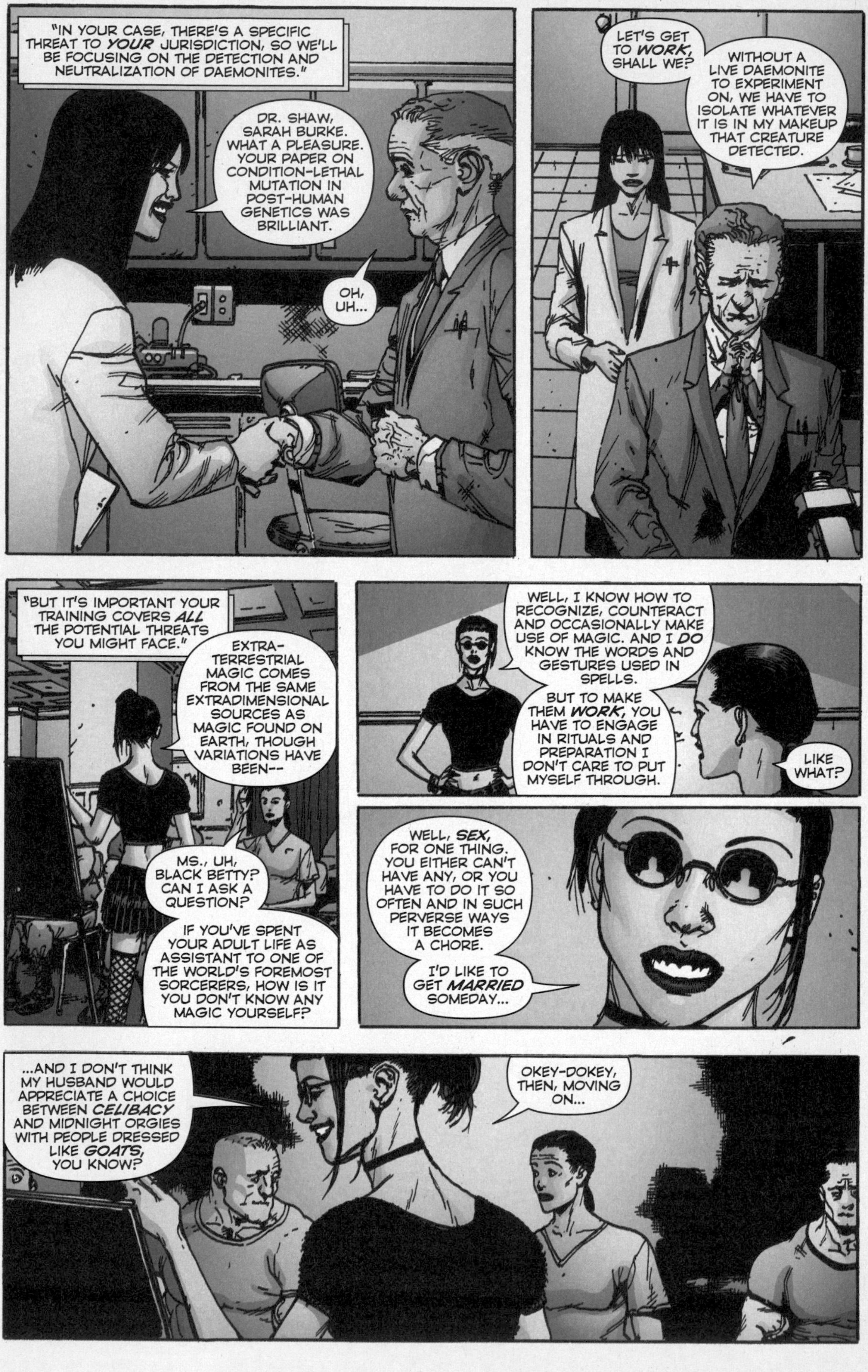
"IN YOUR CASE, THERE'S A SPECIFIC THREAT TO YOUR JURISDICTION, SO WE'LL BE FOCUSING ON THE DETECTION AND NEUTRALIZATION OF DAEMONITES."
DR. SHAW, SARAH BURKE. WHAT A PLEASURE. YOUR PAPER ON CONDITION-LETHAL MUTATION IN POST-HUMAN GENETICS WAS BRILLIANT.
OH, UH...
LET'S GET TO WORK, SHALL WE?
WITHOUT A LIVE DAEMONITE TO EXPERIMENT ON, WE HAVE TO ISOLATE WHATEVER IT IS IN MY MAKEUP THAT CREATURE DETECTED.
"BUT IT'S IMPORTANT YOUR TRAINING COVERS ALL THE POTENTIAL THREATS YOU MIGHT FACE."
EXTRA-TERRESTRIAL MAGIC COMES FROM THE SAME EXTRADIMENSIONAL SOURCES AS MAGIC FOUND ON EARTH, THOUGH VARIATIONS HAVE BEEN--
MS., UH, BLACK BETTY? CAN I ASK A QUESTION?
IF YOU'VE SPENT YOUR ADULT LIFE AS ASSISTANT TO ONE OF THE WORLD'S FOREMOST SORCERERS, HOW IS IT YOU DON'T KNOW ANY MAGIC YOURSELF?
WELL, I KNOW HOW TO RECOGNIZE, COUNTERACT AND OCCASIONALLY MAKE USE OF MAGIC. AND I DO KNOW THE WORDS AND GESTURES USED IN SPELLS.
BUT TO MAKE THEM WORK, YOU HAVE TO ENGAGE IN RITUALS AND PREPARATION I DON'T CARE TO PUT MYSELF THROUGH.
LIKE WHAT?
WELL, SEX, FOR ONE THING. YOU EITHER CAN'T HAVE ANY, OR YOU HAVE TO DO IT SO OFTEN AND IN SUCH PERVERSE WAYS IT BECOMES A CHORE.
I'D LIKE TO GET MARRIED SOMEDAY...
...AND I DON'T THINK MY HUSBAND WOULD APPRECIATE A CHOICE BETWEEN CELIBACY AND MIDNIGHT ORGIES WITH PEOPLE DRESSED LIKE GOATS, YOU KNOW?
OKEY-DOKEY, THEN, MOVING ON...

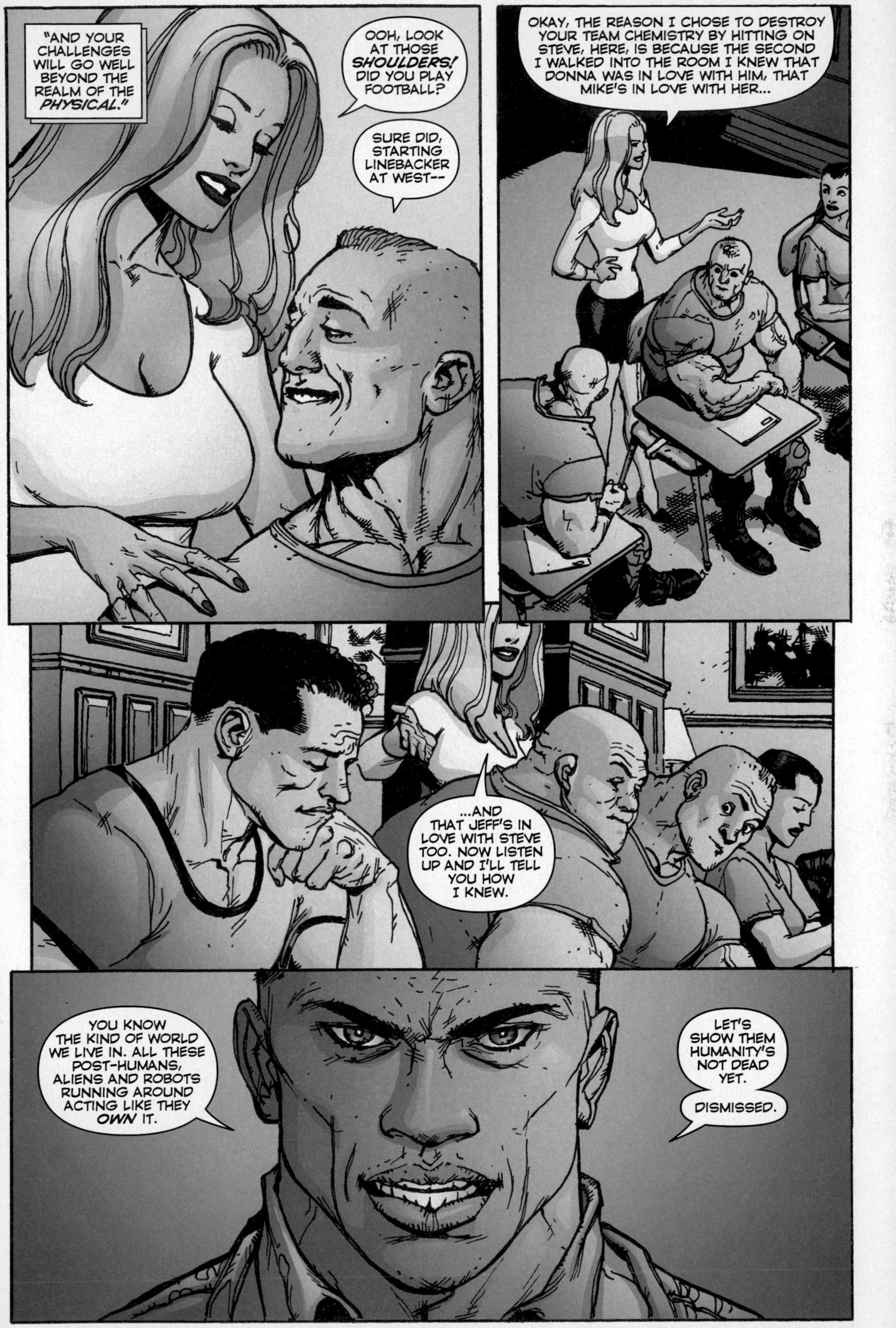
"AND YOUR CHALLENGES WILL GO WELL BEYOND THE REALM OF THE PHYSICAL."
OOH, LOOK AT THOSE SHOULDERS! DID YOU PLAY FOOTBALL?
SURE DID, STARTING LINEBACKER AT WEST--
OKAY, THE REASON I CHOSE TO DESTROY YOUR TEAM CHEMISTRY BY HITTING ON STEVE, HERE, IS BECAUSE THE SECOND I WALKED INTO THE ROOM I KNEW THAT DONNA WAS IN LOVE WITH HIM, THAT MIKE'S IN LOVE WITH HER...
...AND THAT JEFF'S IN LOVE WITH STEVE TOO. NOW LISTEN UP AND I'LL TELL YOU HOW I KNEW.
YOU KNOW THE KIND OF WORLD WE LIVE IN. ALL THESE POST-HUMANS, ALIENS AND ROBOTS RUNNING AROUND ACTING LIKE THEY OWN IT.
LET'S SHOW THEM HUMANITY'S NOT DEAD YET.
DISMISSED.

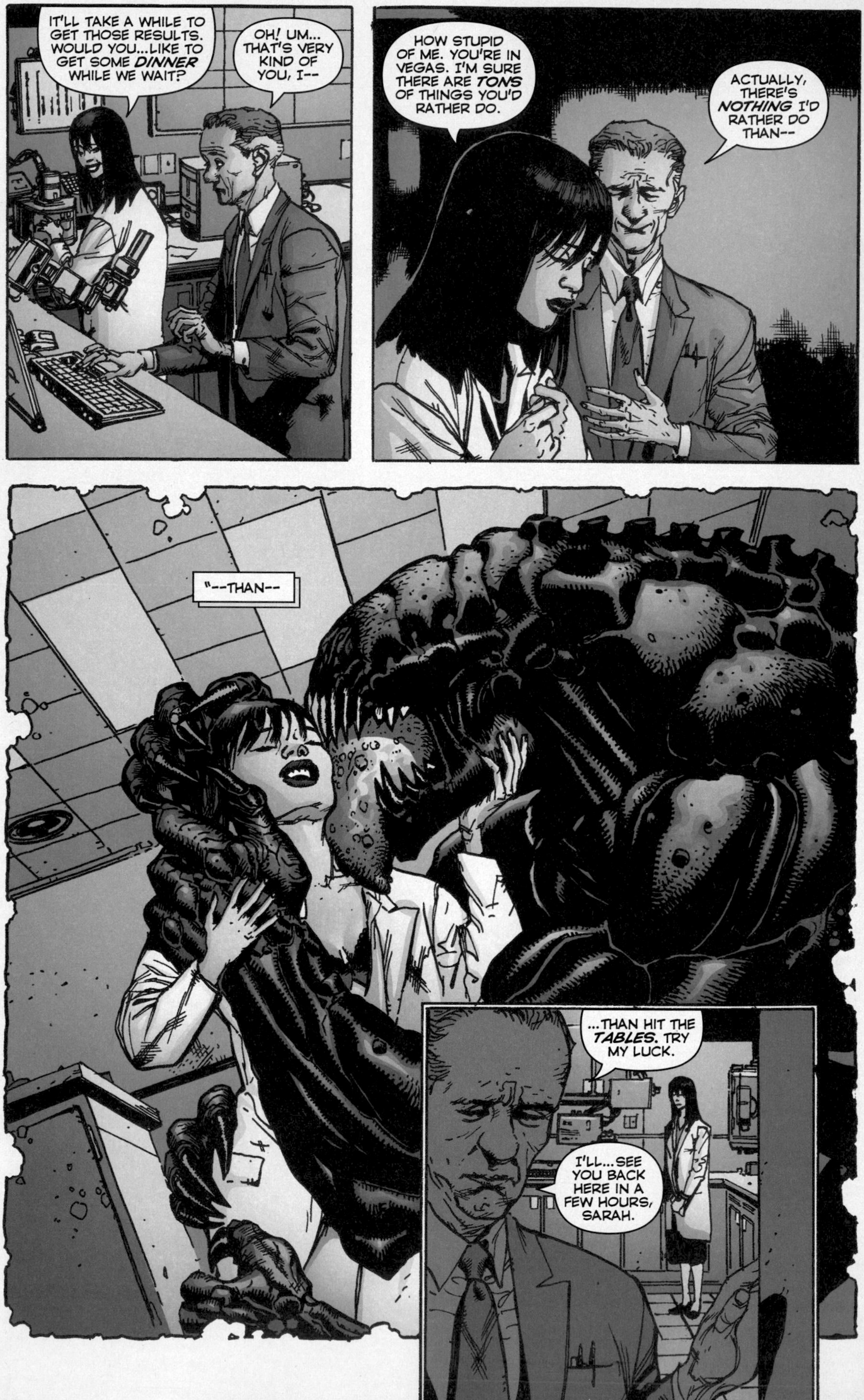
IT'LL TAKE A WHILE TO GET THOSE RESULTS. WOULD YOU...LIKE TO GET SOME DINNER WHILE WE WAIT?
OH! UM... THAT'S VERY KIND OF YOU, I--
HOW STUPID OF ME. YOU'RE IN VEGAS. I'M SURE THERE ARE TONS OF THINGS YOU'D RATHER DO.
ACTUALLY, THERE'S NOTHING I'D RATHER DO THAN--
"--THAN--
...THAN HIT THE TABLES. TRY MY LUCK.
I'LL...SEE YOU BACK HERE IN A FEW HOURS, SARAH.

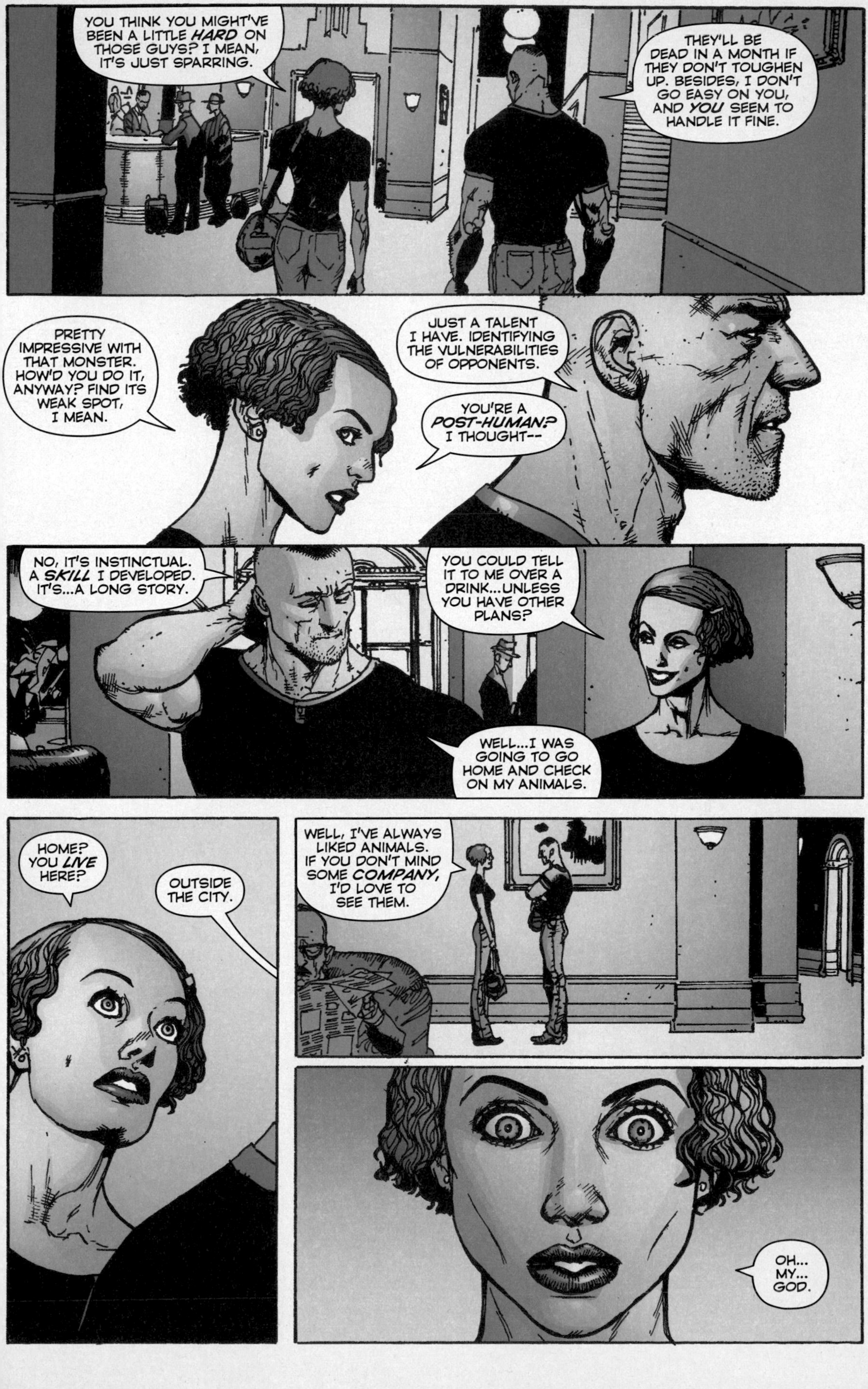
YOU THINK YOU MIGHT'VE BEEN A LITTLE HARD ON THOSE GUYS? I MEAN, IT'S JUST SPARRING.
THEY'LL BE DEAD IN A MONTH IF THEY DON'T TOUGHEN UP. BESIDES, I DON'T GO EASY ON YOU, AND YOU SEEM TO HANDLE IT FINE.
PRETTY IMPRESSIVE WITH THAT MONSTER. HOW'D YOU DO IT, ANYWAY? FIND ITS WEAK SPOT, I MEAN.
JUST A TALENT I HAVE. IDENTIFYING THE VULNERABILITIES OF OPPONENTS.
YOU'RE A POST-HUMAN? I THOUGHT--
NO, IT'S INSTINCTUAL. A SKILL I DEVELOPED. IT'S...A LONG STORY.
YOU COULD TELL IT TO ME OVER A DRINK...UNLESS YOU HAVE OTHER PLANS?
WELL...I WAS GOING TO GO HOME AND CHECK ON MY ANIMALS.
HOME? YOU LIVE HERE?
OUTSIDE THE CITY.
WELL, I'VE ALWAYS LIKED ANIMALS. IF YOU DON'T MIND SOME COMPANY, I'D LOVE TO SEE THEM.
OH... MY... GOD.

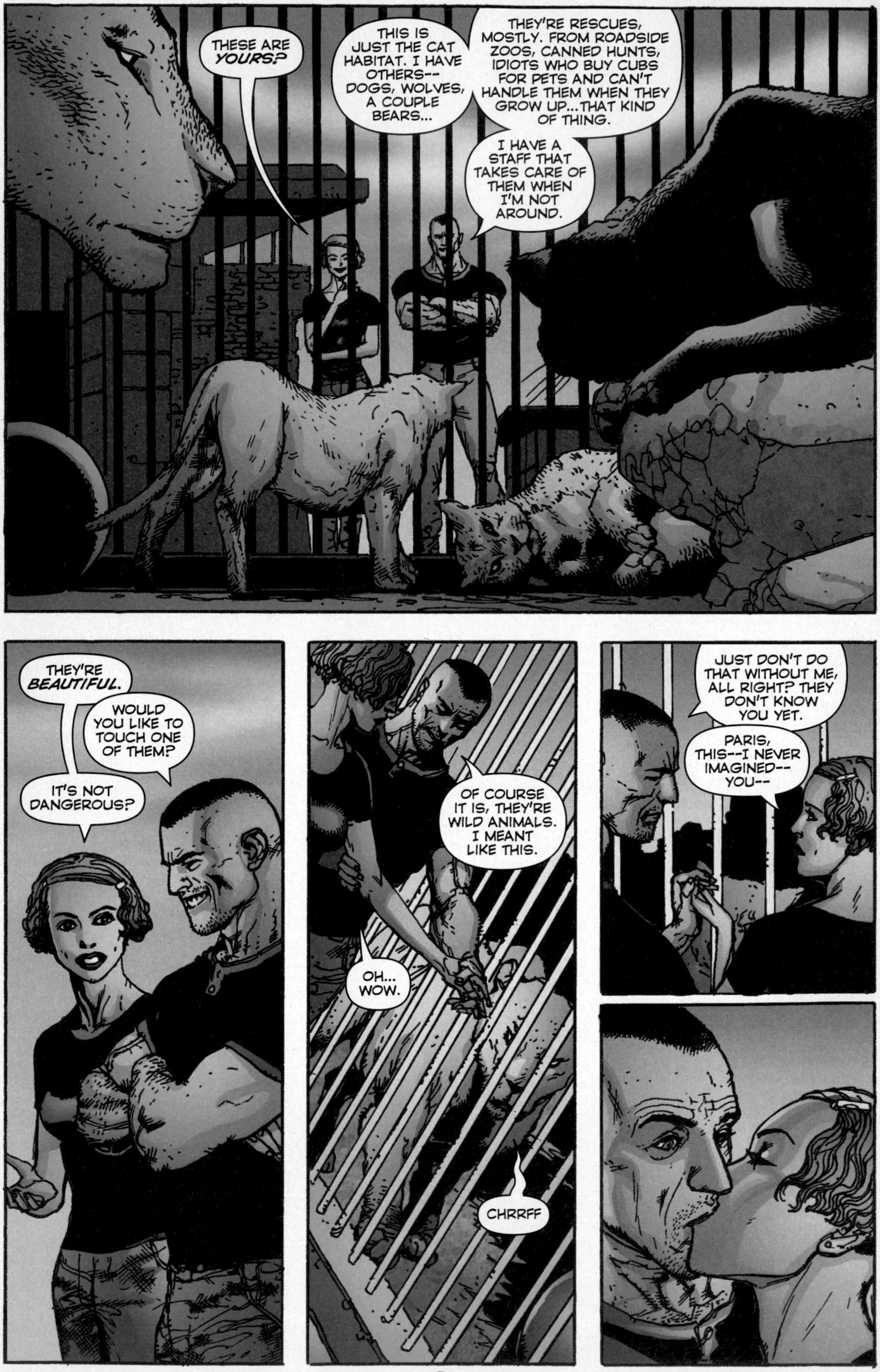
THESE ARE *YOURS?*
THIS IS JUST THE CAT HABITAT. I HAVE OTHERS-- DOGS, WOLVES, A COUPLE BEARS...
THEY'RE RESCUES, MOSTLY. FROM ROADSIDE ZOOS, CANNED HUNTS, IDIOTS WHO BUY CUBS FOR PETS AND CAN'T HANDLE THEM WHEN THEY GROW UP...THAT KIND OF THING.
I HAVE A STAFF THAT TAKES CARE OF THEM WHEN I'M NOT AROUND.
THEY'RE ***BEAUTIFUL***.
WOULD YOU LIKE TO TOUCH ONE OF THEM?
IT'S NOT DANGEROUS?
OF COURSE IT IS, THEY'RE WILD ANIMALS. I MEANT LIKE THIS.
OH... WOW.
CHRRFF
JUST DON'T DO THAT WITHOUT ME, ALL RIGHT? THEY DON'T KNOW YOU YET.
PARIS, THIS--I NEVER IMAGINED-- YOU--

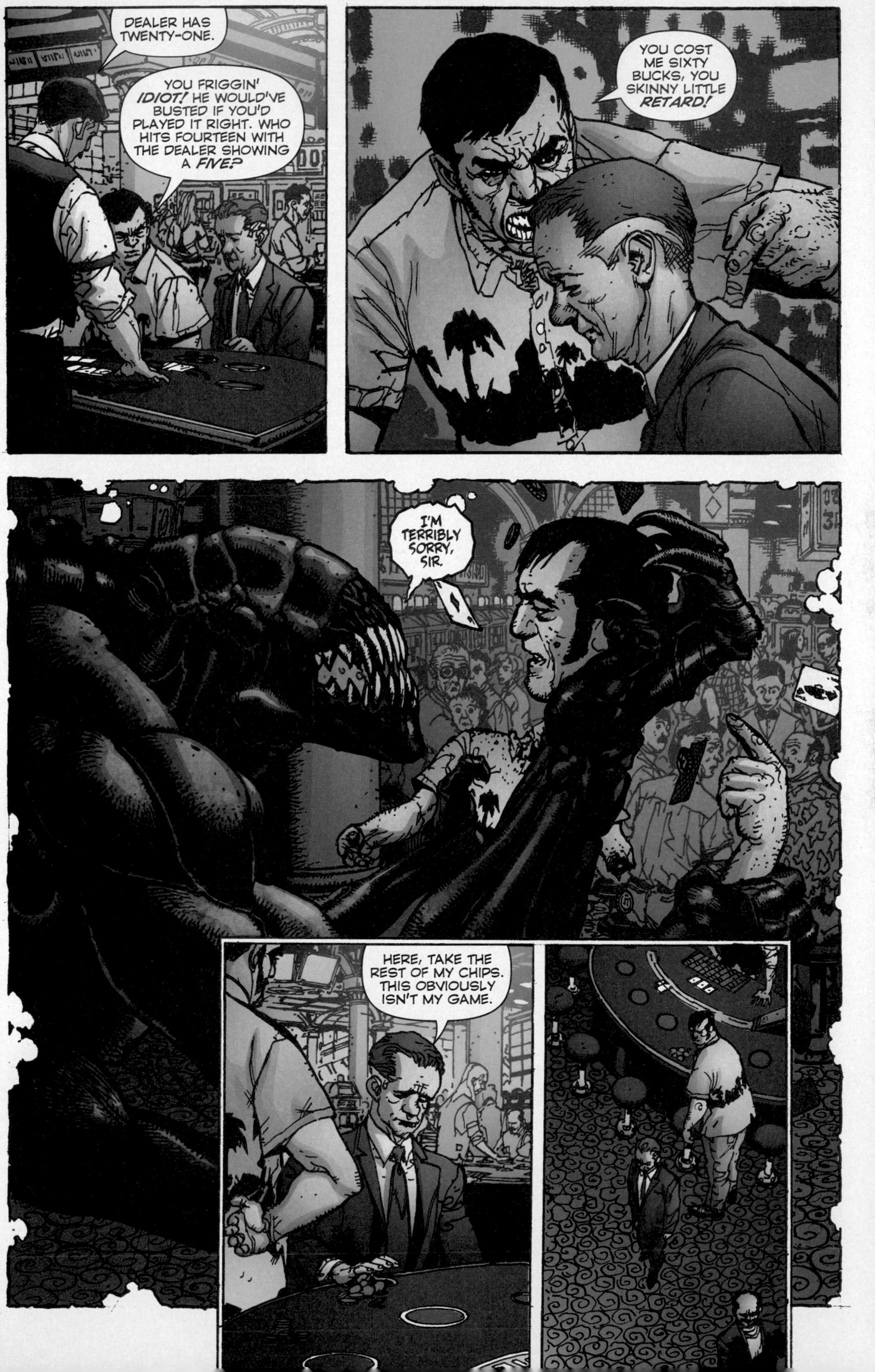
DEALER HAS TWENTY-ONE.
YOU FRIGGIN' *IDIOT!* HE WOULD'VE BUSTED IF YOU'D PLAYED IT RIGHT. WHO HITS FOURTEEN WITH THE DEALER SHOWING A *FIVE?*
YOU COST ME SIXTY BUCKS, YOU SKINNY LITTLE *RETARD!*
I'M TERRIBLY SORRY, SIR.
HERE, TAKE THE REST OF MY CHIPS. THIS OBVIOUSLY ISN'T MY GAME.

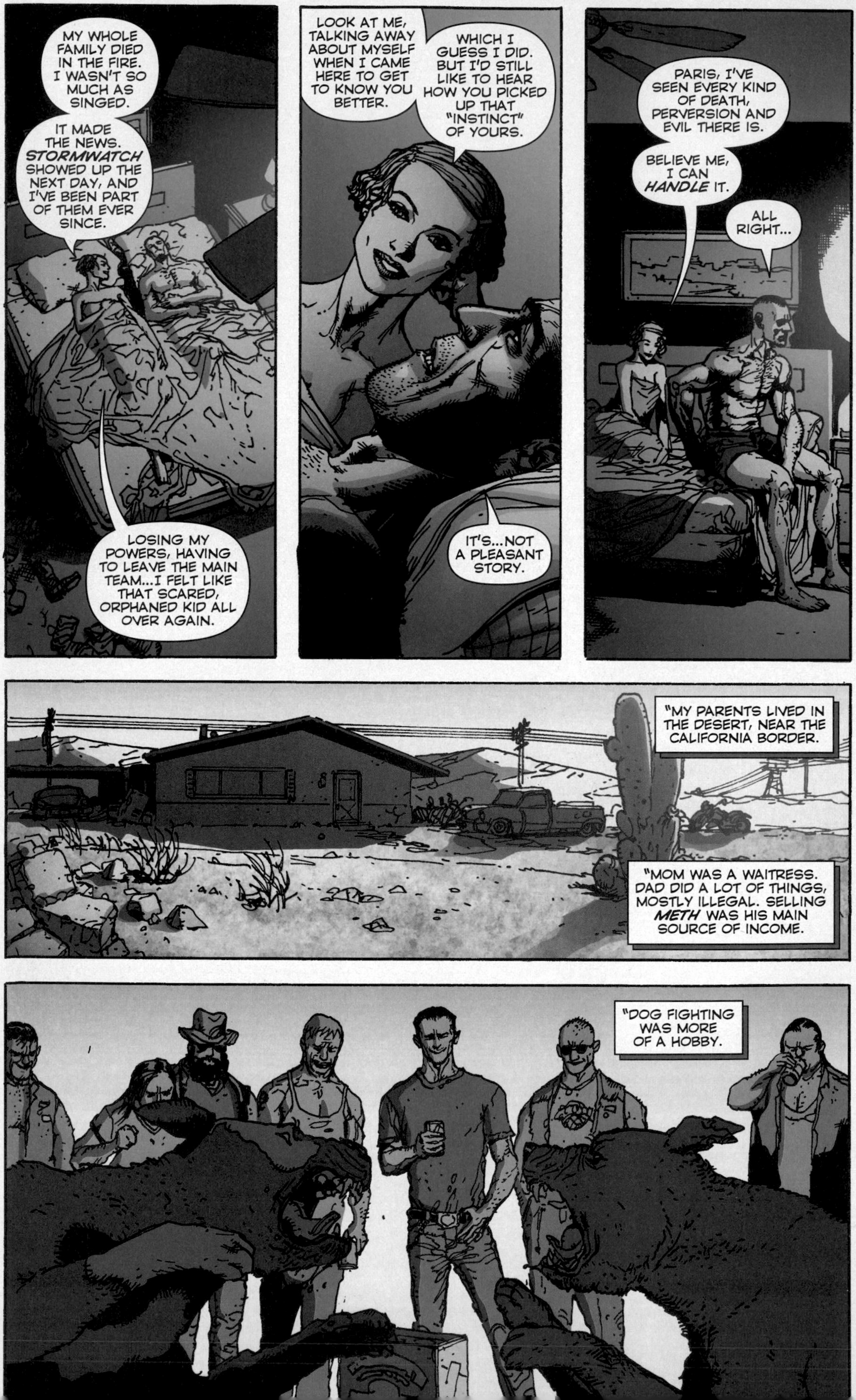
MY WHOLE FAMILY DIED IN THE FIRE. I WASN'T SO MUCH AS SINGED.
IT MADE THE NEWS. STORMWATCH SHOWED UP THE NEXT DAY, AND I'VE BEEN PART OF THEM EVER SINCE.
LOSING MY POWERS, HAVING TO LEAVE THE MAIN TEAM...I FELT LIKE THAT SCARED, ORPHANED KID ALL OVER AGAIN.
LOOK AT ME, TALKING AWAY ABOUT MYSELF WHEN I CAME HERE TO GET TO KNOW YOU BETTER.
WHICH I GUESS I DID. BUT I'D STILL LIKE TO HEAR HOW YOU PICKED UP THAT "INSTINCT" OF YOURS.
IT'S...NOT A PLEASANT STORY.
PARIS, I'VE SEEN EVERY KIND OF DEATH, PERVERSION AND EVIL THERE IS.
BELIEVE ME, I CAN HANDLE IT.
ALL RIGHT...
"MY PARENTS LIVED IN THE DESERT, NEAR THE CALIFORNIA BORDER.
"MOM WAS A WAITRESS. DAD DID A LOT OF THINGS, MOSTLY ILLEGAL. SELLING METH WAS HIS MAIN SOURCE OF INCOME.
"DOG FIGHTING WAS MORE OF A HOBBY.

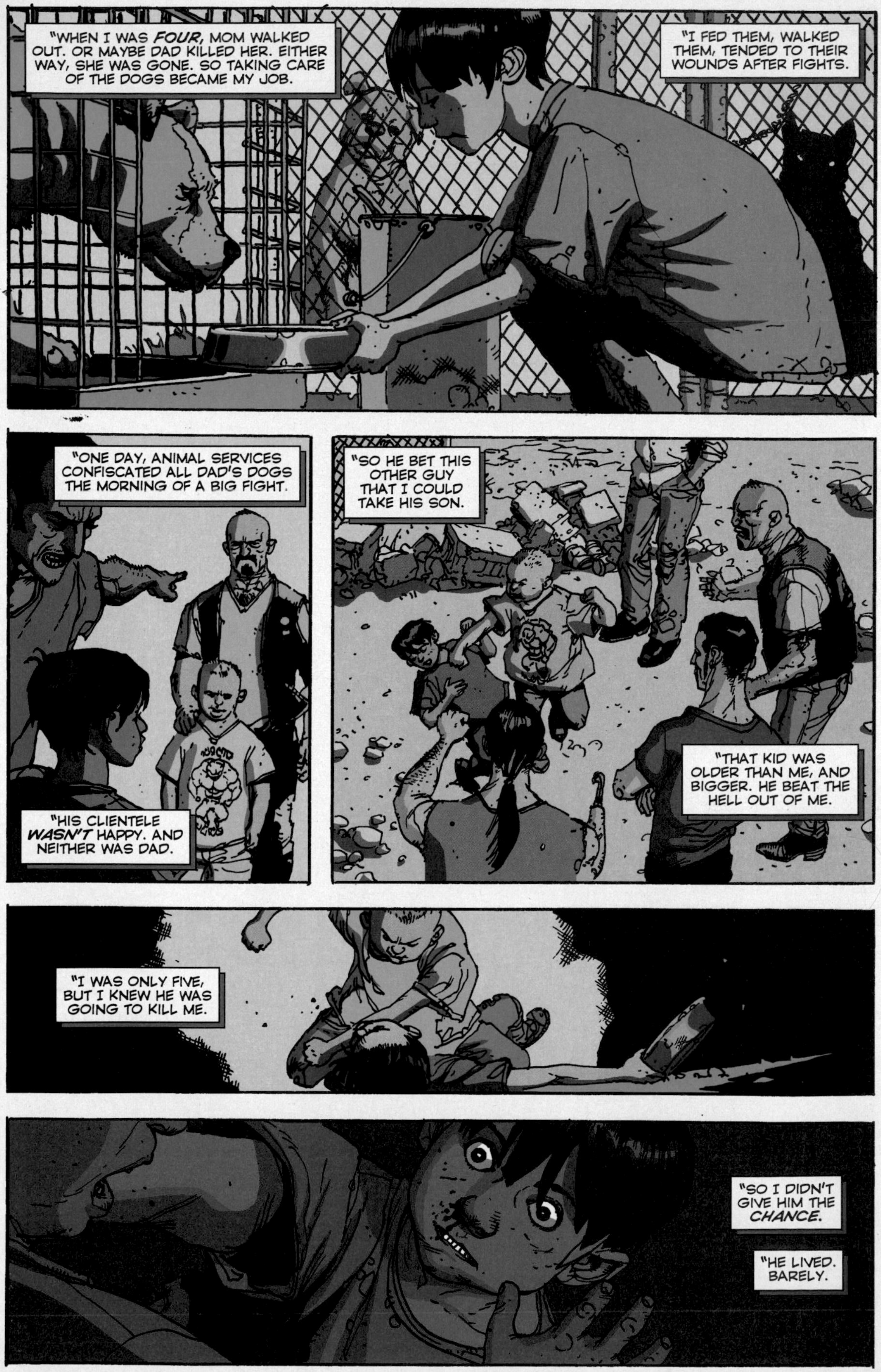
"WHEN I WAS *FOUR,* MOM WALKED OUT. OR MAYBE DAD KILLED HER. EITHER WAY, SHE WAS GONE. SO TAKING CARE OF THE DOGS BECAME MY JOB.
"I FED THEM, WALKED THEM, TENDED TO THEIR WOUNDS AFTER FIGHTS.
"ONE DAY, ANIMAL SERVICES CONFISCATED ALL DAD'S DOGS THE MORNING OF A BIG FIGHT.
"HIS CLIENTELE *WASN'T* HAPPY. AND NEITHER WAS DAD.
"SO HE BET THIS OTHER GUY THAT I COULD TAKE HIS SON.
"THAT KID WAS OLDER THAN ME, AND BIGGER. HE BEAT THE HELL OUT OF ME.
"I WAS ONLY FIVE, BUT I KNEW HE WAS GOING TO KILL ME.
"SO I DIDN'T GIVE HIM THE *CHANCE.*
"HE LIVED. BARELY.

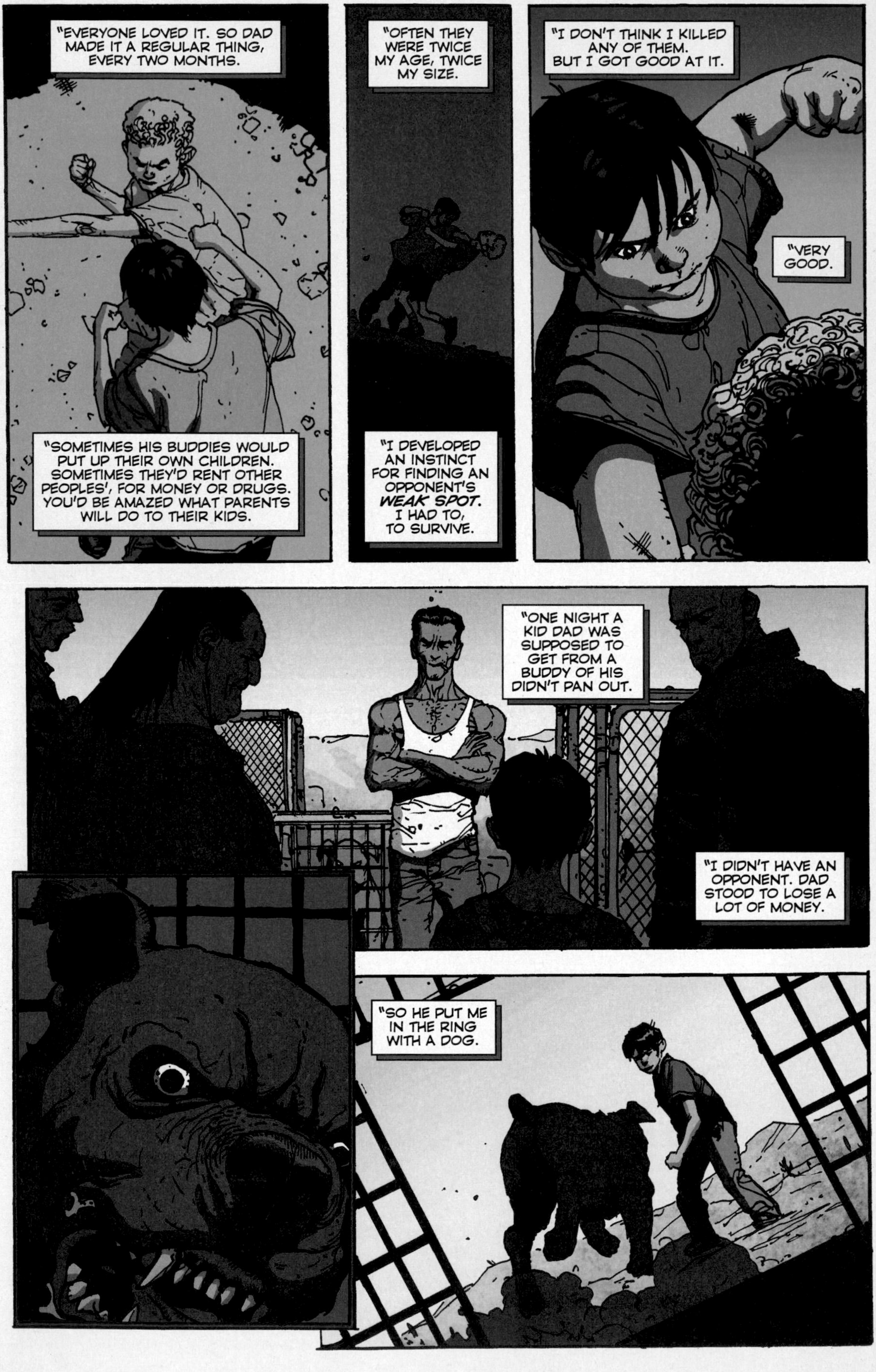
"EVERYONE LOVED IT. SO DAD MADE IT A REGULAR THING, EVERY TWO MONTHS.
"SOMETIMES HIS BUDDIES WOULD PUT UP THEIR OWN CHILDREN. SOMETIMES THEY'D RENT OTHER PEOPLES', FOR MONEY OR DRUGS. YOU'D BE AMAZED WHAT PARENTS WILL DO TO THEIR KIDS.
"OFTEN THEY WERE TWICE MY AGE, TWICE MY SIZE.
"I DEVELOPED AN INSTINCT FOR FINDING AN OPPONENT'S *WEAK SPOT*. I HAD TO, TO SURVIVE.
"I DON'T THINK I KILLED ANY OF THEM. BUT I GOT GOOD AT IT.
"VERY GOOD.
"ONE NIGHT A KID DAD WAS SUPPOSED TO GET FROM A BUDDY OF HIS DIDN'T PAN OUT.
"I DIDN'T HAVE AN OPPONENT. DAD STOOD TO LOSE A LOT OF MONEY.
"SO HE PUT ME IN THE RING WITH A DOG.

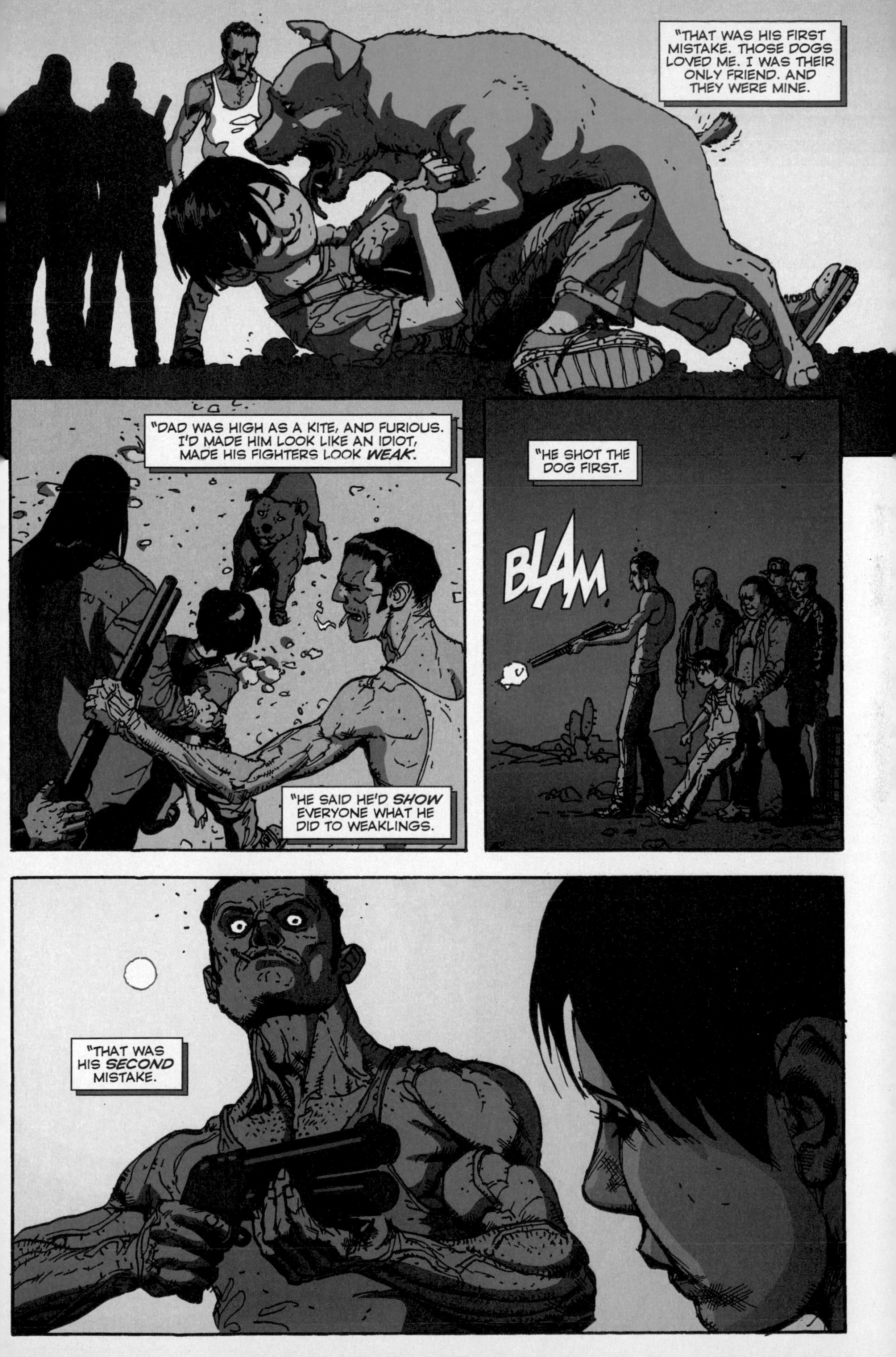
"THAT WAS HIS FIRST MISTAKE. THOSE DOGS LOVED ME. I WAS THEIR ONLY FRIEND. AND THEY WERE MINE.
"DAD WAS HIGH AS A KITE, AND FURIOUS. I'D MADE HIM LOOK LIKE AN IDIOT, MADE HIS FIGHTERS LOOK *WEAK*.
"HE SAID HE'D *SHOW* EVERYONE WHAT HE DID TO WEAKLINGS.
"HE SHOT THE DOG FIRST.
BLAM
"THAT WAS HIS *SECOND* MISTAKE.

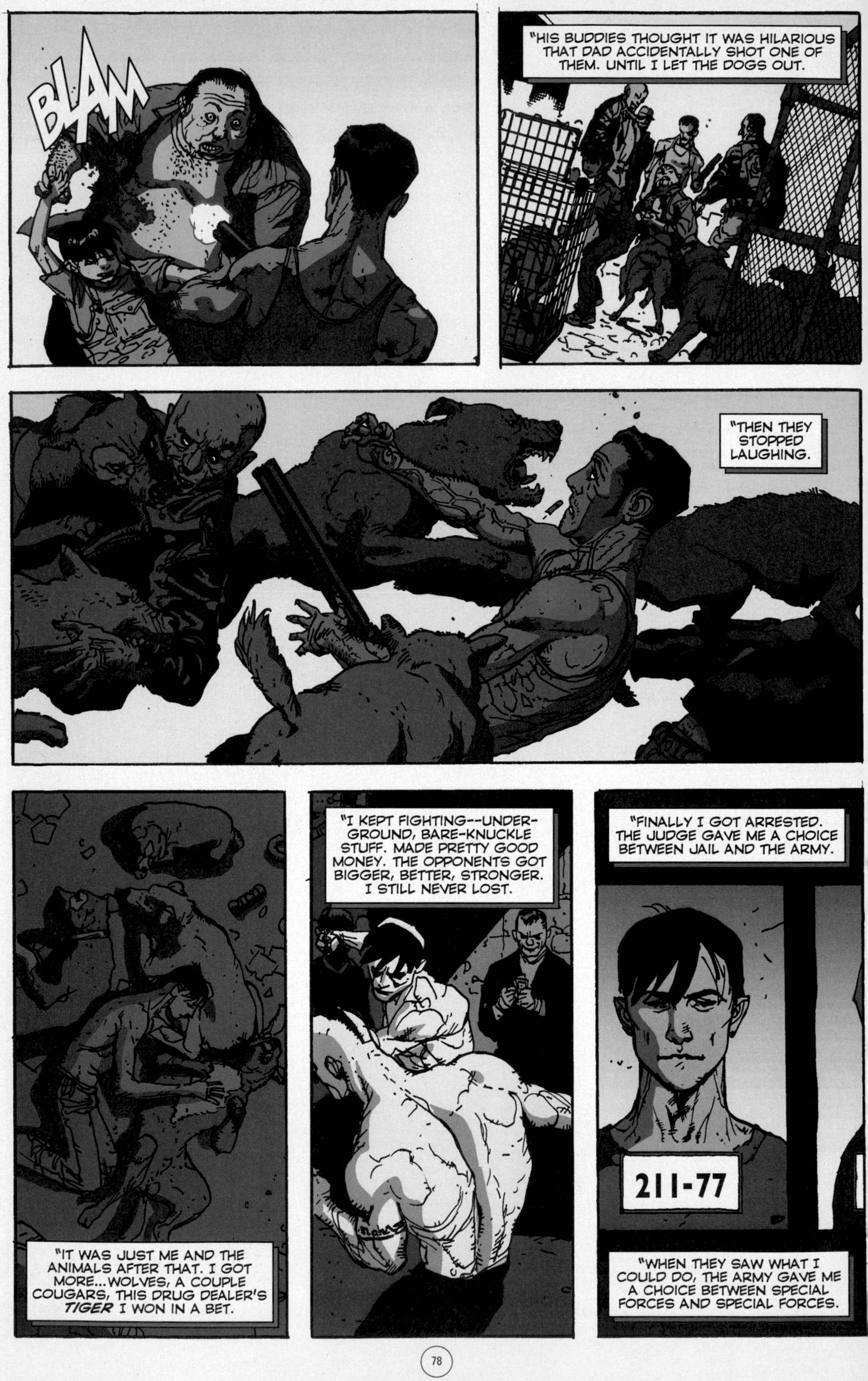
BLAM
"HIS BUDDIES THOUGHT IT WAS HILARIOUS THAT DAD ACCIDENTALLY SHOT ONE OF THEM. UNTIL I LET THE DOGS OUT.
"THEN THEY STOPPED LAUGHING.
"IT WAS JUST ME AND THE ANIMALS AFTER THAT. I GOT MORE...WOLVES, A COUPLE COUGARS, THIS DRUG DEALER'S *TIGER* I WON IN A BET.
"I KEPT FIGHTING--UNDER-GROUND, BARE-KNUCKLE STUFF. MADE PRETTY GOOD MONEY. THE OPPONENTS GOT BIGGER, BETTER, STRONGER. I STILL NEVER LOST.
"FINALLY I GOT ARRESTED. THE JUDGE GAVE ME A CHOICE BETWEEN JAIL AND THE ARMY.
211-77
"WHEN THEY SAW WHAT I COULD DO, THE ARMY GAVE ME A CHOICE BETWEEN SPECIAL FORCES AND SPECIAL FORCES.

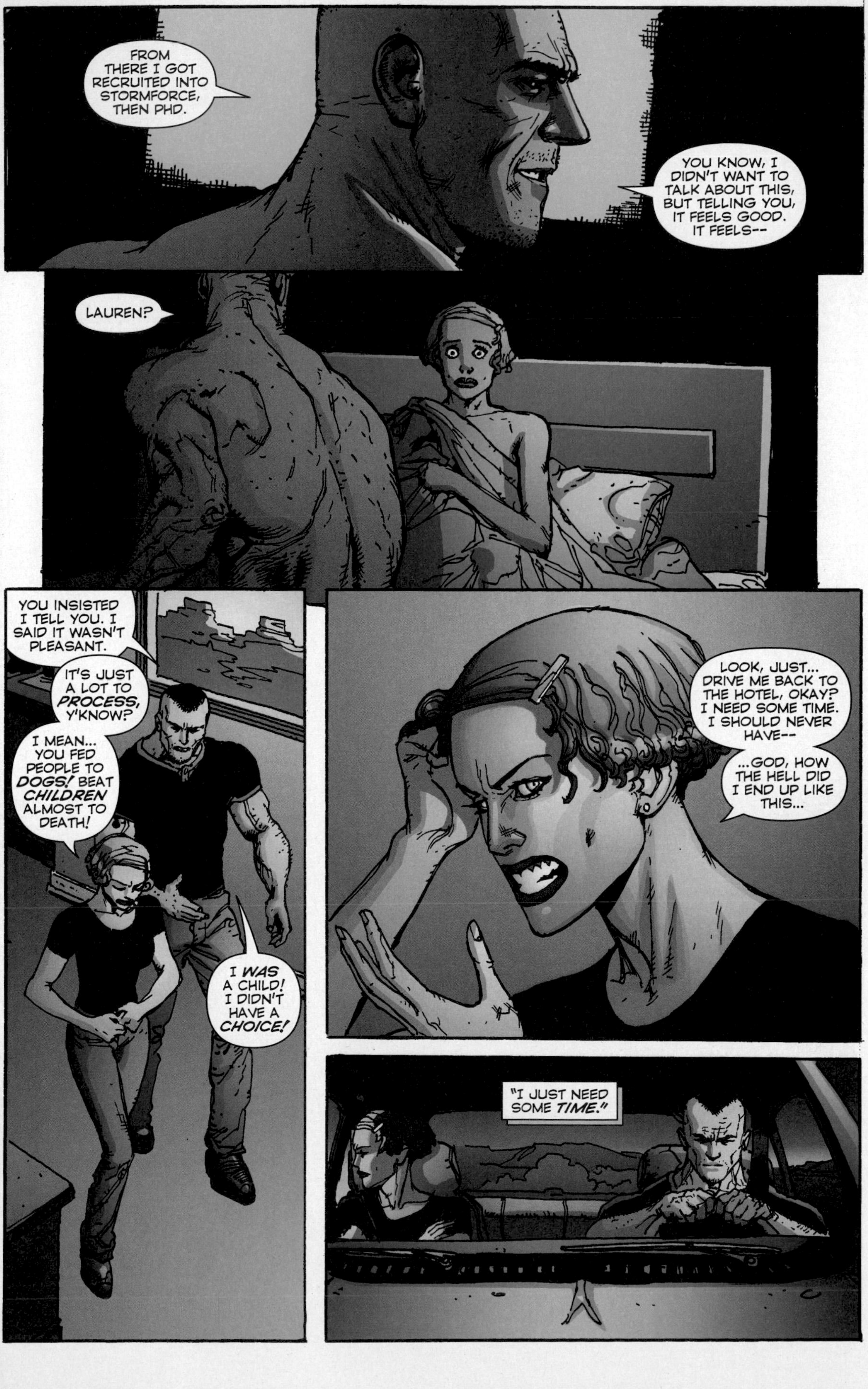
FROM THERE I GOT RECRUITED INTO STORMFORCE, THEN PHD.
YOU KNOW, I DIDN'T WANT TO TALK ABOUT THIS, BUT TELLING YOU, IT FEELS GOOD. IT FEELS--
LAUREN?
YOU INSISTED I TELL YOU. I SAID IT WASN'T PLEASANT.
IT'S JUST A LOT TO PROCESS, Y'KNOW?
I MEAN... YOU FED PEOPLE TO DOGS! BEAT CHILDREN ALMOST TO DEATH!
I WAS A CHILD! I DIDN'T HAVE A CHOICE!
LOOK, JUST... DRIVE ME BACK TO THE HOTEL, OKAY? I NEED SOME TIME. I SHOULD NEVER HAVE--
...GOD, HOW THE HELL DID I END UP LIKE THIS...
"I JUST NEED SOME TIME."

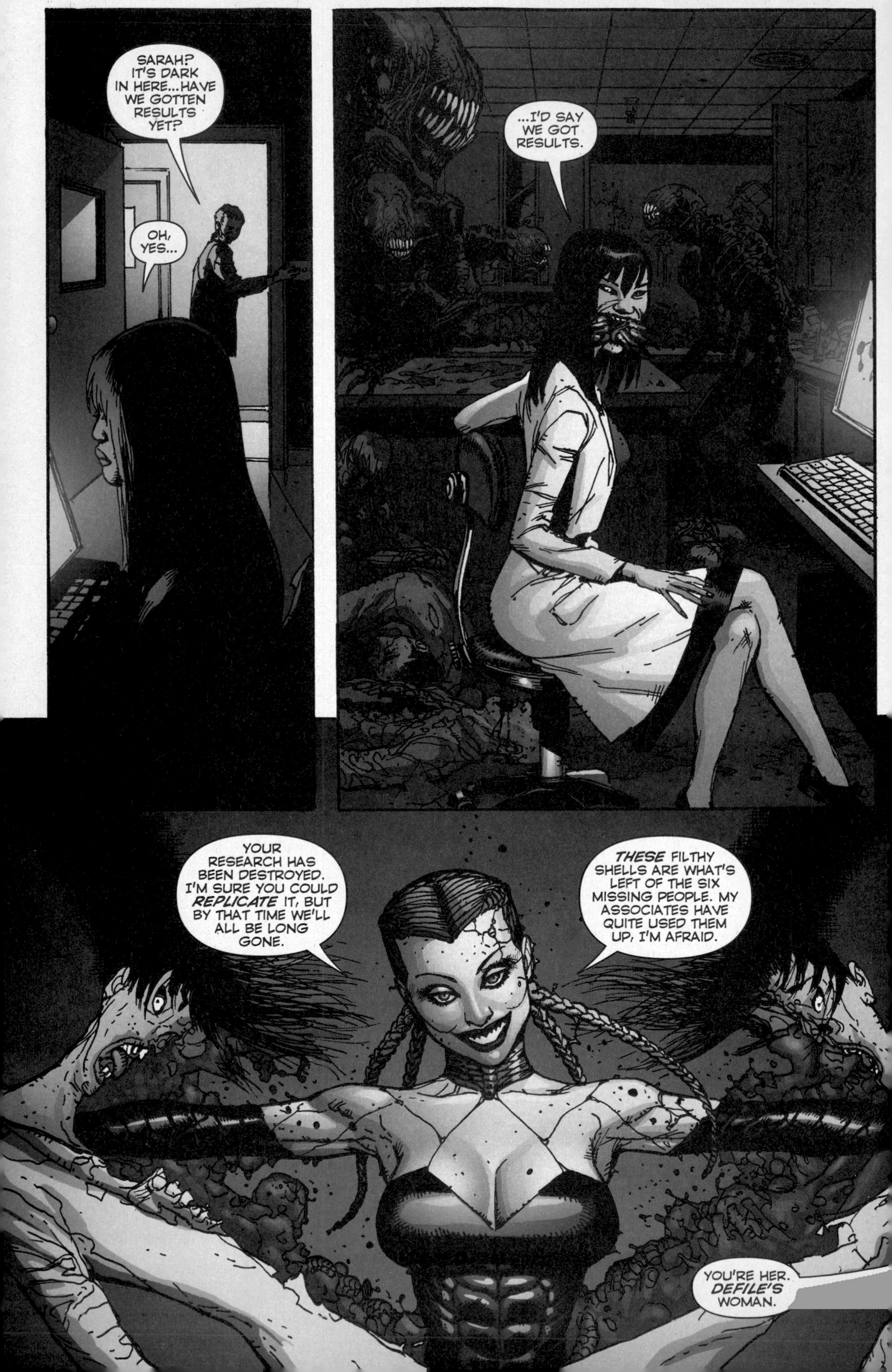
SARAH? IT'S DARK IN HERE...HAVE WE GOTTEN RESULTS YET?
OH, YES...
...I'D SAY WE GOT RESULTS.
YOUR RESEARCH HAS BEEN DESTROYED. I'M SURE YOU COULD REPLICATE IT, BUT BY THAT TIME WE'LL ALL BE LONG GONE.
THESE FILTHY SHELLS ARE WHAT'S LEFT OF THE SIX MISSING PEOPLE. MY ASSOCIATES HAVE QUITE USED THEM UP, I'M AFRAID.
YOU'RE HER. DEFILE'S WOMAN.

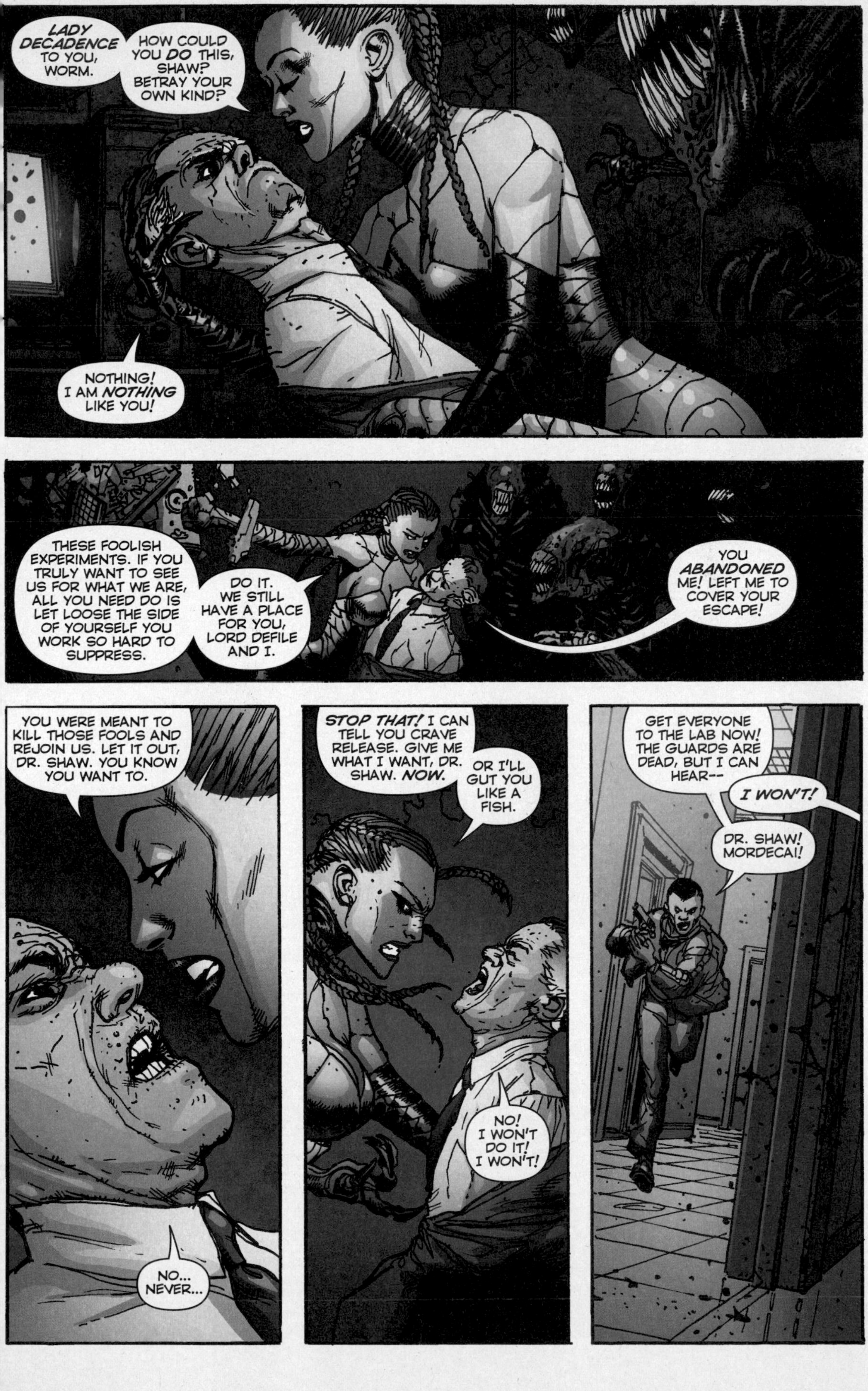
LADY DECADENCE TO YOU, WORM.
HOW COULD YOU DO THIS, SHAW? BETRAY YOUR OWN KIND?
NOTHING! I AM NOTHING LIKE YOU!
THESE FOOLISH EXPERIMENTS. IF YOU TRULY WANT TO SEE US FOR WHAT WE ARE, ALL YOU NEED DO IS LET LOOSE THE SIDE OF YOURSELF YOU WORK SO HARD TO SUPPRESS.
DO IT. WE STILL HAVE A PLACE FOR YOU, LORD DEFILE AND I.
YOU ABANDONED ME! LEFT ME TO COVER YOUR ESCAPE!
YOU WERE MEANT TO KILL THOSE FOOLS AND REJOIN US. LET IT OUT, DR. SHAW. YOU KNOW YOU WANT TO.
NO... NEVER...
STOP THAT! I CAN TELL YOU CRAVE RELEASE. GIVE ME WHAT I WANT, DR. SHAW. NOW.
OR I'LL GUT YOU LIKE A FISH.
NO! I WON'T DO IT! I WON'T!
GET EVERYONE TO THE LAB NOW! THE GUARDS ARE DEAD, BUT I CAN HEAR--
I WON'T!
DR. SHAW! MORDECAI!

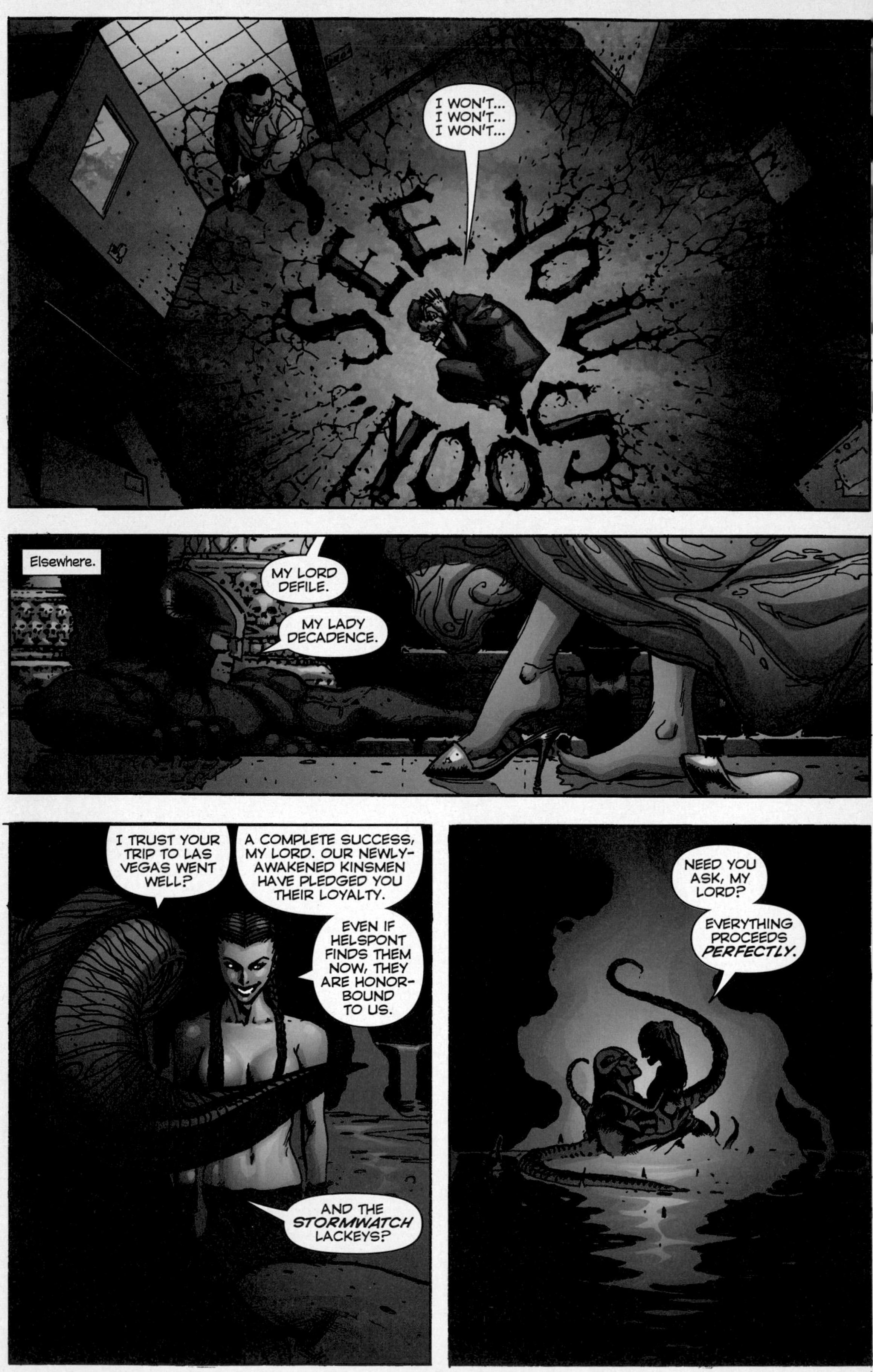
I WON'T...
I WON'T...
I WON'T...
SHE
YOU
SOON
Elsewhere.
MY LORD DEFILE.
MY LADY DECADENCE.
I TRUST YOUR TRIP TO LAS VEGAS WENT WELL?
A COMPLETE SUCCESS, MY LORD. OUR NEWLY-AWAKENED KINSMEN HAVE PLEDGED YOU THEIR LOYALTY.
EVEN IF HELSPONT FINDS THEM NOW, THEY ARE HONOR-BOUND TO US.
AND THE *STORMWATCH* LACKEYS?
NEED YOU ASK, MY LORD?
EVERYTHING PROCEEDS *PERFECTLY*.

Chapter 4: Ladies Night

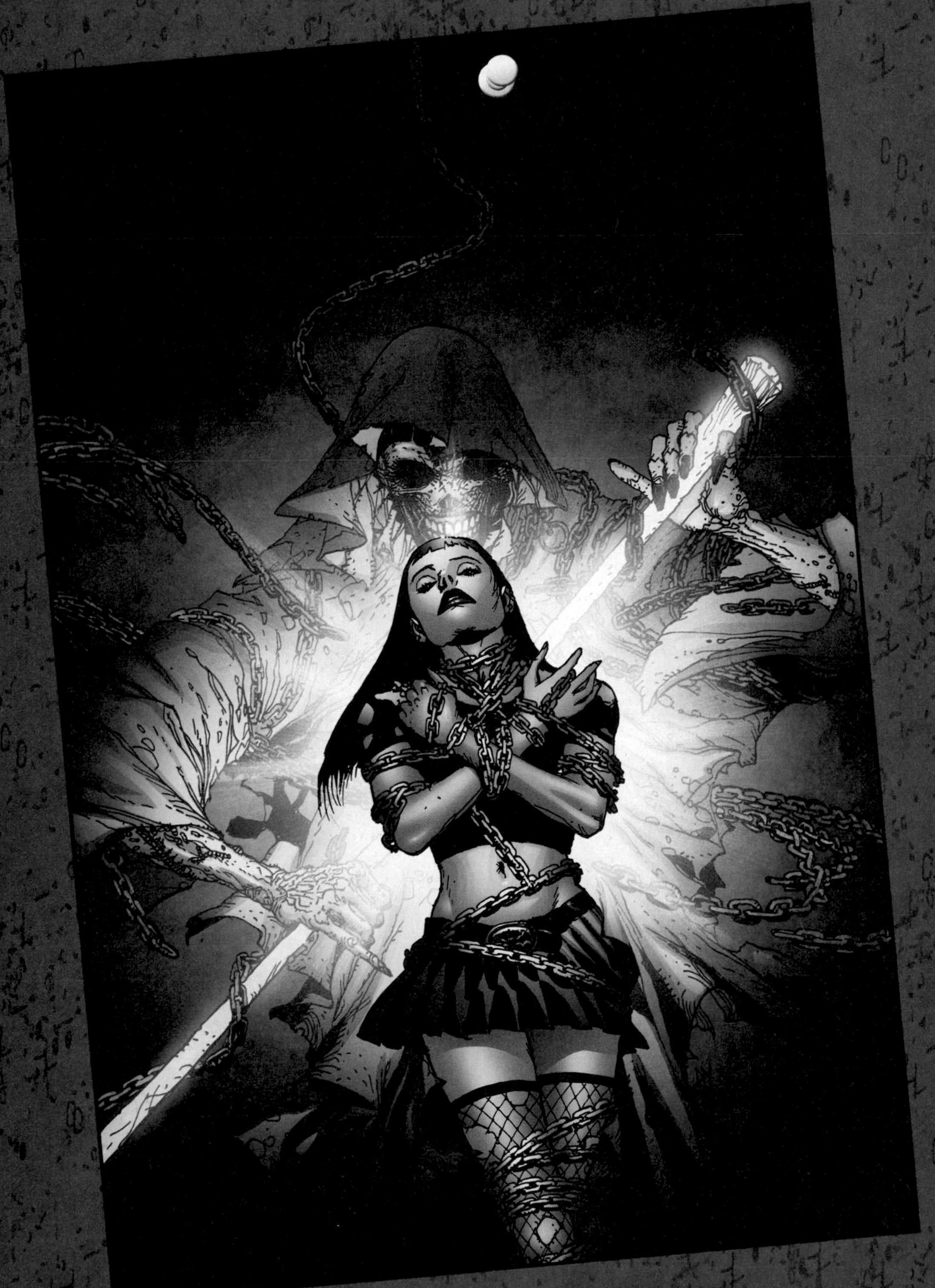

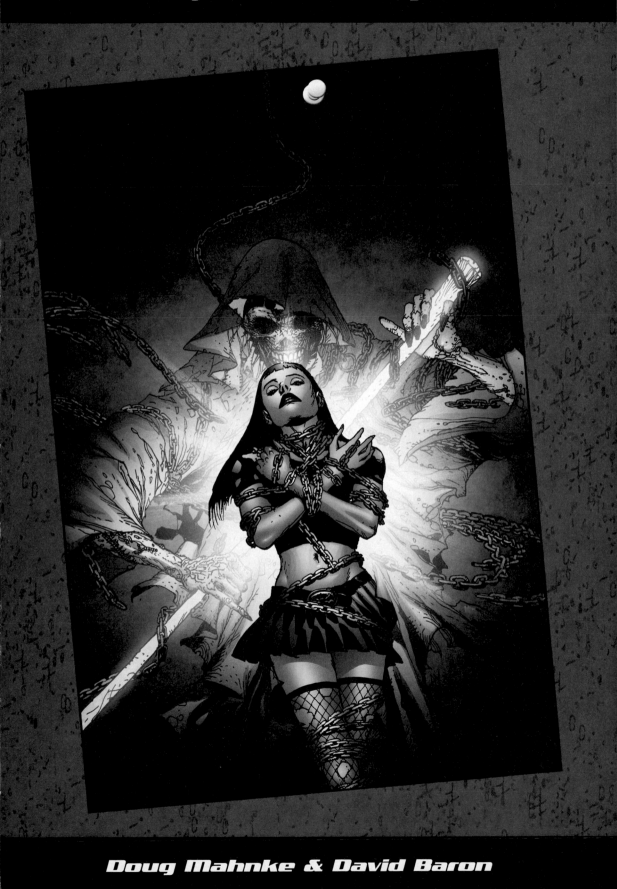

Doug Mahnke & David Baron

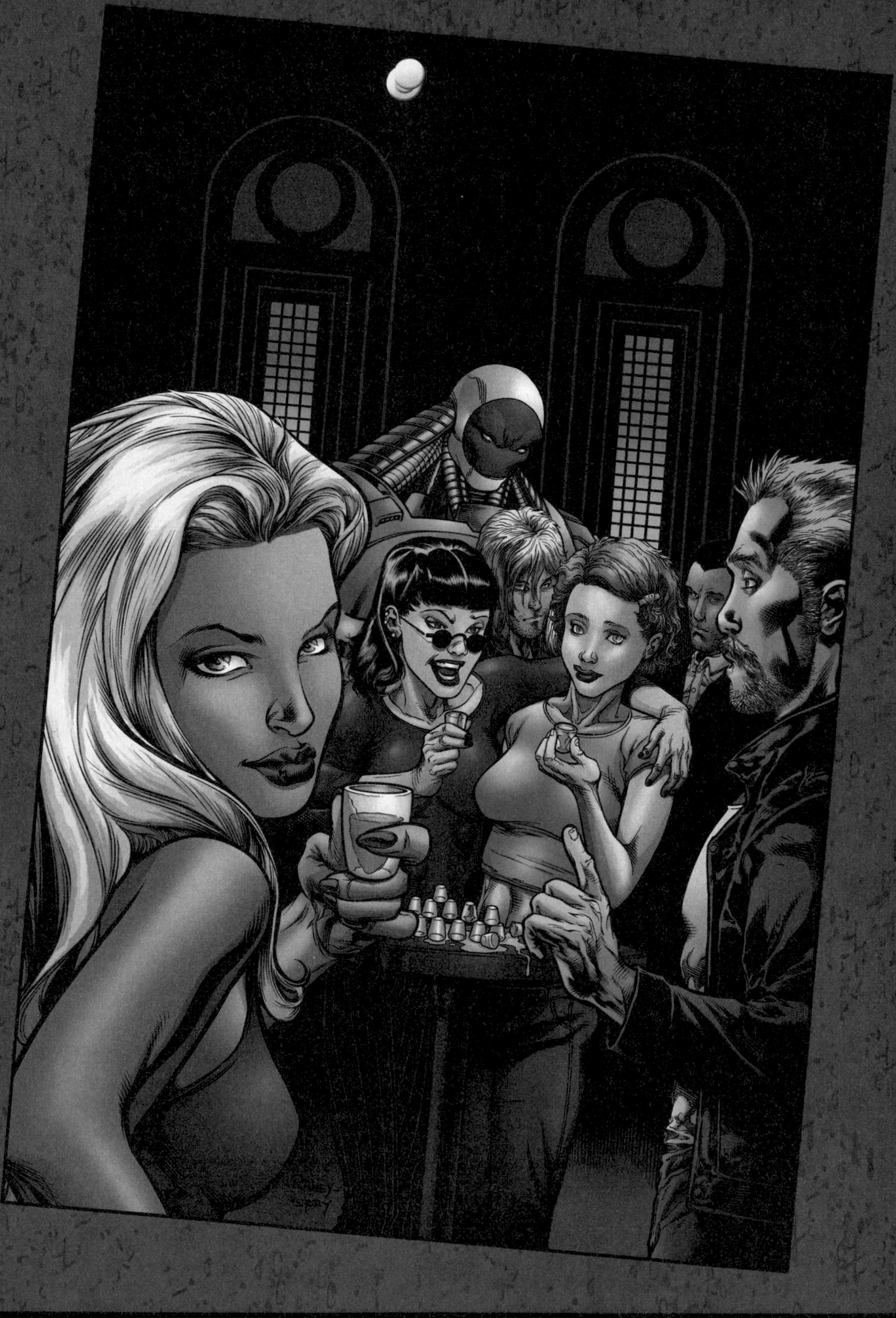

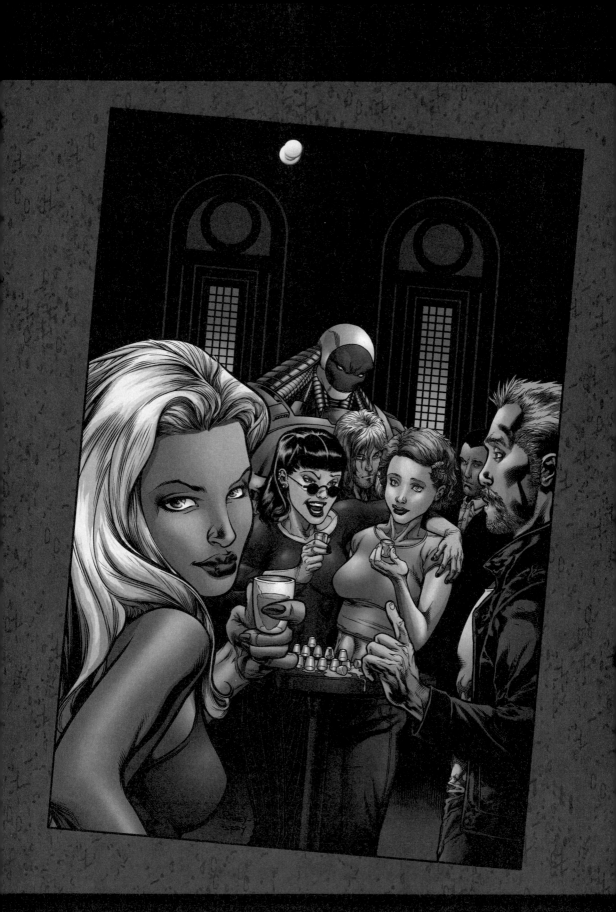

Tom Raney, Karl Story & Gina Going-Raney

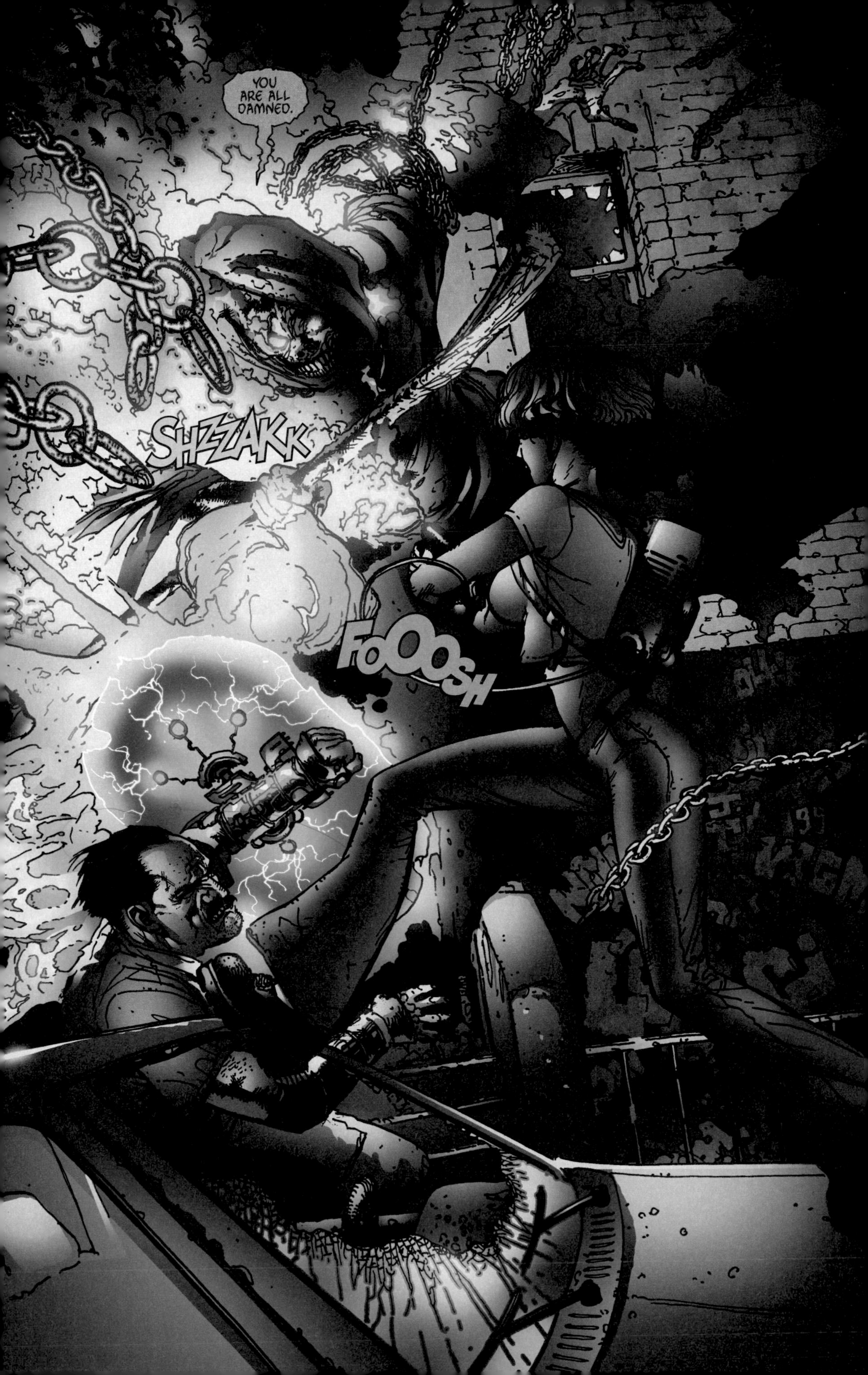
YOU ARE ALL DAMNED.
SHZZAKK
FOOOSH

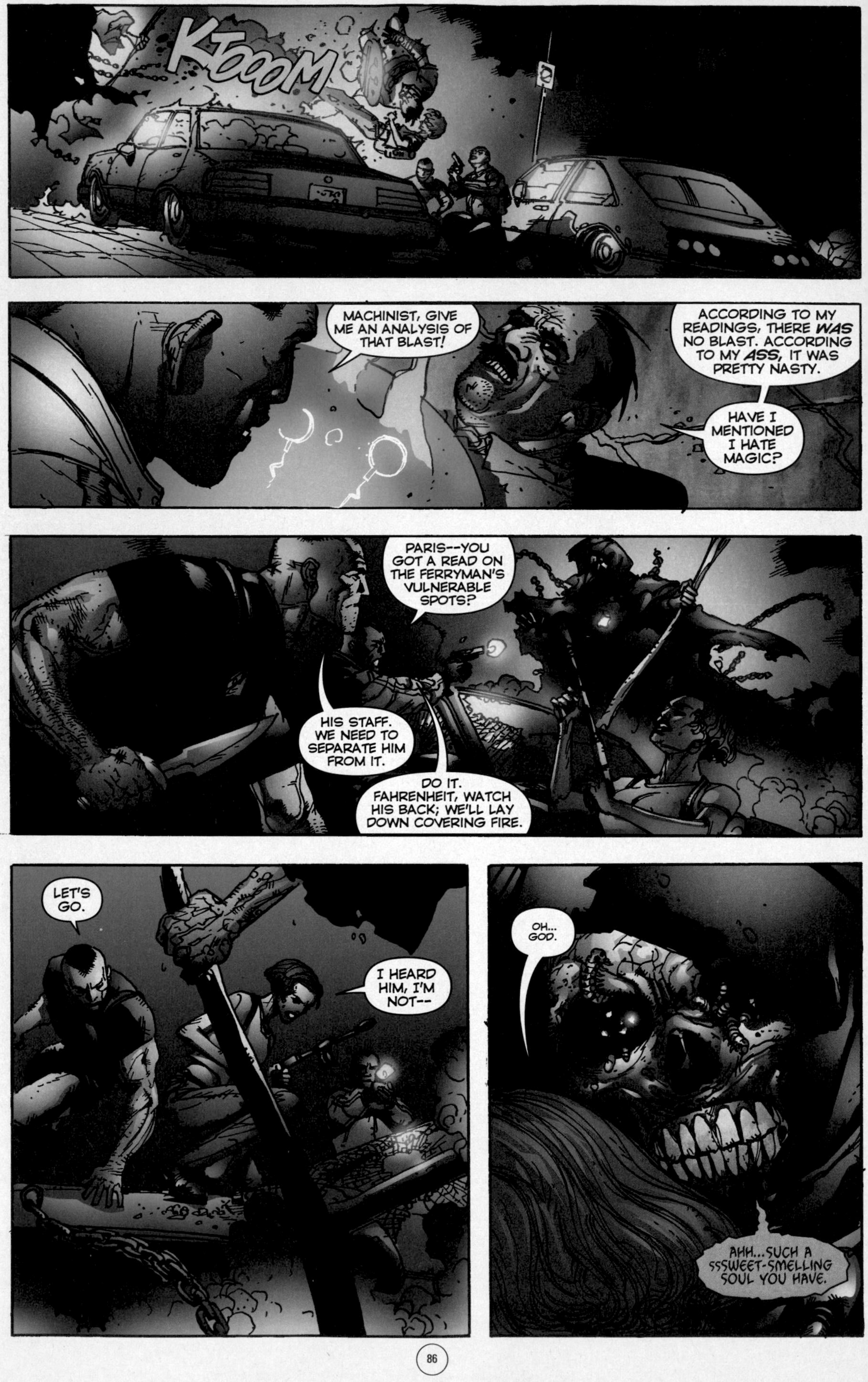
KIOOOM
MACHINIST, GIVE ME AN ANALYSIS OF THAT BLAST!
ACCORDING TO MY READINGS, THERE WAS NO BLAST. ACCORDING TO MY ASS, IT WAS PRETTY NASTY.
HAVE I MENTIONED I HATE MAGIC?
PARIS--YOU GOT A READ ON THE FERRYMAN'S VULNERABLE SPOTS?
HIS STAFF. WE NEED TO SEPARATE HIM FROM IT.
DO IT. FAHRENHEIT, WATCH HIS BACK; WE'LL LAY DOWN COVERING FIRE.
LET'S GO.
I HEARD HIM, I'M NOT--
OH... GOD.
AHH...SUCH A SSSWEET-SMELLING SOUL YOU HAVE.

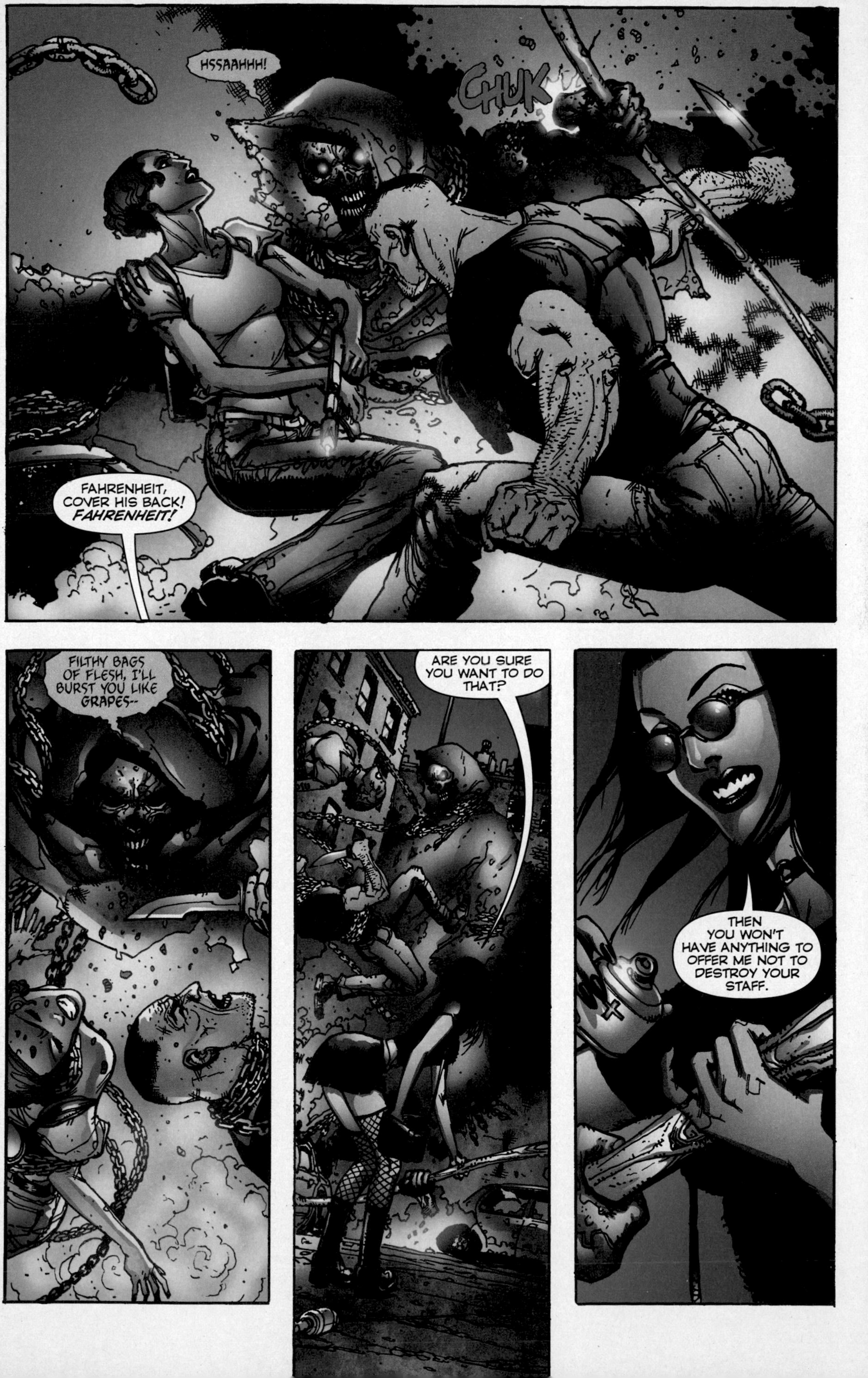
HSSAAHHH!
CHUK
FAHRENHEIT, COVER HIS BACK! FAHRENHEIT!
FILTHY BAGS OF FLESH, I'LL BURST YOU LIKE GRAPES--
ARE YOU SURE YOU WANT TO DO THAT?
THEN YOU WON'T HAVE ANYTHING TO OFFER ME NOT TO DESTROY YOUR STAFF.

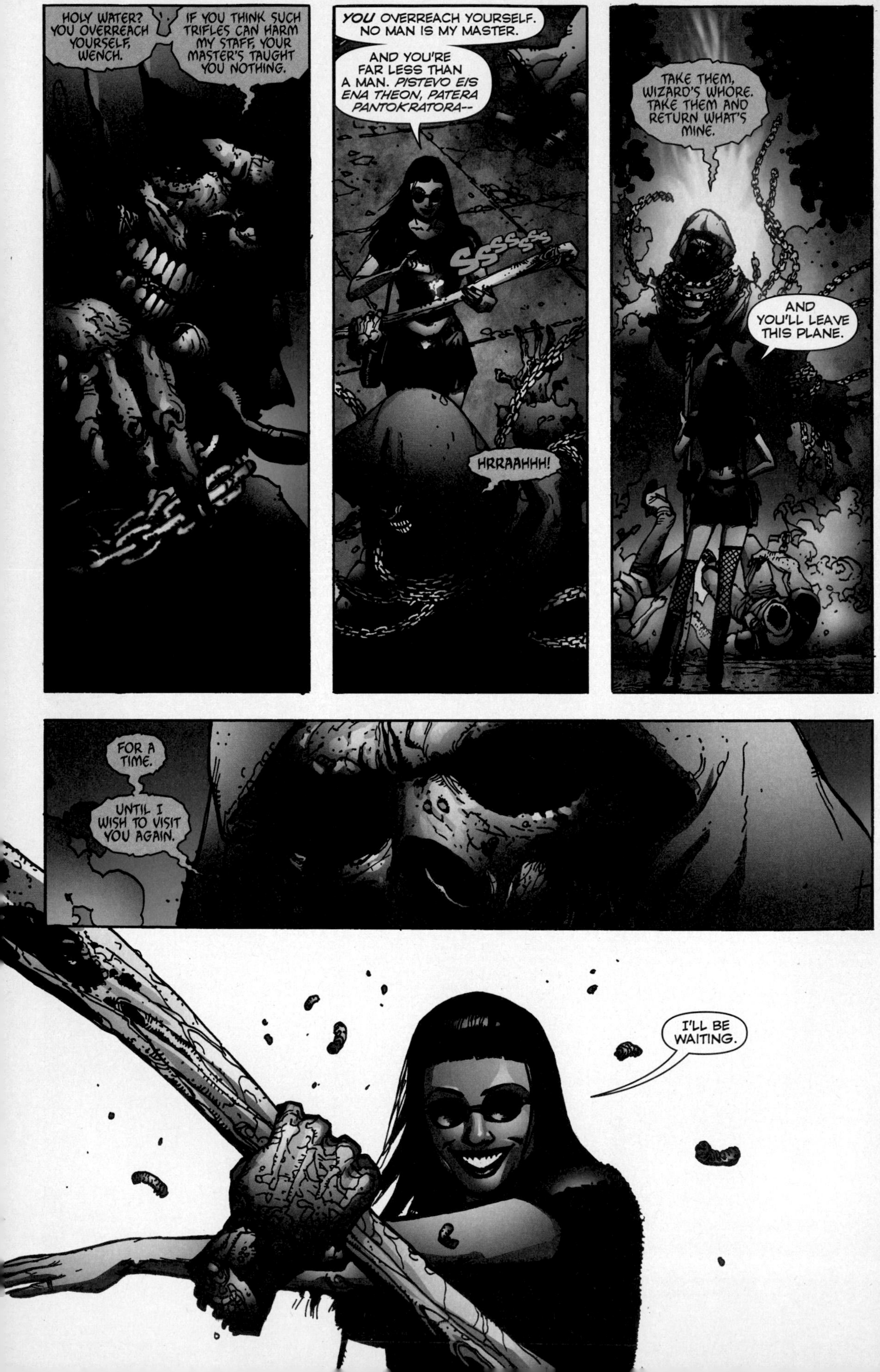
HOLY WATER? YOU OVERREACH YOURSELF, WENCH.
IF YOU THINK SUCH TRIFLES CAN HARM MY STAFF, YOUR MASTER'S TAUGHT YOU NOTHING.
YOU OVERREACH YOURSELF. NO MAN IS MY MASTER.
AND YOU'RE FAR LESS THAN A MAN. *PISTEVO EIS ENA THEON, PATERA PANTOKRATORA--*
SSSSSSS
HRRAAHHH!
TAKE THEM, WIZARD'S WHORE. TAKE THEM AND RETURN WHAT'S MINE.
AND YOU'LL LEAVE THIS PLANE.
FOR A TIME.
UNTIL I WISH TO VISIT YOU AGAIN.
I'LL BE WAITING.

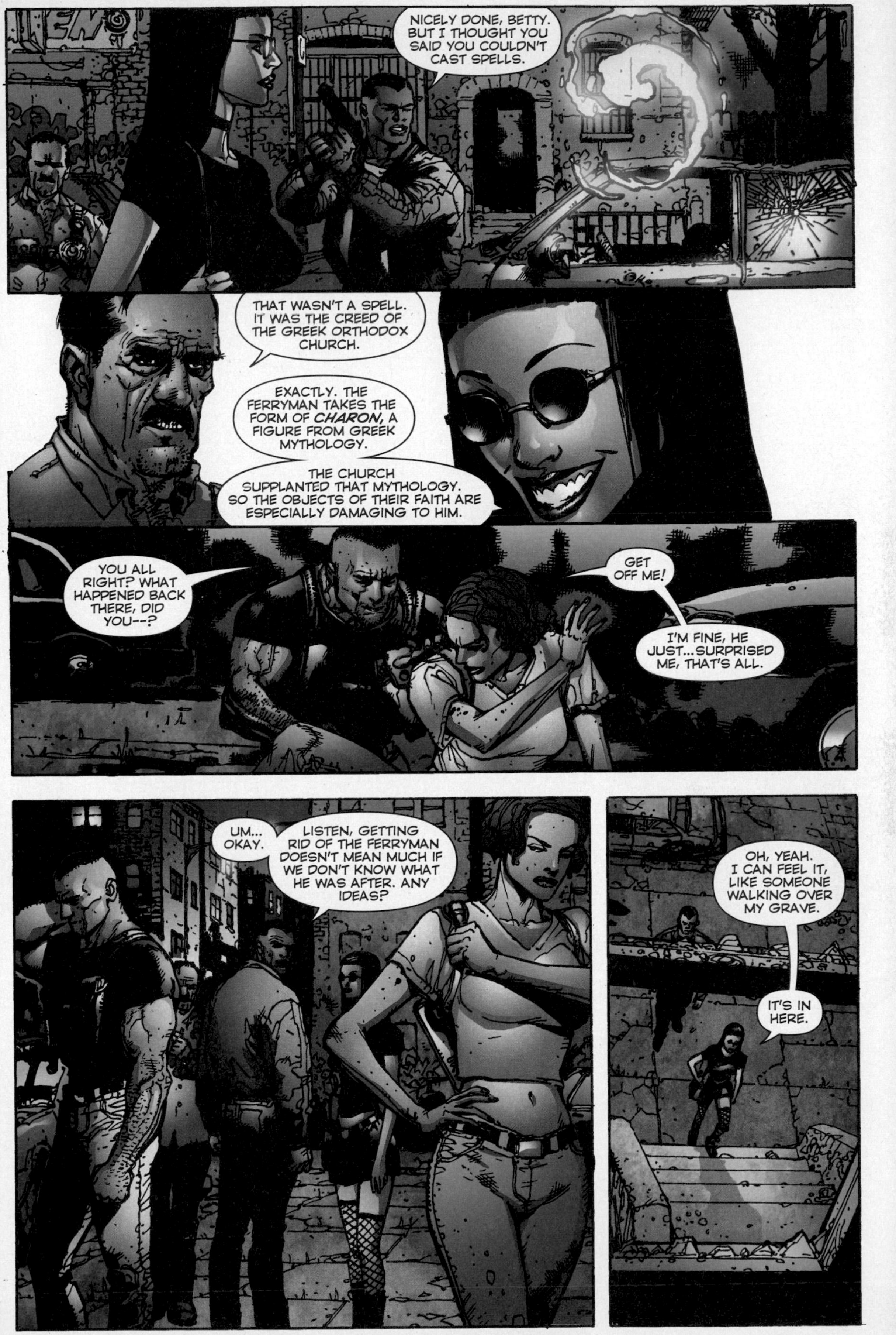
NICELY DONE, BETTY. BUT I THOUGHT YOU SAID YOU COULDN'T CAST SPELLS.
THAT WASN'T A SPELL. IT WAS THE CREED OF THE GREEK ORTHODOX CHURCH.
EXACTLY. THE FERRYMAN TAKES THE FORM OF CHARON, A FIGURE FROM GREEK MYTHOLOGY.
THE CHURCH SUPPLANTED THAT MYTHOLOGY. SO THE OBJECTS OF THEIR FAITH ARE ESPECIALLY DAMAGING TO HIM.
YOU ALL RIGHT? WHAT HAPPENED BACK THERE, DID YOU--?
GET OFF ME!
I'M FINE, HE JUST...SURPRISED ME, THAT'S ALL.
UM... OKAY.
LISTEN, GETTING RID OF THE FERRYMAN DOESN'T MEAN MUCH IF WE DON'T KNOW WHAT HE WAS AFTER. ANY IDEAS?
OH, YEAH. I CAN FEEL IT, LIKE SOMEONE WALKING OVER MY GRAVE.
IT'S IN HERE.

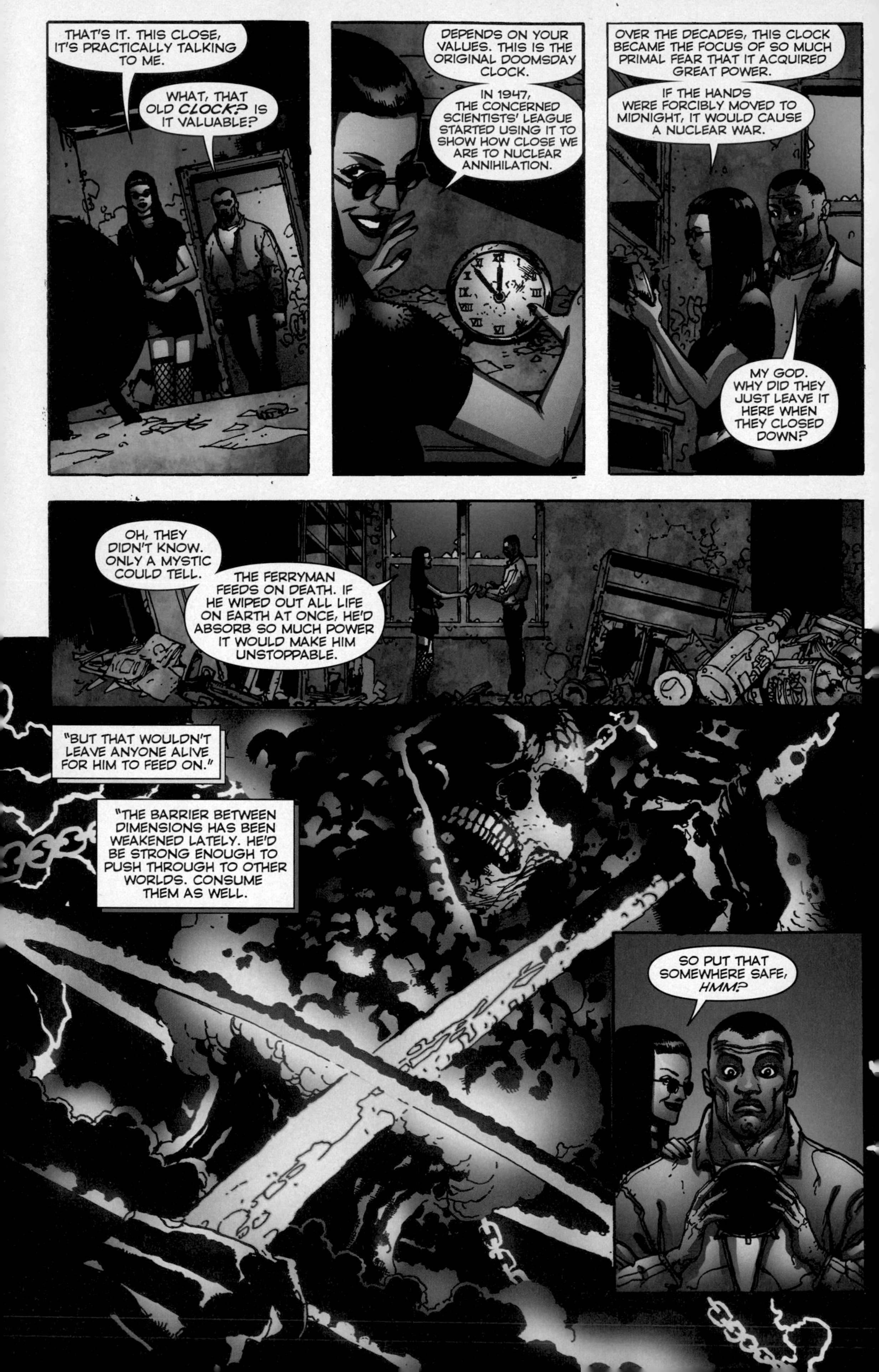
THAT'S IT. THIS CLOSE, IT'S PRACTICALLY TALKING TO ME.
WHAT, THAT OLD *CLOCK?* IS IT VALUABLE?
DEPENDS ON YOUR VALUES. THIS IS THE ORIGINAL DOOMSDAY CLOCK.
IN 1947, THE CONCERNED SCIENTISTS' LEAGUE STARTED USING IT TO SHOW HOW CLOSE WE ARE TO NUCLEAR ANNIHILATION.
OVER THE DECADES, THIS CLOCK BECAME THE FOCUS OF SO MUCH PRIMAL FEAR THAT IT ACQUIRED GREAT POWER.
IF THE HANDS WERE FORCIBLY MOVED TO MIDNIGHT, IT WOULD CAUSE A NUCLEAR WAR.
MY GOD. WHY DID THEY JUST LEAVE IT HERE WHEN THEY CLOSED DOWN?
OH, THEY DIDN'T KNOW. ONLY A MYSTIC COULD TELL.
THE FERRYMAN FEEDS ON DEATH. IF HE WIPED OUT ALL LIFE ON EARTH AT ONCE, HE'D ABSORB SO MUCH POWER IT WOULD MAKE HIM UNSTOPPABLE.
"BUT THAT WOULDN'T LEAVE ANYONE ALIVE FOR HIM TO FEED ON."
"THE BARRIER BETWEEN DIMENSIONS HAS BEEN WEAKENED LATELY. HE'D BE STRONG ENOUGH TO PUSH THROUGH TO OTHER WORLDS. CONSUME THEM AS WELL.
SO PUT THAT SOMEWHERE SAFE, *HMM?*

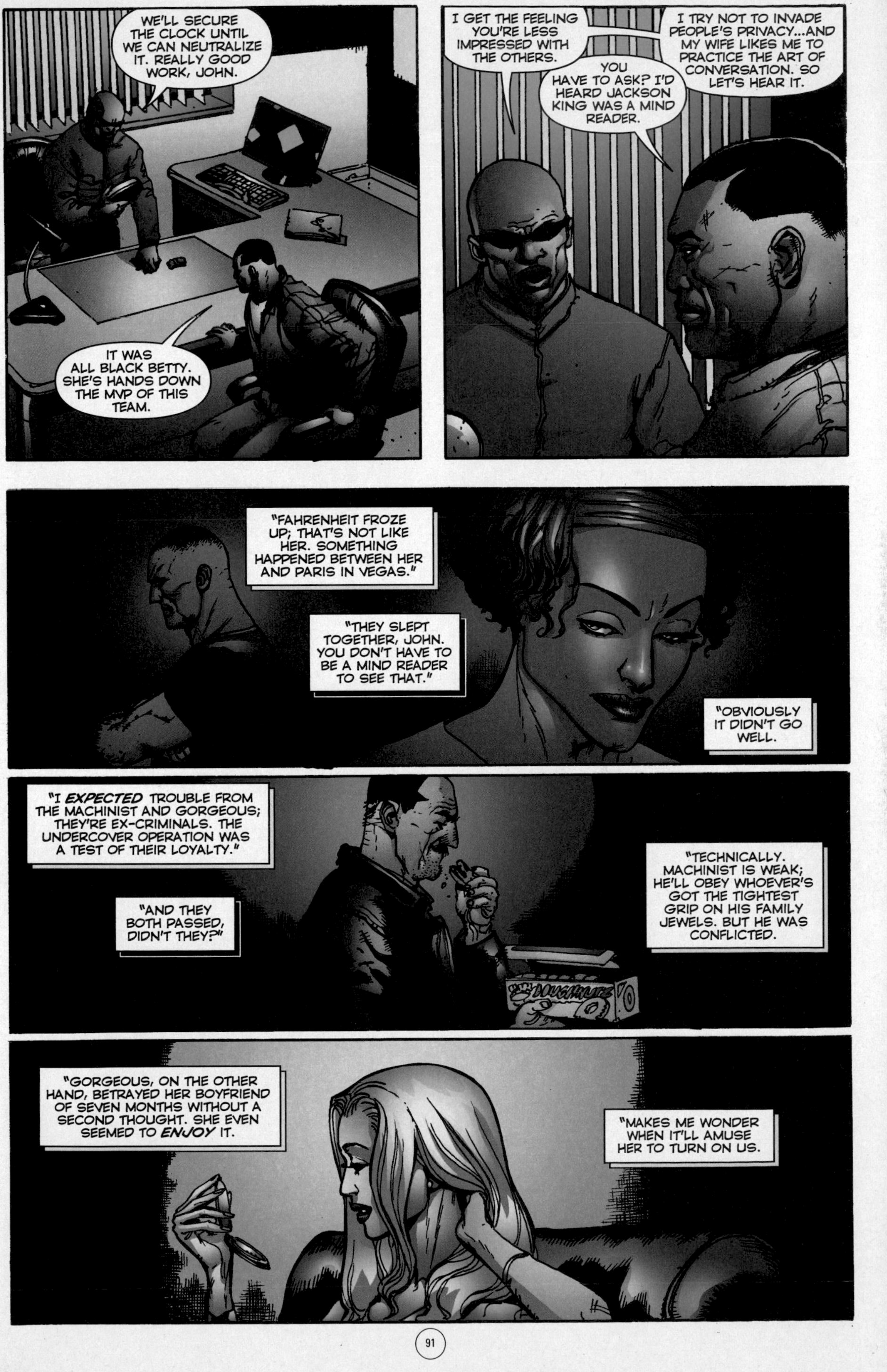
WE'LL SECURE THE CLOCK UNTIL WE CAN NEUTRALIZE IT. REALLY GOOD WORK, JOHN.
IT WAS ALL BLACK BETTY. SHE'S HANDS DOWN THE MVP OF THIS TEAM.
I GET THE FEELING YOU'RE LESS IMPRESSED WITH THE OTHERS.
I TRY NOT TO INVADE PEOPLE'S PRIVACY...AND MY WIFE LIKES ME TO PRACTICE THE ART OF CONVERSATION. SO LET'S HEAR IT.
YOU HAVE TO ASK? I'D HEARD JACKSON KING WAS A MIND READER.
"FAHRENHEIT FROZE UP; THAT'S NOT LIKE HER. SOMETHING HAPPENED BETWEEN HER AND PARIS IN VEGAS."
"THEY SLEPT TOGETHER, JOHN. YOU DON'T HAVE TO BE A MIND READER TO SEE THAT."
"OBVIOUSLY IT DIDN'T GO WELL.
"I EXPECTED TROUBLE FROM THE MACHINIST AND GORGEOUS; THEY'RE EX-CRIMINALS. THE UNDERCOVER OPERATION WAS A TEST OF THEIR LOYALTY."
"AND THEY BOTH PASSED, DIDN'T THEY?"
"TECHNICALLY. MACHINIST IS WEAK; HE'LL OBEY WHOEVER'S GOT THE TIGHTEST GRIP ON HIS FAMILY JEWELS. BUT HE WAS CONFLICTED.
"GORGEOUS, ON THE OTHER HAND, BETRAYED HER BOYFRIEND OF SEVEN MONTHS WITHOUT A SECOND THOUGHT. SHE EVEN SEEMED TO ENJOY IT.
"MAKES ME WONDER WHEN IT'LL AMUSE HER TO TURN ON US.

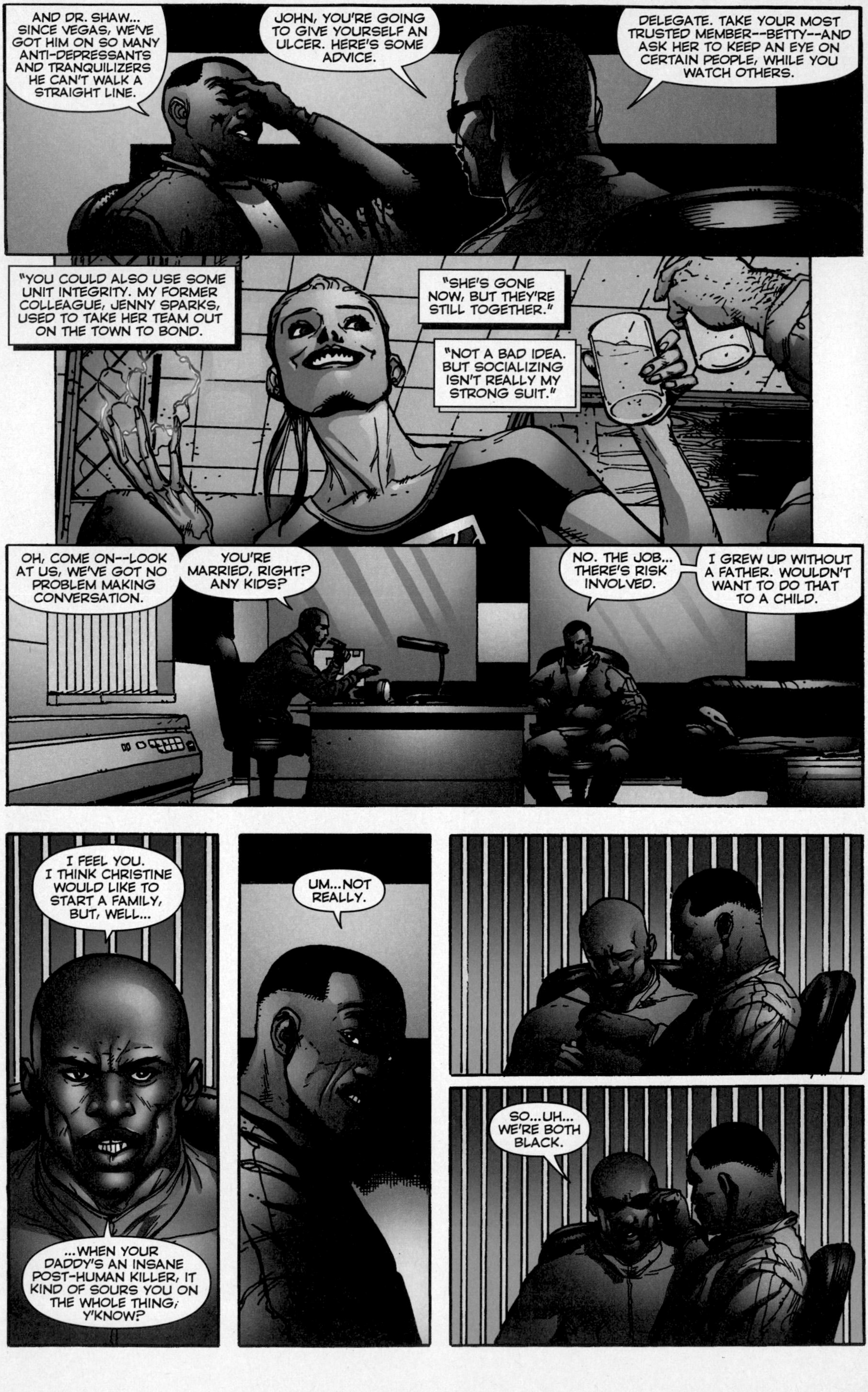
AND DR. SHAW... SINCE VEGAS, WE'VE GOT HIM ON SO MANY ANTI-DEPRESSANTS AND TRANQUILIZERS HE CAN'T WALK A STRAIGHT LINE.
JOHN, YOU'RE GOING TO GIVE YOURSELF AN ULCER. HERE'S SOME ADVICE.
DELEGATE. TAKE YOUR MOST TRUSTED MEMBER--BETTY--AND ASK HER TO KEEP AN EYE ON CERTAIN PEOPLE, WHILE YOU WATCH OTHERS.
"YOU COULD ALSO USE SOME UNIT INTEGRITY. MY FORMER COLLEAGUE, JENNY SPARKS, USED TO TAKE HER TEAM OUT ON THE TOWN TO BOND.
"SHE'S GONE NOW, BUT THEY'RE STILL TOGETHER."
"NOT A BAD IDEA. BUT SOCIALIZING ISN'T REALLY MY STRONG SUIT."
OH, COME ON--LOOK AT US, WE'VE GOT NO PROBLEM MAKING CONVERSATION.
YOU'RE MARRIED, RIGHT? ANY KIDS?
NO. THE JOB... THERE'S RISK INVOLVED.
I GREW UP WITHOUT A FATHER. WOULDN'T WANT TO DO THAT TO A CHILD.
I FEEL YOU. I THINK CHRISTINE WOULD LIKE TO START A FAMILY, BUT, WELL...
...WHEN YOUR DADDY'S AN INSANE POST-HUMAN KILLER, IT KIND OF SOURS YOU ON THE WHOLE THING, Y'KNOW?
UM...NOT REALLY.
SO...UH... WE'RE BOTH BLACK.

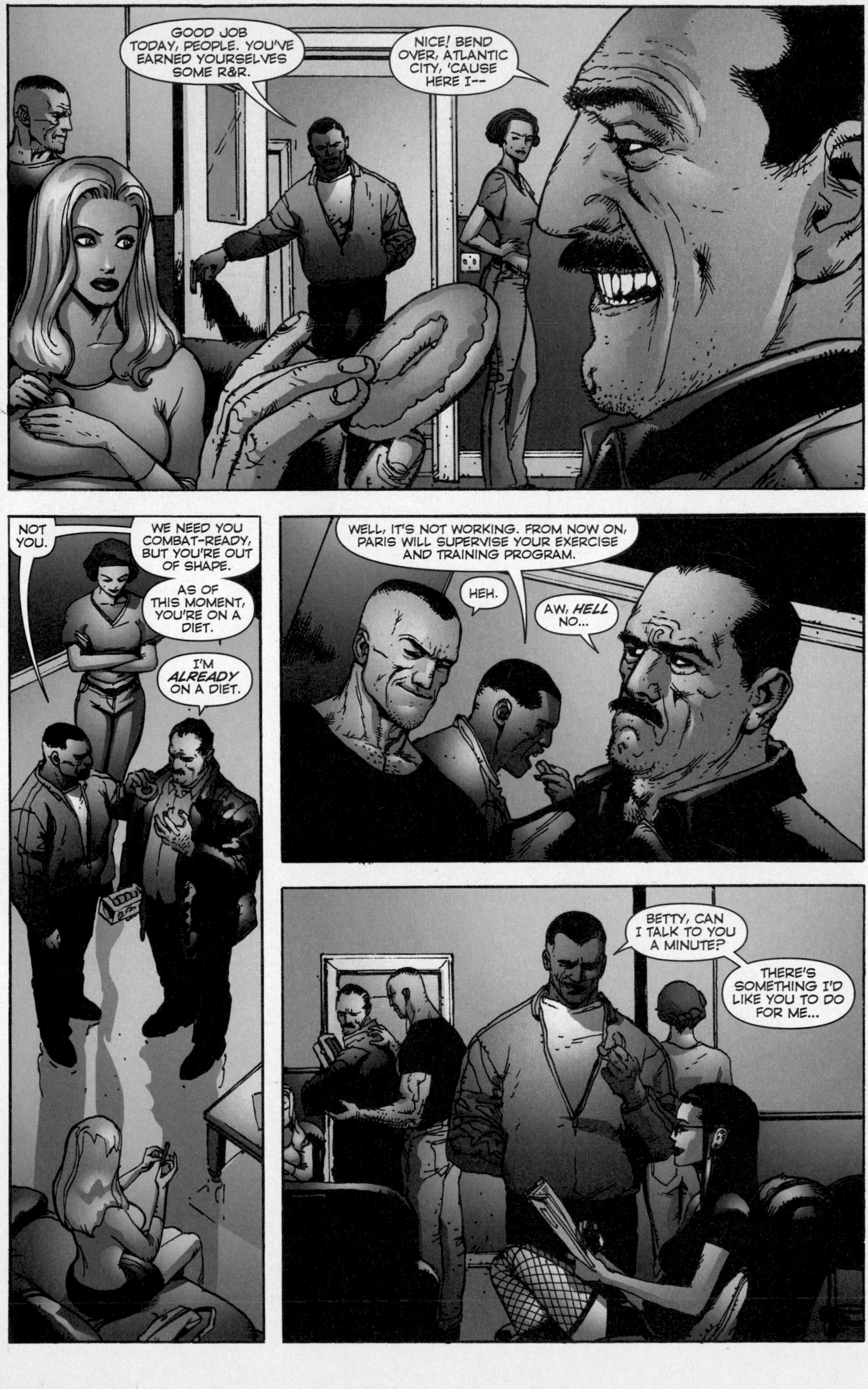
GOOD JOB TODAY, PEOPLE. YOU'VE EARNED YOURSELVES SOME R&R.
NICE! BEND OVER, ATLANTIC CITY, 'CAUSE HERE I--
NOT YOU.
WE NEED YOU COMBAT-READY, BUT YOU'RE OUT OF SHAPE.
AS OF THIS MOMENT, YOU'RE ON A DIET.
I'M *ALREADY* ON A DIET.
WELL, IT'S NOT WORKING. FROM NOW ON, PARIS WILL SUPERVISE YOUR EXERCISE AND TRAINING PROGRAM.
HEH.
AW, ***HELL*** NO...
BETTY, CAN I TALK TO YOU A MINUTE?
THERE'S SOMETHING I'D LIKE YOU TO DO FOR ME...

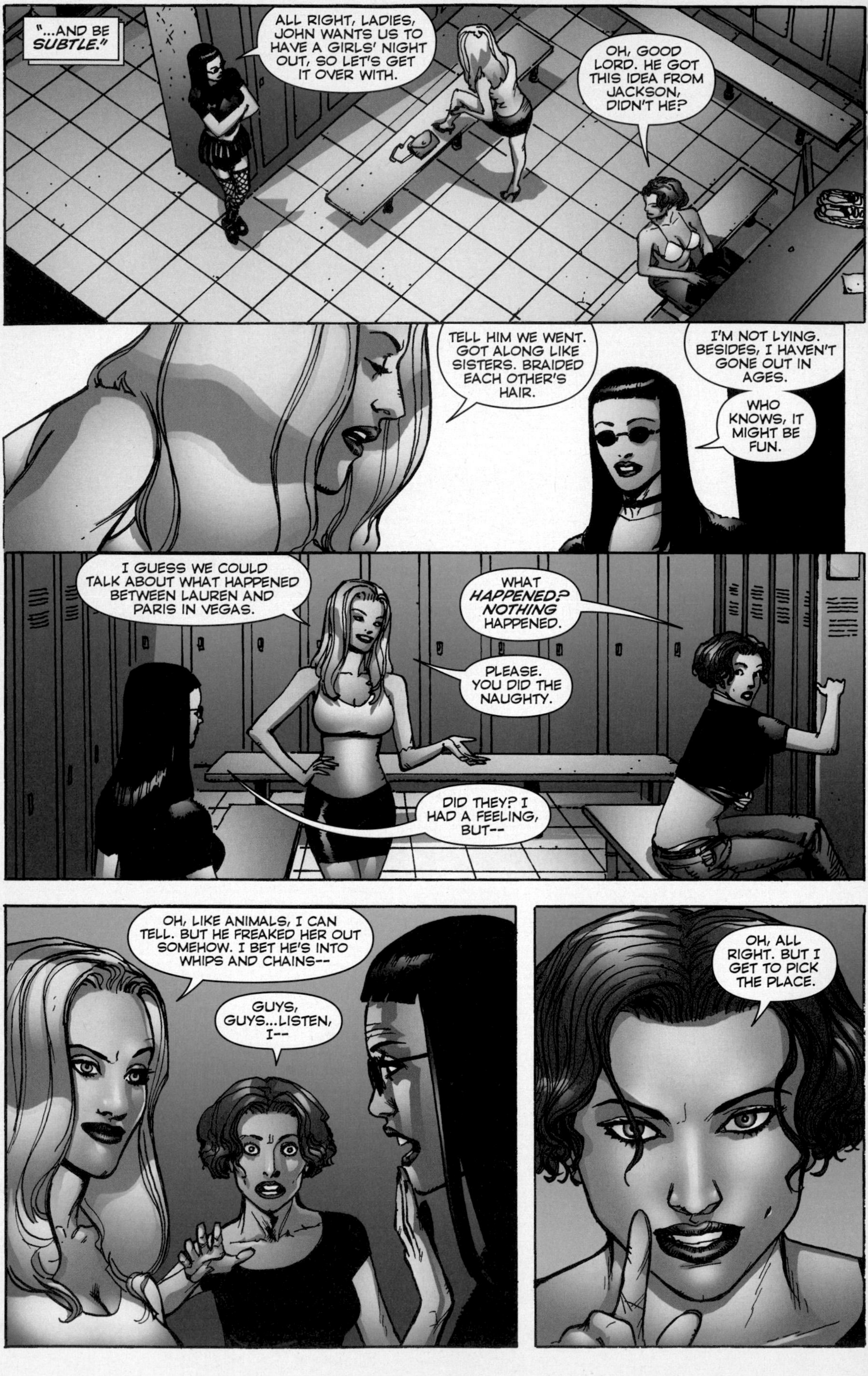
"...AND BE *SUBTLE.*"
ALL RIGHT, LADIES, JOHN WANTS US TO HAVE A GIRLS' NIGHT OUT, SO LET'S GET IT OVER WITH.
OH, GOOD LORD. HE GOT THIS IDEA FROM JACKSON, DIDN'T HE?
TELL HIM WE WENT. GOT ALONG LIKE SISTERS. BRAIDED EACH OTHER'S HAIR.
I'M NOT LYING. BESIDES, I HAVEN'T GONE OUT IN AGES.
WHO KNOWS, IT MIGHT BE FUN.
I GUESS WE COULD TALK ABOUT WHAT HAPPENED BETWEEN LAUREN AND PARIS IN VEGAS.
WHAT *HAPPENED? NOTHING* HAPPENED.
PLEASE. YOU DID THE NAUGHTY.
DID THEY? I HAD A FEELING, BUT--
OH, LIKE ANIMALS, I CAN TELL. BUT HE FREAKED HER OUT SOMEHOW. I BET HE'S INTO WHIPS AND CHAINS--
GUYS, GUYS...LISTEN, I--
OH, ALL RIGHT. BUT I GET TO PICK THE PLACE.

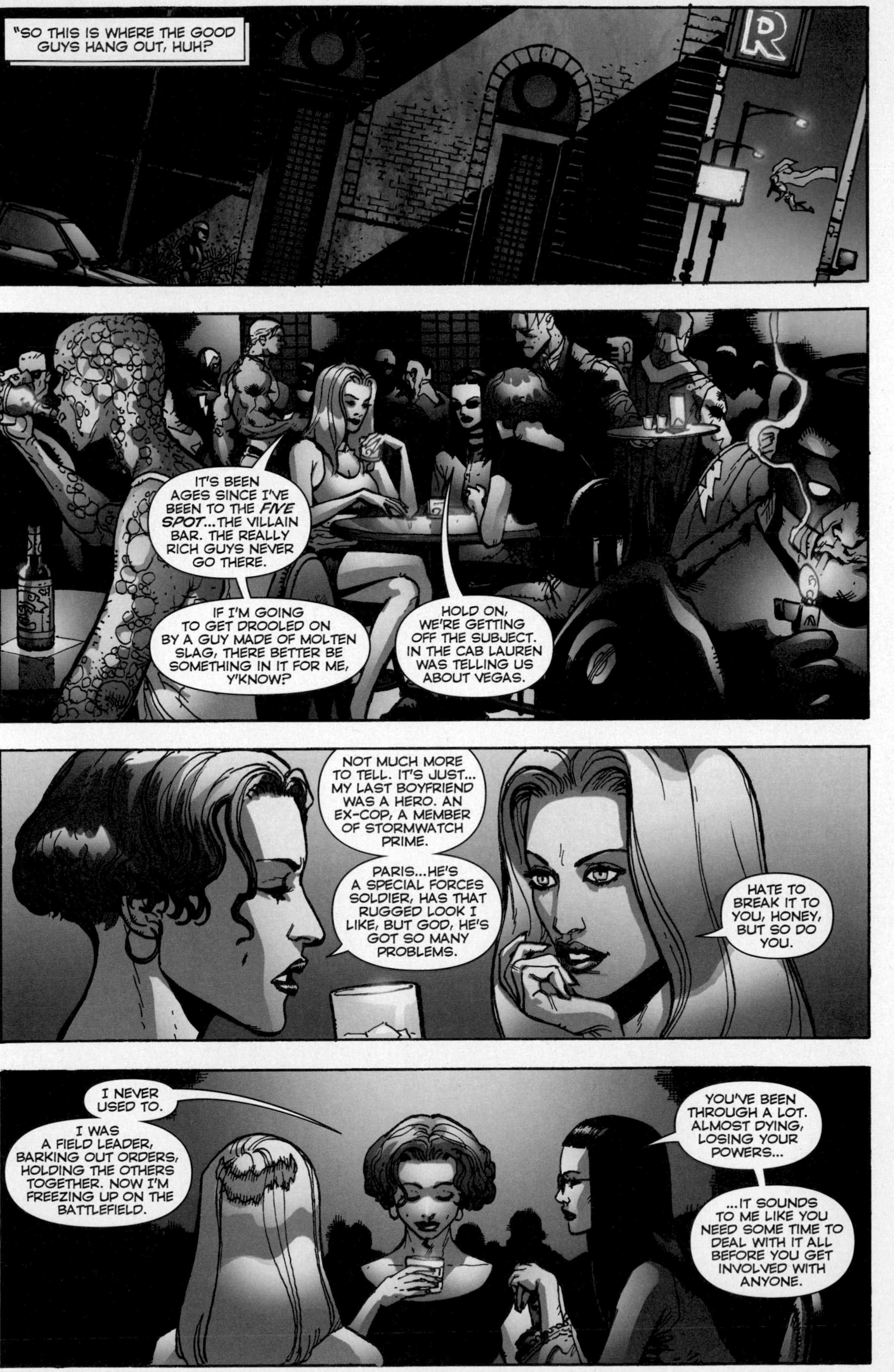
"SO THIS IS WHERE THE GOOD GUYS HANG OUT, HUH?
IT'S BEEN AGES SINCE I'VE BEEN TO THE *FIVE SPOT*...THE VILLAIN BAR. THE REALLY RICH GUYS NEVER GO THERE.
IF I'M GOING TO GET DROOLED ON BY A GUY MADE OF MOLTEN SLAG, THERE BETTER BE SOMETHING IN IT FOR ME, Y'KNOW?
HOLD ON, WE'RE GETTING OFF THE SUBJECT. IN THE CAB LAUREN WAS TELLING US ABOUT VEGAS.
NOT MUCH MORE TO TELL. IT'S JUST... MY LAST BOYFRIEND WAS A HERO. AN EX-COP, A MEMBER OF STORMWATCH PRIME.
PARIS...HE'S A SPECIAL FORCES SOLDIER, HAS THAT RUGGED LOOK I LIKE, BUT GOD, HE'S GOT SO MANY PROBLEMS.
HATE TO BREAK IT TO YOU, HONEY, BUT SO DO YOU.
I NEVER USED TO.
I WAS A FIELD LEADER, BARKING OUT ORDERS, HOLDING THE OTHERS TOGETHER. NOW I'M FREEZING UP ON THE BATTLEFIELD.
YOU'VE BEEN THROUGH A LOT. ALMOST DYING, LOSING YOUR POWERS...
...IT SOUNDS TO ME LIKE YOU NEED SOME TIME TO DEAL WITH IT ALL BEFORE YOU GET INVOLVED WITH ANYONE.

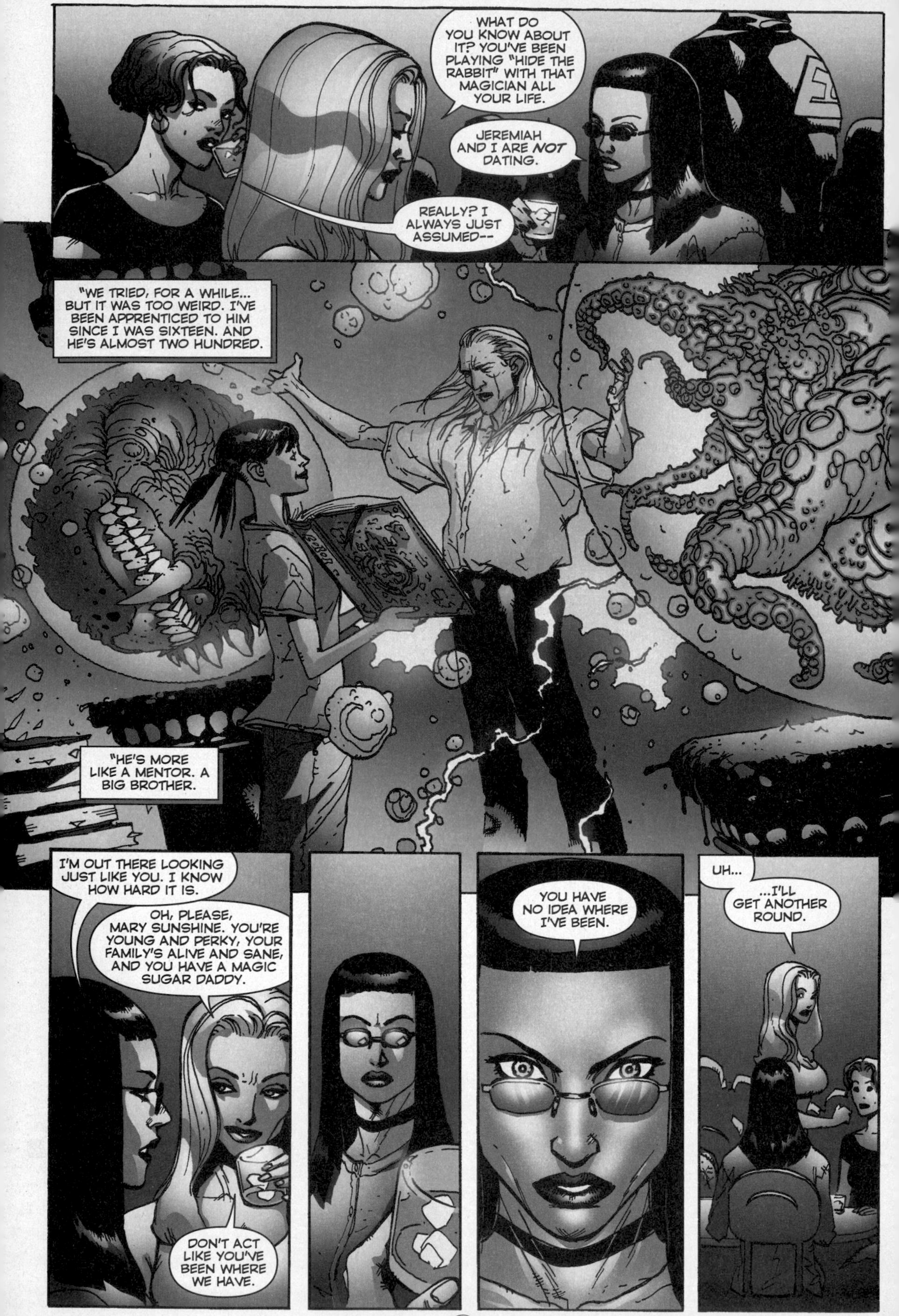
WHAT DO YOU KNOW ABOUT IT? YOU'VE BEEN PLAYING "HIDE THE RABBIT" WITH THAT MAGICIAN ALL YOUR LIFE.
JEREMIAH AND I ARE *NOT* DATING.
REALLY? I ALWAYS JUST ASSUMED--
"WE TRIED, FOR A WHILE... BUT IT WAS TOO WEIRD. I'VE BEEN APPRENTICED TO HIM SINCE I WAS SIXTEEN. AND HE'S ALMOST TWO HUNDRED.
"HE'S MORE LIKE A MENTOR. A BIG BROTHER.
I'M OUT THERE LOOKING JUST LIKE YOU. I KNOW HOW HARD IT IS.
OH, PLEASE, MARY SUNSHINE. YOU'RE YOUNG AND PERKY, YOUR FAMILY'S ALIVE AND SANE, AND YOU HAVE A MAGIC SUGAR DADDY.
DON'T ACT LIKE YOU'VE BEEN WHERE WE HAVE.
YOU HAVE NO IDEA WHERE I'VE BEEN.
UH...
...I'LL GET ANOTHER ROUND.

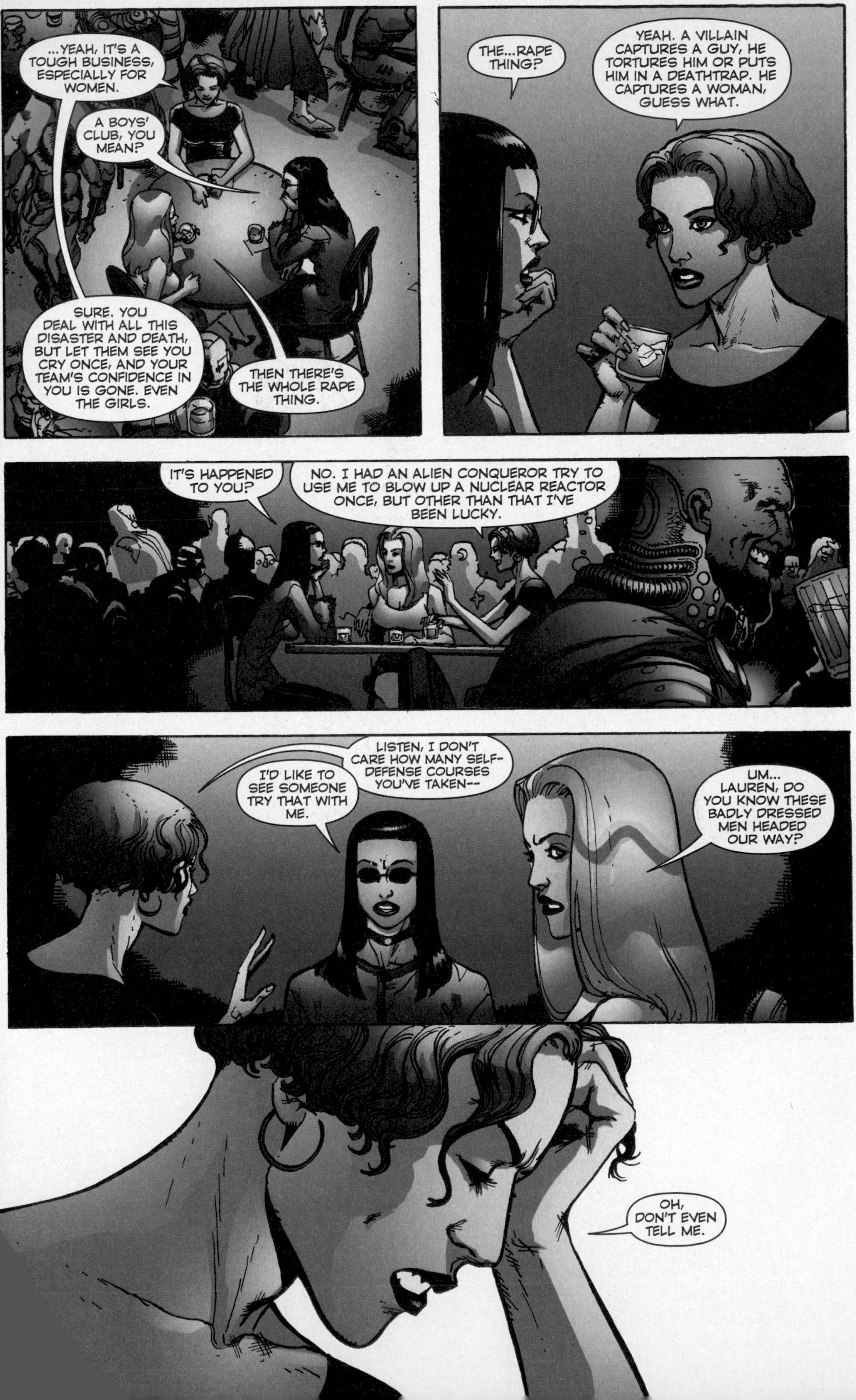
...YEAH, IT'S A TOUGH BUSINESS, ESPECIALLY FOR WOMEN.
A BOYS' CLUB, YOU MEAN?
SURE. YOU DEAL WITH ALL THIS DISASTER AND DEATH, BUT LET THEM SEE YOU CRY ONCE, AND YOUR TEAM'S CONFIDENCE IN YOU IS GONE. EVEN THE GIRLS.
THEN THERE'S THE WHOLE RAPE THING.
THE...RAPE THING?
YEAH. A VILLAIN CAPTURES A GUY, HE TORTURES HIM OR PUTS HIM IN A DEATHTRAP. HE CAPTURES A WOMAN, GUESS WHAT.
IT'S HAPPENED TO YOU?
NO. I HAD AN ALIEN CONQUEROR TRY TO USE ME TO BLOW UP A NUCLEAR REACTOR ONCE, BUT OTHER THAN THAT I'VE BEEN LUCKY.
I'D LIKE TO SEE SOMEONE TRY THAT WITH ME.
LISTEN, I DON'T CARE HOW MANY SELF-DEFENSE COURSES YOU'VE TAKEN--
UM... LAUREN, DO YOU KNOW THESE BADLY DRESSED MEN HEADED OUR WAY?
OH, DON'T EVEN TELL ME.

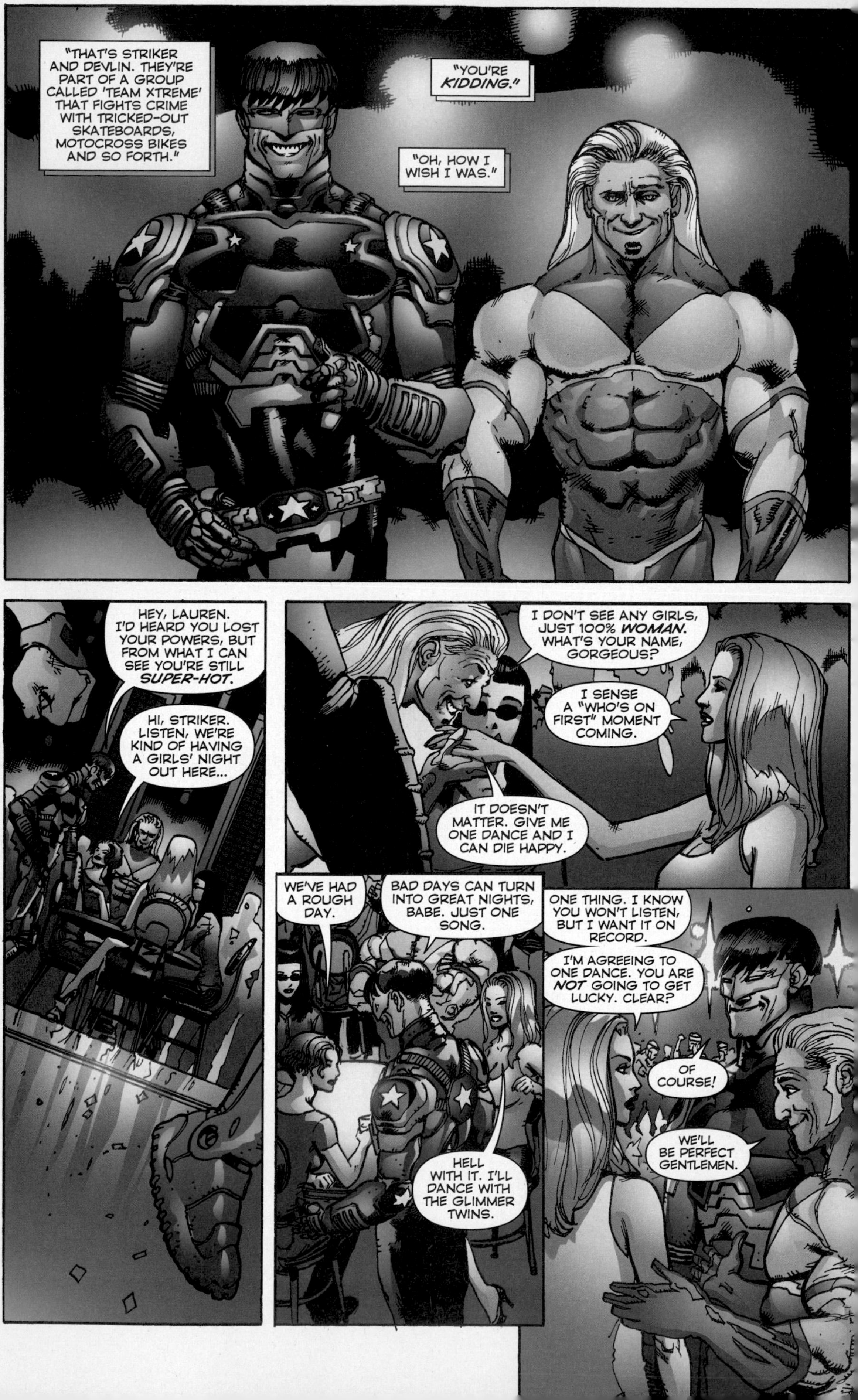
"THAT'S STRIKER AND DEVLIN. THEY'RE PART OF A GROUP CALLED 'TEAM XTREME' THAT FIGHTS CRIME WITH TRICKED-OUT SKATEBOARDS, MOTOCROSS BIKES AND SO FORTH."
"YOU'RE *KIDDING*."
"OH, HOW I WISH I WAS."
HEY, LAUREN. I'D HEARD YOU LOST YOUR POWERS, BUT FROM WHAT I CAN SEE YOU'RE STILL ***SUPER-HOT***.
HI, STRIKER. LISTEN, WE'RE KIND OF HAVING A GIRLS' NIGHT OUT HERE...
I DON'T SEE ANY GIRLS, JUST 100% ***WOMAN***. WHAT'S YOUR NAME, GORGEOUS?
I SENSE A "WHO'S ON FIRST" MOMENT COMING.
IT DOESN'T MATTER. GIVE ME ONE DANCE AND I CAN DIE HAPPY.
WE'VE HAD A ROUGH DAY.
BAD DAYS CAN TURN INTO GREAT NIGHTS, BABE. JUST ONE SONG.
HELL WITH IT. I'LL DANCE WITH THE GLIMMER TWINS.
ONE THING. I KNOW YOU WON'T LISTEN, BUT I WANT IT ON RECORD.
I'M AGREEING TO ONE DANCE. YOU ARE ***NOT*** GOING TO GET LUCKY. CLEAR?
OF COURSE!
WE'LL BE PERFECT GENTLEMEN.

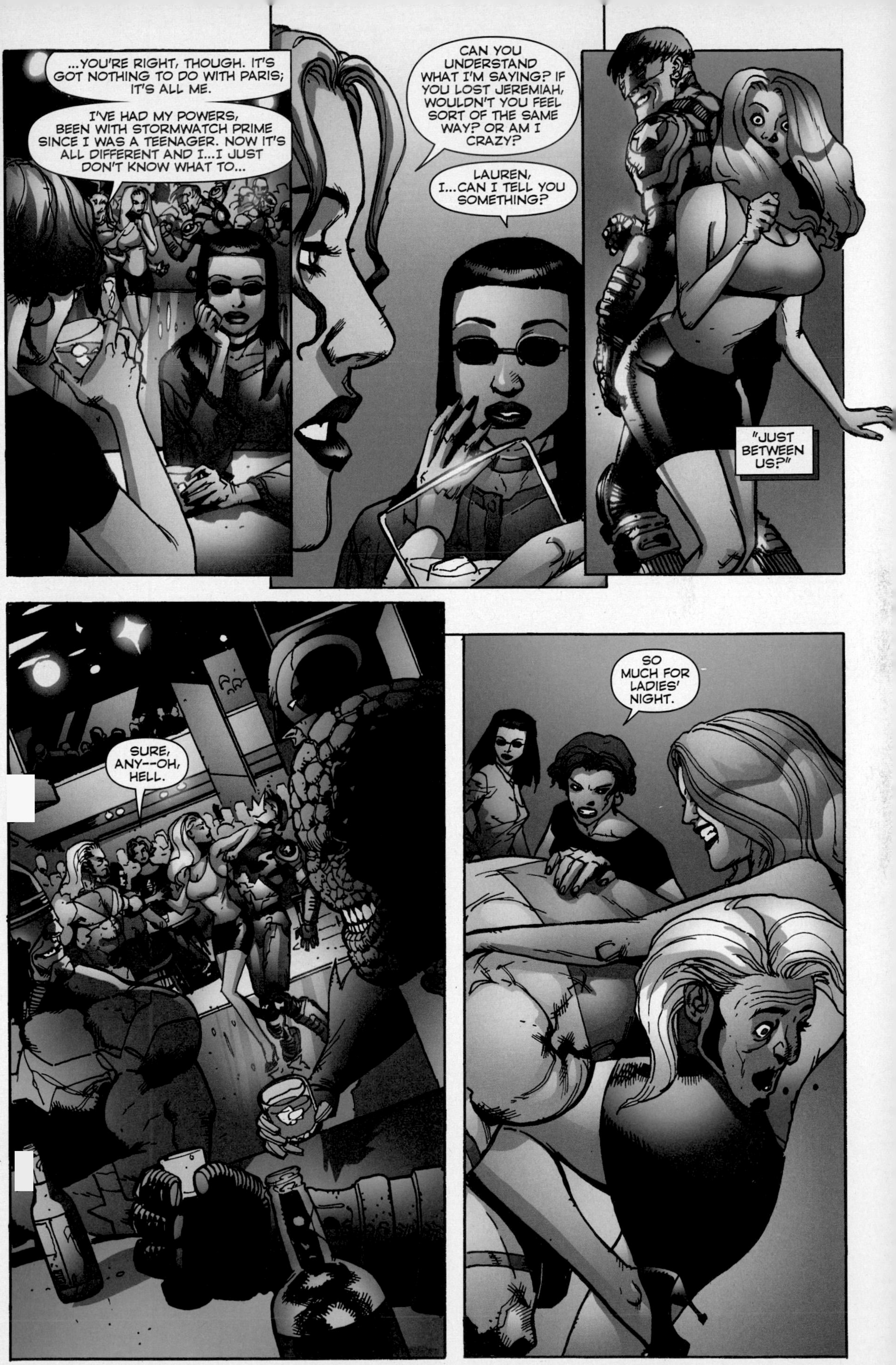
...YOU'RE RIGHT, THOUGH. IT'S GOT NOTHING TO DO WITH PARIS; IT'S ALL ME.
I'VE HAD MY POWERS, BEEN WITH STORMWATCH PRIME SINCE I WAS A TEENAGER. NOW IT'S ALL DIFFERENT AND I...I JUST DON'T KNOW WHAT TO...
CAN YOU UNDERSTAND WHAT I'M SAYING? IF YOU LOST JEREMIAH, WOULDN'T YOU FEEL SORT OF THE SAME WAY? OR AM I CRAZY?
LAUREN, I...CAN I TELL YOU SOMETHING?
"JUST BETWEEN US?"
SURE, ANY--OH, HELL.
SO MUCH FOR LADIES' NIGHT.

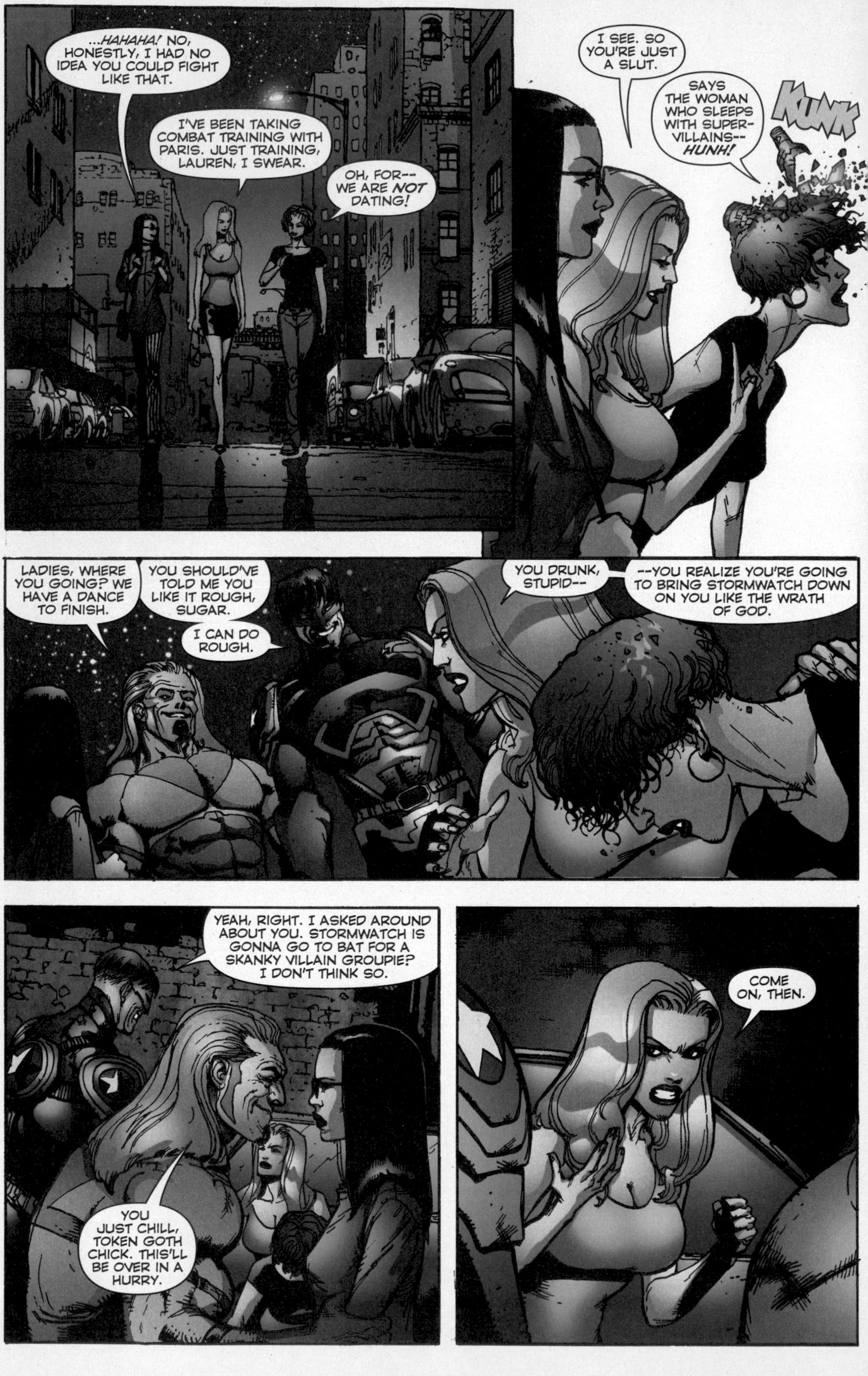
...HAHAHA! NO, HONESTLY, I HAD NO IDEA YOU COULD FIGHT LIKE THAT.
I'VE BEEN TAKING COMBAT TRAINING WITH PARIS. JUST TRAINING, LAUREN, I SWEAR.
OH, FOR-- WE ARE NOT DATING!
I SEE. SO YOU'RE JUST A SLUT.
SAYS THE WOMAN WHO SLEEPS WITH SUPER-VILLAINS-- HUNH!
KUNK
LADIES, WHERE YOU GOING? WE HAVE A DANCE TO FINISH.
YOU SHOULD'VE TOLD ME YOU LIKE IT ROUGH, SUGAR.
I CAN DO ROUGH.
YOU DRUNK, STUPID--
--YOU REALIZE YOU'RE GOING TO BRING STORMWATCH DOWN ON YOU LIKE THE WRATH OF GOD.
YEAH, RIGHT. I ASKED AROUND ABOUT YOU. STORMWATCH IS GONNA GO TO BAT FOR A SKANKY VILLAIN GROUPIE? I DON'T THINK SO.
YOU JUST CHILL, TOKEN GOTH CHICK. THIS'LL BE OVER IN A HURRY.
COME ON, THEN.

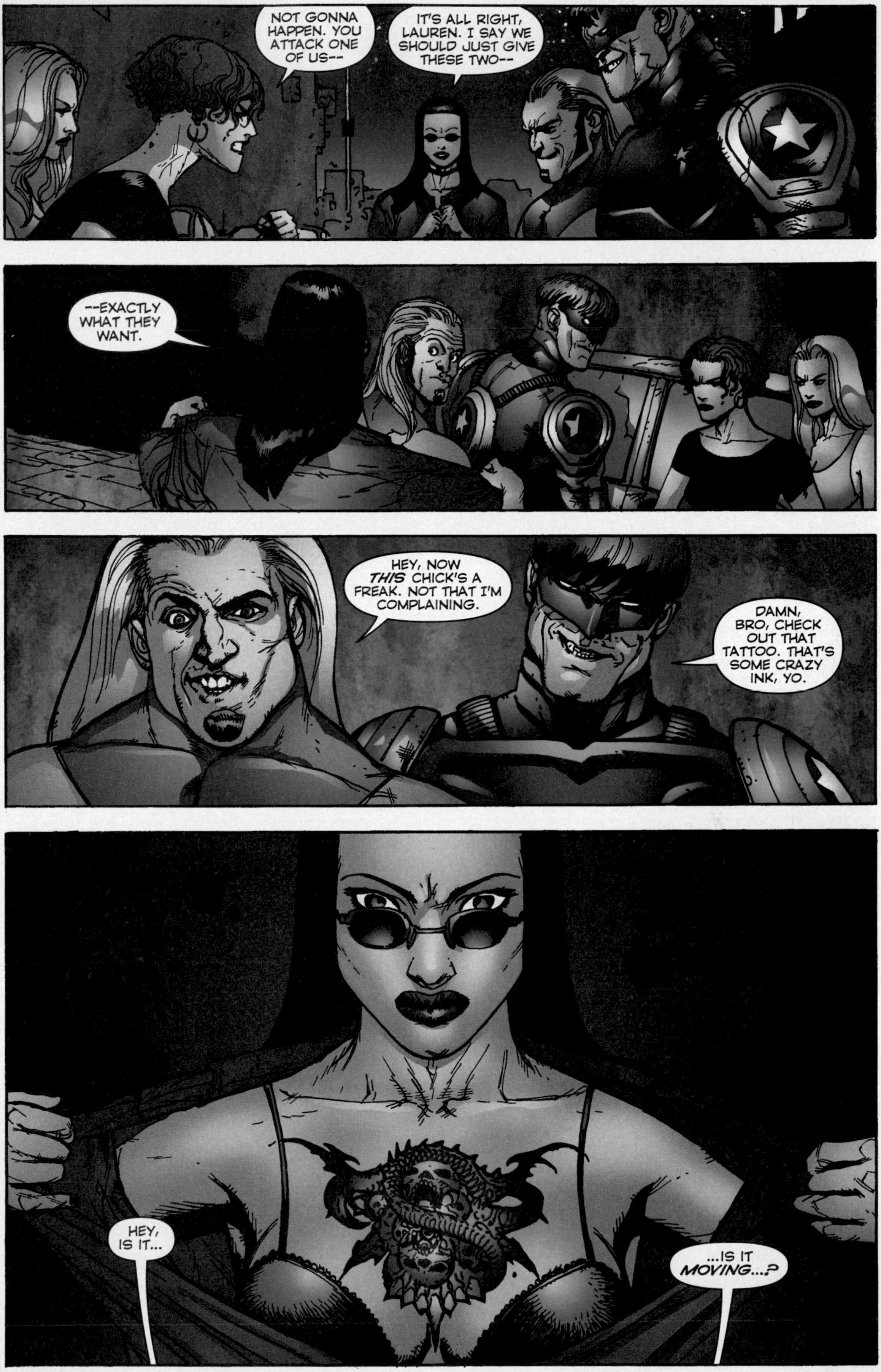
NOT GONNA HAPPEN. YOU ATTACK ONE OF US--
IT'S ALL RIGHT, LAUREN. I SAY WE SHOULD JUST GIVE THESE TWO--
--EXACTLY WHAT THEY WANT.
HEY, NOW *THIS* CHICK'S A FREAK. NOT THAT I'M COMPLAINING.
DAMN, BRO, CHECK OUT THAT TATTOO. THAT'S SOME CRAZY INK, YO.
HEY, IS IT...
...IS IT *MOVING*...?

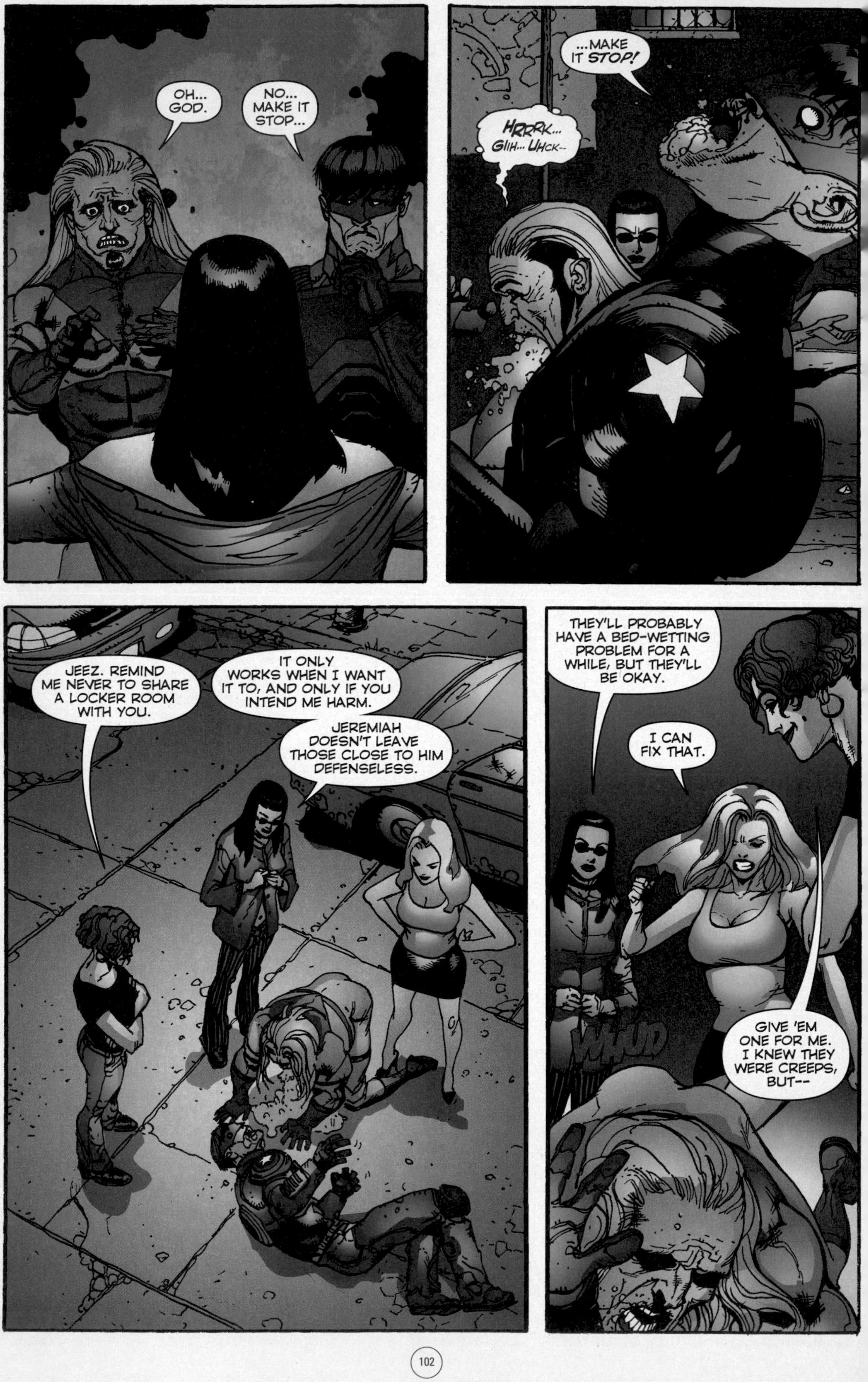
OH... GOD.
NO... MAKE IT STOP...
...MAKE IT STOP!
HRRRK... GIIH... UHCK--
JEEZ. REMIND ME NEVER TO SHARE A LOCKER ROOM WITH YOU.
IT ONLY WORKS WHEN I WANT IT TO, AND ONLY IF YOU INTEND ME HARM.
JEREMIAH DOESN'T LEAVE THOSE CLOSE TO HIM DEFENSELESS.
THEY'LL PROBABLY HAVE A BED-WETTING PROBLEM FOR A WHILE, BUT THEY'LL BE OKAY.
I CAN FIX THAT.
WHUD
GIVE 'EM ONE FOR ME. I KNEW THEY WERE CREEPS, BUT--

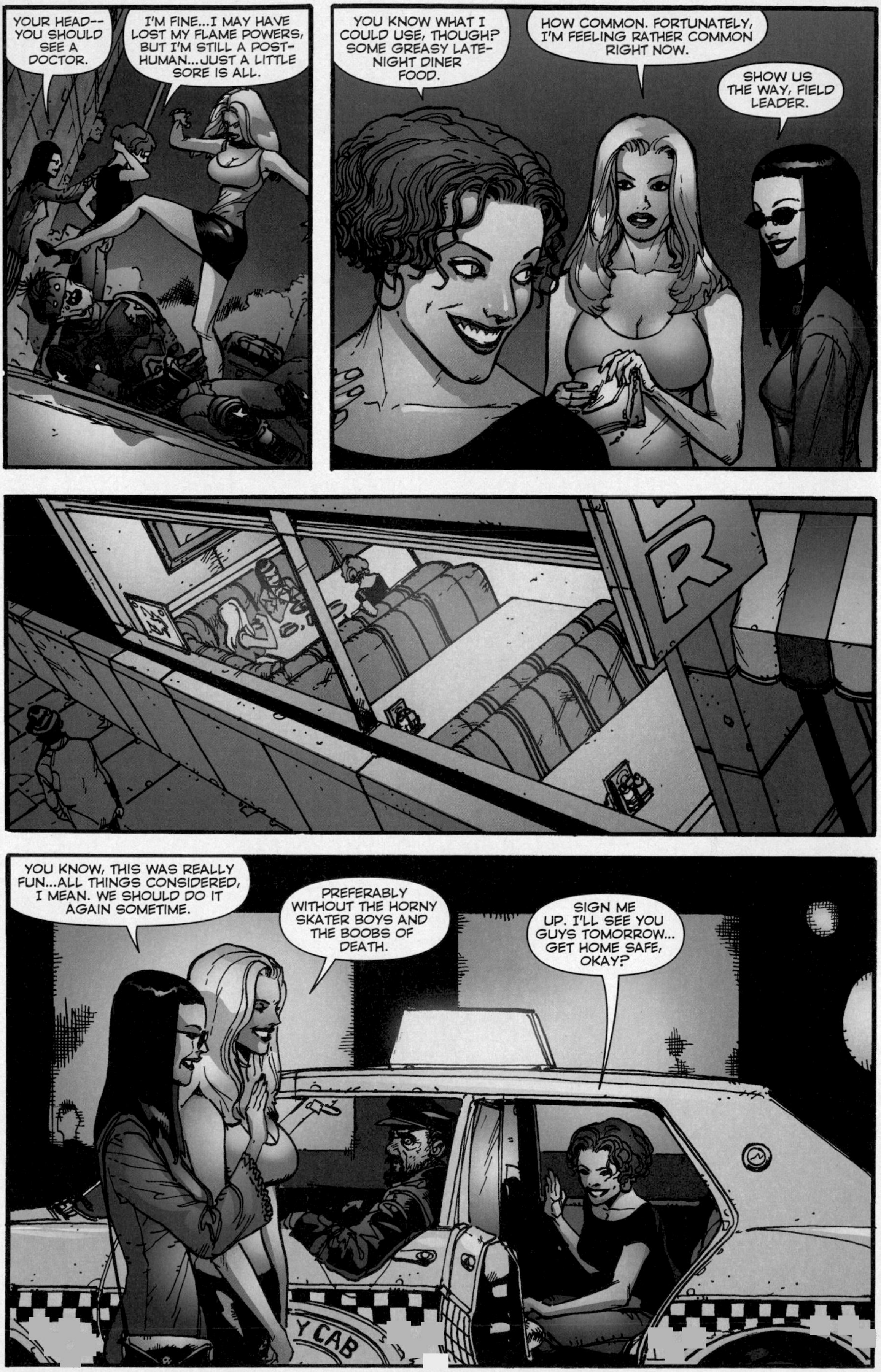
YOUR HEAD-- YOU SHOULD SEE A DOCTOR.
I'M FINE...I MAY HAVE LOST MY FLAME POWERS, BUT I'M STILL A POST-HUMAN...JUST A LITTLE SORE IS ALL.
YOU KNOW WHAT I COULD USE, THOUGH? SOME GREASY LATE-NIGHT DINER FOOD.
HOW COMMON. FORTUNATELY, I'M FEELING RATHER COMMON RIGHT NOW.
SHOW US THE WAY, FIELD LEADER.
YOU KNOW, THIS WAS REALLY FUN...ALL THINGS CONSIDERED, I MEAN. WE SHOULD DO IT AGAIN SOMETIME.
PREFERABLY WITHOUT THE HORNY SKATER BOYS AND THE BOOBS OF DEATH.
SIGN ME UP. I'LL SEE YOU GUYS TOMORROW... GET HOME SAFE, OKAY?
Y CAB

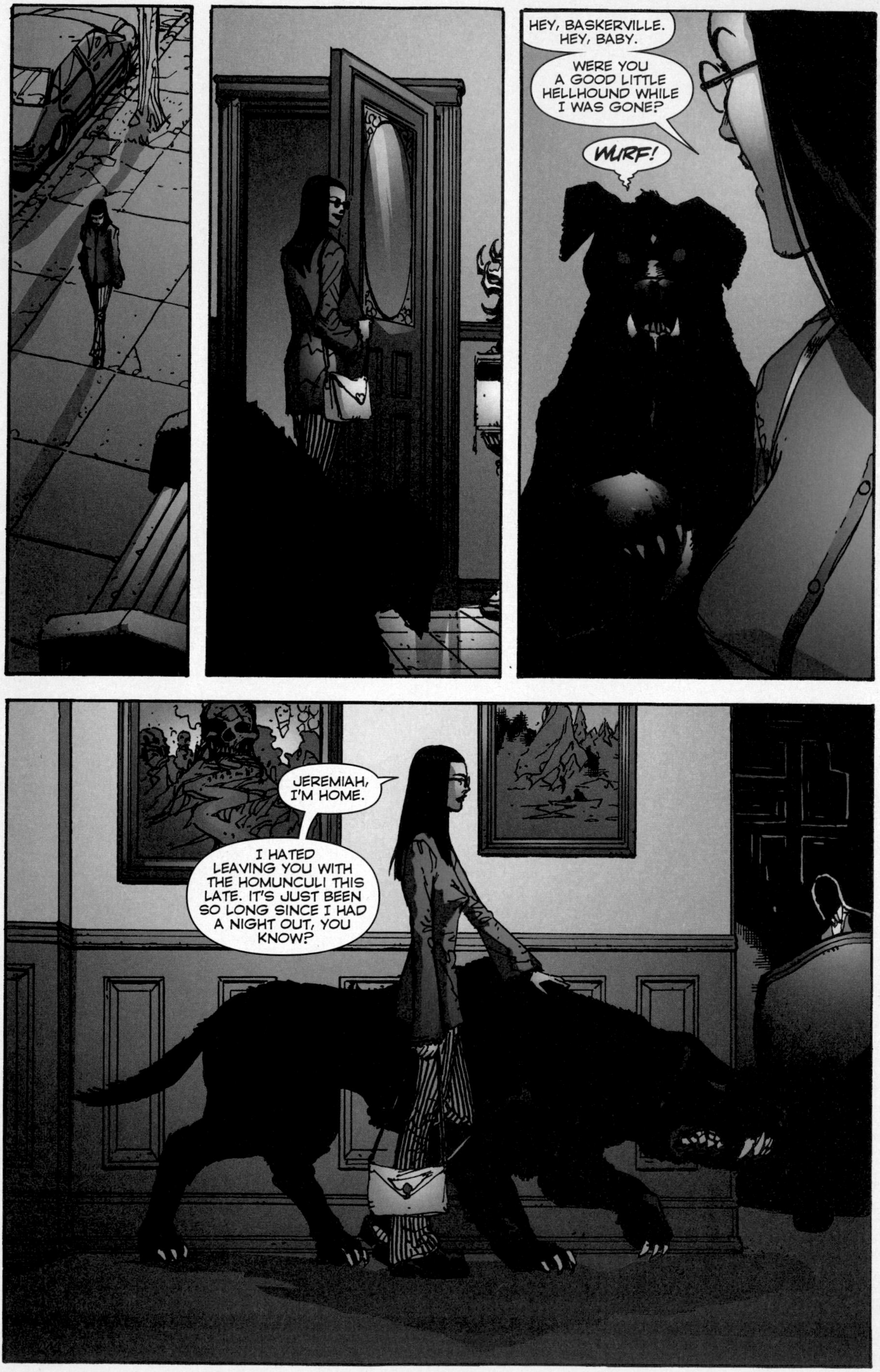
HEY, BASKERVILLE. HEY, BABY.
WERE YOU A GOOD LITTLE HELLHOUND WHILE I WAS GONE?
WURF!
JEREMIAH, I'M HOME.
I HATED LEAVING YOU WITH THE HOMUNCULI THIS LATE. IT'S JUST BEEN SO LONG SINCE I HAD A NIGHT OUT, YOU KNOW?

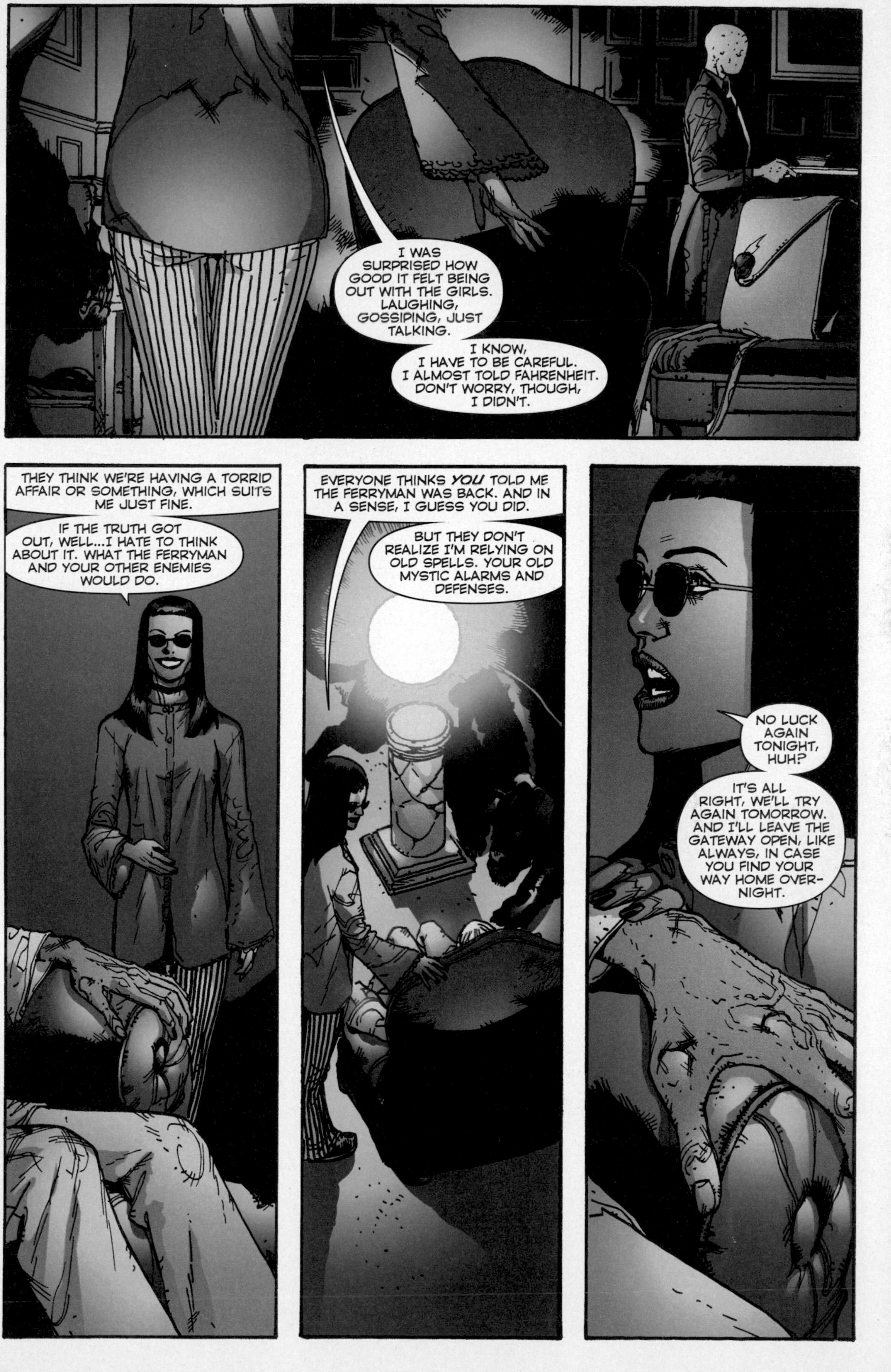
I WAS SURPRISED HOW GOOD IT FELT BEING OUT WITH THE GIRLS. LAUGHING, GOSSIPING, JUST TALKING.
I KNOW, I HAVE TO BE CAREFUL. I ALMOST TOLD FAHRENHEIT. DON'T WORRY, THOUGH, I DIDN'T.
THEY THINK WE'RE HAVING A TORRID AFFAIR OR SOMETHING, WHICH SUITS ME JUST FINE.
IF THE TRUTH GOT OUT, WELL...I HATE TO THINK ABOUT IT. WHAT THE FERRYMAN AND YOUR OTHER ENEMIES WOULD DO.
EVERYONE THINKS *YOU* TOLD ME THE FERRYMAN WAS BACK. AND IN A SENSE, I GUESS YOU DID.
BUT THEY DON'T REALIZE I'M RELYING ON OLD SPELLS. YOUR OLD MYSTIC ALARMS AND DEFENSES.
NO LUCK AGAIN TONIGHT, HUH?
IT'S ALL RIGHT, WE'LL TRY AGAIN TOMORROW. AND I'LL LEAVE THE GATEWAY OPEN, LIKE ALWAYS, IN CASE YOU FIND YOUR WAY HOME OVER-NIGHT.

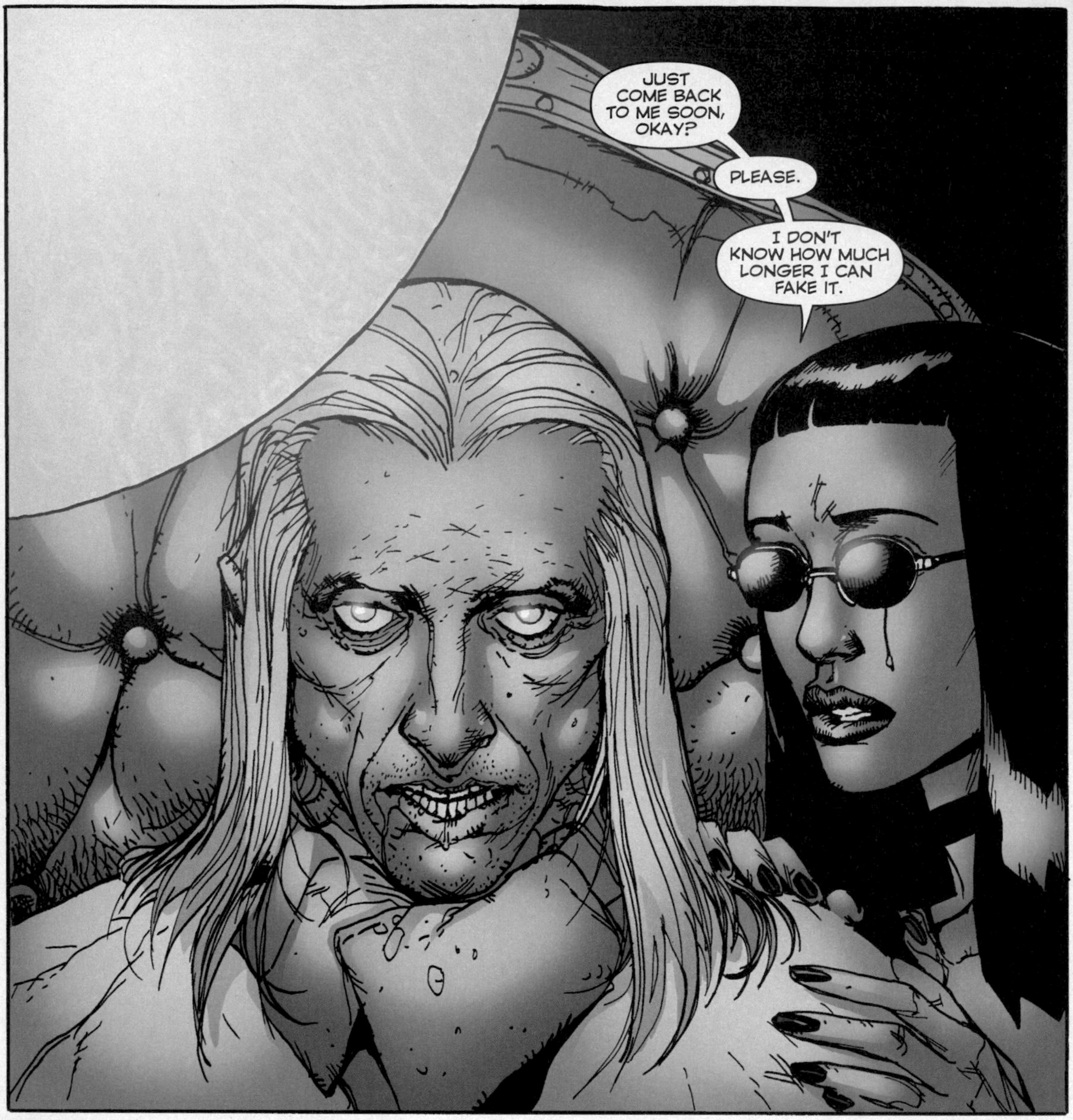
JUST COME BACK TO ME SOON, OKAY?
PLEASE.
I DON'T KNOW HOW MUCH LONGER I CAN FAKE IT.

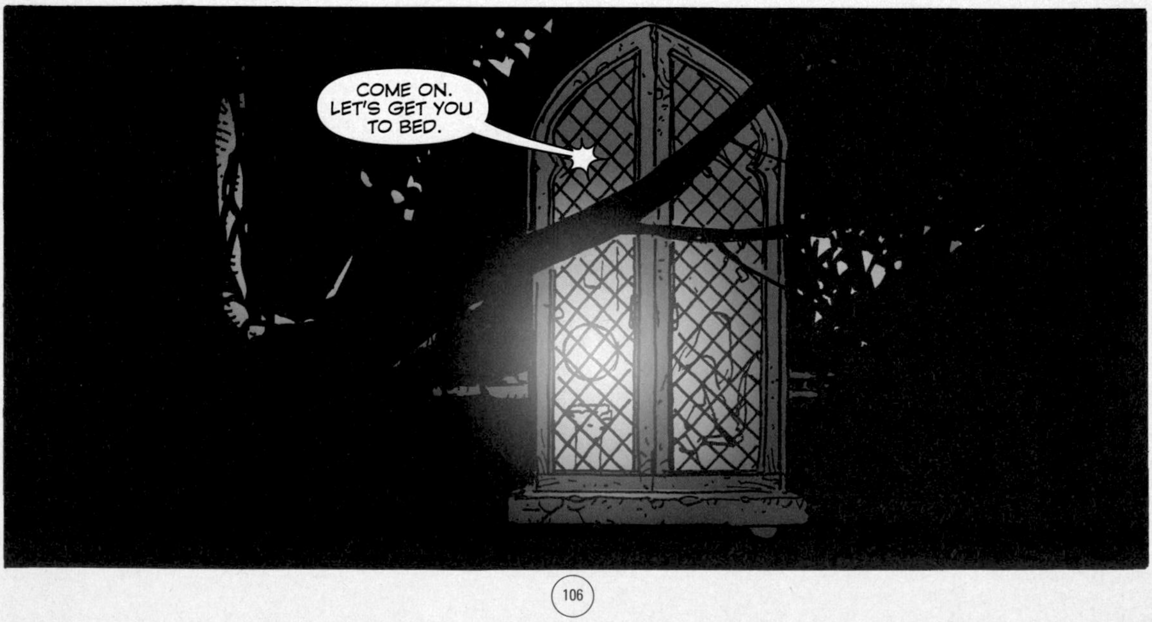
COME ON. LET'S GET YOU TO BED.

Chapter 5: A Day at the Office

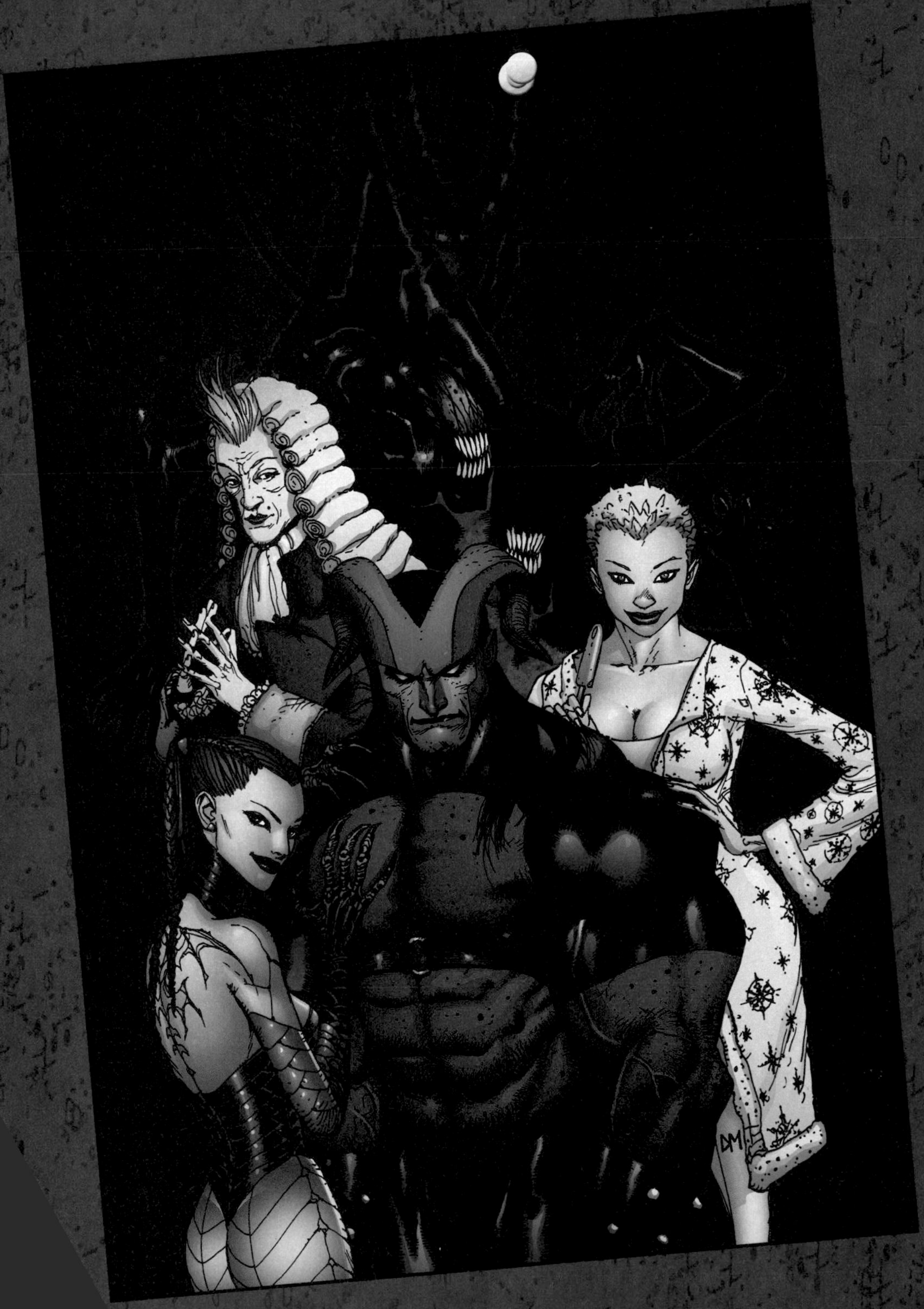

Doug Mahnke & David Baron

Variant Cover Sketches

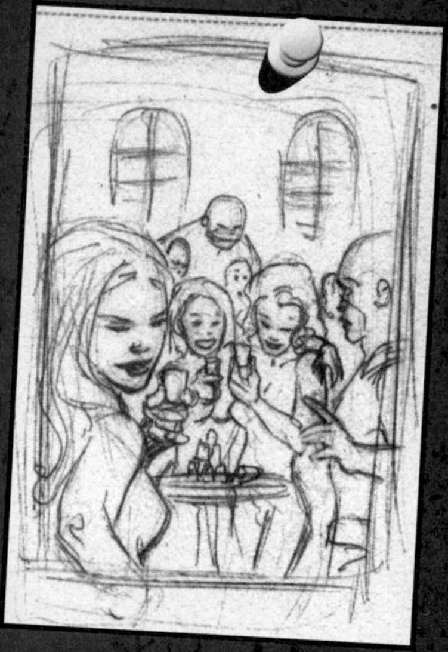

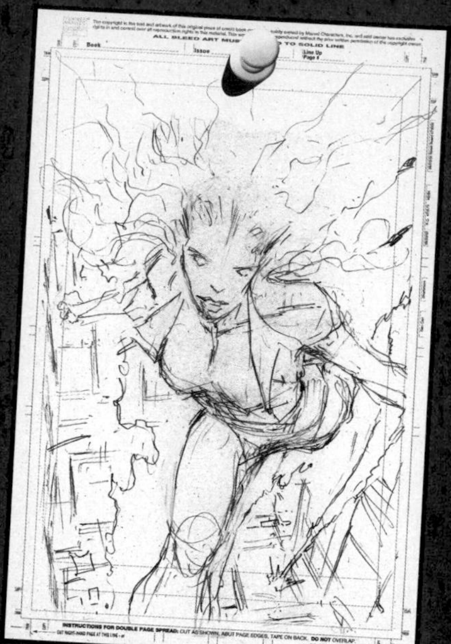

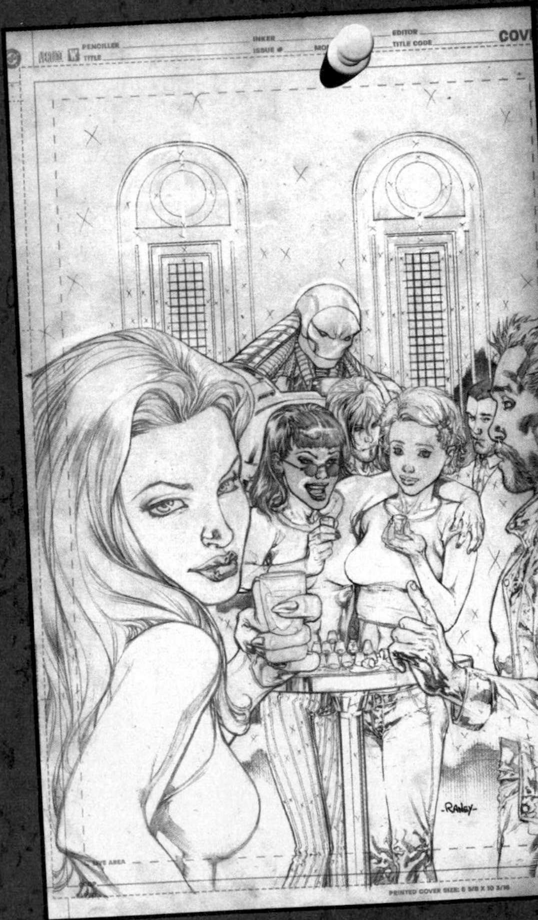
RANEY

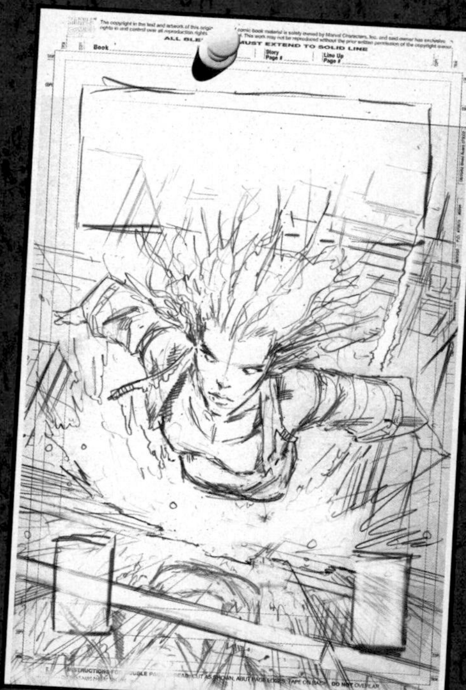

Tom Raney & Trevor Hairsine

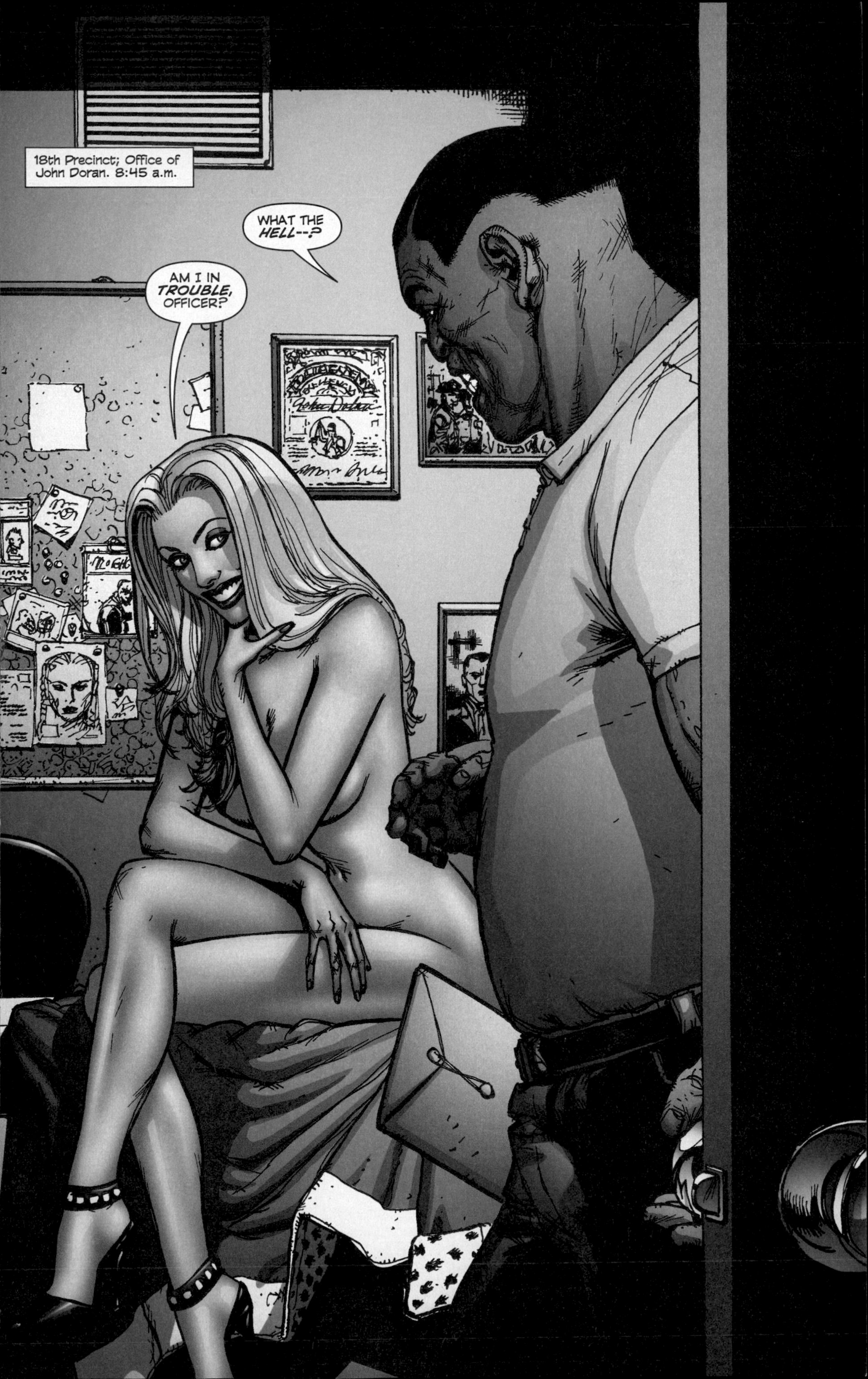
18th Precinct; Office of John Doran. 8:45 a.m.
WHAT THE HELL--?
AM I IN TROUBLE, OFFICER?

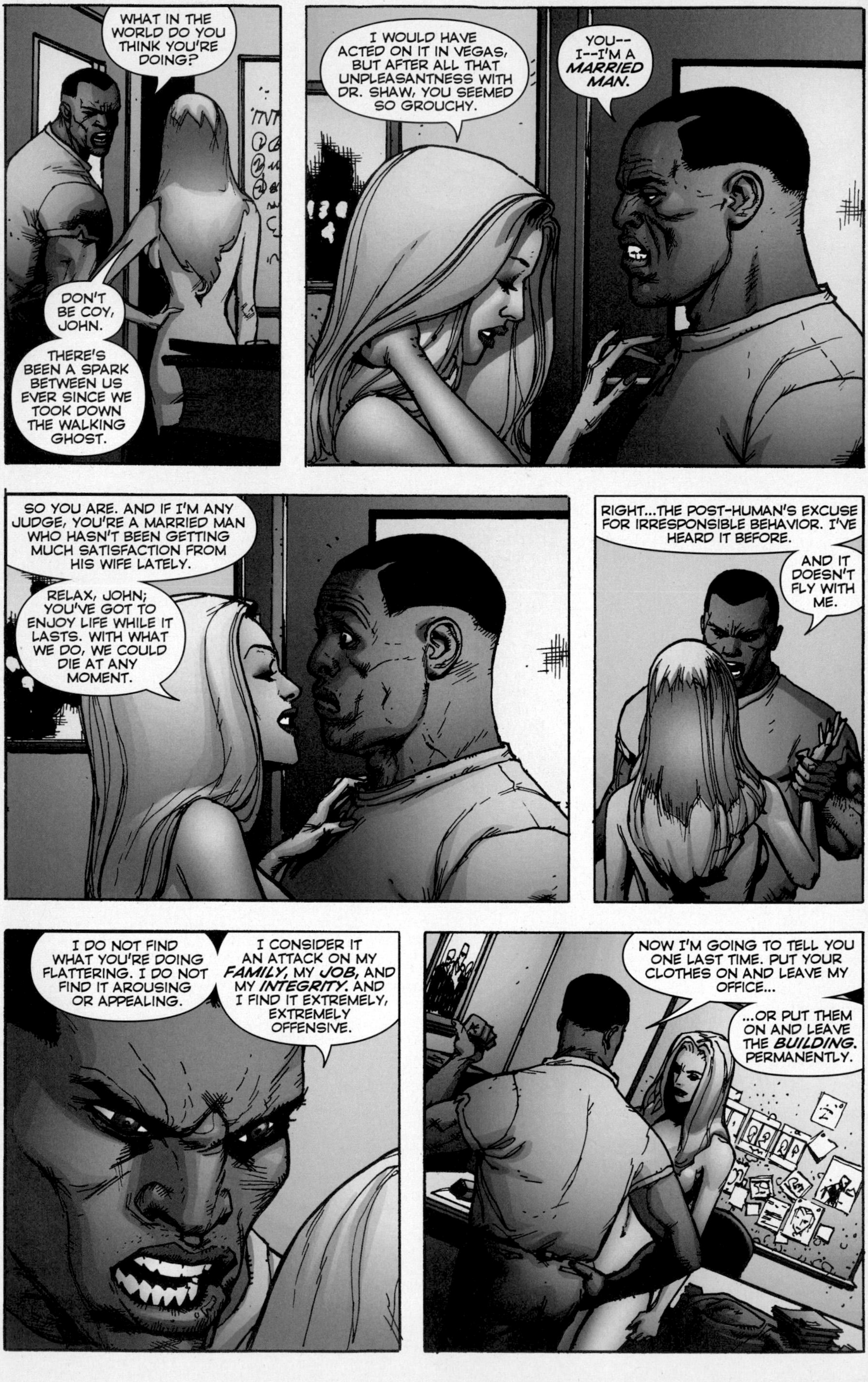
WHAT IN THE WORLD DO YOU THINK YOU'RE DOING?
DON'T BE COY, JOHN.
THERE'S BEEN A SPARK BETWEEN US EVER SINCE WE TOOK DOWN THE WALKING GHOST.
I WOULD HAVE ACTED ON IT IN VEGAS, BUT AFTER ALL THAT UNPLEASANTNESS WITH DR. SHAW, YOU SEEMED SO GROUCHY.
YOU-- I--I'M A *MARRIED MAN.*
SO YOU ARE. AND IF I'M ANY JUDGE, YOU'RE A MARRIED MAN WHO HASN'T BEEN GETTING MUCH SATISFACTION FROM HIS WIFE LATELY.
RELAX, JOHN; YOU'VE GOT TO ENJOY LIFE WHILE IT LASTS. WITH WHAT WE DO, WE COULD DIE AT ANY MOMENT.
RIGHT...THE POST-HUMAN'S EXCUSE FOR IRRESPONSIBLE BEHAVIOR. I'VE HEARD IT BEFORE.
AND IT DOESN'T FLY WITH ME.
I DO NOT FIND WHAT YOU'RE DOING FLATTERING. I DO NOT FIND IT AROUSING OR APPEALING.
I CONSIDER IT AN ATTACK ON MY *FAMILY,* MY *JOB,* AND MY *INTEGRITY.* AND I FIND IT EXTREMELY, EXTREMELY OFFENSIVE.
NOW I'M GOING TO TELL YOU ONE LAST TIME. PUT YOUR CLOTHES ON AND LEAVE MY OFFICE...
...OR PUT THEM ON AND LEAVE THE *BUILDING.* PERMANENTLY.

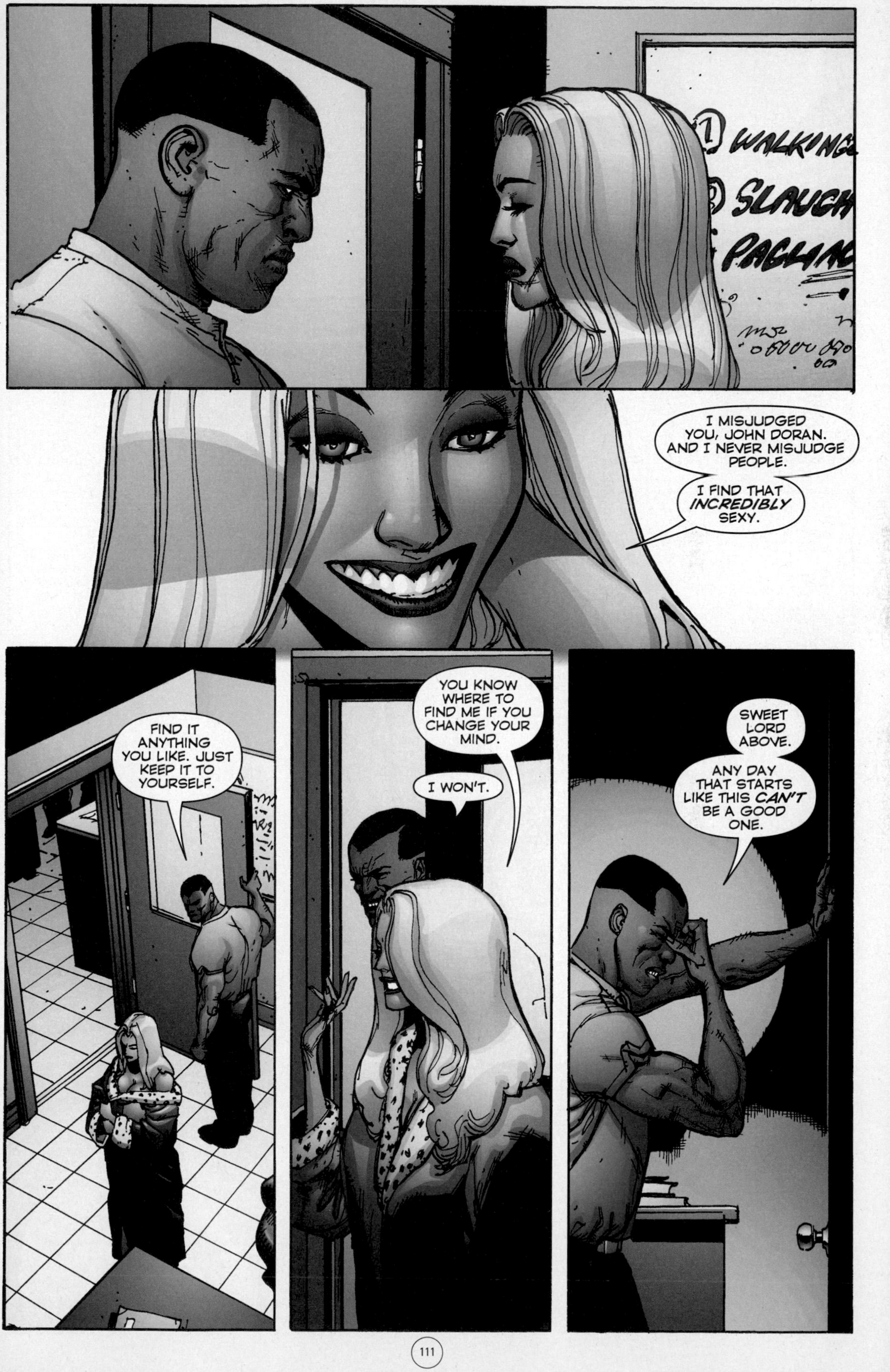
I MISJUDGED YOU, JOHN DORAN. AND I NEVER MISJUDGE PEOPLE.
I FIND THAT *INCREDIBLY* SEXY.
FIND IT ANYTHING YOU LIKE. JUST KEEP IT TO YOURSELF.
YOU KNOW WHERE TO FIND ME IF YOU CHANGE YOUR MIND.
I WON'T.
SWEET LORD ABOVE.
ANY DAY THAT STARTS LIKE THIS *CAN'T* BE A GOOD ONE.

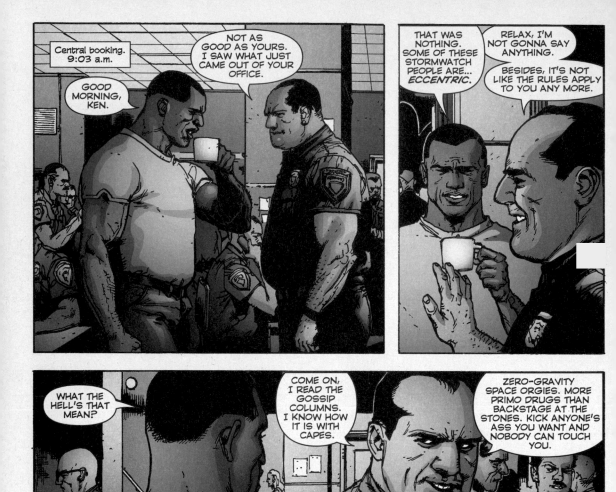

Central booking. 9:03 a.m.

GOOD MORNING, KEN.

NOT AS GOOD AS YOURS. I SAW WHAT JUST CAME OUT OF YOUR OFFICE.

THAT WAS NOTHING. SOME OF THESE STORMWATCH PEOPLE ARE... *ECCENTRIC*.

RELAX, I'M NOT GONNA SAY ANYTHING.

BESIDES, IT'S NOT LIKE THE RULES APPLY TO YOU ANY MORE.

WHAT THE HELL'S THAT MEAN?

COME ON, I READ THE GOSSIP COLUMNS. I KNOW HOW IT IS WITH CAPES.

ZERO-GRAVITY SPACE ORGIES. MORE PRIMO DRUGS THAN BACKSTAGE AT THE STONES. KICK ANYONE'S ASS YOU WANT AND NOBODY CAN TOUCH YOU.

KEN, IT'S NOT LIKE THAT. NOT WITH US.

NOT WITH *ME*.

I'M STILL DOING THE JOB, JUST LIKE ALWAYS.

SURE THING, JOHN.

I GOTTA GO, THERE'S A HORNY NAKED SUPER-CHICK WAITING FOR ME.

YOU KNOW... JUST ANOTHER DAY AT THE OFFICE.

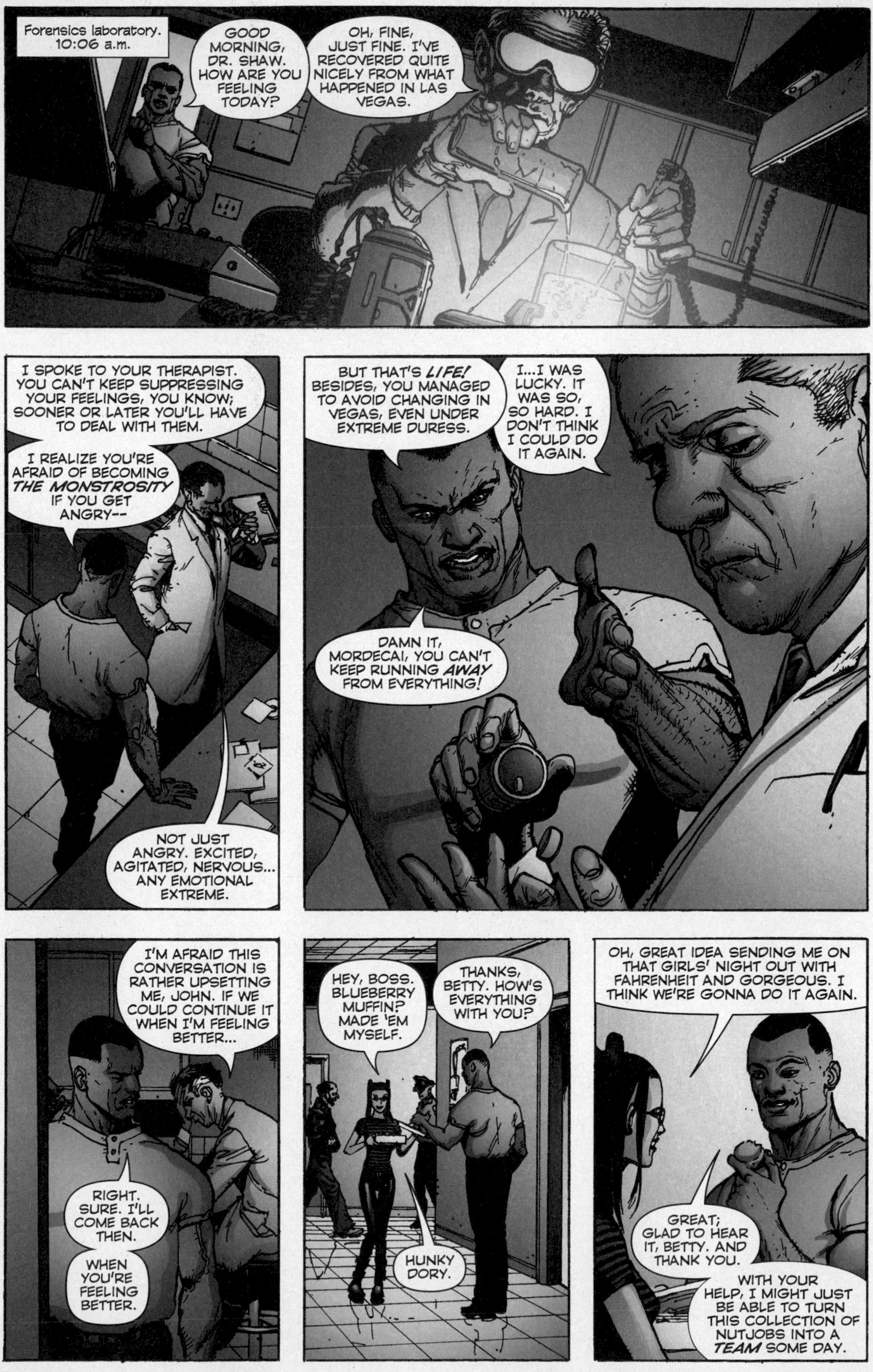
Forensics laboratory. 10:06 a.m.
GOOD MORNING, DR. SHAW. HOW ARE YOU FEELING TODAY?
OH, FINE, JUST FINE. I'VE RECOVERED QUITE NICELY FROM WHAT HAPPENED IN LAS VEGAS.
I SPOKE TO YOUR THERAPIST. YOU CAN'T KEEP SUPPRESSING YOUR FEELINGS, YOU KNOW; SOONER OR LATER YOU'LL HAVE TO DEAL WITH THEM.
I REALIZE YOU'RE AFRAID OF BECOMING THE MONSTROSITY IF YOU GET ANGRY--
NOT JUST ANGRY. EXCITED, AGITATED, NERVOUS... ANY EMOTIONAL EXTREME.
BUT THAT'S LIFE! BESIDES, YOU MANAGED TO AVOID CHANGING IN VEGAS, EVEN UNDER EXTREME DURESS.
I...I WAS LUCKY. IT WAS SO, SO HARD. I DON'T THINK I COULD DO IT AGAIN.
DAMN IT, MORDECAI, YOU CAN'T KEEP RUNNING AWAY FROM EVERYTHING!
I'M AFRAID THIS CONVERSATION IS RATHER UPSETTING ME, JOHN. IF WE COULD CONTINUE IT WHEN I'M FEELING BETTER...
RIGHT. SURE. I'LL COME BACK THEN.
WHEN YOU'RE FEELING BETTER.
HEY, BOSS. BLUEBERRY MUFFIN? MADE 'EM MYSELF.
THANKS, BETTY. HOW'S EVERYTHING WITH YOU?
HUNKY DORY.
OH, GREAT IDEA SENDING ME ON THAT GIRLS' NIGHT OUT WITH FAHRENHEIT AND GORGEOUS. I THINK WE'RE GONNA DO IT AGAIN.
GREAT; GLAD TO HEAR IT, BETTY. AND THANK YOU.
WITH YOUR HELP, I MIGHT JUST BE ABLE TO TURN THIS COLLECTION OF NUTJOBS INTO A TEAM SOME DAY.

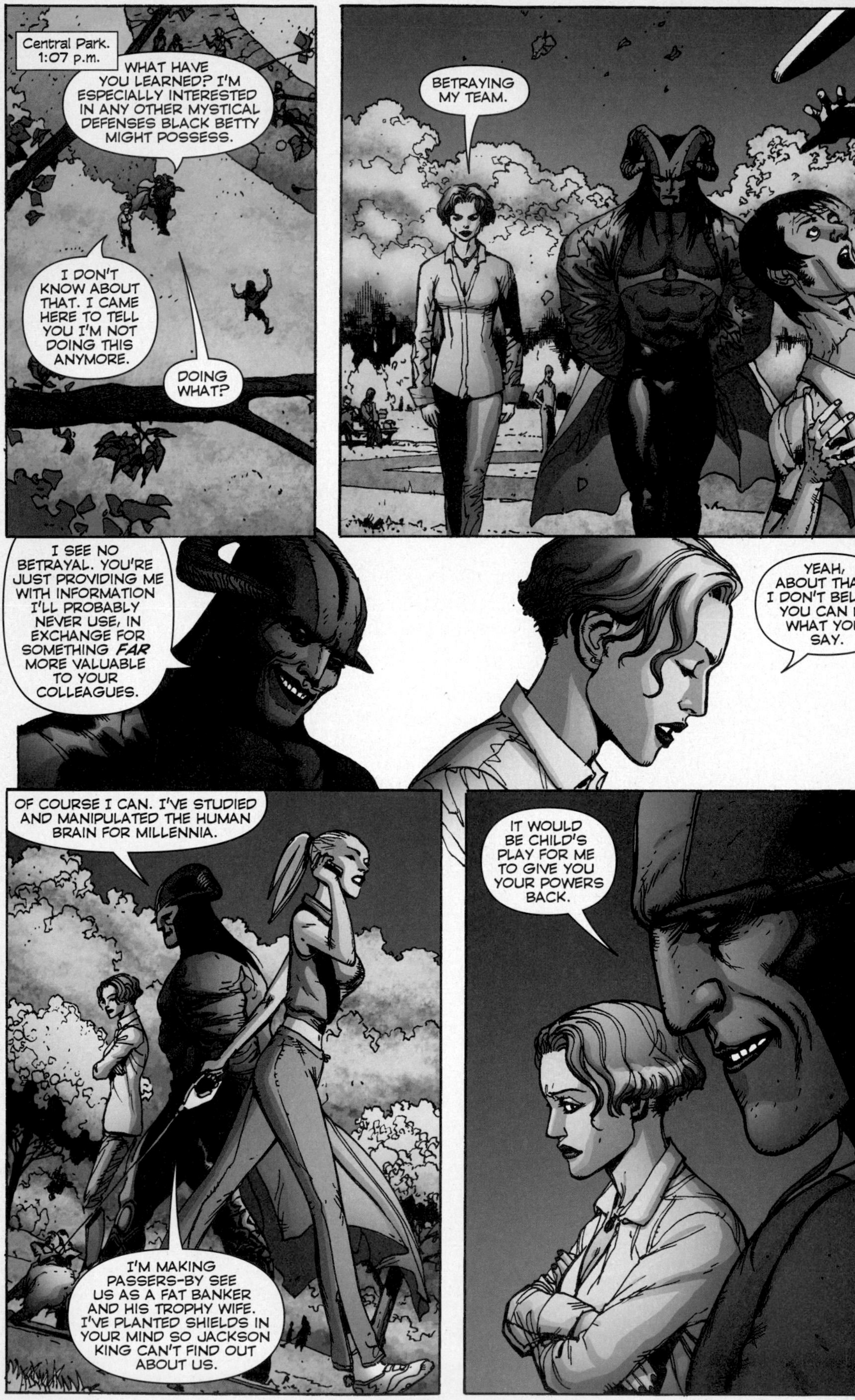
Central Park.
1:07 p.m.
WHAT HAVE YOU LEARNED? I'M ESPECIALLY INTERESTED IN ANY OTHER MYSTICAL DEFENSES BLACK BETTY MIGHT POSSESS.
I DON'T KNOW ABOUT THAT. I CAME HERE TO TELL YOU I'M NOT DOING THIS ANYMORE.
DOING WHAT?
BETRAYING MY TEAM.
I SEE NO BETRAYAL. YOU'RE JUST PROVIDING ME WITH INFORMATION I'LL PROBABLY NEVER USE, IN EXCHANGE FOR SOMETHING *FAR* MORE VALUABLE TO YOUR COLLEAGUES.
YEAH, ABOUT THAT. I DON'T BELIEVE YOU CAN DO WHAT YOU SAY.
OF COURSE I CAN. I'VE STUDIED AND MANIPULATED THE HUMAN BRAIN FOR MILLENNIA.
I'M MAKING PASSERS-BY SEE US AS A FAT BANKER AND HIS TROPHY WIFE. I'VE PLANTED SHIELDS IN YOUR MIND SO JACKSON KING CAN'T FIND OUT ABOUT US.
IT WOULD BE CHILD'S PLAY FOR ME TO GIVE YOU YOUR POWERS BACK.

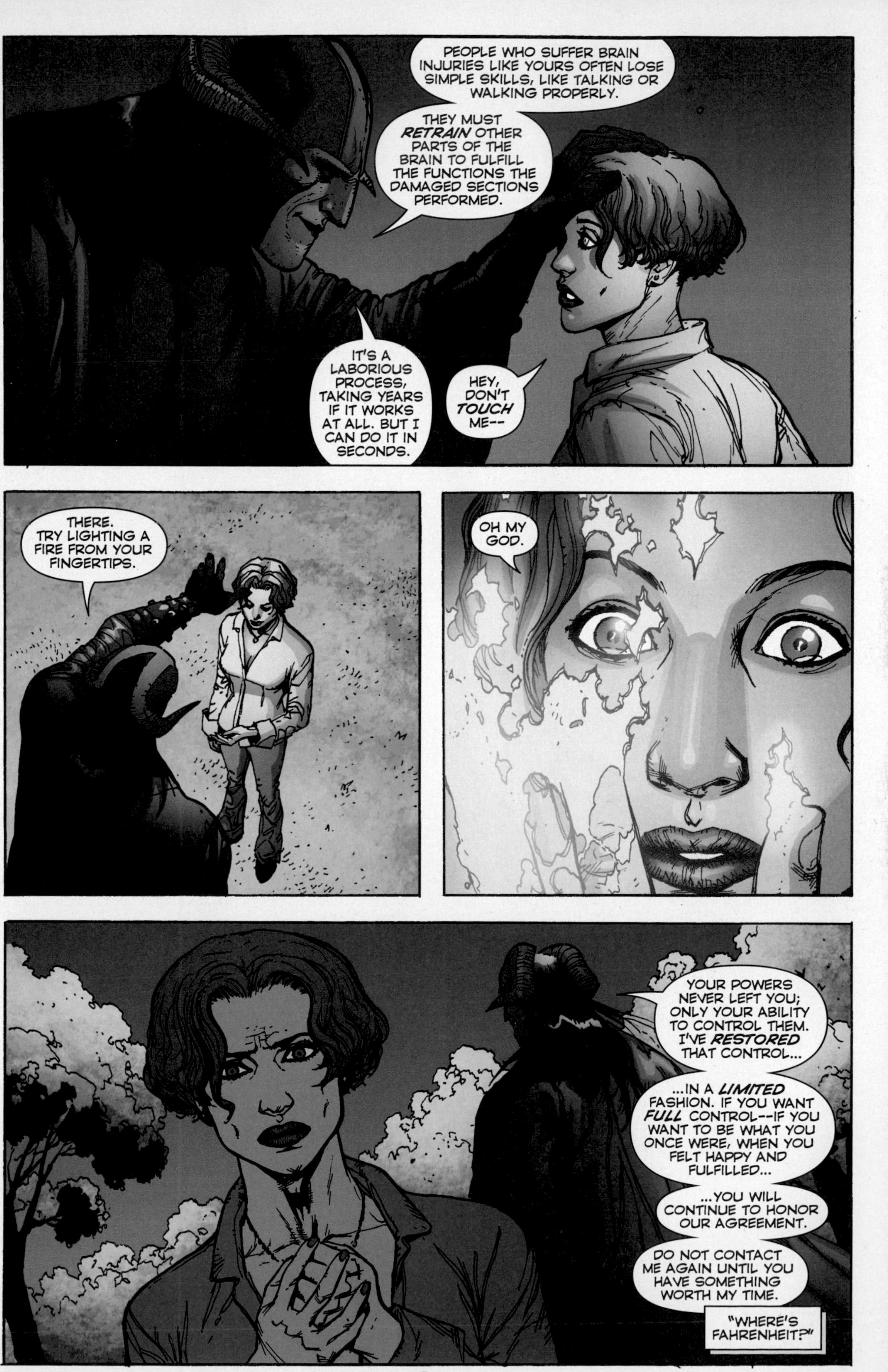
PEOPLE WHO SUFFER BRAIN INJURIES LIKE YOURS OFTEN LOSE SIMPLE SKILLS, LIKE TALKING OR WALKING PROPERLY.
THEY MUST *RETRAIN* OTHER PARTS OF THE BRAIN TO FULFILL THE FUNCTIONS THE DAMAGED SECTIONS PERFORMED.
IT'S A LABORIOUS PROCESS, TAKING YEARS IF IT WORKS AT ALL. BUT I CAN DO IT IN SECONDS.
HEY, DON'T *TOUCH* ME--
THERE. TRY LIGHTING A FIRE FROM YOUR FINGERTIPS.
OH MY GOD.
YOUR POWERS NEVER LEFT YOU; ONLY YOUR ABILITY TO CONTROL THEM. I'VE *RESTORED* THAT CONTROL...
...IN A *LIMITED* FASHION. IF YOU WANT *FULL* CONTROL--IF YOU WANT TO BE WHAT YOU ONCE WERE, WHEN YOU FELT HAPPY AND FULFILLED...
...YOU WILL CONTINUE TO HONOR OUR AGREEMENT.
DO NOT CONTACT ME AGAIN UNTIL YOU HAVE SOMETHING WORTH MY TIME.
"WHERE'S FAHRENHEIT?"

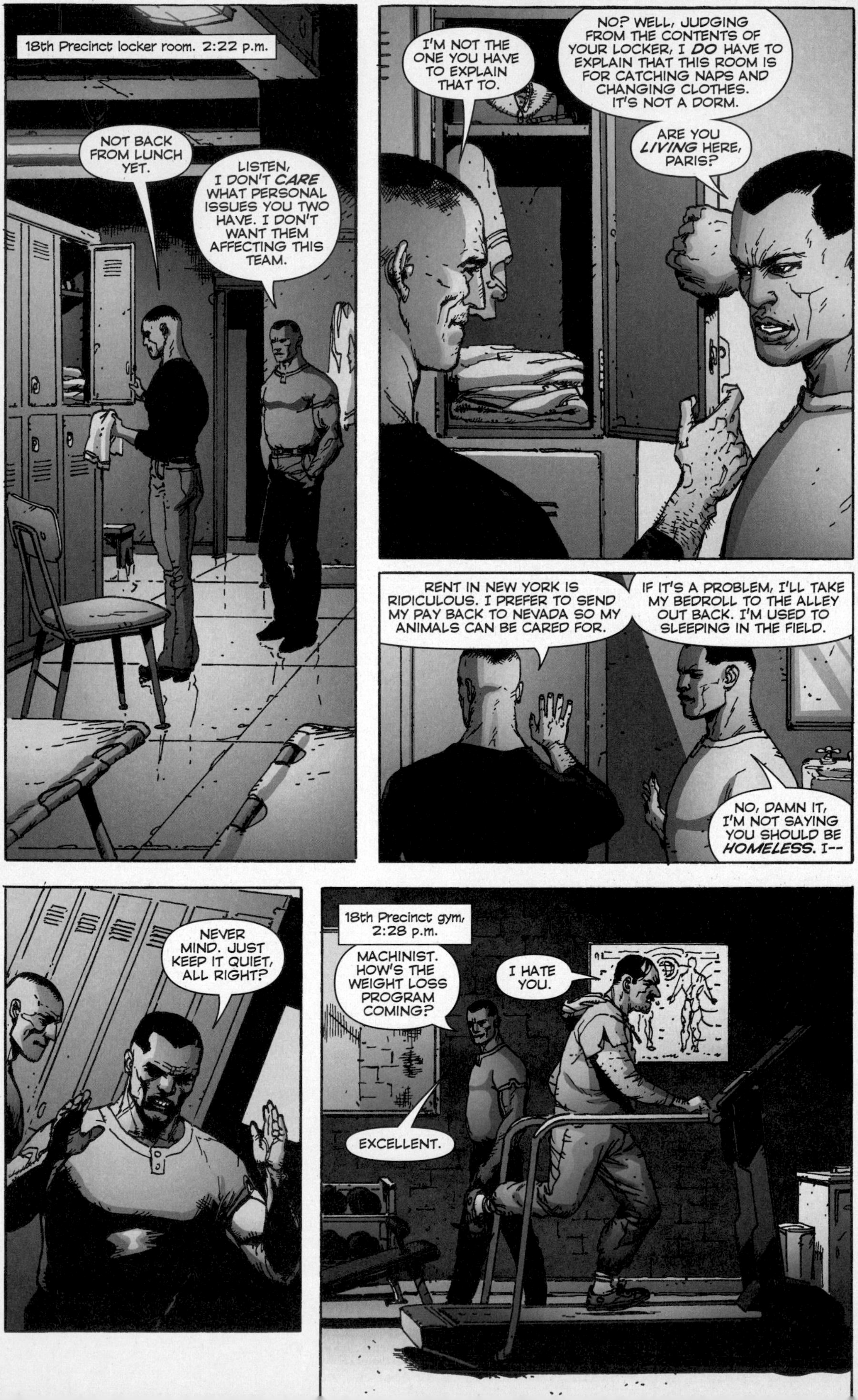
18th Precinct locker room. 2:22 p.m.
NOT BACK FROM LUNCH YET.
LISTEN, I DON'T CARE WHAT PERSONAL ISSUES YOU TWO HAVE. I DON'T WANT THEM AFFECTING THIS TEAM.
I'M NOT THE ONE YOU HAVE TO EXPLAIN THAT TO.
NO? WELL, JUDGING FROM THE CONTENTS OF YOUR LOCKER, I DO HAVE TO EXPLAIN THAT THIS ROOM IS FOR CATCHING NAPS AND CHANGING CLOTHES. IT'S NOT A DORM.
ARE YOU LIVING HERE, PARIS?
RENT IN NEW YORK IS RIDICULOUS. I PREFER TO SEND MY PAY BACK TO NEVADA SO MY ANIMALS CAN BE CARED FOR.
IF IT'S A PROBLEM, I'LL TAKE MY BEDROLL TO THE ALLEY OUT BACK. I'M USED TO SLEEPING IN THE FIELD.
NO, DAMN IT, I'M NOT SAYING YOU SHOULD BE HOMELESS. I--
NEVER MIND. JUST KEEP IT QUIET, ALL RIGHT?
18th Precinct gym, 2:28 p.m.
MACHINIST. HOW'S THE WEIGHT LOSS PROGRAM COMING?
I HATE YOU.
EXCELLENT.

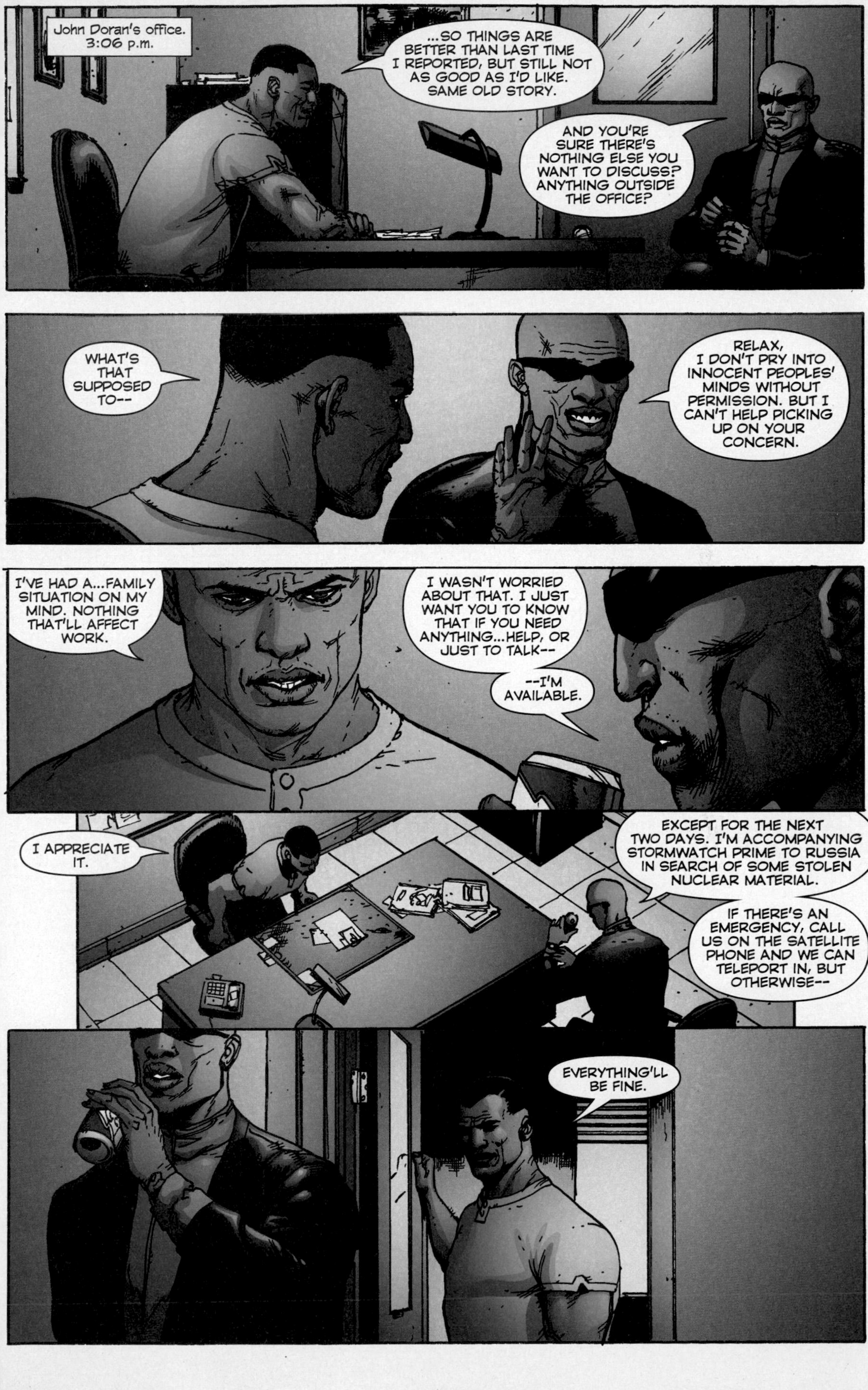
John Doran's office. 3:06 p.m.
...SO THINGS ARE BETTER THAN LAST TIME I REPORTED, BUT STILL NOT AS GOOD AS I'D LIKE. SAME OLD STORY.
AND YOU'RE SURE THERE'S NOTHING ELSE YOU WANT TO DISCUSS? ANYTHING OUTSIDE THE OFFICE?
WHAT'S THAT SUPPOSED TO--
RELAX, I DON'T PRY INTO INNOCENT PEOPLES' MINDS WITHOUT PERMISSION. BUT I CAN'T HELP PICKING UP ON YOUR CONCERN.
I'VE HAD A...FAMILY SITUATION ON MY MIND. NOTHING THAT'LL AFFECT WORK.
I WASN'T WORRIED ABOUT THAT. I JUST WANT YOU TO KNOW THAT IF YOU NEED ANYTHING...HELP, OR JUST TO TALK--
--I'M AVAILABLE.
I APPRECIATE IT.
EXCEPT FOR THE NEXT TWO DAYS. I'M ACCOMPANYING STORMWATCH PRIME TO RUSSIA IN SEARCH OF SOME STOLEN NUCLEAR MATERIAL.
IF THERE'S AN EMERGENCY, CALL US ON THE SATELLITE PHONE AND WE CAN TELEPORT IN, BUT OTHERWISE--
EVERYTHING'LL BE FINE.

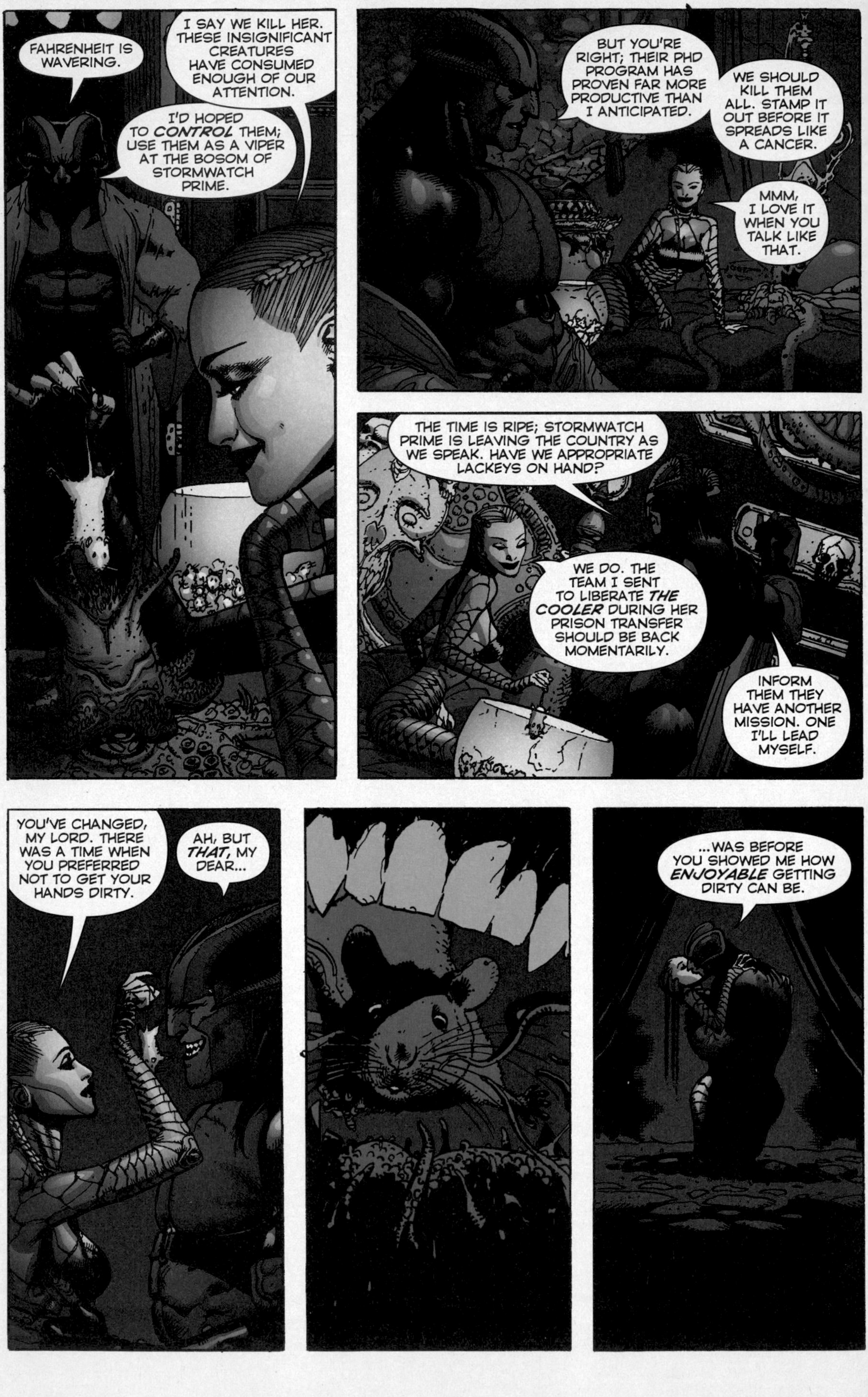
FAHRENHEIT IS WAVERING.
I SAY WE KILL HER. THESE INSIGNIFICANT CREATURES HAVE CONSUMED ENOUGH OF OUR ATTENTION.
I'D HOPED TO CONTROL THEM; USE THEM AS A VIPER AT THE BOSOM OF STORMWATCH PRIME.
BUT YOU'RE RIGHT; THEIR PHD PROGRAM HAS PROVEN FAR MORE PRODUCTIVE THAN I ANTICIPATED.
WE SHOULD KILL THEM ALL. STAMP IT OUT BEFORE IT SPREADS LIKE A CANCER.
MMM, I LOVE IT WHEN YOU TALK LIKE THAT.
THE TIME IS RIPE; STORMWATCH PRIME IS LEAVING THE COUNTRY AS WE SPEAK. HAVE WE APPROPRIATE LACKEYS ON HAND?
WE DO. THE TEAM I SENT TO LIBERATE THE COOLER DURING HER PRISON TRANSFER SHOULD BE BACK MOMENTARILY.
INFORM THEM THEY HAVE ANOTHER MISSION. ONE I'LL LEAD MYSELF.
YOU'VE CHANGED, MY LORD. THERE WAS A TIME WHEN YOU PREFERRED NOT TO GET YOUR HANDS DIRTY.
AH, BUT THAT, MY DEAR...
...WAS BEFORE YOU SHOWED ME HOW ENJOYABLE GETTING DIRTY CAN BE.

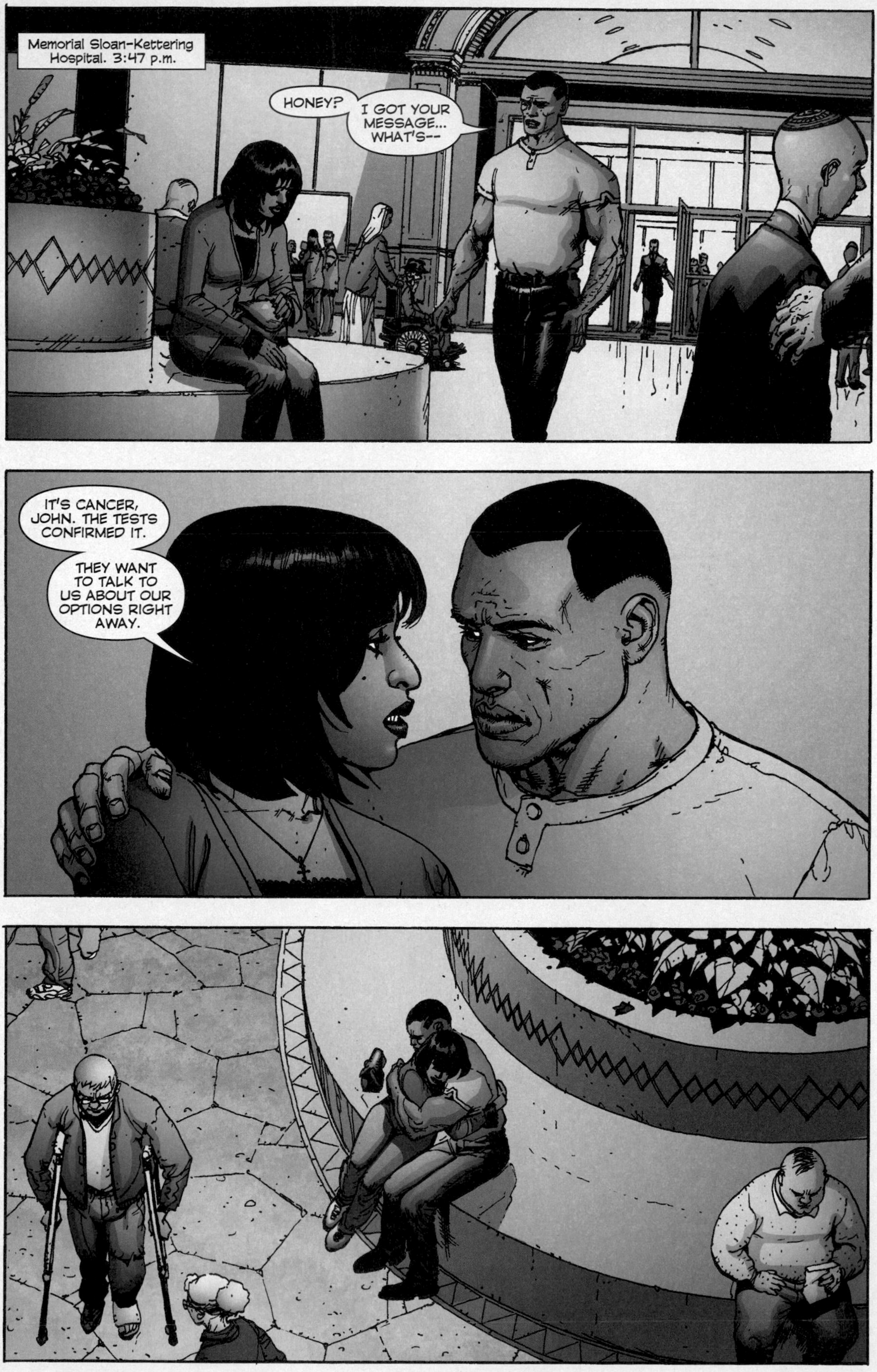
Memorial Sloan-Kettering Hospital. 3:47 p.m.
HONEY?
I GOT YOUR MESSAGE... WHAT'S--
IT'S CANCER, JOHN. THE TESTS CONFIRMED IT.
THEY WANT TO TALK TO US ABOUT OUR OPTIONS RIGHT AWAY.

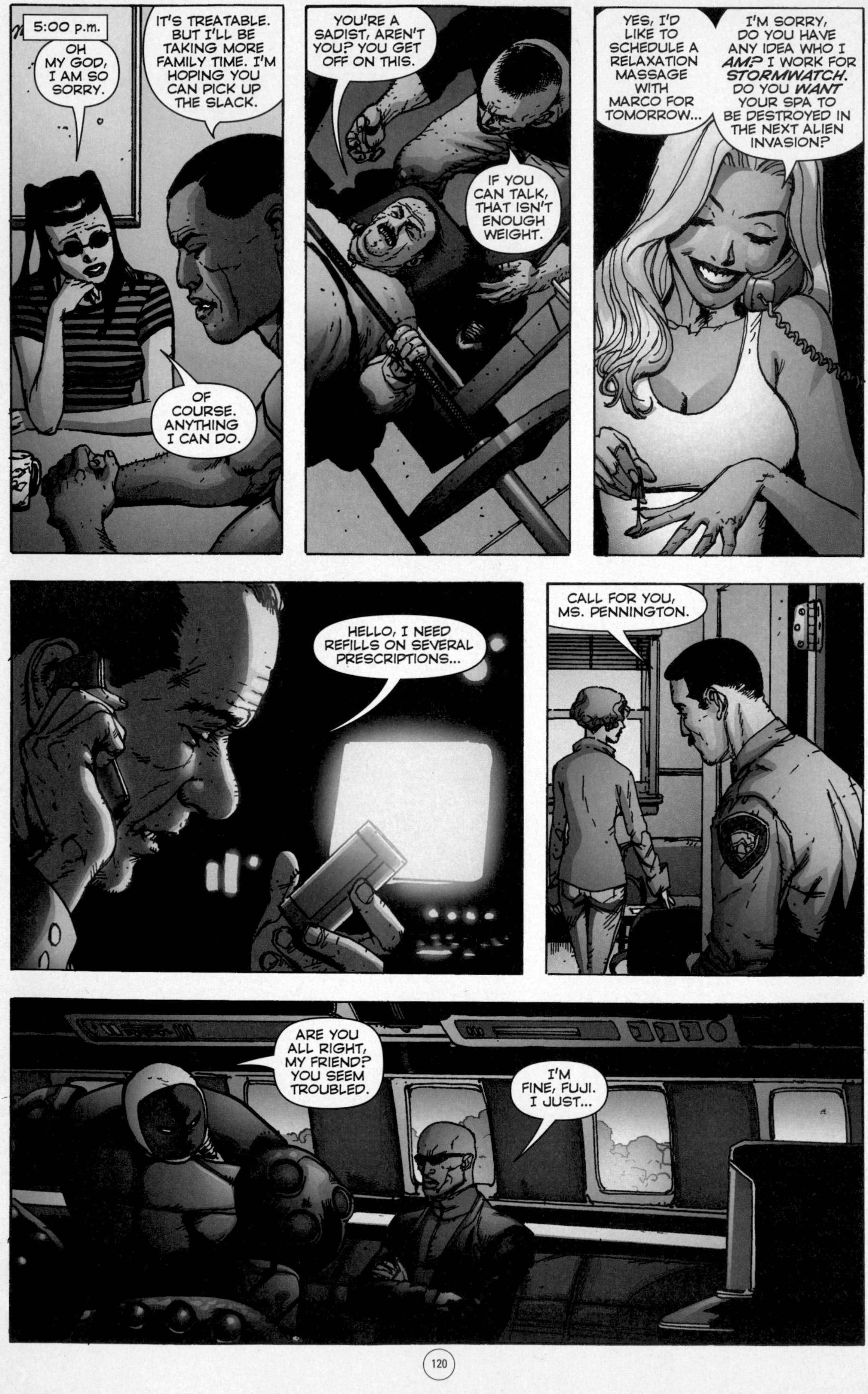
5:00 p.m.
OH MY GOD, I AM SO SORRY.
IT'S TREATABLE. BUT I'LL BE TAKING MORE FAMILY TIME. I'M HOPING YOU CAN PICK UP THE SLACK.
OF COURSE. ANYTHING I CAN DO.
YOU'RE A SADIST, AREN'T YOU? YOU GET OFF ON THIS.
IF YOU CAN TALK, THAT ISN'T ENOUGH WEIGHT.
YES, I'D LIKE TO SCHEDULE A RELAXATION MASSAGE WITH MARCO FOR TOMORROW...
I'M SORRY, DO YOU HAVE ANY IDEA WHO I AM? I WORK FOR STORMWATCH. DO YOU WANT YOUR SPA TO BE DESTROYED IN THE NEXT ALIEN INVASION?
HELLO, I NEED REFILLS ON SEVERAL PRESCRIPTIONS...
CALL FOR YOU, MS. PENNINGTON.
ARE YOU ALL RIGHT, MY FRIEND? YOU SEEM TROUBLED.
I'M FINE, FUJI. I JUST...

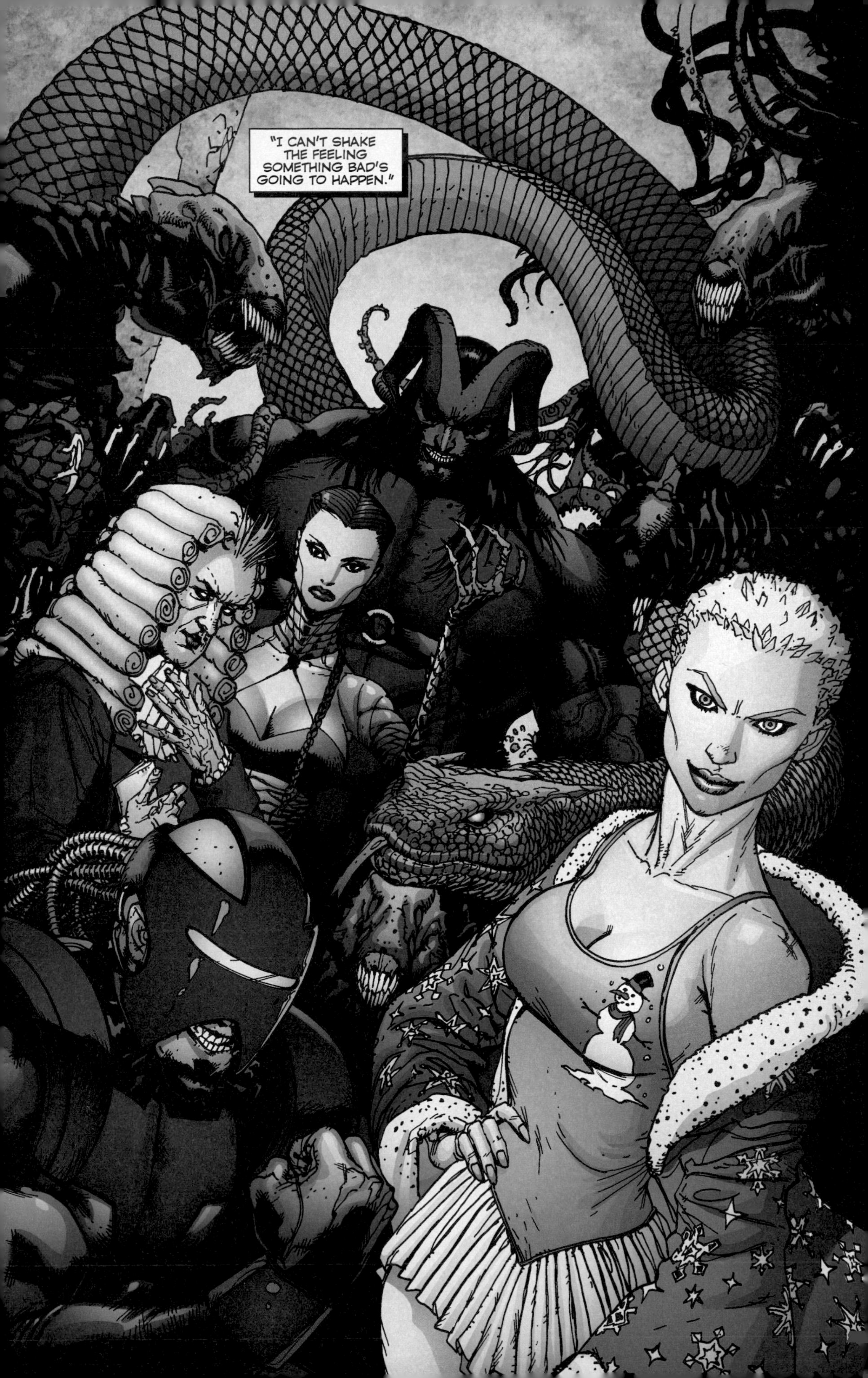
"I CAN'T SHAKE THE FEELING SOMETHING BAD'S GOING TO HAPPEN."

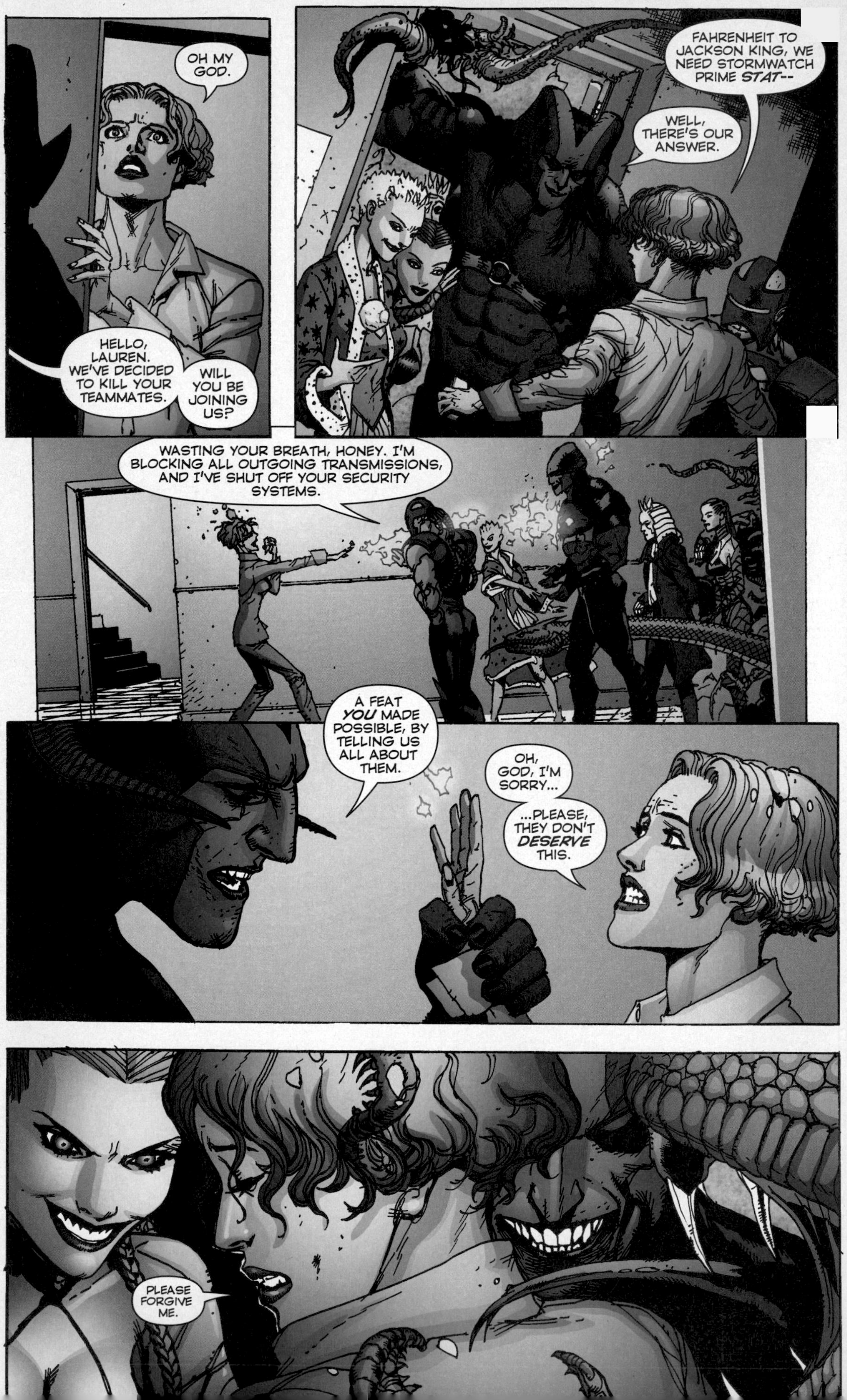
OH MY GOD.
HELLO, LAUREN. WE'VE DECIDED TO KILL YOUR TEAMMATES.
WILL YOU BE JOINING US?
FAHRENHEIT TO JACKSON KING, WE NEED STORMWATCH PRIME STAT--
WELL, THERE'S OUR ANSWER.
WASTING YOUR BREATH, HONEY. I'M BLOCKING ALL OUTGOING TRANSMISSIONS, AND I'VE SHUT OFF YOUR SECURITY SYSTEMS.
A FEAT YOU MADE POSSIBLE, BY TELLING US ALL ABOUT THEM.
OH, GOD, I'M SORRY...
...PLEASE, THEY DON'T DESERVE THIS.
PLEASE FORGIVE ME.

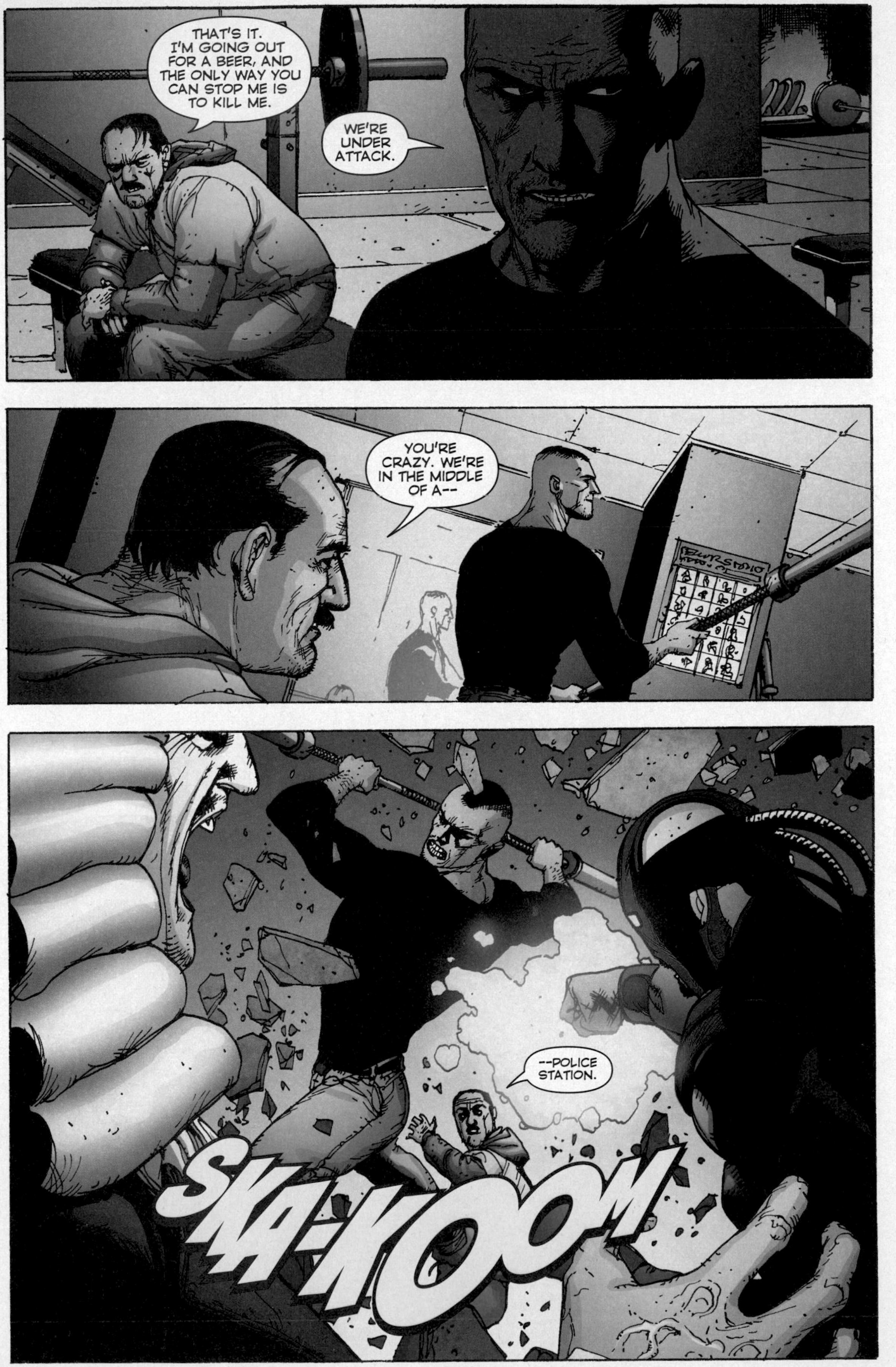
THAT'S IT. I'M GOING OUT FOR A BEER, AND THE ONLY WAY YOU CAN STOP ME IS TO KILL ME.
WE'RE UNDER ATTACK.
YOU'RE CRAZY. WE'RE IN THE MIDDLE OF A--
--POLICE STATION.
SKA-KOOM

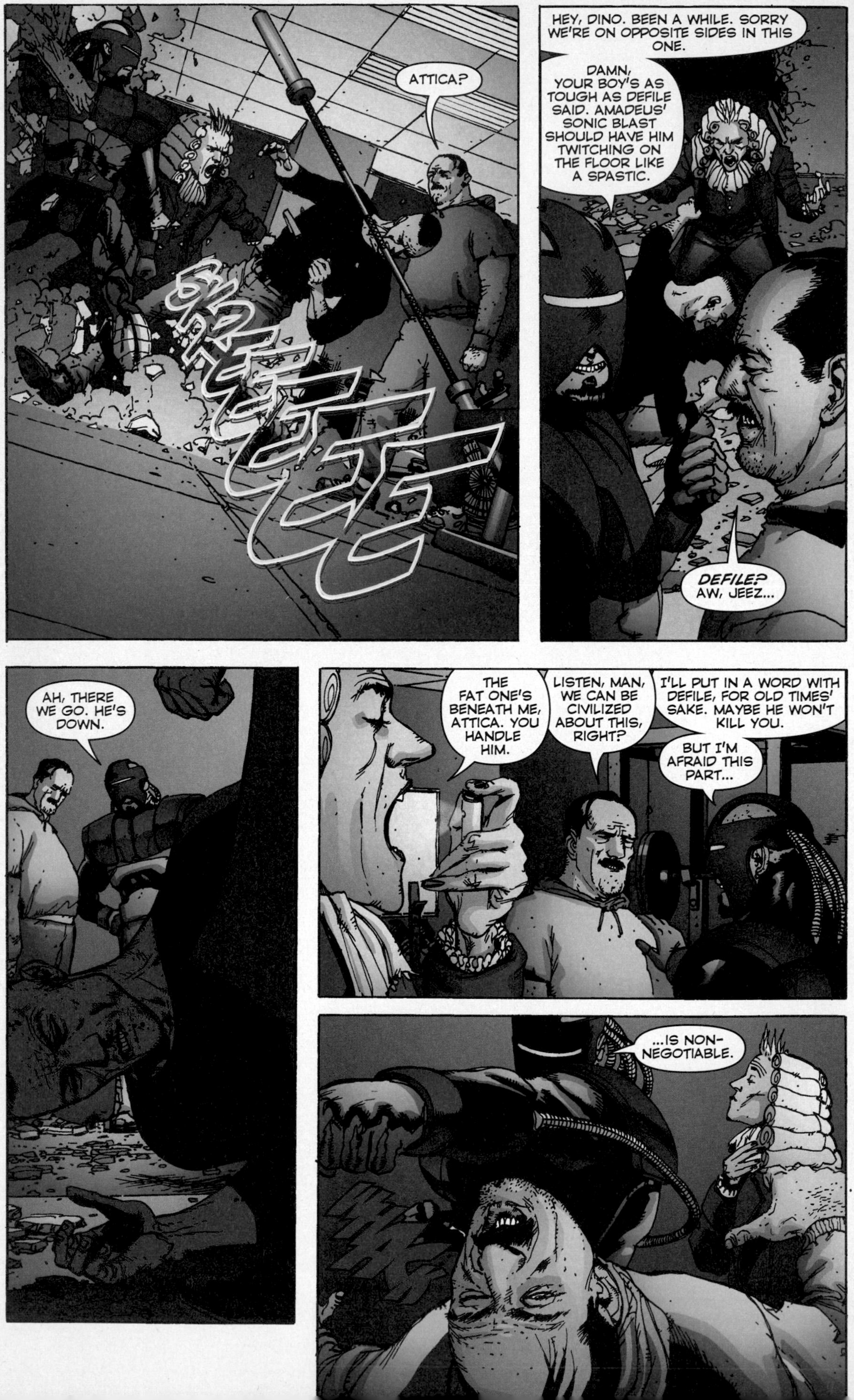
ATTICA?
HEY, DINO. BEEN A WHILE. SORRY WE'RE ON OPPOSITE SIDES IN THIS ONE.
DAMN, YOUR BOY'S AS TOUGH AS DEFILE SAID. AMADEUS' SONIC BLAST SHOULD HAVE HIM TWITCHING ON THE FLOOR LIKE A SPASTIC.
DEFILE? AW, JEEZ...
AH, THERE WE GO. HE'S DOWN.
THE FAT ONE'S BENEATH ME, ATTICA. YOU HANDLE HIM.
LISTEN, MAN, WE CAN BE CIVILIZED ABOUT THIS, RIGHT?
I'LL PUT IN A WORD WITH DEFILE, FOR OLD TIMES' SAKE. MAYBE HE WON'T KILL YOU.
BUT I'M AFRAID THIS PART...
...IS NON-NEGOTIABLE.

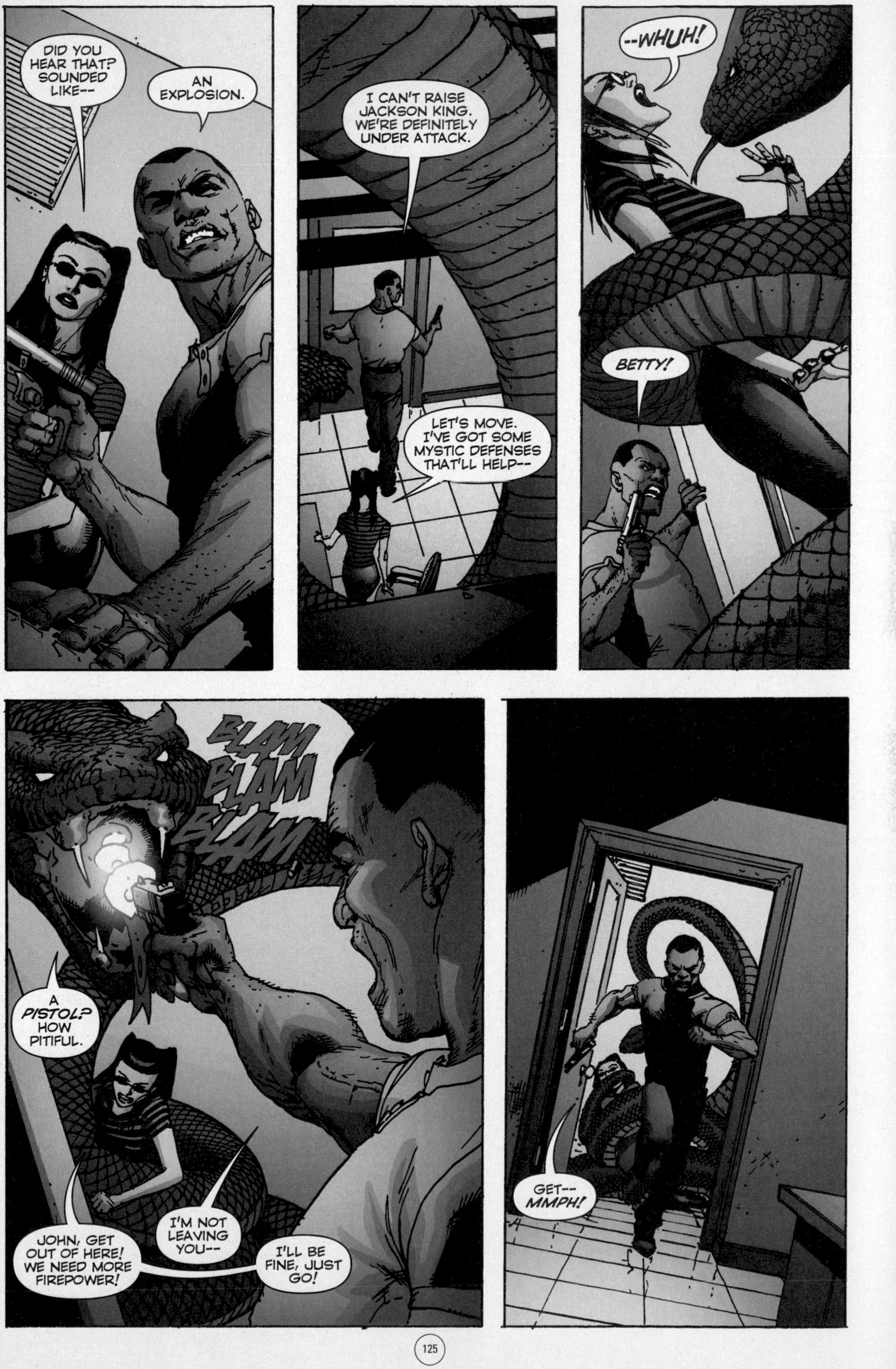
DID YOU HEAR THAT? SOUNDED LIKE--
AN EXPLOSION.
I CAN'T RAISE JACKSON KING. WE'RE DEFINITELY UNDER ATTACK.
LET'S MOVE. I'VE GOT SOME MYSTIC DEFENSES THAT'LL HELP--
--WHUH!
BETTY!
BLAM BLAM BLAM
A PISTOL? HOW PITIFUL.
JOHN, GET OUT OF HERE! WE NEED MORE FIREPOWER!
I'M NOT LEAVING YOU--
I'LL BE FINE, JUST GO!
GET-- MMPH!

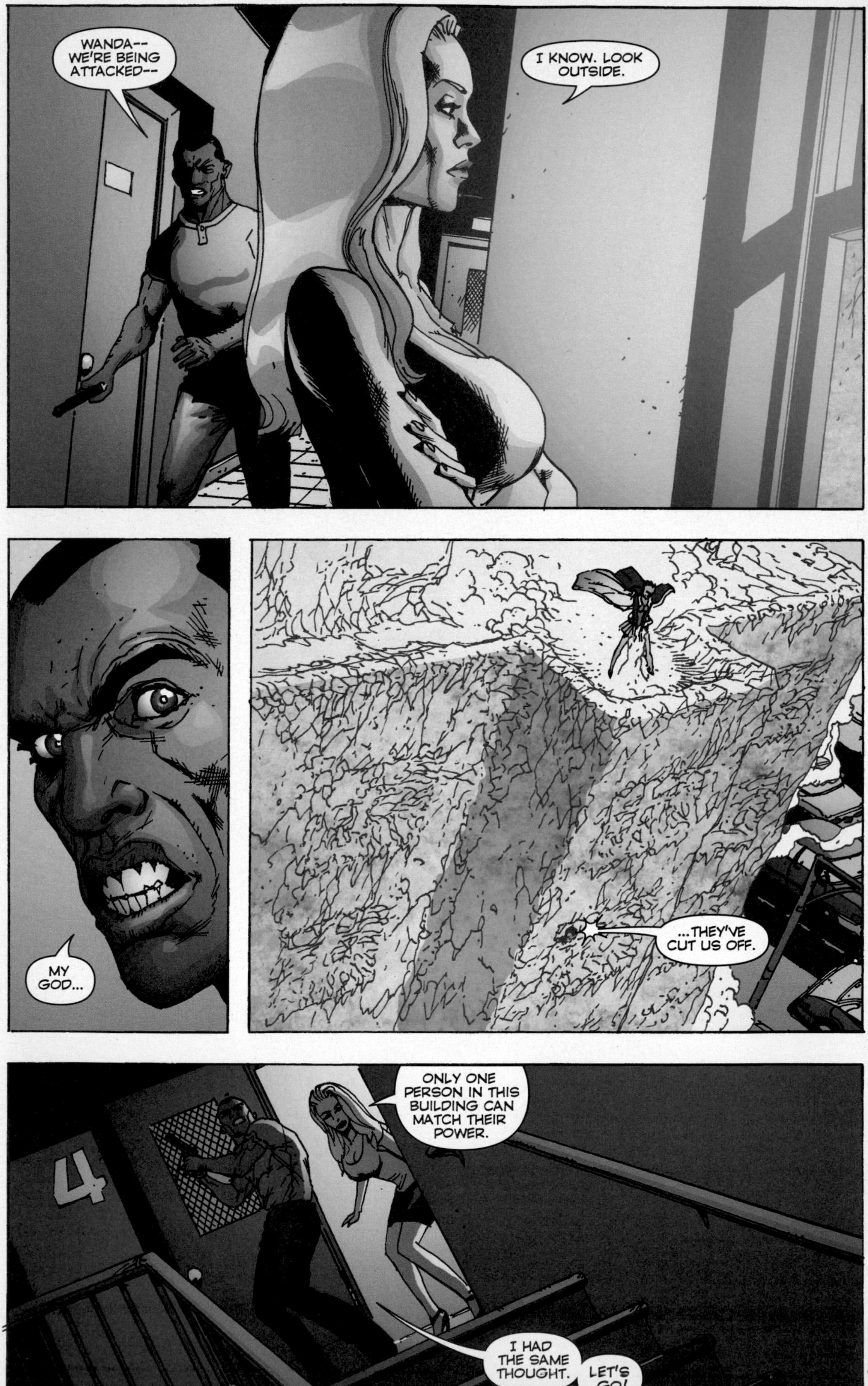
WANDA-- WE'RE BEING ATTACKED--
I KNOW. LOOK OUTSIDE.
MY GOD...
...THEY'VE CUT US OFF.
ONLY ONE PERSON IN THIS BUILDING CAN MATCH THEIR POWER.
I HAD THE SAME THOUGHT.
LET'S GO!
4

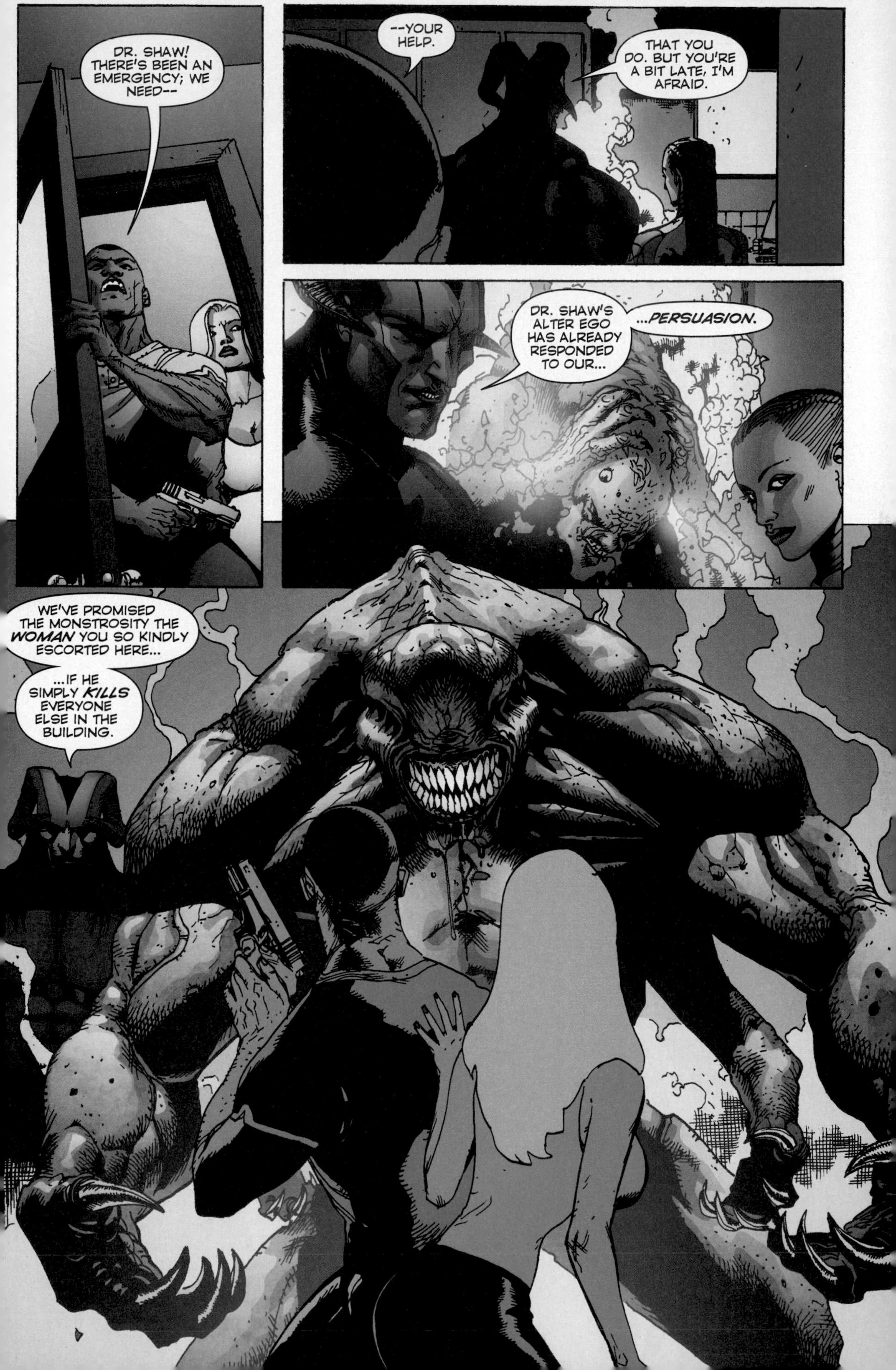
DR. SHAW! THERE'S BEEN AN EMERGENCY; WE NEED--
--YOUR HELP.
THAT YOU DO. BUT YOU'RE A BIT LATE, I'M AFRAID.
DR. SHAW'S ALTER EGO HAS ALREADY RESPONDED TO OUR...
...PERSUASION.
WE'VE PROMISED THE MONSTROSITY THE WOMAN YOU SO KINDLY ESCORTED HERE...
...IF HE SIMPLY KILLS EVERYONE ELSE IN THE BUILDING.

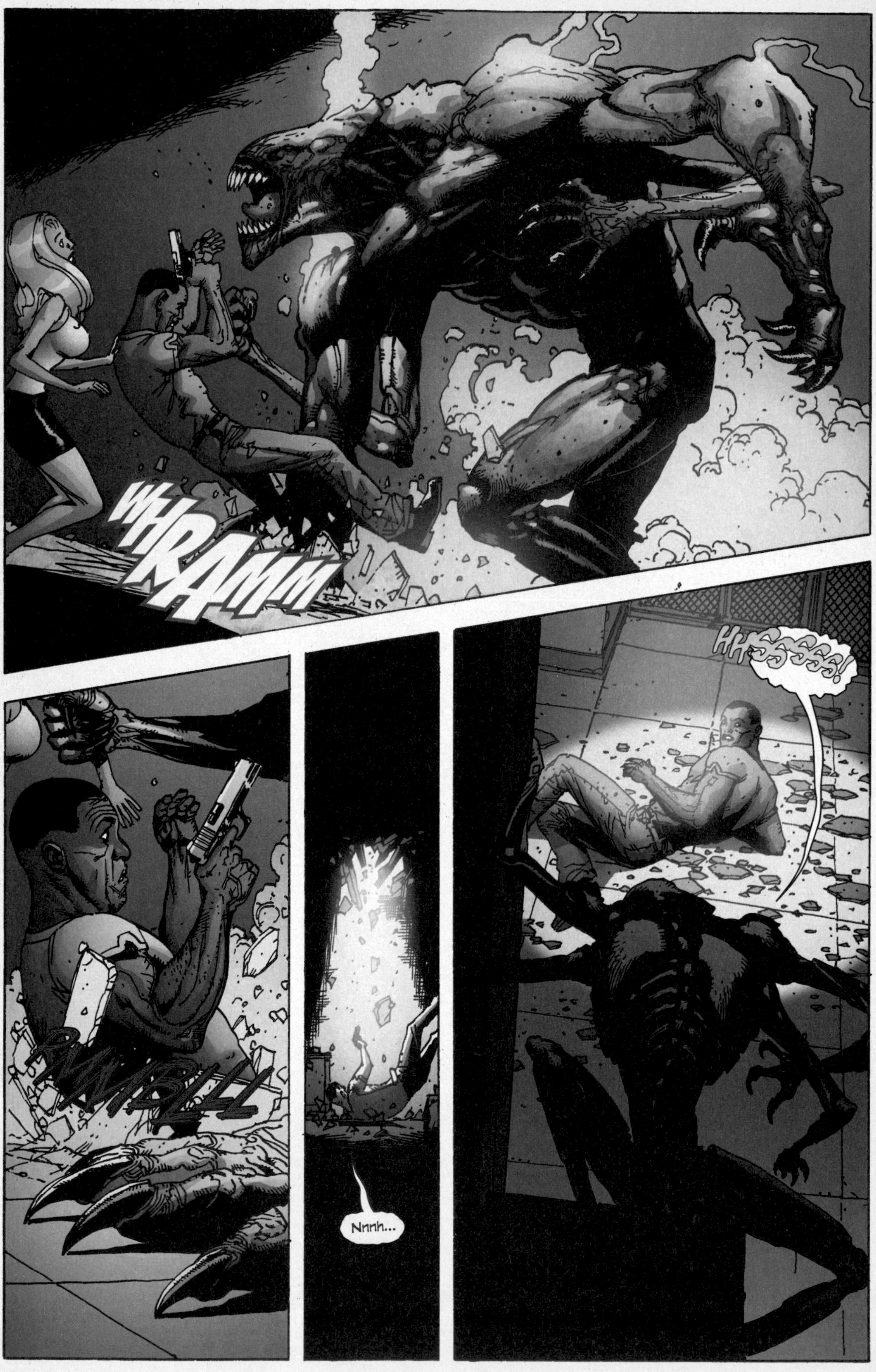
WHRAMM
RMMBLLL
Nnnh...
HHSSSSS!

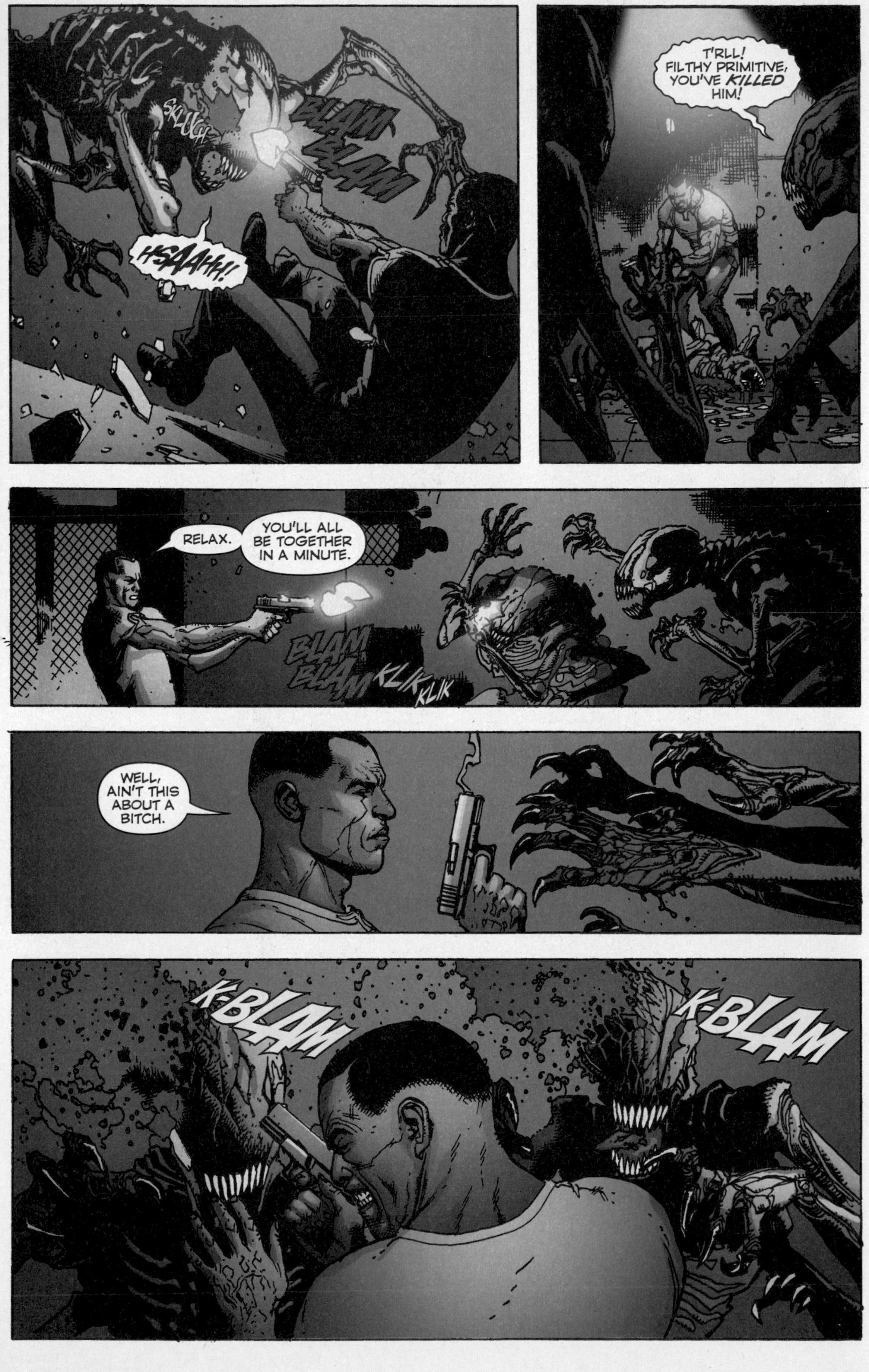
SKLUCH
BLAM BLAM
HSAAHH!
T'RLL! FILTHY PRIMITIVE, YOU'VE KILLED HIM!
RELAX.
YOU'LL ALL BE TOGETHER IN A MINUTE.
BLAM BLAM KLIK KLIK
WELL, AIN'T THIS ABOUT A BITCH.
K-BLAM
K-BLAM

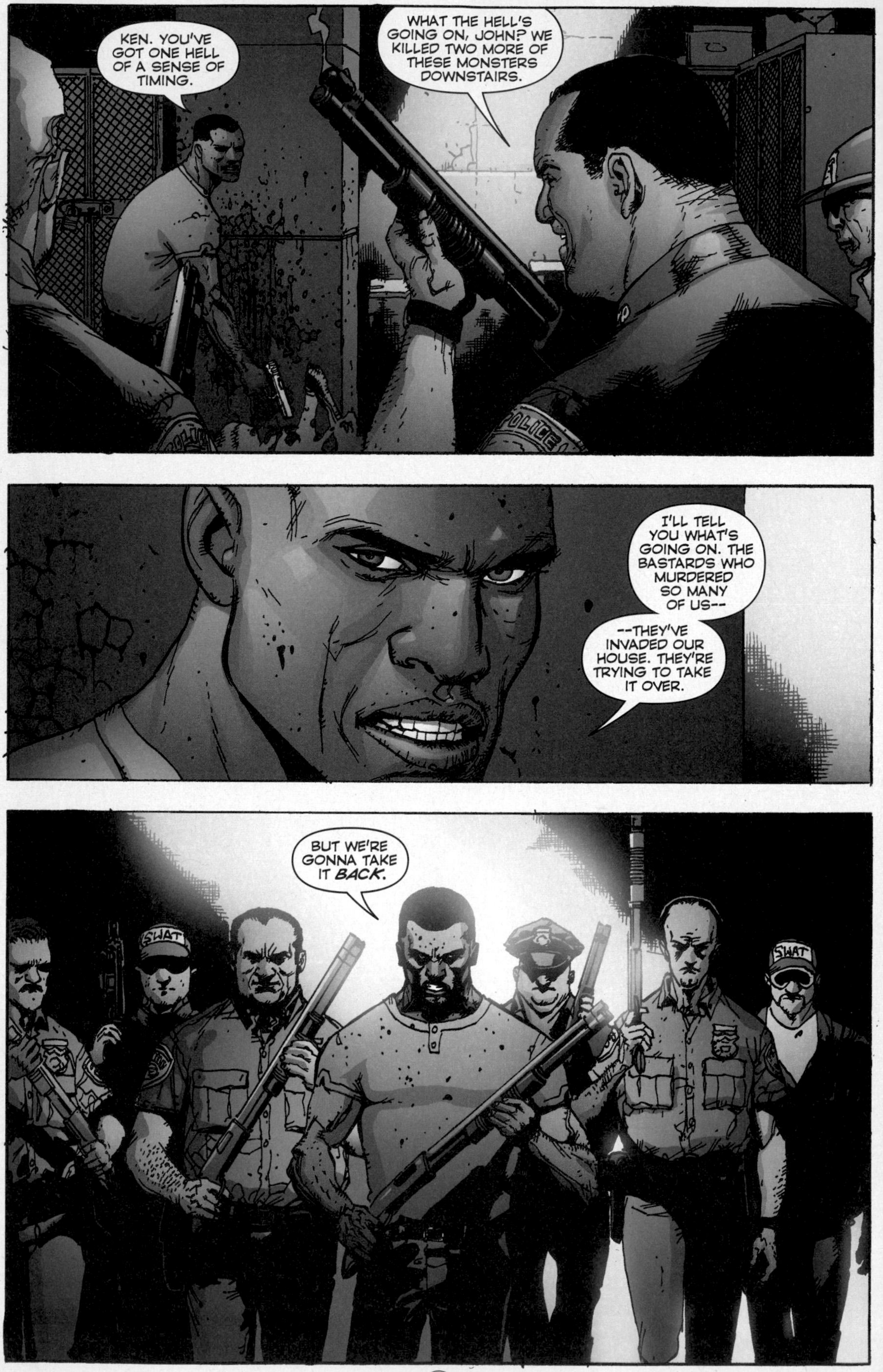
KEN. YOU'VE GOT ONE HELL OF A SENSE OF TIMING.
WHAT THE HELL'S GOING ON, JOHN? WE KILLED TWO MORE OF THESE MONSTERS DOWNSTAIRS.
I'LL TELL YOU WHAT'S GOING ON. THE BASTARDS WHO MURDERED SO MANY OF US--
--THEY'VE INVADED OUR HOUSE. THEY'RE TRYING TO TAKE IT OVER.
BUT WE'RE GONNA TAKE IT *BACK*.
SWAT
SWAT

Chapter 6: Assault on Precinct 13

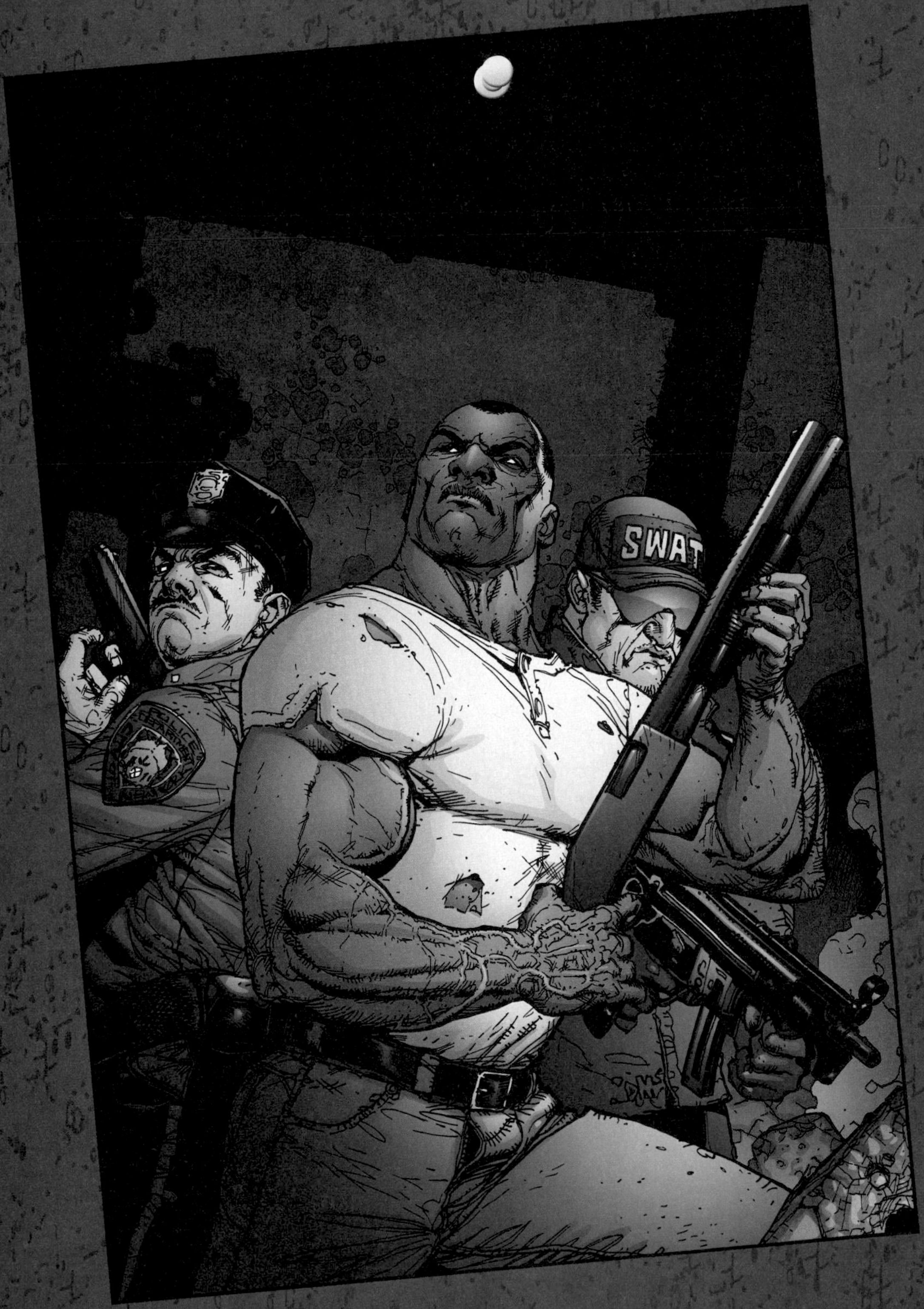

SWAT

Doug Mahnke & David Baron

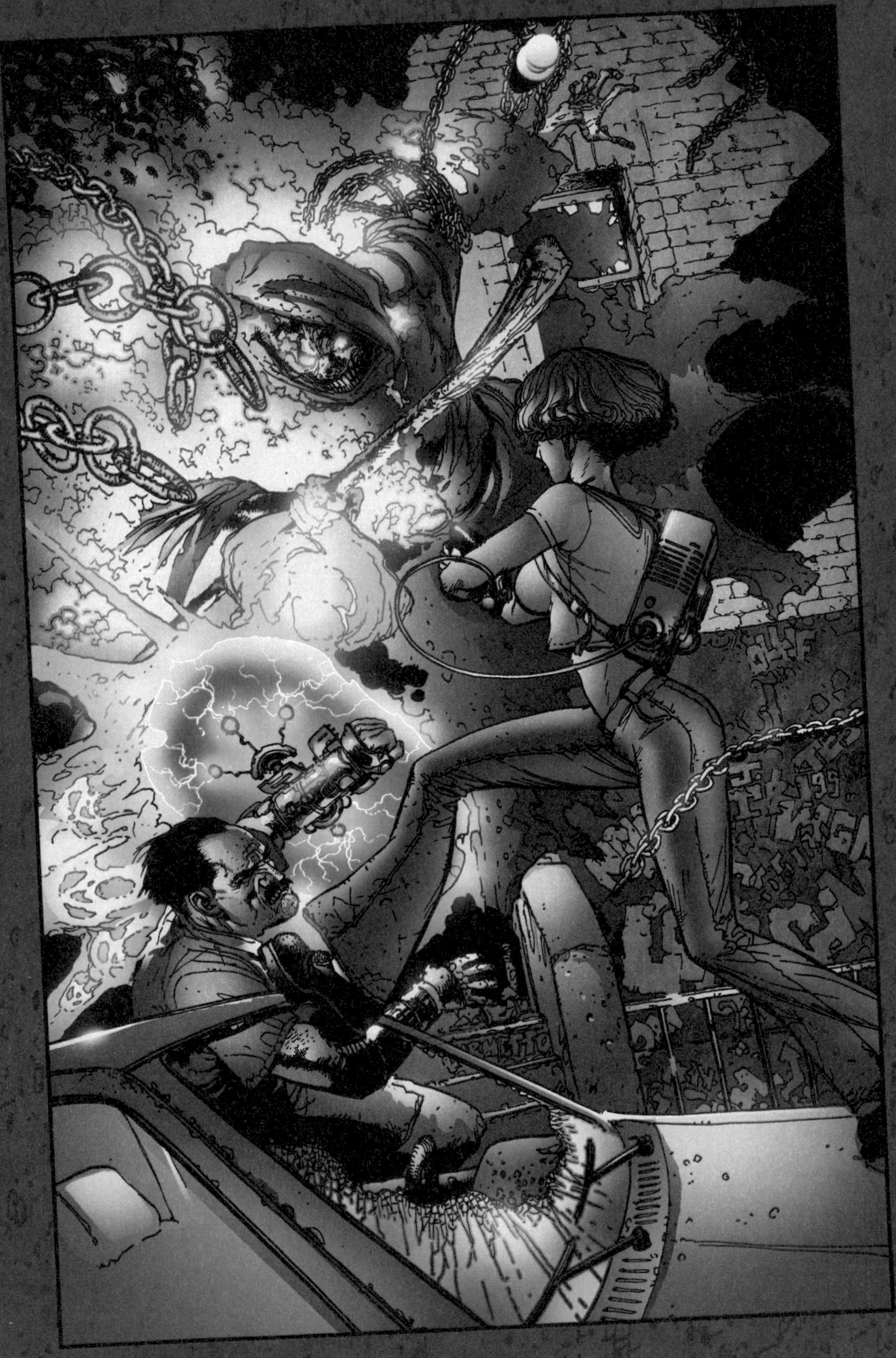

Doug Mahnke & Peter Pantazis

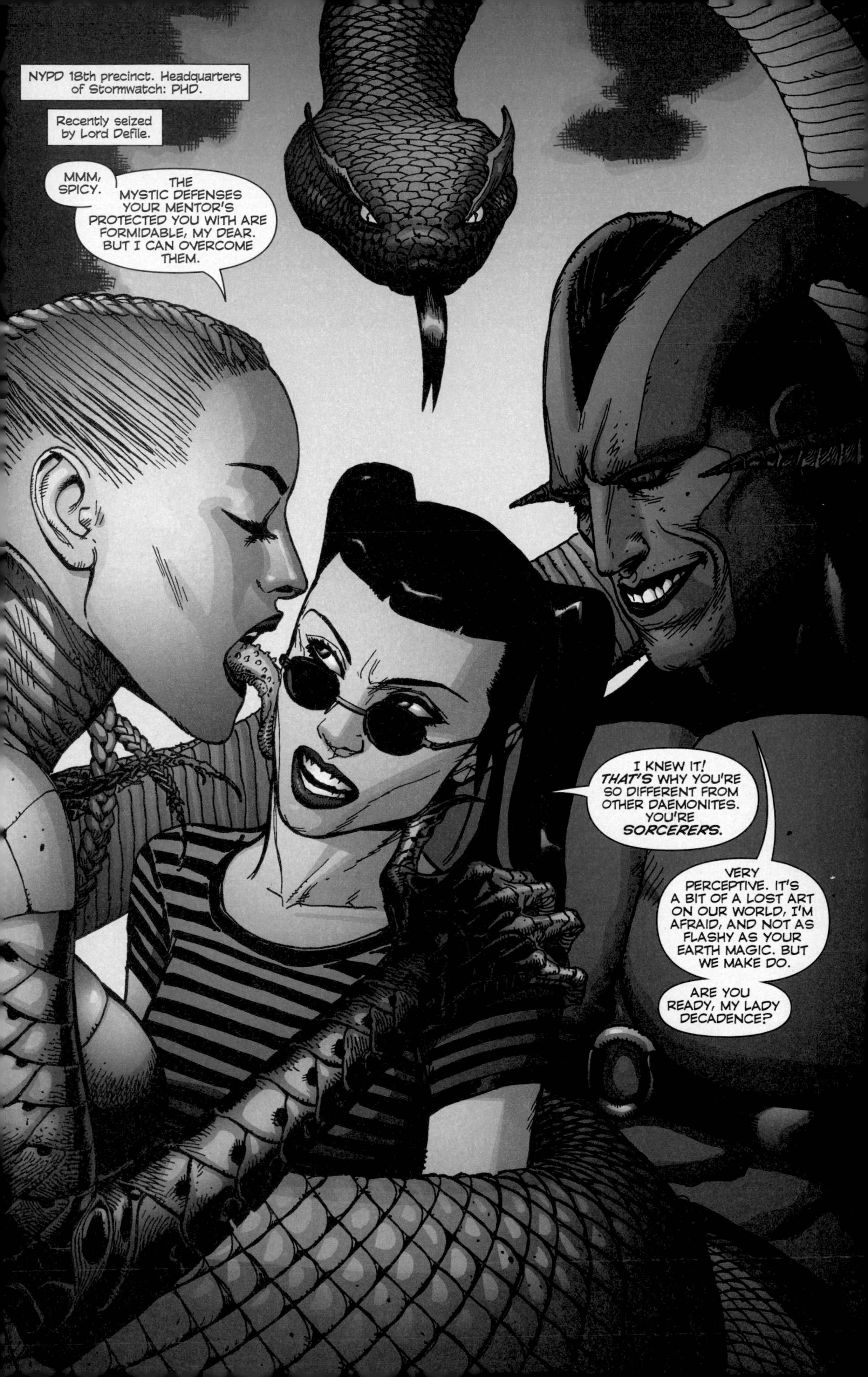
NYPD 18th precinct. Headquarters of Stormwatch: PHD.
Recently seized by Lord Defile.
MMM, SPICY.
THE MYSTIC DEFENSES YOUR MENTOR'S PROTECTED YOU WITH ARE FORMIDABLE, MY DEAR. BUT I CAN OVERCOME THEM.
I KNEW IT! THAT'S WHY YOU'RE SO DIFFERENT FROM OTHER DAEMONITES. YOU'RE SORCERERS.
VERY PERCEPTIVE. IT'S A BIT OF A LOST ART ON OUR WORLD, I'M AFRAID, AND NOT AS FLASHY AS YOUR EARTH MAGIC. BUT WE MAKE DO.
ARE YOU READY, MY LADY DECADENCE?

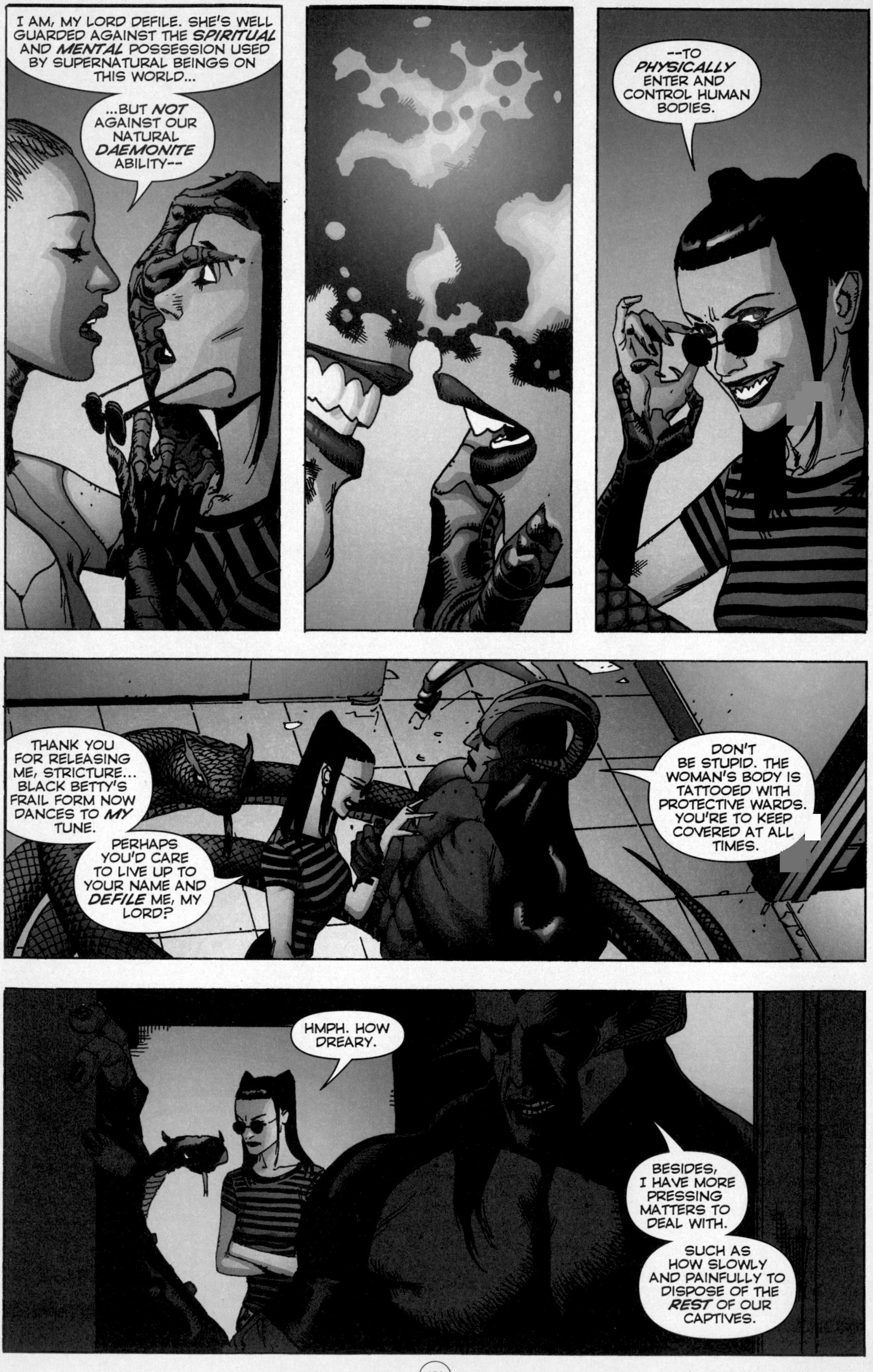

I AM, MY LORD DEFILE. SHE'S WELL GUARDED AGAINST THE SPIRITUAL AND MENTAL POSSESSION USED BY SUPERNATURAL BEINGS ON THIS WORLD...
...BUT NOT AGAINST OUR NATURAL DAEMONITE ABILITY--
--TO PHYSICALLY ENTER AND CONTROL HUMAN BODIES.
THANK YOU FOR RELEASING ME, STRICTURE... BLACK BETTY'S FRAIL FORM NOW DANCES TO MY TUNE.
PERHAPS YOU'D CARE TO LIVE UP TO YOUR NAME AND DEFILE ME, MY LORD?
DON'T BE STUPID. THE WOMAN'S BODY IS TATTOOED WITH PROTECTIVE WARDS. YOU'RE TO KEEP COVERED AT ALL TIMES.
HMPH. HOW DREARY.
BESIDES, I HAVE MORE PRESSING MATTERS TO DEAL WITH.
SUCH AS HOW SLOWLY AND PAINFULLY TO DISPOSE OF THE REST OF OUR CAPTIVES.

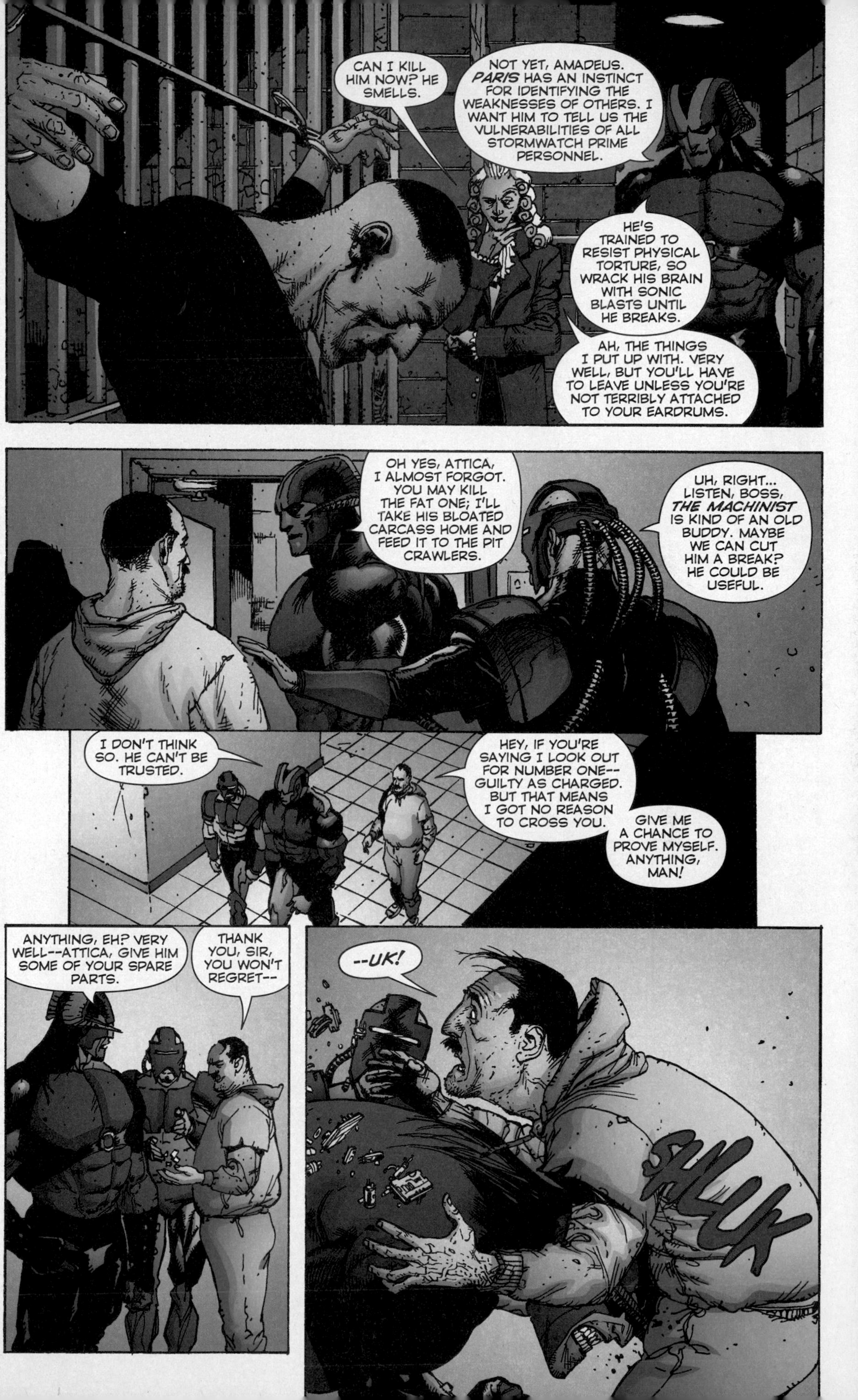
CAN I KILL HIM NOW? HE SMELLS.
NOT YET, AMADEUS. PARIS HAS AN INSTINCT FOR IDENTIFYING THE WEAKNESSES OF OTHERS. I WANT HIM TO TELL US THE VULNERABILITIES OF ALL STORMWATCH PRIME PERSONNEL.
HE'S TRAINED TO RESIST PHYSICAL TORTURE, SO WRACK HIS BRAIN WITH SONIC BLASTS UNTIL HE BREAKS.
AH, THE THINGS I PUT UP WITH. VERY WELL, BUT YOU'LL HAVE TO LEAVE UNLESS YOU'RE NOT TERRIBLY ATTACHED TO YOUR EARDRUMS.
OH YES, ATTICA, I ALMOST FORGOT. YOU MAY KILL THE FAT ONE; I'LL TAKE HIS BLOATED CARCASS HOME AND FEED IT TO THE PIT CRAWLERS.
UH, RIGHT... LISTEN, BOSS, THE MACHINIST IS KIND OF AN OLD BUDDY. MAYBE WE CAN CUT HIM A BREAK? HE COULD BE USEFUL.
I DON'T THINK SO. HE CAN'T BE TRUSTED.
HEY, IF YOU'RE SAYING I LOOK OUT FOR NUMBER ONE--GUILTY AS CHARGED. BUT THAT MEANS I GOT NO REASON TO CROSS YOU.
GIVE ME A CHANCE TO PROVE MYSELF. ANYTHING, MAN!
ANYTHING, EH? VERY WELL--ATTICA, GIVE HIM SOME OF YOUR SPARE PARTS.
THANK YOU, SIR, YOU WON'T REGRET--
--UK!
SHLUK

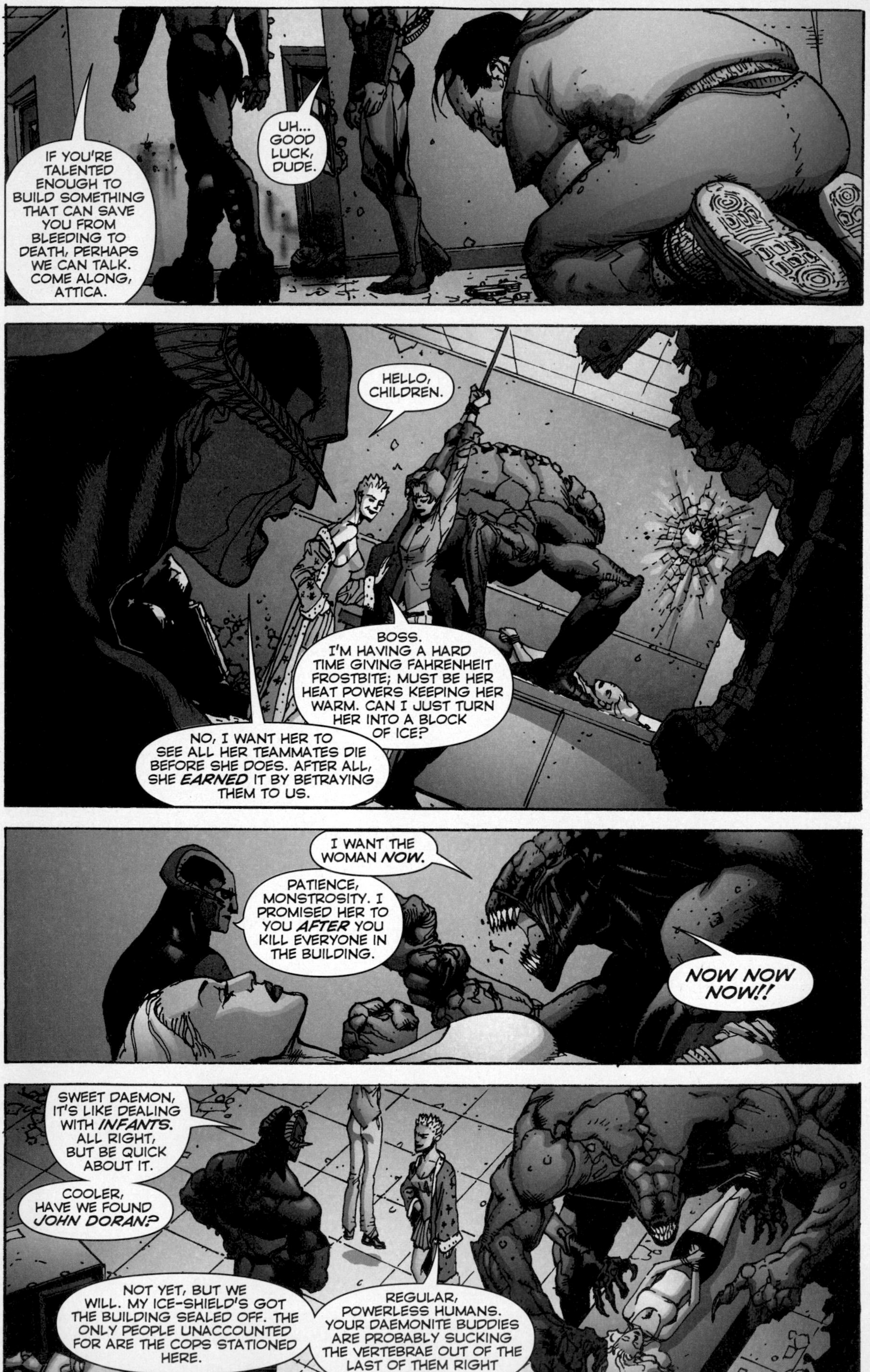
IF YOU'RE TALENTED ENOUGH TO BUILD SOMETHING THAT CAN SAVE YOU FROM BLEEDING TO DEATH, PERHAPS WE CAN TALK. COME ALONG, ATTICA.
UH... GOOD LUCK, DUDE.
HELLO, CHILDREN.
BOSS. I'M HAVING A HARD TIME GIVING FAHRENHEIT FROSTBITE; MUST BE HER HEAT POWERS KEEPING HER WARM. CAN I JUST TURN HER INTO A BLOCK OF ICE?
NO, I WANT HER TO SEE ALL HER TEAMMATES DIE BEFORE SHE DOES. AFTER ALL, SHE *EARNED* IT BY BETRAYING THEM TO US.
I WANT THE WOMAN *NOW.*
PATIENCE, MONSTROSITY. I PROMISED HER TO YOU *AFTER* YOU KILL EVERYONE IN THE BUILDING.
NOW NOW NOW!!
SWEET DAEMON, IT'S LIKE DEALING WITH *INFANTS.* ALL RIGHT, BUT BE QUICK ABOUT IT.
COOLER, HAVE WE FOUND *JOHN DORAN?*
NOT YET, BUT WE WILL. MY ICE-SHIELD'S GOT THE BUILDING SEALED OFF. THE ONLY PEOPLE UNACCOUNTED FOR ARE THE COPS STATIONED HERE.
REGULAR, POWERLESS HUMANS. YOUR DAEMONITE BUDDIES ARE PROBABLY SUCKING THE VERTEBRAE OUT OF THE LAST OF THEM RIGHT NOW.

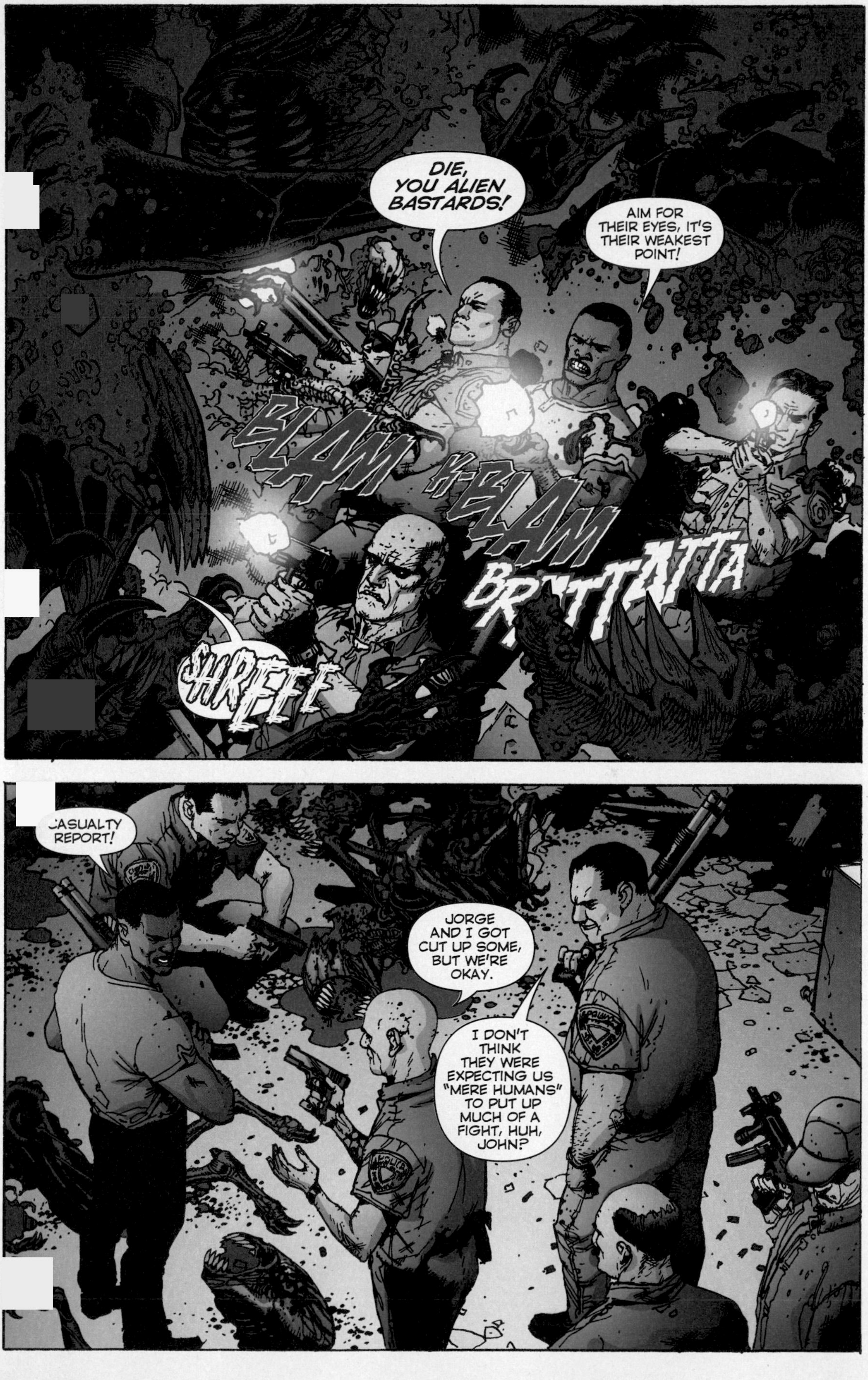
DIE, YOU ALIEN BASTARDS!
AIM FOR THEIR EYES, IT'S THEIR WEAKEST POINT!
BLAM
K-BLAM
BRTTTATTA
SHREEE
CASUALTY REPORT!
JORGE AND I GOT CUT UP SOME, BUT WE'RE OKAY.
I DON'T THINK THEY WERE EXPECTING US "MERE HUMANS" TO PUT UP MUCH OF A FIGHT, HUH, JOHN?

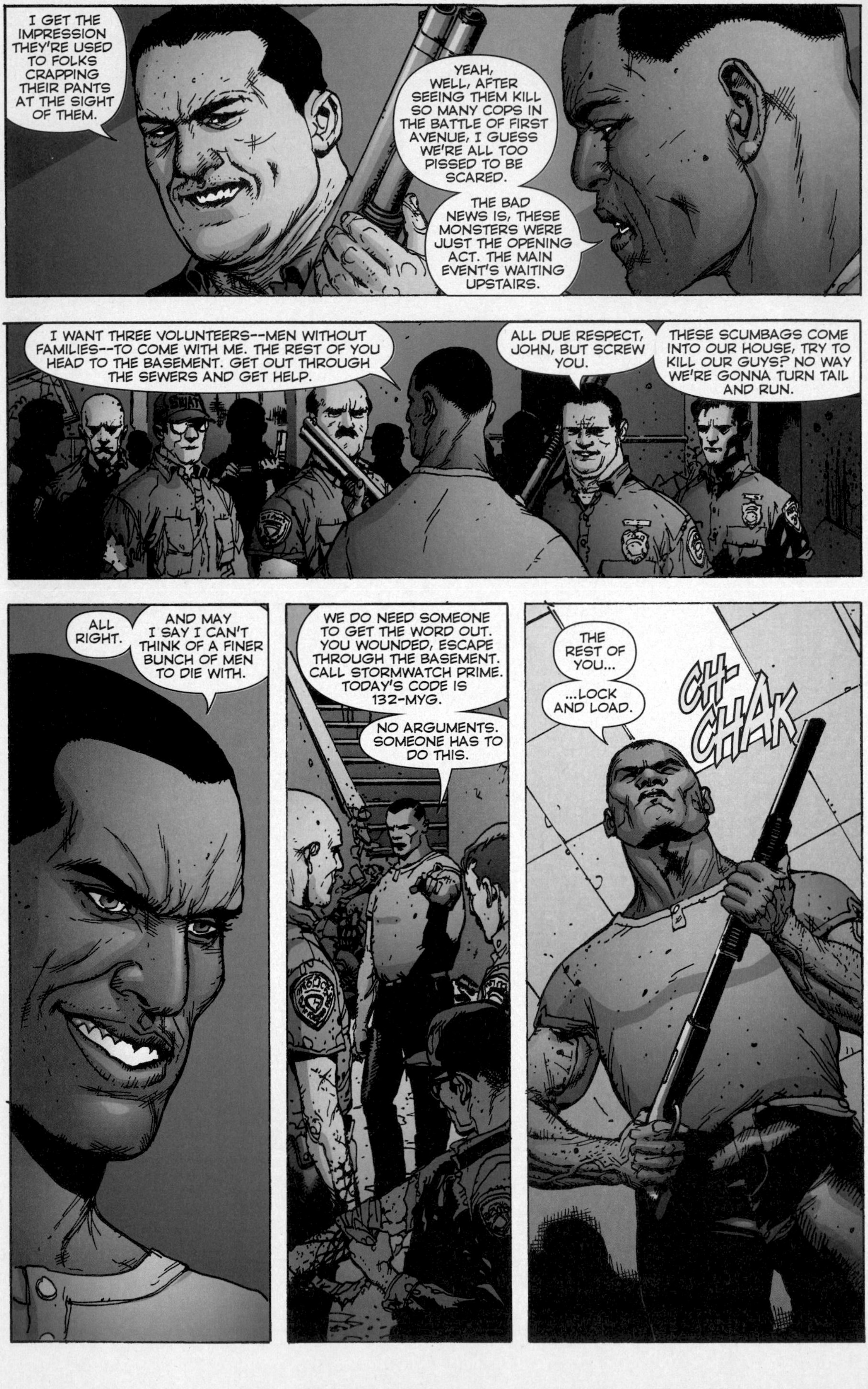
I GET THE IMPRESSION THEY'RE USED TO FOLKS CRAPPING THEIR PANTS AT THE SIGHT OF THEM.
YEAH, WELL, AFTER SEEING THEM KILL SO MANY COPS IN THE BATTLE OF FIRST AVENUE, I GUESS WE'RE ALL TOO PISSED TO BE SCARED.
THE BAD NEWS IS, THESE MONSTERS WERE JUST THE OPENING ACT. THE MAIN EVENT'S WAITING UPSTAIRS.
I WANT THREE VOLUNTEERS--MEN WITHOUT FAMILIES--TO COME WITH ME. THE REST OF YOU HEAD TO THE BASEMENT. GET OUT THROUGH THE SEWERS AND GET HELP.
ALL DUE RESPECT, JOHN, BUT SCREW YOU.
THESE SCUMBAGS COME INTO OUR HOUSE, TRY TO KILL OUR GUYS? NO WAY WE'RE GONNA TURN TAIL AND RUN.
ALL RIGHT.
AND MAY I SAY I CAN'T THINK OF A FINER BUNCH OF MEN TO DIE WITH.
WE DO NEED SOMEONE TO GET THE WORD OUT. YOU WOUNDED, ESCAPE THROUGH THE BASEMENT. CALL STORMWATCH PRIME. TODAY'S CODE IS 132-MYG.
NO ARGUMENTS. SOMEONE HAS TO DO THIS.
THE REST OF YOU...
...LOCK AND LOAD.
CH-CHAK

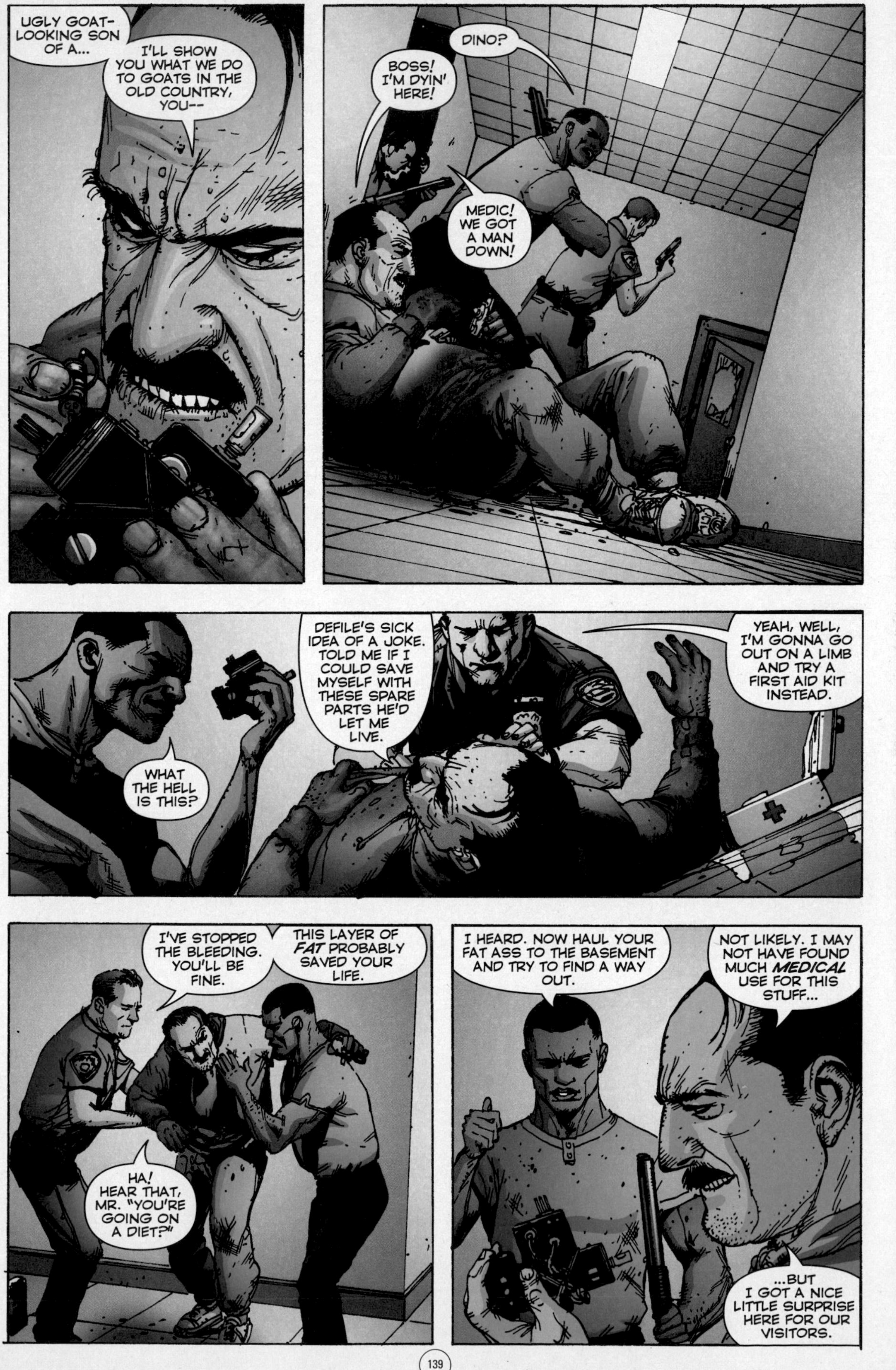

UGLY GOAT-LOOKING SON OF A...
I'LL SHOW YOU WHAT WE DO TO GOATS IN THE OLD COUNTRY, YOU--
BOSS! I'M DYIN' HERE!
DINO?
MEDIC! WE GOT A MAN DOWN!
WHAT THE HELL IS THIS?
DEFILE'S SICK IDEA OF A JOKE. TOLD ME IF I COULD SAVE MYSELF WITH THESE SPARE PARTS HE'D LET ME LIVE.
YEAH, WELL, I'M GONNA GO OUT ON A LIMB AND TRY A FIRST AID KIT INSTEAD.
I'VE STOPPED THE BLEEDING. YOU'LL BE FINE.
THIS LAYER OF *FAT* PROBABLY SAVED YOUR LIFE.
HA! HEAR THAT, MR. "YOU'RE GOING ON A DIET?"
I HEARD. NOW HAUL YOUR FAT ASS TO THE BASEMENT AND TRY TO FIND A WAY OUT.
NOT LIKELY. I MAY NOT HAVE FOUND MUCH *MEDICAL* USE FOR THIS STUFF...
...BUT I GOT A NICE LITTLE SURPRISE HERE FOR OUR VISITORS.

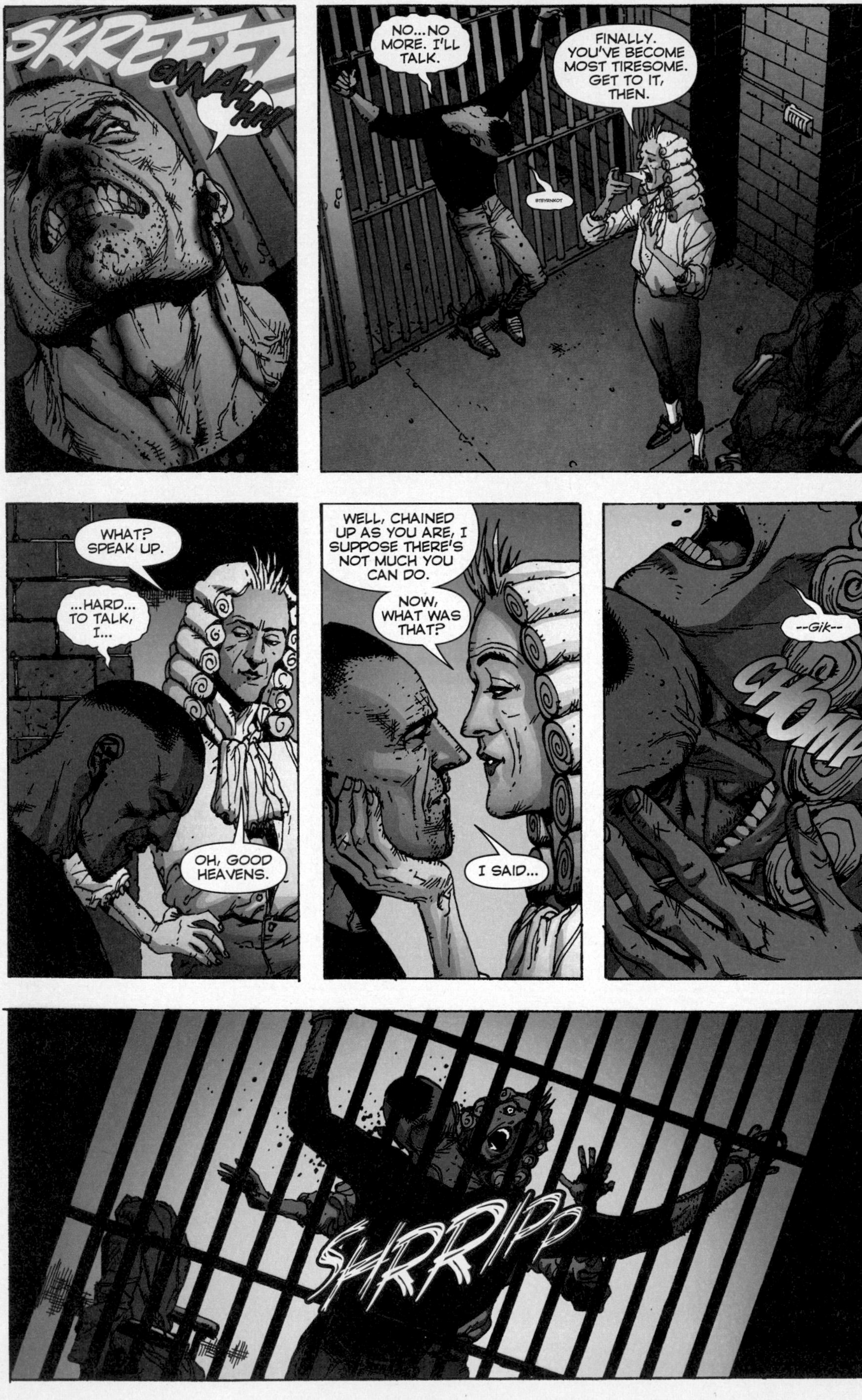
SKREEE
GNNAHHH!
NO... NO MORE. I'LL TALK.
FINALLY. YOU'VE BECOME MOST TIRESOME. GET TO IT, THEN.
BTEYRNKOT
WHAT? SPEAK UP.
...HARD... TO TALK, I...
OH, GOOD HEAVENS.
WELL, CHAINED UP AS YOU ARE, I SUPPOSE THERE'S NOT MUCH YOU CAN DO.
NOW, WHAT WAS THAT?
I SAID...
--Gik--
CHOMP
SHRRIPP

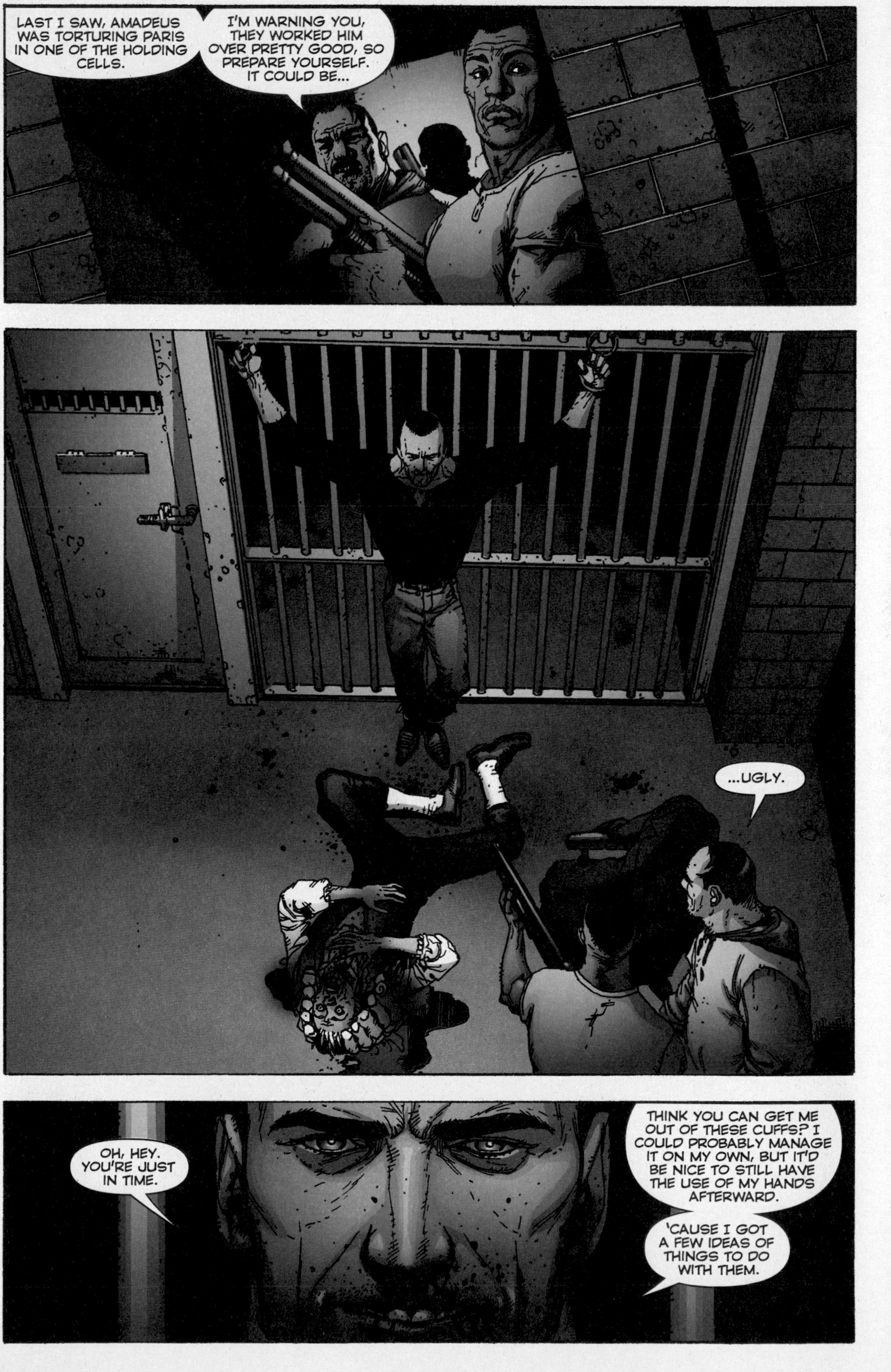
LAST I SAW, AMADEUS WAS TORTURING PARIS IN ONE OF THE HOLDING CELLS.
I'M WARNING YOU, THEY WORKED HIM OVER PRETTY GOOD, SO PREPARE YOURSELF. IT COULD BE...
...UGLY.
OH, HEY. YOU'RE JUST IN TIME.
THINK YOU CAN GET ME OUT OF THESE CUFFS? I COULD PROBABLY MANAGE IT ON MY OWN, BUT IT'D BE NICE TO STILL HAVE THE USE OF MY HANDS AFTERWARD.
'CAUSE I GOT A FEW IDEAS OF THINGS TO DO WITH THEM.

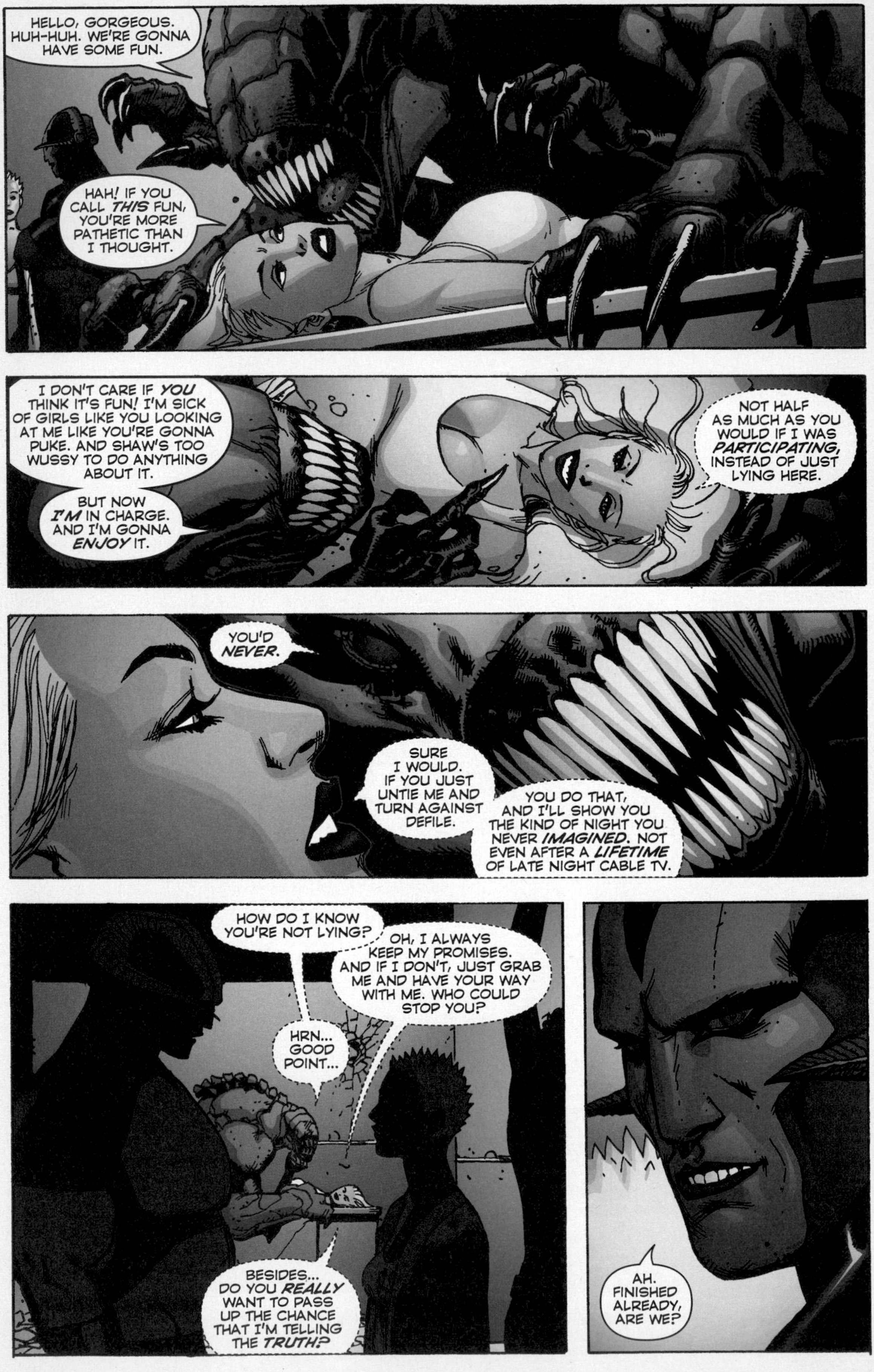
HELLO, GORGEOUS. HUH-HUH. WE'RE GONNA HAVE SOME FUN.
HAH! IF YOU CALL THIS FUN, YOU'RE MORE PATHETIC THAN I THOUGHT.
I DON'T CARE IF YOU THINK IT'S FUN! I'M SICK OF GIRLS LIKE YOU LOOKING AT ME LIKE YOU'RE GONNA PUKE. AND SHAW'S TOO WUSSY TO DO ANYTHING ABOUT IT.
BUT NOW I'M IN CHARGE. AND I'M GONNA ENJOY IT.
NOT HALF AS MUCH AS YOU WOULD IF I WAS PARTICIPATING, INSTEAD OF JUST LYING HERE.
YOU'D NEVER.
SURE I WOULD. IF YOU JUST UNTIE ME AND TURN AGAINST DEFILE.
YOU DO THAT, AND I'LL SHOW YOU THE KIND OF NIGHT YOU NEVER IMAGINED. NOT EVEN AFTER A LIFETIME OF LATE NIGHT CABLE TV.
HOW DO I KNOW YOU'RE NOT LYING?
OH, I ALWAYS KEEP MY PROMISES. AND IF I DON'T, JUST GRAB ME AND HAVE YOUR WAY WITH ME. WHO COULD STOP YOU?
HRN... GOOD POINT...
BESIDES... DO YOU REALLY WANT TO PASS UP THE CHANCE THAT I'M TELLING THE TRUTH?
AH. FINISHED ALREADY, ARE WE?

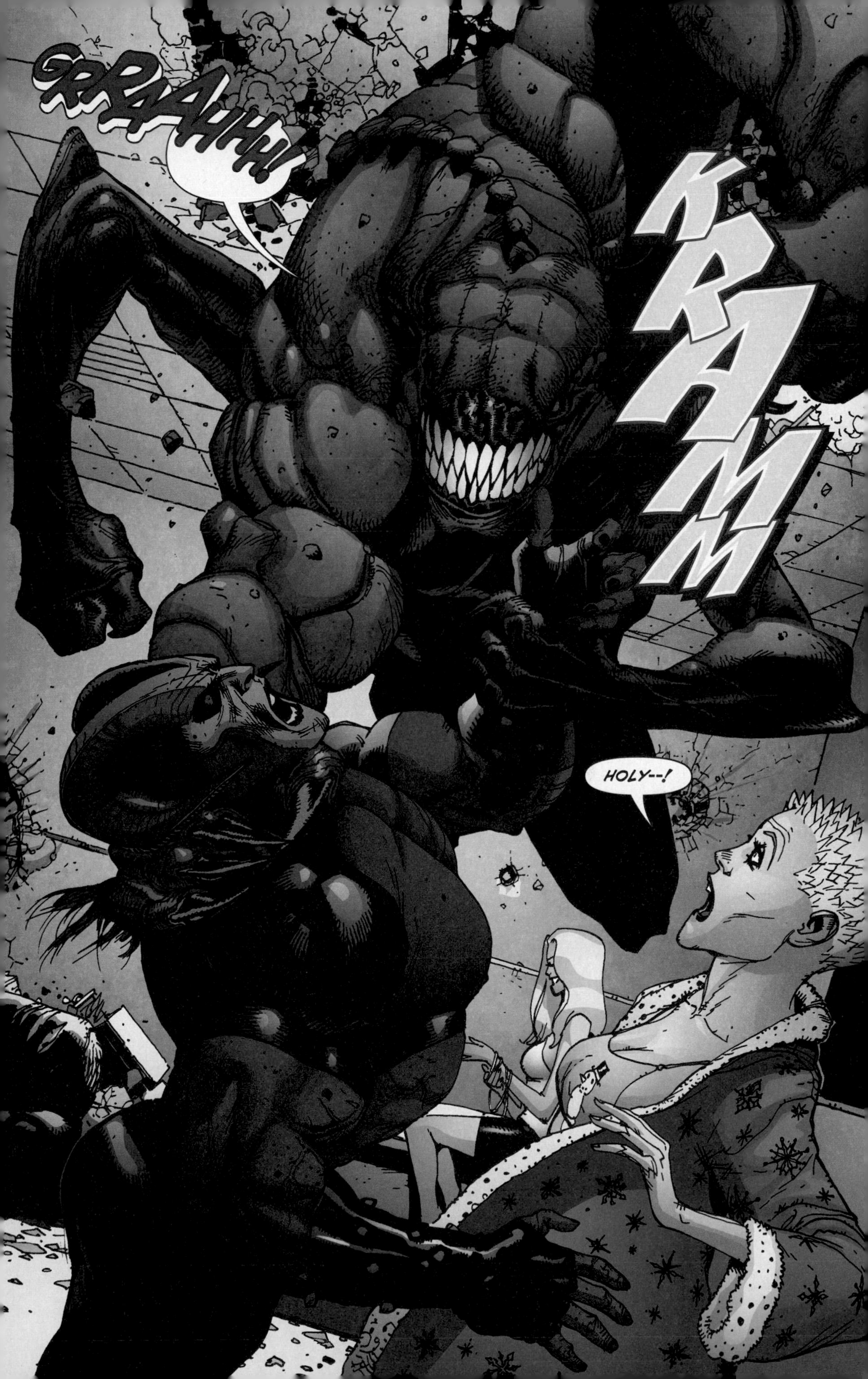
GRRAHHH!
KRAM
HOLY--!

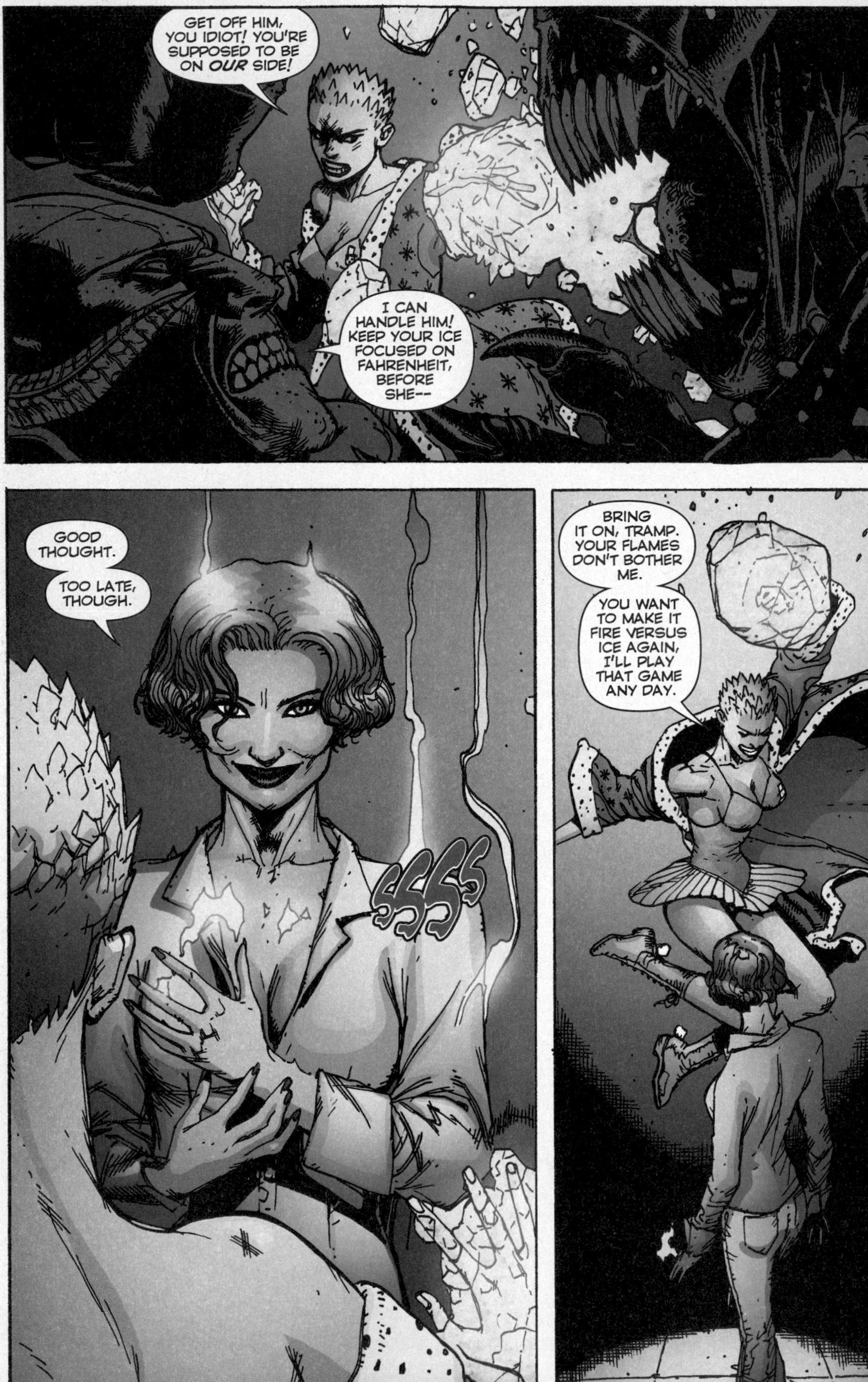
GET OFF HIM, YOU IDIOT! YOU'RE SUPPOSED TO BE ON *OUR* SIDE!
I CAN HANDLE HIM! KEEP YOUR ICE FOCUSED ON FAHRENHEIT, BEFORE SHE--
GOOD THOUGHT.
TOO LATE, THOUGH.
SSSS
BRING IT ON, TRAMP. YOUR FLAMES DON'T BOTHER ME.
YOU WANT TO MAKE IT FIRE VERSUS ICE AGAIN, I'LL PLAY THAT GAME ANY DAY.

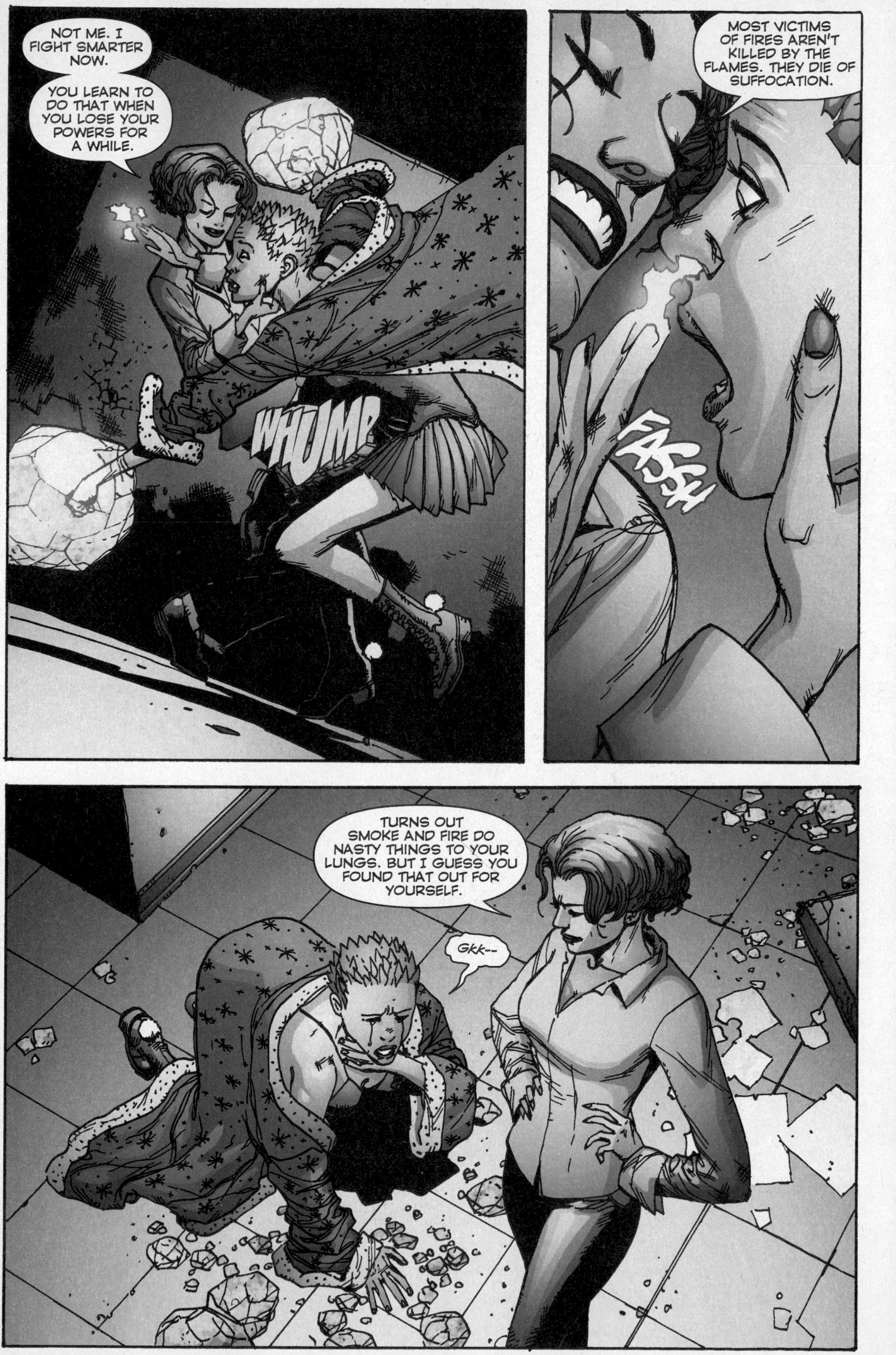
NOT ME. I FIGHT SMARTER NOW.
YOU LEARN TO DO THAT WHEN YOU LOSE YOUR POWERS FOR A WHILE.
WHUMP
MOST VICTIMS OF FIRES AREN'T KILLED BY THE FLAMES. THEY DIE OF SUFFOCATION.
FASSH
TURNS OUT SMOKE AND FIRE DO NASTY THINGS TO YOUR LUNGS. BUT I GUESS YOU FOUND THAT OUT FOR YOURSELF.
GKK--

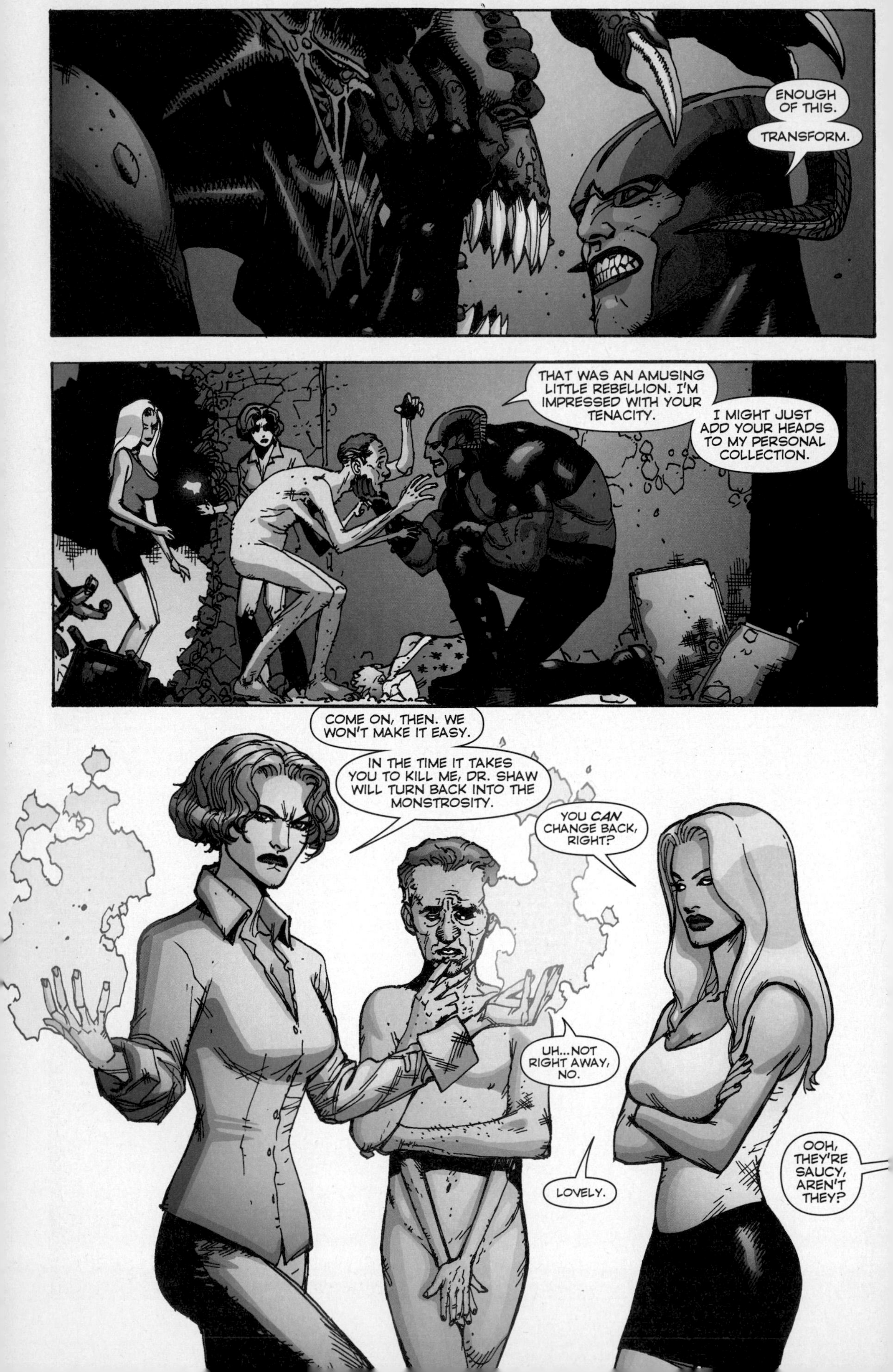
ENOUGH OF THIS.
TRANSFORM.
THAT WAS AN AMUSING LITTLE REBELLION. I'M IMPRESSED WITH YOUR TENACITY.
I MIGHT JUST ADD YOUR HEADS TO MY PERSONAL COLLECTION.
COME ON, THEN. WE WON'T MAKE IT EASY.
IN THE TIME IT TAKES YOU TO KILL ME, DR. SHAW WILL TURN BACK INTO THE MONSTROSITY.
YOU *CAN* CHANGE BACK, RIGHT?
UH...NOT RIGHT AWAY, NO.
LOVELY.
OOH, THEY'RE SAUCY, AREN'T THEY?

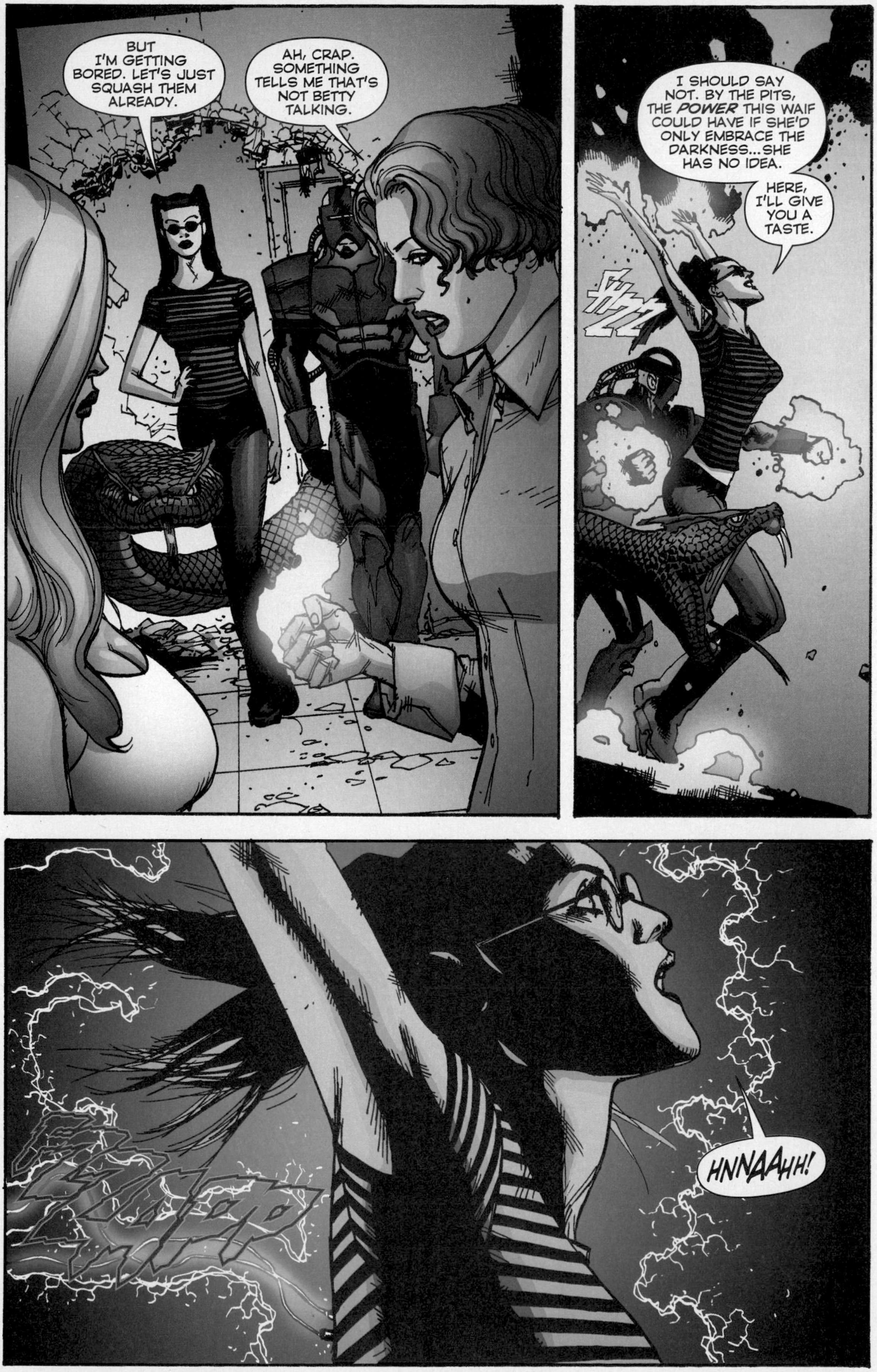
BUT I'M GETTING BORED. LET'S JUST SQUASH THEM ALREADY.
AH, CRAP. SOMETHING TELLS ME THAT'S NOT BETTY TALKING.
I SHOULD SAY NOT. BY THE PITS, THE *POWER* THIS WAIF COULD HAVE IF SHE'D ONLY EMBRACE THE DARKNESS...SHE HAS NO IDEA.
HERE, I'LL GIVE YOU A TASTE.
HNNAAHH!

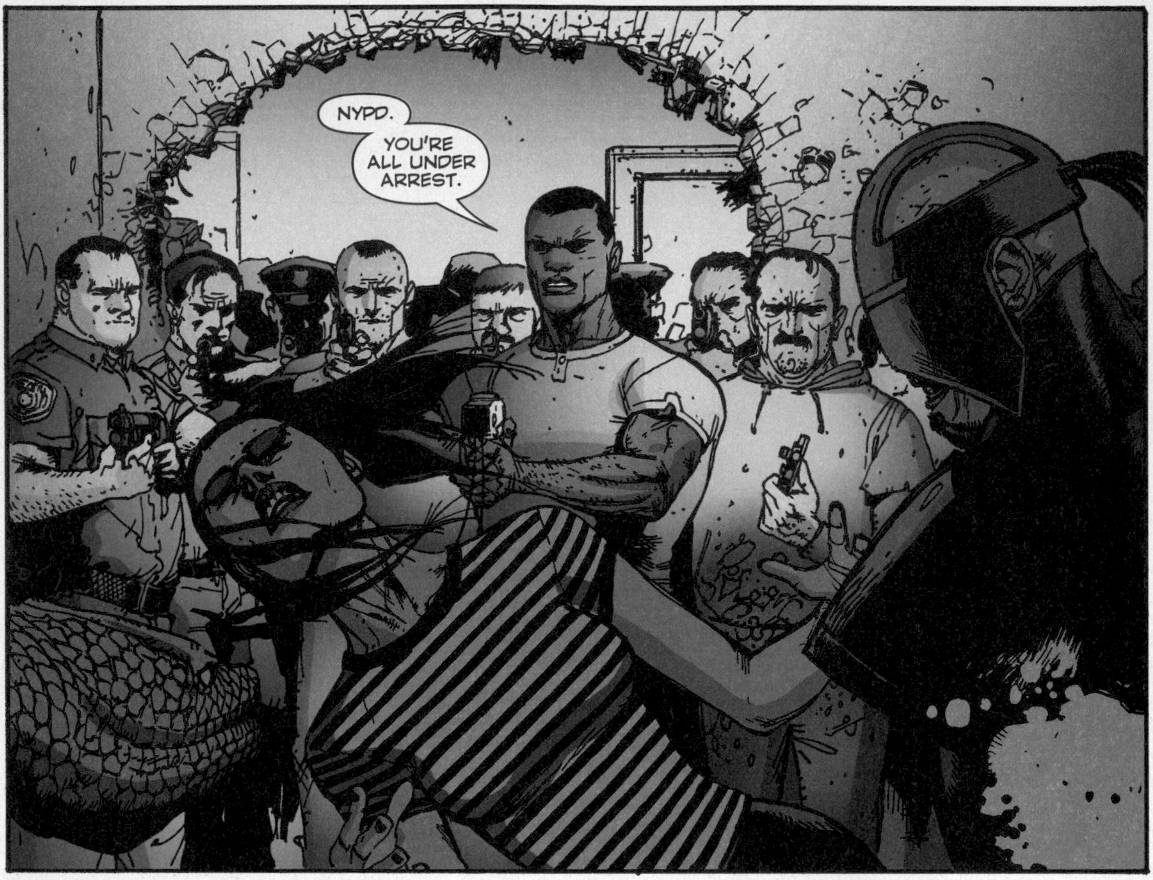
NYPD.
YOU'RE ALL UNDER ARREST.

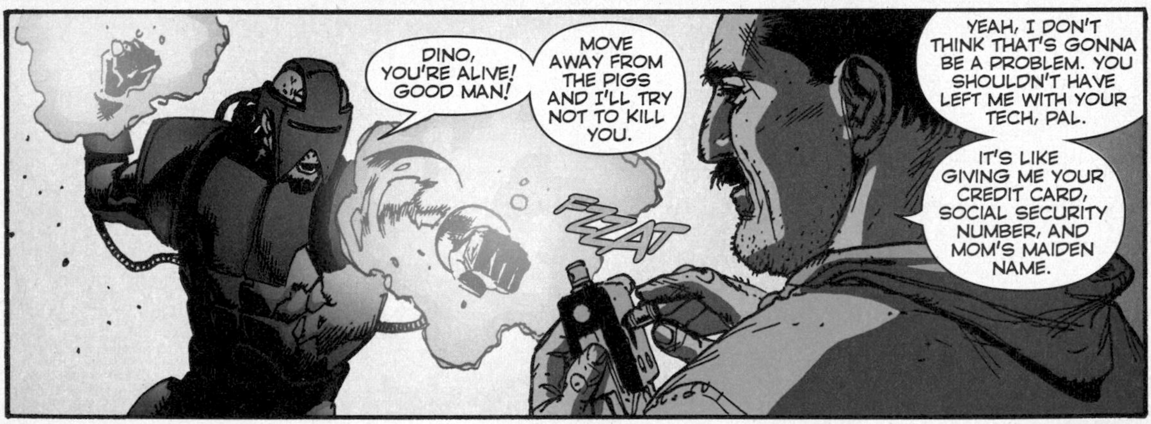
DINO, YOU'RE ALIVE! GOOD MAN!
MOVE AWAY FROM THE PIGS AND I'LL TRY NOT TO KILL YOU.
YEAH, I DON'T THINK THAT'S GONNA BE A PROBLEM. YOU SHOULDN'T HAVE LEFT ME WITH YOUR TECH, PAL.
IT'S LIKE GIVING ME YOUR CREDIT CARD, SOCIAL SECURITY NUMBER, AND MOM'S MAIDEN NAME.
FZZAT

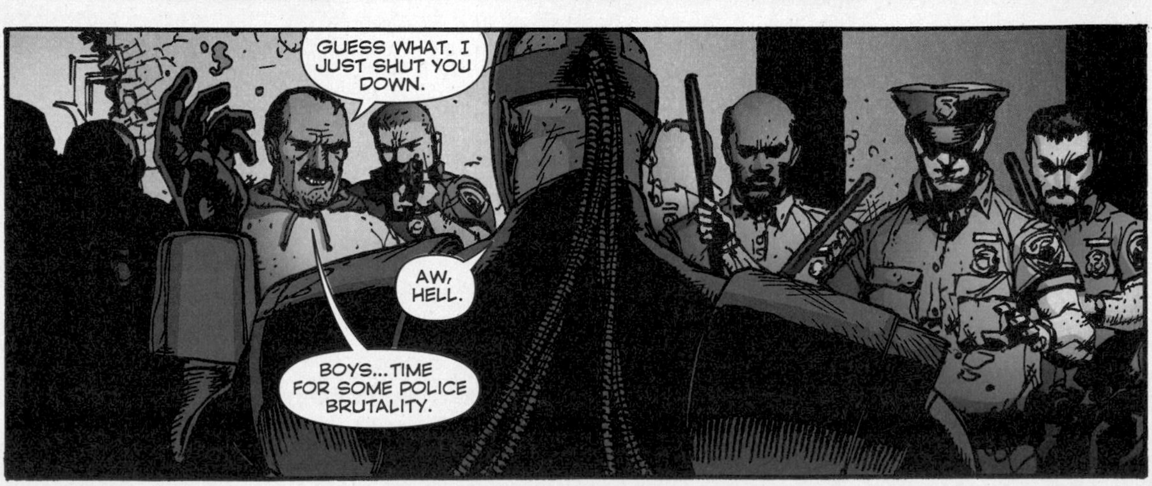
GUESS WHAT. I JUST SHUT YOU DOWN.
AW, HELL.
BOYS...TIME FOR SOME POLICE BRUTALITY.

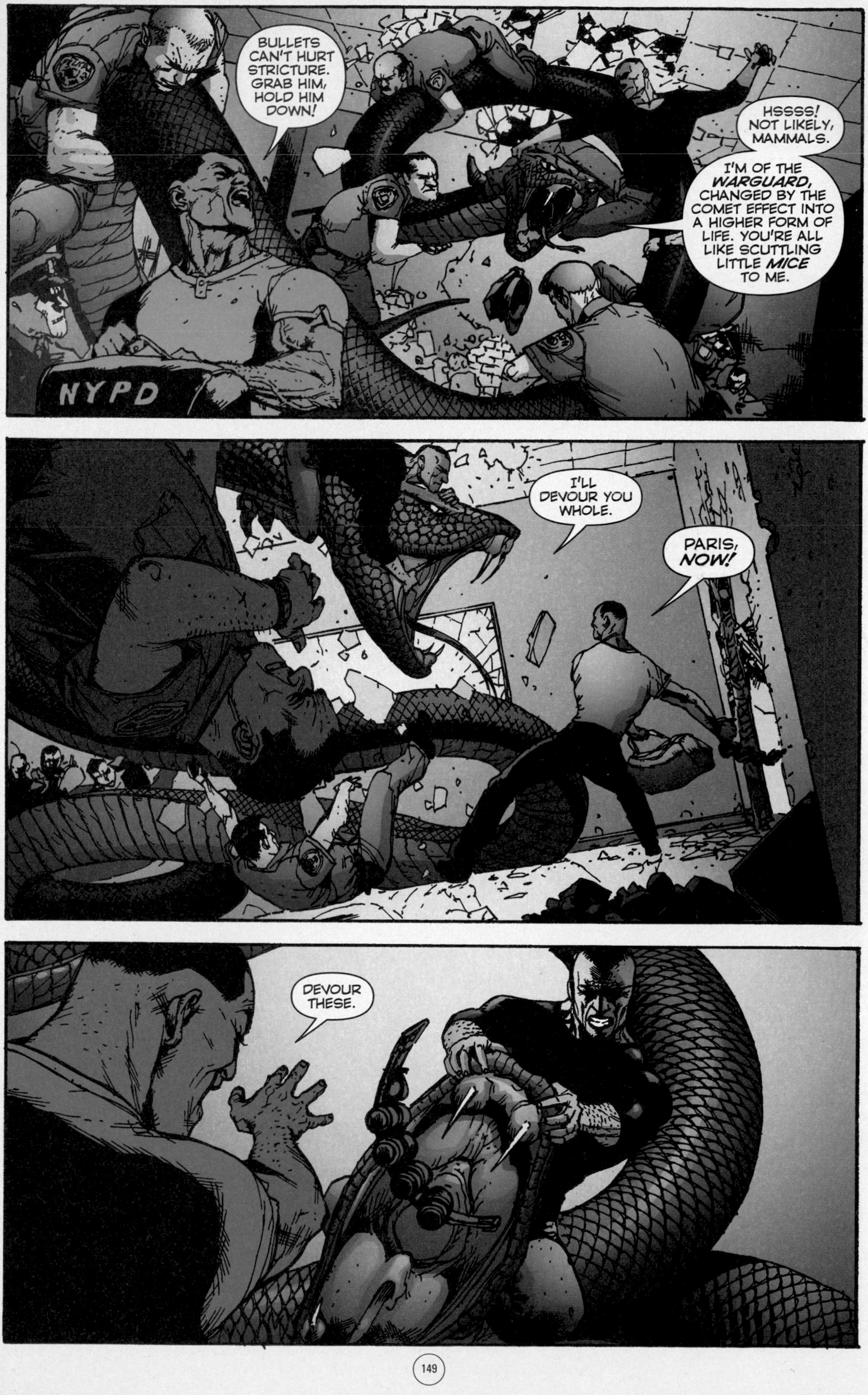
BULLETS CAN'T HURT STRICTURE. GRAB HIM, HOLD HIM DOWN!
HSSSS! NOT LIKELY, MAMMALS.
I'M OF THE WARGUARD, CHANGED BY THE COMET EFFECT INTO A HIGHER FORM OF LIFE. YOU'RE ALL LIKE SCUTTLING LITTLE MICE TO ME.
NYPD
I'LL DEVOUR YOU WHOLE.
PARIS, NOW!
DEVOUR THESE.

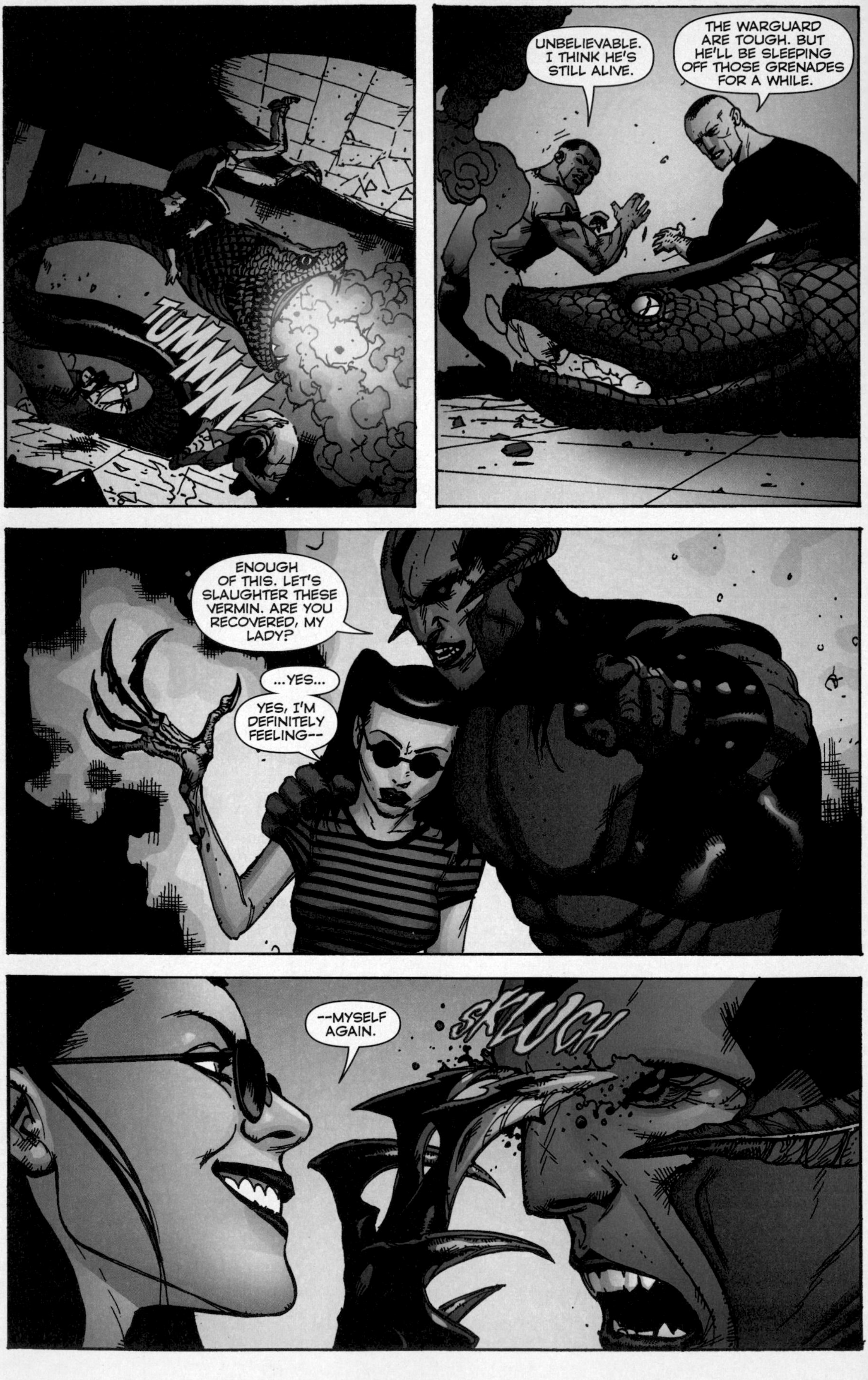
TUMMM
UNBELIEVABLE. I THINK HE'S STILL ALIVE.
THE WARGUARD ARE TOUGH. BUT HE'LL BE SLEEPING OFF THOSE GRENADES FOR A WHILE.
ENOUGH OF THIS. LET'S SLAUGHTER THESE VERMIN. ARE YOU RECOVERED, MY LADY?
...YES...
YES, I'M DEFINITELY FEELING--
--MYSELF AGAIN.
SKLUCH

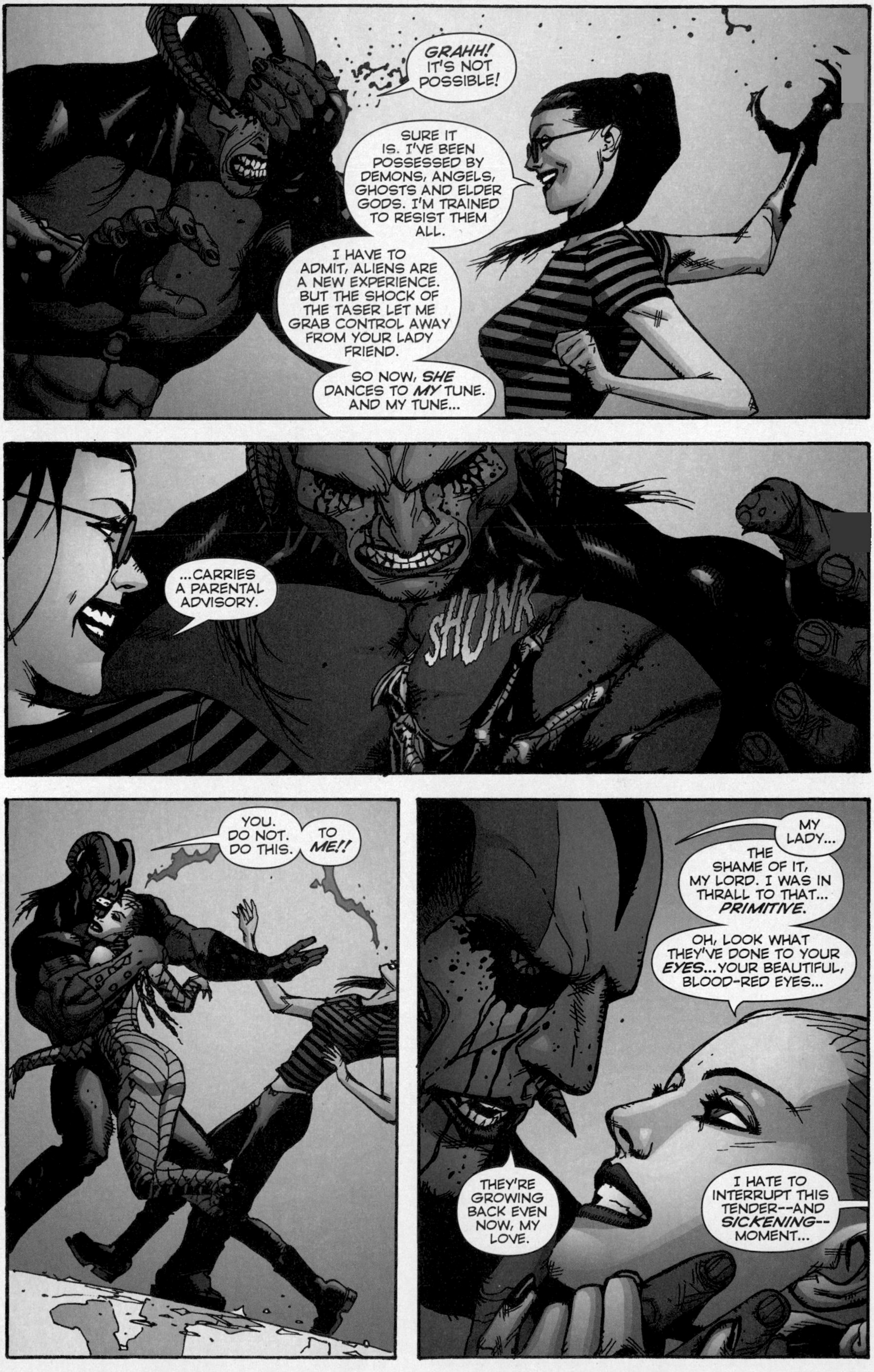
GRAHH! IT'S NOT POSSIBLE!
SURE IT IS. I'VE BEEN POSSESSED BY DEMONS, ANGELS, GHOSTS AND ELDER GODS. I'M TRAINED TO RESIST THEM ALL.
I HAVE TO ADMIT, ALIENS ARE A NEW EXPERIENCE. BUT THE SHOCK OF THE TASER LET ME GRAB CONTROL AWAY FROM YOUR LADY FRIEND.
SO NOW, SHE DANCES TO MY TUNE. AND MY TUNE...
...CARRIES A PARENTAL ADVISORY.
SHUNK
YOU. DO NOT. DO THIS.
TO ME!!
MY LADY...
THE SHAME OF IT, MY LORD. I WAS IN THRALL TO THAT... PRIMITIVE.
OH, LOOK WHAT THEY'VE DONE TO YOUR EYES...YOUR BEAUTIFUL, BLOOD-RED EYES...
THEY'RE GROWING BACK EVEN NOW, MY LOVE.
I HATE TO INTERRUPT THIS TENDER--AND SICKENING--MOMENT...

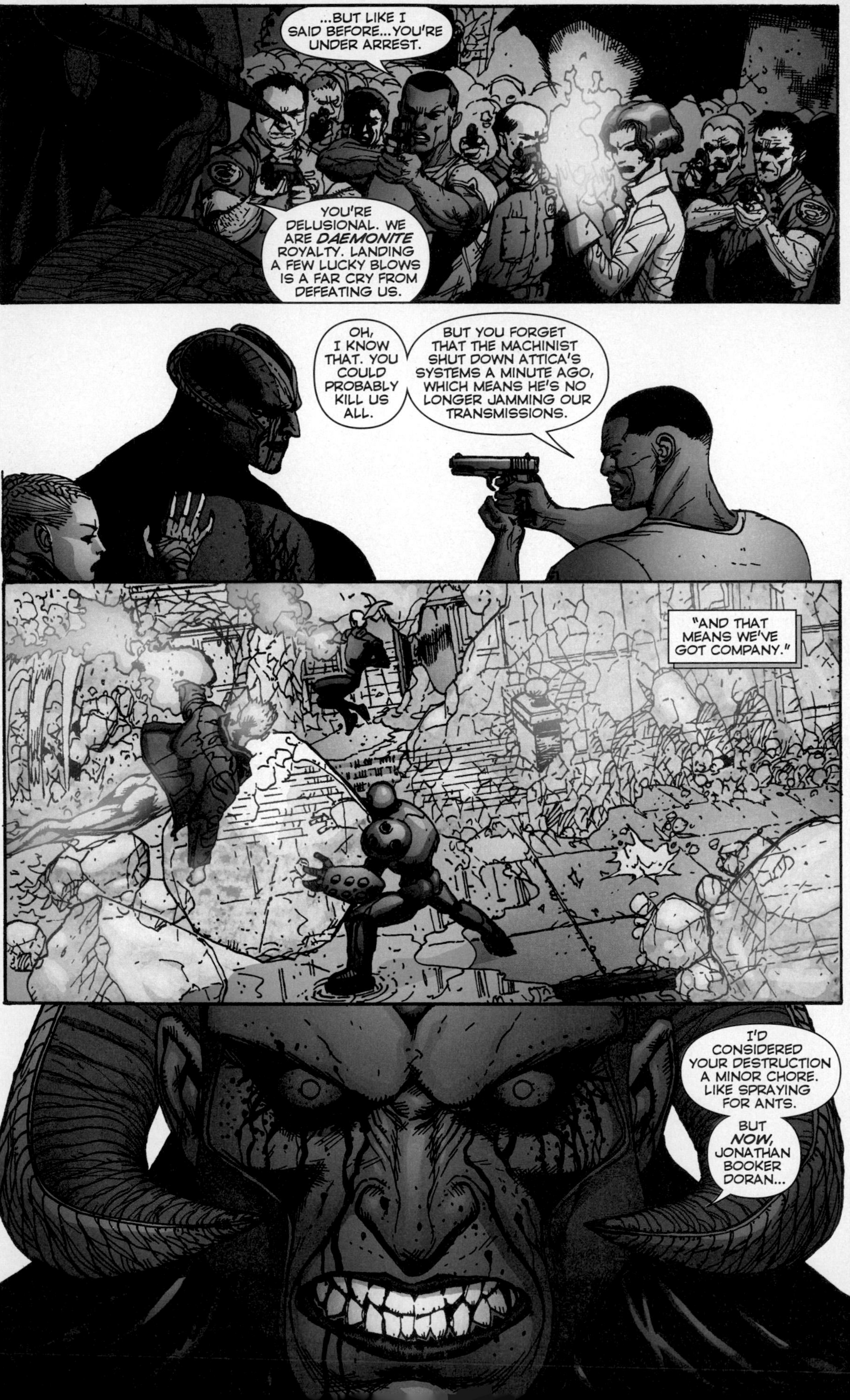
...BUT LIKE I SAID BEFORE...YOU'RE UNDER ARREST.
YOU'RE DELUSIONAL. WE ARE *DAEMONITE* ROYALTY. LANDING A FEW LUCKY BLOWS IS A FAR CRY FROM DEFEATING US.
OH, I KNOW THAT. YOU COULD PROBABLY KILL US ALL.
BUT YOU FORGET THAT THE MACHINIST SHUT DOWN ATTICA'S SYSTEMS A MINUTE AGO, WHICH MEANS HE'S NO LONGER JAMMING OUR TRANSMISSIONS.
"AND THAT MEANS WE'VE GOT COMPANY."
I'D CONSIDERED YOUR DESTRUCTION A MINOR CHORE. LIKE SPRAYING FOR ANTS.
BUT *NOW,* JONATHAN BOOKER DORAN...

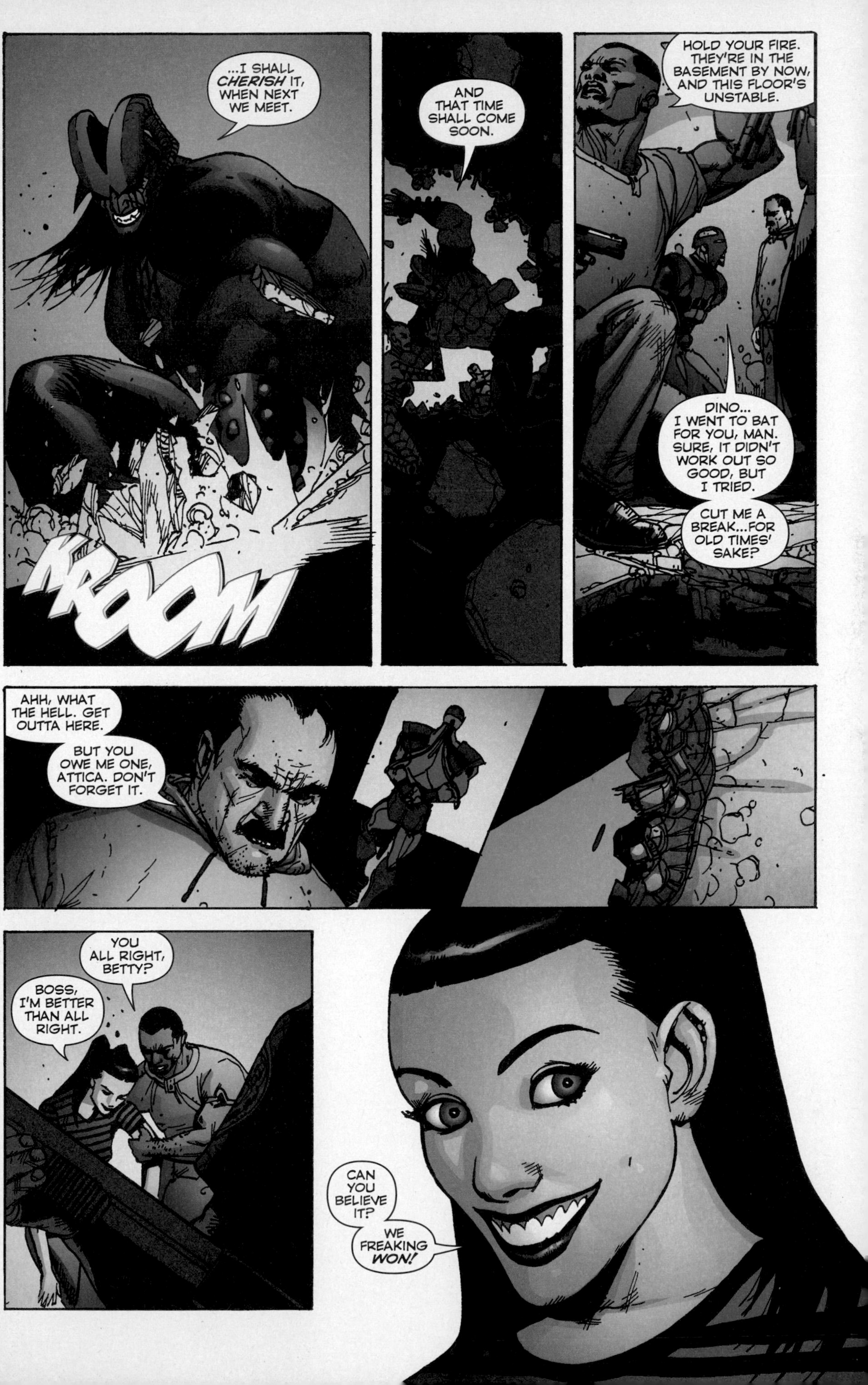
...I SHALL *CHERISH* IT, WHEN NEXT WE MEET.
KROOM
AND THAT TIME SHALL COME SOON.
HOLD YOUR FIRE. THEY'RE IN THE BASEMENT BY NOW, AND THIS FLOOR'S UNSTABLE.
DINO... I WENT TO BAT FOR YOU, MAN. SURE, IT DIDN'T WORK OUT SO GOOD, BUT I TRIED.
CUT ME A BREAK...FOR OLD TIMES' SAKE?
AHH, WHAT THE HELL. GET OUTTA HERE.
BUT YOU OWE ME ONE, ATTICA. DON'T FORGET IT.
YOU ALL RIGHT, BETTY?
BOSS, I'M BETTER THAN ALL RIGHT.
CAN YOU BELIEVE IT?
WE FREAKING *WON!*

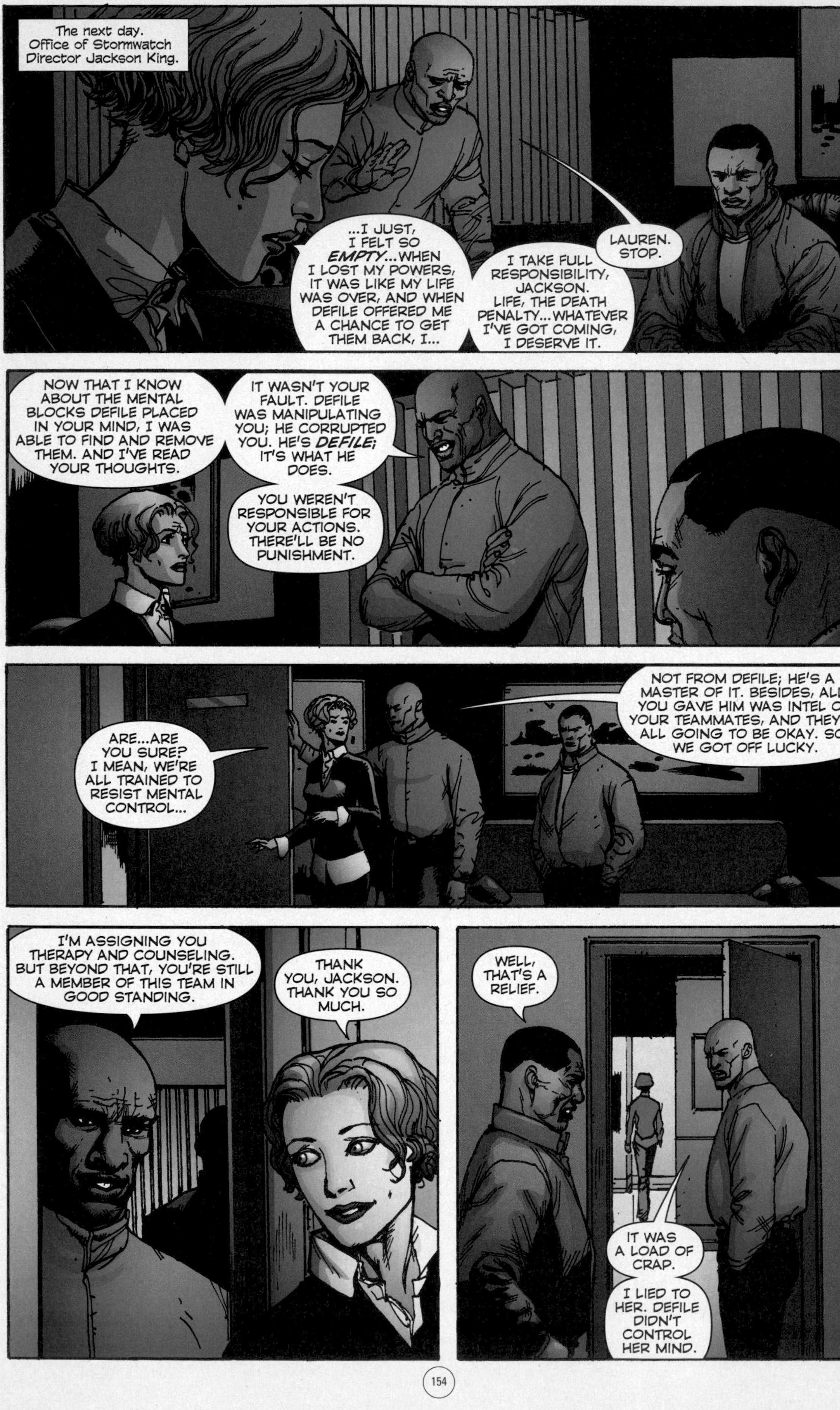
The next day. Office of Stormwatch Director Jackson King.
...I JUST, I FELT SO EMPTY...WHEN I LOST MY POWERS, IT WAS LIKE MY LIFE WAS OVER, AND WHEN DEFILE OFFERED ME A CHANCE TO GET THEM BACK, I...
I TAKE FULL RESPONSIBILITY, JACKSON. LIFE, THE DEATH PENALTY...WHATEVER I'VE GOT COMING, I DESERVE IT.
LAUREN. STOP.
NOW THAT I KNOW ABOUT THE MENTAL BLOCKS DEFILE PLACED IN YOUR MIND, I WAS ABLE TO FIND AND REMOVE THEM. AND I'VE READ YOUR THOUGHTS.
IT WASN'T YOUR FAULT. DEFILE WAS MANIPULATING YOU; HE CORRUPTED YOU. HE'S DEFILE; IT'S WHAT HE DOES.
YOU WEREN'T RESPONSIBLE FOR YOUR ACTIONS. THERE'LL BE NO PUNISHMENT.
ARE...ARE YOU SURE? I MEAN, WE'RE ALL TRAINED TO RESIST MENTAL CONTROL...
NOT FROM DEFILE; HE'S A MASTER OF IT. BESIDES, ALL YOU GAVE HIM WAS INTEL ON YOUR TEAMMATES, AND THEY'RE ALL GOING TO BE OKAY. SO WE GOT OFF LUCKY.
I'M ASSIGNING YOU THERAPY AND COUNSELING. BUT BEYOND THAT, YOU'RE STILL A MEMBER OF THIS TEAM IN GOOD STANDING.
THANK YOU, JACKSON. THANK YOU SO MUCH.
WELL, THAT'S A RELIEF.
IT WAS A LOAD OF CRAP.
I LIED TO HER. DEFILE DIDN'T CONTROL HER MIND.

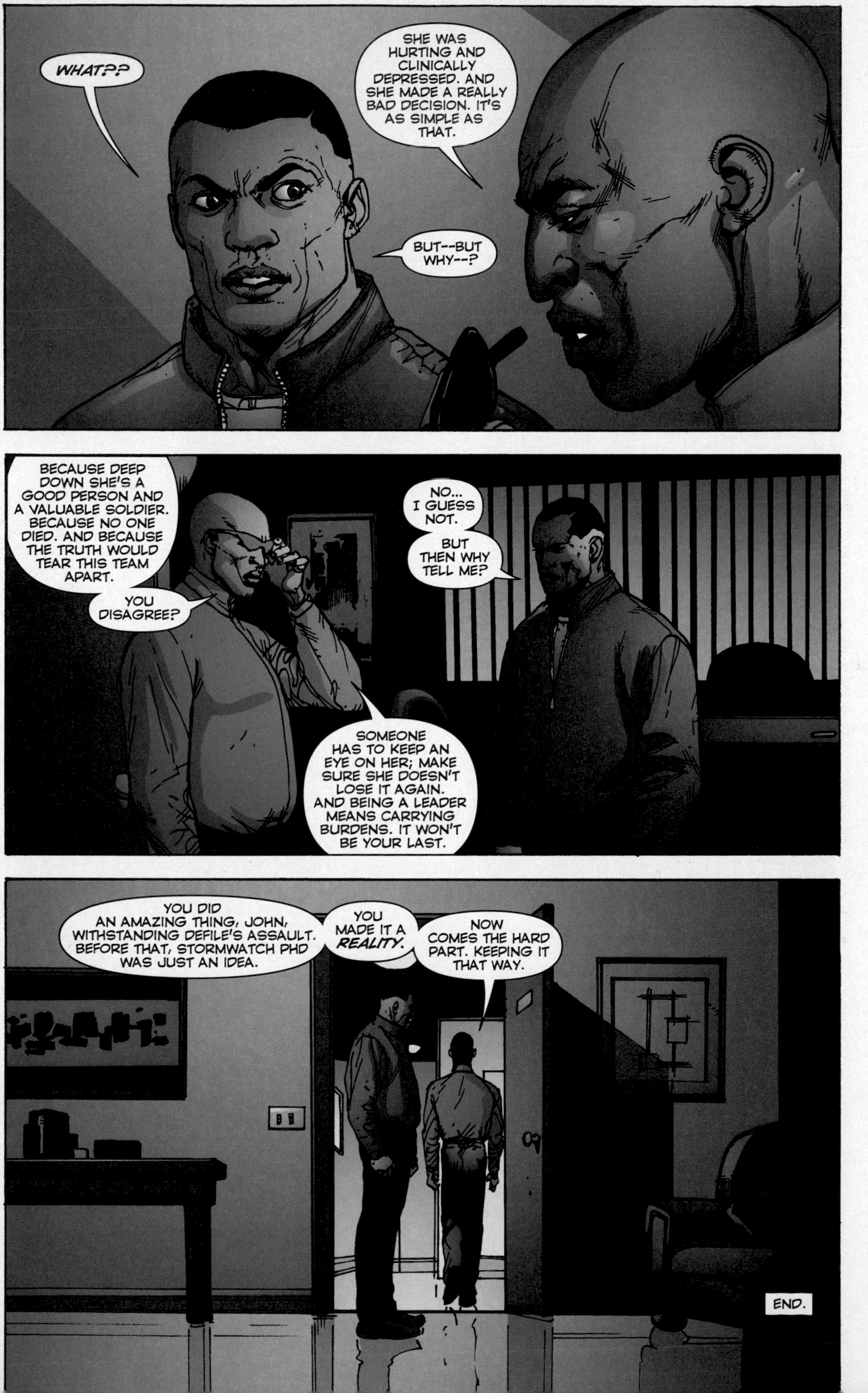
WHAT??
SHE WAS HURTING AND CLINICALLY DEPRESSED. AND SHE MADE A REALLY BAD DECISION. IT'S AS SIMPLE AS THAT.
BUT--BUT WHY--?
BECAUSE DEEP DOWN SHE'S A GOOD PERSON AND A VALUABLE SOLDIER. BECAUSE NO ONE DIED. AND BECAUSE THE TRUTH WOULD TEAR THIS TEAM APART.
YOU DISAGREE?
NO... I GUESS NOT.
BUT THEN WHY TELL ME?
SOMEONE HAS TO KEEP AN EYE ON HER; MAKE SURE SHE DOESN'T LOSE IT AGAIN. AND BEING A LEADER MEANS CARRYING BURDENS. IT WON'T BE YOUR LAST.
YOU DID AN AMAZING THING, JOHN, WITHSTANDING DEFILE'S ASSAULT. BEFORE THAT, STORMWATCH PHD WAS JUST AN IDEA.
YOU MADE IT A *REALITY*.
NOW COMES THE HARD PART. KEEPING IT THAT WAY.
END.

Sketches by Doug Mahnke

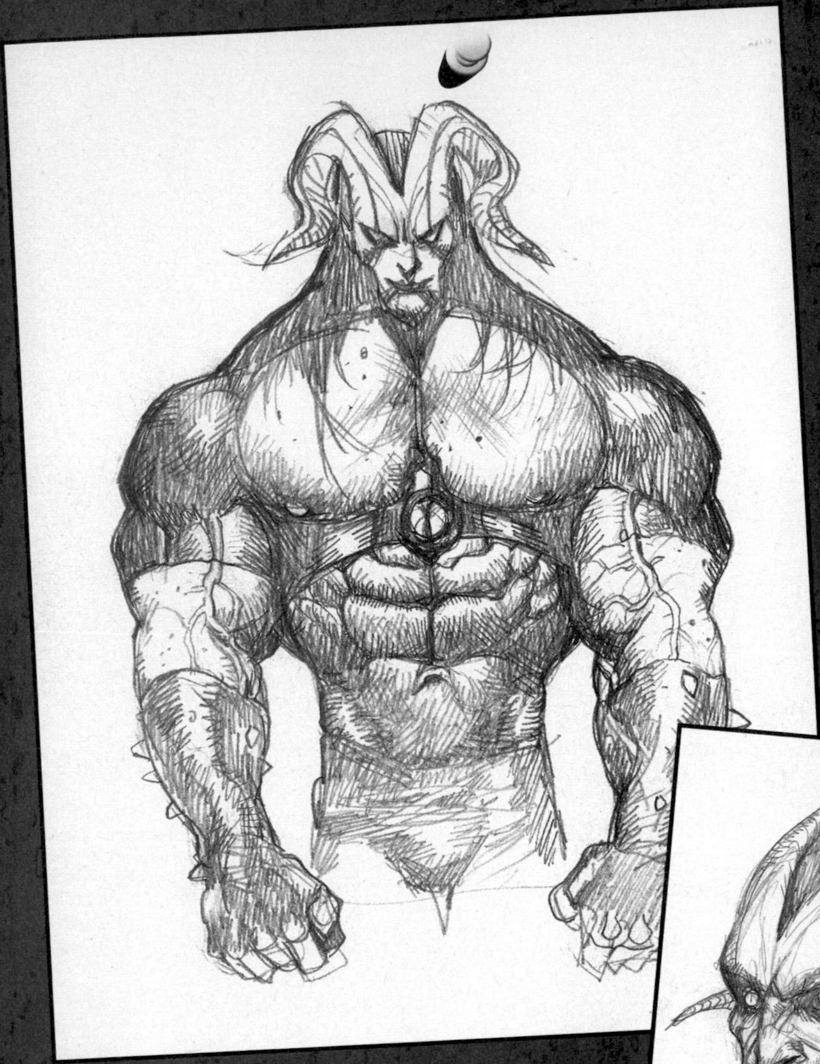

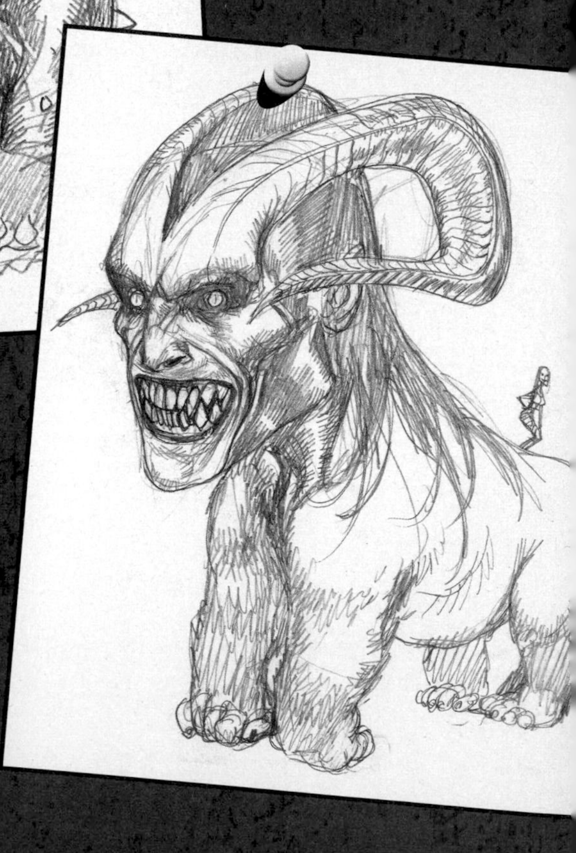

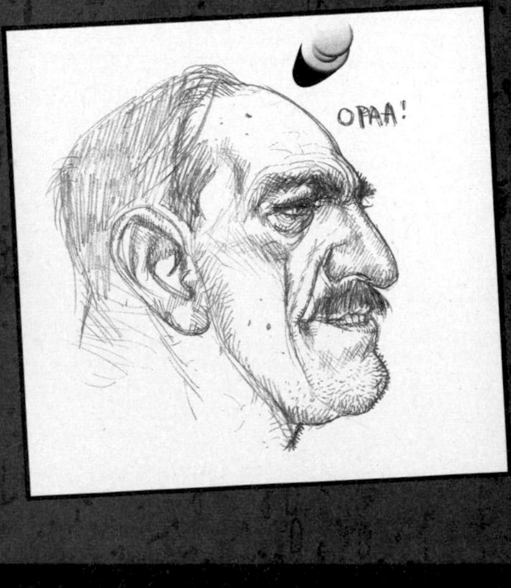
OPAA!

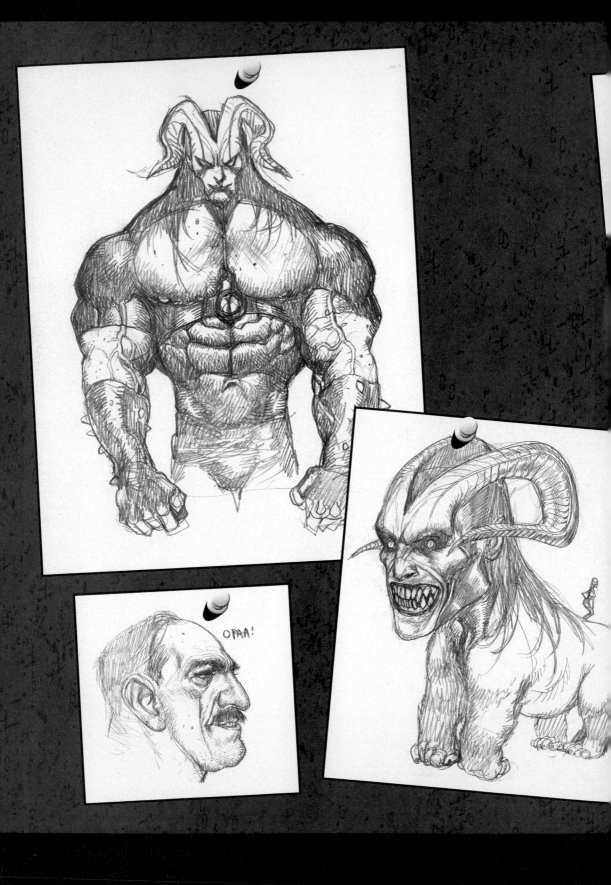

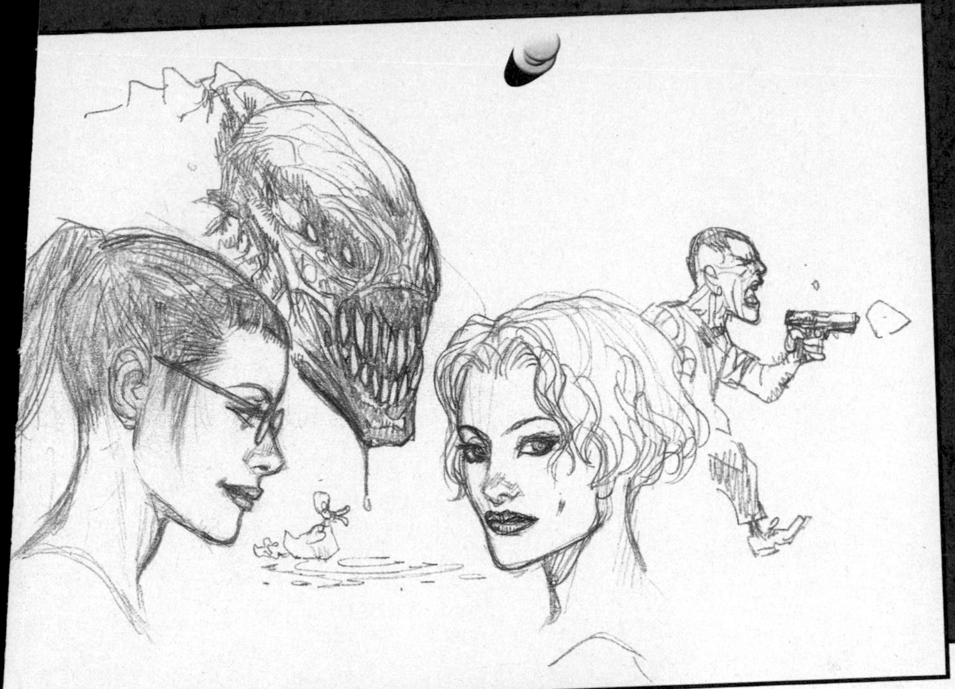
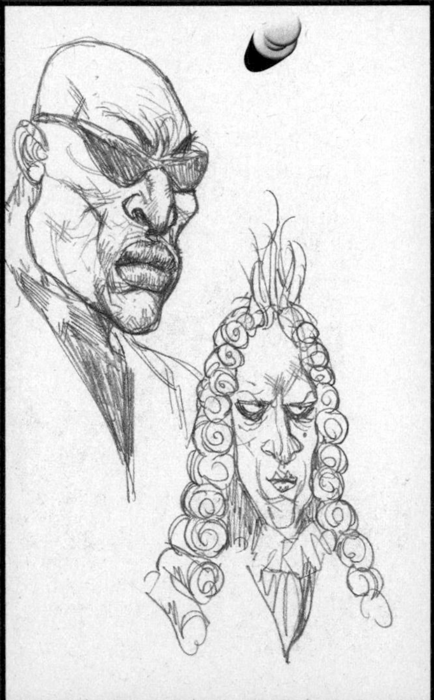
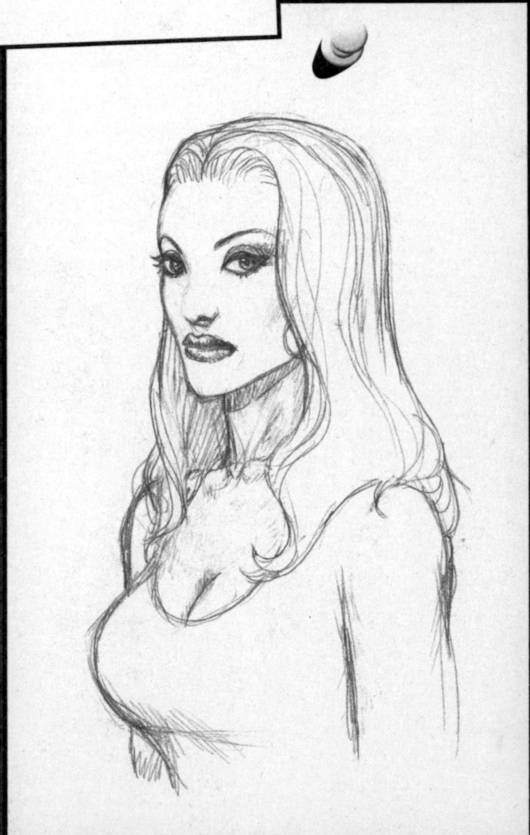

Cover Sketches by Doug Mahnke

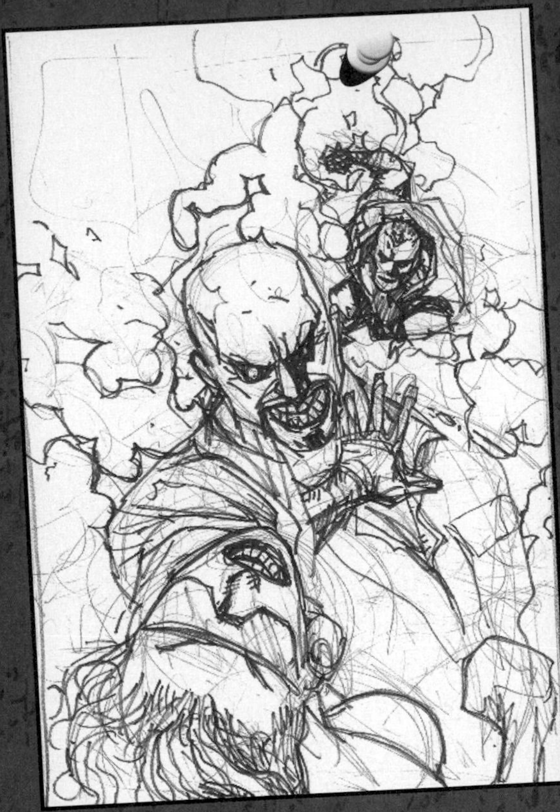

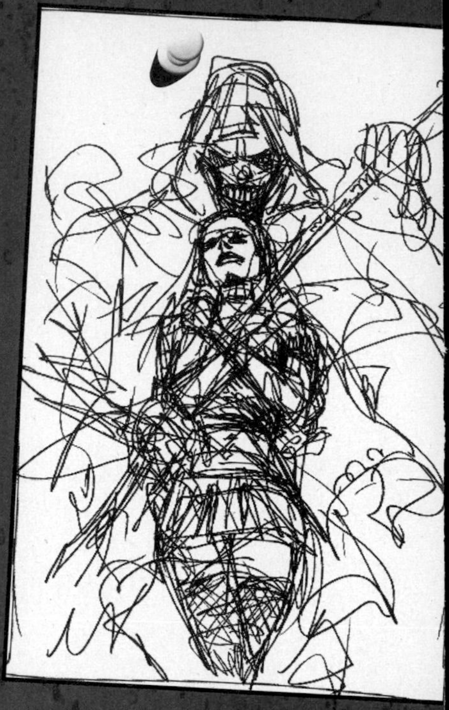

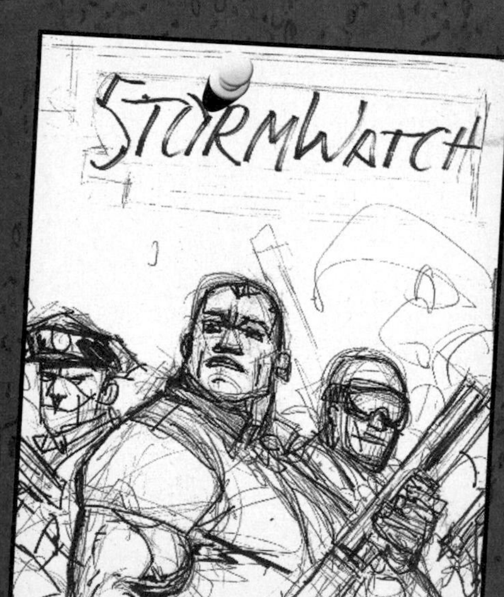
STORMWATCH

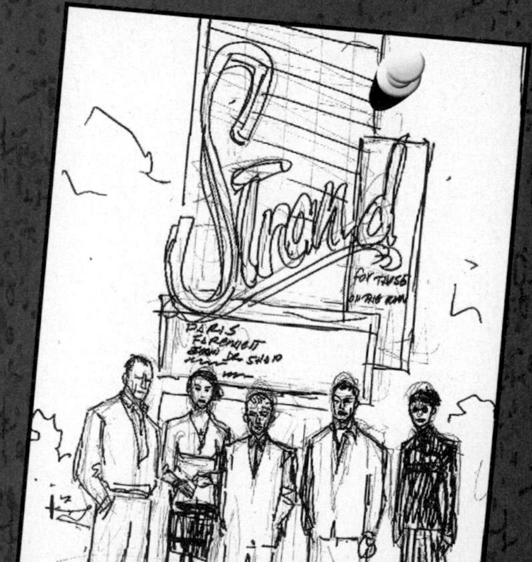
Strand

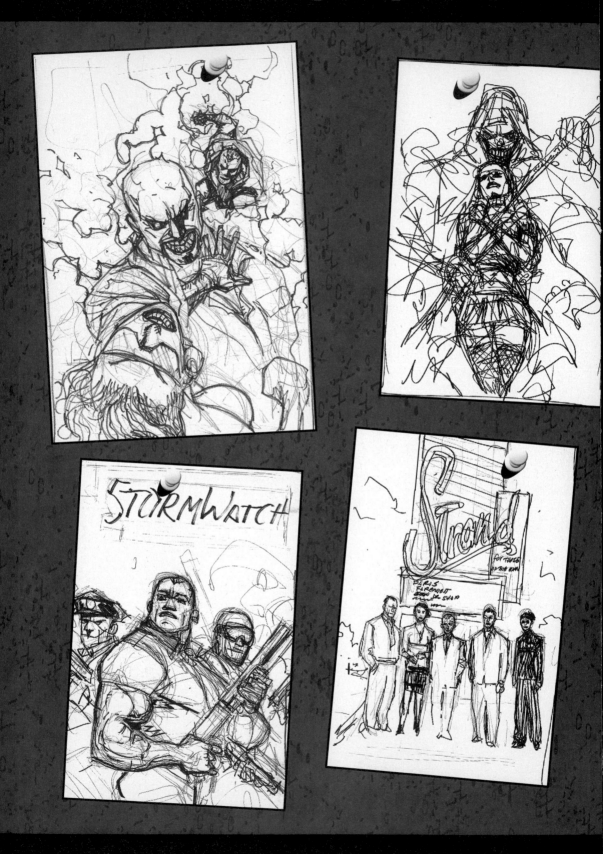

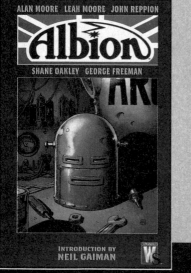